From Ignatius to Francis

From Ignatius to Francis

The Jesuits in History

Michael Walsh

LITURGICAL PRESS
ACADEMIC

Collegeville, Minnesota
www.litpress.org

Cover design by John Vineyard. Ignatius image courtesy of Getty Images.
Pope Francis image courtesy of Wikimedia Commons.

1	2	3	4	5	6	7	8	9

Library of Congress Cataloging-in-Publication Data

Names: Walsh, Michael J., 1937– author.
Title: From Ignatius to Francis : the Jesuits in history / Michael Walsh.
Description: Collegeville, Minnesota : Liturgical Press Academic, [2022] |
    Includes bibliographical references and index. | Summary: "While
    recounting the more significant events in the history of the Jesuit order, this
    book pays particular attention to the controversies that have surrounded it,
    especially those concerning human freedom"— Provided by publisher.
Identifiers: LCCN 2022013924 (print) | LCCN 2022013925 (ebook) |
    ISBN 9780814684917 (paperback) | ISBN 9780814684672 (epub) |
    ISBN 9780814668979 (pdf)
Subjects: LCSH: Jesuits—History. | BISAC: RELIGION / Christianity /
    Catholic | RELIGION / Christian Church / History
Classification: LCC BX3706.3 .W35 2022 (print) | LCC BX3706.3 (ebook) |
    DDC 271/.53—dc23/eng/20220613
LC record available at https://lccn.loc.gov/2022013924
LC ebook record available at https://lccn.loc.gov/2022013925

*In memory of Kathleen Walsh, my wife of 46 years,
who didn't live quite long enough to see this book completed*

Contents

Preface

A very long time ago I found myself in conversation with a distinguished Jesuit historian. There were, I was well aware, many histories of the Society of Jesus available, most, like this one, in single volumes. My proposal, as a brash new graduate in history, was that what was needed was a Cambridge-style history, one in several volumes. For those not familiar with them, the Cambridge University Press histories are typically multiauthored volumes, with the essay titles in each volume carefully chosen to provide comprehensive coverage of the chosen topic.

My Jesuit historian interlocutor, and I honestly cannot remember who it was except that he was not British, demurred. The time was not yet ripe, he said; there was still so much to learn. He was, of course, right about there being so much more to learn. But then there always is. In preparation for this book I entered an alert for "Jesuit" in an academic search engine. Each day there arrives in my inbox a notice commonly listing forty or so, sometimes more, new articles added to the database, not all of them perhaps of great value, but some among them certainly reporting valuable new research.

Since that conversation, perhaps nearly half a century ago, many more volumes have appeared. There is still no Cambridge history, but there is a *Cambridge Encyclopedia* and a *Cambridge Companion*—though in my view the *Oxford Handbook* is far more satisfactory than either. But as my view is that a Cambridge-style history is still needed, why, then, have I produced yet another single-volume version of the 450-year story of the Catholic Church's largest and most controversial religious order?

As I have indicated, many studies of the Society keep appearing. One reason for writing the book is to bring some of this new research to a wider audience. A second reason is that most, if not all, histories give prominence to what Jesuits *did*. That is important, of course, and

1

indispensable in what claims to be a history, but in this new book I want to give rather more coverage of what Jesuits *thought*. Not, as will be seen, that they all thought the same, but there are some major controversies where Jesuit theologians were ranged against others in the Church, and I have tried to give a fair amount of space, at least for a general history, to these debates.

I have to confess, however, the main reason I wrote the book is that I was asked to do so. Half a dozen years ago I was approached by an evangelical publishing house to write a life of Luther. I said Martin Luther was not my kind of topic. The commissioning editor then kindly asked what I would like to write. In the mid-1980s I had been (very) marginally involved in the film *The Mission*, starring Jeremy Irons and Robert de Niro. One of the film's producers, David, now Lord, Puttnam, asked me to write book about it: not about the film as such but about the historical context of the Jesuit reductions in Paraguay. In the end, the book never happened, but my interest in the project remained. I bought books and read articles, and so when asked by the obliging editor what I would like to write I suggested as a possible topic the Jesuit reductions. That was too narrow in scope for them, said the publisher. On the other hand, a general history of the Jesuits would suit very well.

With that encouragement, I began to write and research. Then the publisher became insolvent. Happily the idea of a history of the Society, especially in the light of the election of a Jesuit to be pope, eventually went on to find a home with Liturgical Press in the United States and Canterbury Press in the United Kingdom. For that, and to them, I am very grateful. I am also grateful to the editors for their patience. Because of problems arising from the pandemic, and hence the difficulty in accessing material, it has taken much longer to write than I, or they, anticipated.

But the Jesuit historian was in a sense quite right. There is never the right moment to write a history of the Society. Nor is there ever enough time or space to tell the complete story. There are always going to be things left out. I am conscious that in this text there are many matters I have not touched upon. I have, for example, said nothing about the Philippines, or about the Marianas Islands, or Cambodia, or Vietnam; there is precious little about Jesuits in Africa or in Eastern Europe. There is a little about science because of the Galileo affair but otherwise nothing about their important work as astronomers, still ongoing, not least in the Vatican Observatory, and nothing at all about art and architecture—though in my defense these have recently been excellently covered in two volumes edited by John W. O'Malley and others titled *The Jesuits: Cultures, Sciences, and the Arts, 1540–1773.*

This, then, is not a complete history of the Jesuits. It is about (some of) the Jesuits in history, hence the book's title. It has been a great story, and it is most certainly not yet over.

Chapter 1

From Inigo to Ignatius

"It is generally agreed among his foes no less than among his friends that Ignatius Loyola was a maker of history." These are the opening words of the saint's biography by the Irish—though a member of the English (now British) province—Jesuit historian James Brodrick, and he adds, "A hundred books can be cited in proof of this statement."[1] Ignatius's life story is fairly well known, not least because he left an account of some of it in his *Reminiscences*, a short biography that he dictated to his secretary, Luis Gonçalves da Cámara, urged on by the man whom Ignatius eventually appointed as vicar general of the Society, Jerónimo Nadal. It begins, however, only with his involvement in, and wounding at, the siege of Pamplona in May 1521: "Until the age of twenty-six he was a man given up to the vanities of this world, and his chief delight used to be in the exercise of arms, with a great and vain desire to gain honour."[2]

That might suggest a birth date of 1495, but from other sources it would seem he was born in 1491 when "Erasmus was twenty-five, Machiavelli twenty-two, Copernicus eighteen, Michelangelo sixteen, Thomas More eleven, and Luther had just turned seven."[3] He was born, in other words, in a year that hovers between the medieval and the Renaissance.

---

[1] James Brodrick, *Saint Ignatius Loyola: The Pilgrim Years* (London: Burns and Oates, 1956), vii. This is the first of an intended two-volume life of the saint, but the second volume did not get written. Brodrick many years ago admitted to the present author in a private conversation that he did not find the second part of Ignatius's life at all interesting.

[2] *Saint Ignatius of Loyola: Personal Writings*, trans. with intro. and notes by Joseph A. Munitiz and Philip Endean (London: Penguin Books, 2004), 13. Ignatius consistently refers to himself in the third person in this narrative.

[3] Jean Lacouture, *Jesuits: A Multibiography* (London: The Harvill Press, 1995), 4.

He might indeed have won fame as a soldier as he hoped. Born in the castle of Loyola, built by his grandfather some thirty years earlier, Inigo López (as Ignatius was baptised) belonged to one of the most important families in Guipúzcoa. It seems his father, Beltrán Yáñez, may have been away from the castle at the time of his birth, fighting with the armies of Ferdinand and Isabella in the siege of Granada, the capture of which finally united the whole of what is now Spain under Christian rule. Inigo's mother, Marina Sánchez de Licone, was of noble birth, related to the counts of Oñate and to the dukes of Nájara. All but one of Inigo's brothers became soldiers, two of them dying in battles in Europe, one in the New World. Inigo, the youngest son, might have been destined for the priesthood rather than the army had not the parish in the family's gift, that of Azpeitia, a village a mile or so north of the castle, been bestowed on the next youngest, Pero López. It is likely that Inigo had also entered the clerical state, though his behavior, or so witnesses thought when a case was brought against Inigo and Pero in 1515, was more that of a young gallant than of a priest: there is even a possibility that he may have fathered a daughter, though the evidence is slight.[4] He escaped the charges against him only through the intervention of Juan Velázquez de Cuellar, a close friend of Inigo's father to whose household in Arévalo he was consigned sometime before his father's death in 1507; his mother had died soon after he was born, and he had spent his first years in the care of the wife of the local blacksmith.

Juan Velázquez was the majordomo of Queen Isabella and treasurer of Castile whose capital, in effect the capital of Spain, was Valladolid, not far from Arévalo. Inigo became a page at the royal court. He was there for some ten years, leaving only after Juan Velázquez's death in 1517. On the advice of Juan Velázquez's widow he next entered the service of the duke of Nájera, a distant relative, who was the viceroy of Navarre, annexed to Castile in 1512 by Ferdinand. This was disputed territory. Francis I, piqued that Charles, the Flanders-born grandson of Ferdinand and Isabella and from 1516

---

[4] The story is told by June Rockett in her biography of Fr. Philip Caraman, *A Gentle Jesuit* (Leominster: Gracewing, 2004), 296–98. Caraman had advanced the theory that Inigo had fathered a daughter on what proved to be very shaky evidence: the author says that the Jesuit censor who cut the passage out of Caraman's text was doing him a favor. Unhappily, Caraman did not think so at the time.

the king of Spain, had been elected in 1519 as Holy Roman Emperor, invaded Navarre and the duke of Nájera, with Inigo in attendance, marched from Pamplona and recaptured the city. The French withdrew but in May 1521 returned with a force of twelve thousand men and laid siege to Pamplona itself. The town council was prepared to surrender and so, it seems, was the commander of the garrison, but Inigo persuaded the defenders to fight on—which they did, until he fell, hit in the legs by a stray shot: "a shot hit him in one leg, completely shattering it, and because the ball passed between both legs, he was badly wounded too."[5]

Despite his professed desire for martial glory,[6] Inigo was more of a diplomat than a professional soldier, and without his own account of these events to his secretary, we would not know that he had been in the siege of Pamplona.

Nevertheless he records the fighting, and his own injury, quite precisely, including the courtesy with which the French treated him, setting his leg and allowing him to convalesce in Pamplona for a fortnight or so before sending him home in a litter to the castle of Loyola.

There he was placed in a room at the top of the castle, and local doctors were summoned. They decreed that the French, however well-meaning, had done a bad job, and the bones of Inigo's leg needed to be broken again and then reset. This was done, but they proved no more skillful than the former team: one bone now protruded over another. The patient was at one point judged to be on the point of death and was given the last sacraments, but he recovered. When sufficiently well again he asked the doctors whether there was anything that could be done about his unsightly leg. The protruding piece could be cut off, they said, though the pain of the operation would be greater than anything he had suffered before. Concerned about the kind of figure he would cut in the world with so badly damaged a leg, he ordered them to go ahead: "That cannonball crushed not only the bones of his leg, but also his ideal, ambitions and dreams of glory. . . . How could he maintain the image of a handsome, dashing

[5] *Reminiscences*, in Munitiz and Endean, *Saint Ignatius of Loyola*, 13. The "ball" is usually taken to be that fired by a canon, but in their notes Munitiz and Endean remark that Ignatius's wording suggests something smaller, cf. *Saint Ignatius of Loyola*, 361.

[6] Munitiz and Endean, *Saint Ignatius of Loyola*, 13.

hero with a misshapen leg and an obvious limp."[7] When some three decades later Inigo—by now calling himself Ignatius—dictated this story, not sparing his readers the pain he endured, he seemed remarkably proud of his stoicism.

Confined to his bed for so long a period, some five months, Inigo asked for something to read. What he wanted were the tales of chivalry that had first fired his imagination, but they were not to be found in the castle. Instead, he had to make do with books thought to have been brought to Loyola by the devout wife of his brother Martín, Magdalena de Araoz, who had once been, if not a lady in waiting to, at least in the retinue of, Queen Isabella. The books were, he says in the *Reminiscences*, a life of Christ and a collection of lives of the saints, in Spanish.

He does not name the books that changed his life, but it is clear what they were. The life of Christ was that by the Carthusian monk, Ludolph of Saxony (1295–1378), a difficult book to categorize because it was part biography drawn from the gospels, part moral exhortation, and part meditation—and in the meditations Ludolph urged his readers to place themselves in the scene they were reflecting on, an approach Ignatius was later to make his own in his *Spiritual Exercises*. The other book, the lives of the saints, was *The Golden Legend*, compiled by the Dominican friar Jacobus de Voragine (1230–1298), who became archbishop of Genoa. Replete with miracles and other extraordinary happenings, it was wildly popular in the Middle Ages and was one of the first books that William Caxton printed in English at Westminster. It is not known who translated into Spanish the version Inigo read, but it was adorned with prologues to each of the lives—they were arranged in order of the liturgical year—written by a monk, whose life as a courtier before he entered the Cistercian Order had many echoes of Inigo's own. Most important, he understood the life of a Christian as a form of holy knighthood. Inigo read the books time and again and copied extracts into a large notebook, writing down the words of Christ in red and those of Christ's mother in blue. In another notebook he added his own reflections. "While reading the lives of Our Lord and the saints, he would stop to think, reasoning with himself: 'How would it be, if I did this which St Francis did,

---

[7] W. W. Meissner, *Ignatius of Loyola: The Psychology of a Saint* (New Haven, CT: Yale University Press, 1992), 55.

and this which St Dominic did? . . . [H]is whole way of thinking was to say to himself: St Francis did this, so I must do it; St Dominic did this, so I must do it.' "[8] For Inigo, a new form of chivalry, a new knighthood, a new way of achieving fame, had been born: he was to imitate the lives of saints. But first he was to make a pilgrimage to Jerusalem.

One night he had a vision of the Virgin Mary holding the Child Jesus. He was sickened by thoughts of his past life and, he says, never again after the vision had temptations against chastity. It brought him, he reported, great consolation.[9] Influenced perhaps by Ludolph of Saxony, he had thought for a time of, like Ludolph, entering the Carthusian Order. He sent a servant to find out about the rule of life at the Charterhouse in Burgos, but eventually he decided, against the advice of his brother Martín, to set out for Jerusalem. First of all, however, he wanted to pay a courtesy call upon the duke of Nájera. His brother Pero went with him and agreed to visit on the way to Aranzazu, a shrine to the Virgin—Our Lady of the Thorn Bush—who is said to have appeared there to a shepherd named Rodrigo in 1468. Situated at four thousand feet in the mountains of southern Guipúzcoa, it was even then as a small shrine (it is now a major basilica) a regular place of pilgrimage for the people of the Basque country, but one not easy to reach at any time: when Inigo and Pero made the journey in February or early March 1522 the road to it would likely have been snowbound, making the journey more difficult, even perilous. Once they had arrived Inigo persuaded Pero to stay the night, and there at the shrine of the Virgin Inigo made a vow of chastity.

From Aranzazu he went on to Oñate to visit his sister and to leave Pero behind, then to Navarrete to call on the duke of Nájera to collect, he hoped, some money owed to him. The duke, however, had been deprived of the viceroyalty and was himself short of funds. The duke's treasurer told Inigo there was no money to be had, but the duke himself demurred, saying there would always be money for a Loyola, and handed over what was owed. Inigo distributed the money among people to whom he was himself in some way indebted,

---

[8] Munitiz and Endean, *Saint Ignatius of Loyola*, 15.

[9] This was, of course, written—or rather dictated—long after the event, by which time "consolation" had for Ignatius become something of a technical term, especially in the context of the *Spiritual Exercises*; see below, p. 15.

and with what remained he asked that an image of the Virgin he had seen, much in need of repair, be well restored. The duke also offered Inigo, still dressed as a Spanish gentleman with a sword at his waist, a position in his entourage. Inigo refused and set out on his mule for the sanctuary of the Black Madonna at Montserrat.

En route to the shrine he encountered a Moor, obviously from the context a Muslim who had converted to Christianity, as many felt obliged to do, especially after the fall of Granada. Inigo must have told his new traveling companion where he was going, and discussion turned on the virginity of Mary. The Moor's version, in Inigo's eyes, besmirched the dignity of Mary. Clearly the Moor realised he had upset Inigo and rode rapidly ahead. Inigo, in his newfound version of chivalry, wondered what he should do and was tempted to defend the Virgin's honor by attacking—he says in his *Reminiscences* "stabbing"—his adversary. He came to a crossroads. He decided to let his mule make his mind up for him: should he take the path the Moor had gone down to a nearby town or follow the main road? Happily, Inigo's mule took the high road, and the Moor was spared.

Inigo's destination was a Benedictine abbey, founded in the eleventh century on the site of a shrine to the Virgin that, according to tradition, housed the black statue with the Christ child in her lap that had been found on a ledge on the side of the mountain in the ninth century. Located some thirty miles northwest of Barcelona, it was, and still is, one of the most potent religious symbols in Spain,[10] razed to the ground and rebuilt several times and more recently the focus in particular of Catalan nationalism. Now huge, perhaps the largest community of Benedictines in the world, but when Inigo arrived, on March 21, 1522, it was a much more modest affair. Nonetheless under its abbot, Garcia Ximénez de Cisneros (c. 1455–1510, abbot from 1493), it was one of the major centers of Catholic devotional revival, especially in methods of prayer. Cisneros had published in 1500 *Ejercitatorio de la vida espiritual*, a book of spiritual instructions for his monks that, in its methodical approach to prayer,[11] must have influenced Inigo in compiling his own *Spiritual Exercises*.

---

[10] Columbus named the island of Montserrat in the Caribbean in honor of the shrine.

[11] Munitiz and Endean, *Saint Ignatius of Loyola*, 362.

On the evening of March 25—the eve of the Feast of the Annunciation—he made a confession of his whole life to a French monk, Jean Chanon, then hung up his sword in the Lady Chapel and spent the rest of the night before the altar in a vigil as knights had traditionally done. He attended Mass the following morning, gave away all his possessions, including his clothes, and dressed himself instead in the rough garb of a pilgrim.[12]

In his vigil at the Lady Chapel of Monserrat Inigo was consciously copying the behavior of the medieval knights whose heroic (if fictional) deeds he had first wanted to read while confined to his bed in the castle of Loyola. The "soldier saint" is a common figure in Christian hagiography, and Inigo is often portrayed as such.[13] The company he founded, the Jesuits, are frequently described as the "shock troops" of the Catholic Church. And as one of his biographers remarks, "When one opens Ignatius' *Spiritual Exercises*, one sets foot in a world of spiritual combat."[14] But the operative word is "spiritual." Inigo was brought up in the household of the treasurer of Castile, not as a soldier but as a courtier. True, he carried a sword and was not afraid occasionally to brandish it, but there is no record of him taking part in any battle except that at Pamplona, which for him ended ignominiously, carried away as he was from the citadel after exhorting his companions to defend what turned out to be indefensible. As will be seen,[15] the *Spiritual Exercises* makes much use of military metaphors, but this kind of language and thought patterns would have been quite usual among those of his class in early sixteenth-century Spain. Nonetheless, setting out as a pilgrim was, for Inigo, at last a definitive break with the life he had lived hitherto.

The destination of his pilgrimage was, as it had always been, Jerusalem, but it proved a much longer journey than he could have imagined. His first stop was the town of Manresa, below the mountain

---

[12] Unfortunately, the beggar who received his clothes was afterward accused of stealing them: Inigo had to vouch for him.

[13] Inigo is portrayed as a soldier, and the discipline of the Jesuits as that of a military machine, in the first biography of Inigo. It was written by Pedro de Ribadeneira, who had served for a time as his secretary, and first published in Latin in 1572. It was soon afterward translated into Spanish and became the standard interpretation of his life. Ribadeneira had access to Inigo's *Reminiscences*, but this was not widely available.

[14] Meissner, *Ignatius of Loyola*, 88.

[15] See below, p. 31.

and on the river Cardoner. He stayed there almost a year, from March 1522 to February 1523, living sometimes in the houses of friends, sometimes in a hospice, sometimes in the local Dominican priory. That is as much as Inigo himself tells us, but from other sources it is known that he sometimes retreated to a cave beside the river, subjecting himself there to harsh penances—too harsh, he came to realize, because during the winter of 1522 and 1523 they brought him to the point of death. He let his hair grow, did not eat meat, and fasted as well as scourging himself.[16] While his austerities weakened him physically, what was clearly much more psychologically damaging were the scruples from which he suffered, wondering anxiously over and over again whether he had honestly declared all his sins to the priest at Montserrat. So anxious did he become that he records he contemplated suicide. These were important experiences in the formulation of his *Spiritual Exercises*—he adds, for example, notes on how to deal with scruples almost at the end of them, and as superior general of the Jesuits he was opposed to extreme penitential practices.

In February 1523 he resumed his journey toward Jerusalem. He made his way to Barcelona to take a ship to Italy. It took him twenty days or so to find one,[17] but eventually he left for Gaeta and from there made his way to Rome, arriving on Palm Sunday and living during his stay in a Spanish hospice on the Piazza Navona. To set off for the Holy Land he needed a papal blessing, and this he got from the dour Dutchman Adrian VI, who once had been Emperor Charles V's tutor. After Easter he resumed his journey, a four-week walk to Venice to find a ship to take him to Jaffa.

The voyage proved anything but straightforward, landing at Famagusta in Cyprus, then crossing the island, and taking another ship from Larnaca. He reached Jaffa on August 25, six weeks after sailing from Venice. It was a difficult time to be going to the Holy Land, as even the single-minded Inigo could not help noticing. The Ottoman Turks had, little more than six months before, captured

[16] This was at one time a common practice in religious orders, and only the seeming intensity of it would have appeared excessive in the sixteenth century.

[17] Not least because he was once again plagued by scruples: the ship's captain, though offering a free passage, wanted him to take food with him whereas Inigo thought he ought to beg for it, even on the ship.

Rhodes, which deterred many from making the journey to Jerusalem, and even those who did so, once they had arrived, found themselves in a territory governed by the Ottomans. The Franciscans, as guardians of the Holy Places, had to tread a difficult path, and when Inigo declared that, having arrived, he was not going home but intended to stay, preaching to those who might listen, he was told firmly but gently that he could not do so, even producing papal documents that threatened excommunication should anyone not obey the Franciscan Guardian. Inigo obeyed, though he slipped away surreptitiously from the party of pilgrims—much to the annoyance of the Franciscans—to revisit the Mount of Olives so that he might see again the supposed footprints of Christ. Those on guard at the Mount of Olives denied him entrance, until he bribed them with a pair of scissors. *he did what?*

Apart from this rather picaresque detail, which occurred just before his departure, Inigo says remarkably little about his time in Jerusalem, though the tour of the Holy Places was a fairly standard one and can be pieced together from other sources. It would have included the place where Christ was held prisoner, the house of Caiaphas and that of Pilate, the house where Mary lived after the crucifixion, the site of the Last Supper, and, as has just been mentioned, the footprints of Christ where he ascended in heaven. It also included the Church of the Holy Sepulchre, where Inigo, as was customary, spent the night alongside with his fellow pilgrims. When, at the start of the third week of the *Spiritual Exercises*, Inigo asks the person making them to recall the story of the Last Supper and what followed and to imagine the events of Christ's passion in the mind's eye, he himself had been there. The images to him were very real—though he never questioned the accuracy of what he had been told. But then few others of his period would have done so.

The return journey proved even more hazardous than the outward one. Battered by storms in the Mediterranean—his ship was on one occasion driven back to Cyprus—it took him three and a half months to travel from Jaffa back to Venice, and he then had to walk across Italy to Genoa, an Italy in the midst of a war between Emperor Charles V and Francis I of France. From Genoa he took a ship to Barcelona, arriving back where he had set out at the end of February 1524, a year after starting out on his pilgrimage.

Rebuffed in his desire to stay in the Holy Land, Inigo had, in his long journey home, plenty of time to think about his future. He determined to study, and for that he needed Latin. He had lessons and became reasonably proficient—sufficiently so after a couple of years for his friends to encourage him to study at the recently established university at Alcalá. Not that he had dedicated himself solely to Latin during this two years in Barcelona. He continued to preach and became a familiar figure in the city, so familiar that, although he still begged for his food, he was given so much more than he needed and was able to distribute to others in need what he had left over. His preaching had brought him disciples, three of them (a fourth joined later), who in March 1524 followed him to Alcalá.

There Inigo attracted even more disciples, and they went about preaching and teaching the catechism as well as, at least in Inigo's case, begging for a living. They also dressed similarly in a "habit" of rough gray cloth—they became known as "the sack-wearers."[18] This was a mistake. It made them look as if they were a religious order or a sect—and sects were suspect in sixteenth-century Spain. It was a time of much religious ferment and enthusiasm, and the inquisitors were watching closely. In particular there was a loosely allied group called the *alumbrados* or "enlightened ones" who abandoned the traditional practices of Catholicism in favour of personal "illumination"—hence the name—which they believed was the surest way to union with God. It was not difficult for Inigo to demonstrate that he was not an *alumbrado* (though some of his followers had been[19]) because in his teaching he emphasised not just the ascetical life, which the *alumbrados* rejected, but also the sacrament of confession, which they also spurned. Inigo was twice interrogated by inquisitors sent from Toledo, the first time simply being told to dress as students rather than as friars. The second time, however, Inigo found himself in the Inquisition's prison. It appears to have had a fairly easy-going regime, for people still came to him for instruction and spiritual guidance, but on his release, after forty-two days, he decided to consult the archbishop of Toledo about his wish to teach the catechism and the problems he had encountered while in Alcalá. The archbishop, the most senior churchman in Spain—the primate—was friendly and encouraging, and when Inigo indicated that he was thinking of moving to the ancient university of Salamanca, which

---

[18] Munitiz and Endean, *Saint Ignatius of Loyola*, 41.
[19] Meissner, *Ignatius of Loyola*, 132.

was the most prestigious in the country, he gave him introductions to people the archbishop indicated would be welcoming.

Salamanca, however, proved even less welcoming than Alcalá had been. Inigo and his four companions arrived there in mid-1527 and almost immediately ran into trouble. On arrival there Inigo sought out, as he had at Manresa, a Dominican friar from the ancient priory of San Esteban (St. Stephen) as his confessor and spiritual director. They had spoken together on only a few occasions when the friar said other members of the community wanted to talk to him and invited him to a meal with the community. He was taken to a chapel and questioned about his preaching. He did not preach, Inigo insisted, but simply talked to people about virtues and vices. He and one of his companions from Alcalá were kept in San Esteban for three days, then chained together[20] and taken off to the town jail, technically as prisoners of the bishop. His two other companions were taken there also, but not put in the same cell.

They were then interrogated by four judges, each of whom had before him a copy of the *Spiritual Exercises*—though it cannot be certain that the version they had was identical with that which was eventually printed. Though they asked him a variety of questions, they appear to have been particularly concerned with the distinction made in the *Exercises* between mortal and venial sin, that is, a sin that condemns the soul to death—hell—and one that does not, a reflection that occurs in sections 35, 36, and 37 of the *Exercises* as they are conventionally numbered. John O'Malley, however, reports that they "paid special attention to the part dealing with 'discernment of spirits,' in which the movements in the soul of consolation and desolation and their role in finding and following the will of God are discussed."[21] If so, and O'Malley provides no reference, then the judges had alighted upon the concept of "election," something that is central to the *Spiritual Exercises*, and to Jesuit spiritual life in general,

---

[20] The chain was such that "every time one of them wanted to do anything, the other would have to go with him" (*Reminiscences*, 46). The imprisonment does not appear to have been particularly arduous, because people could still approach him for spiritual counsel. One of those who came, Inigo remarks, was Francisco de Mendoza, who then taught Greek in the university but later became a cardinal and in 1550 archbishop of Burgos.

[21] John W. O'Malley, *The First Jesuits* (Cambridge, MA: Harvard University Press, 1993), 28.

and the topic in the *Exercises* that is perhaps closest to the teachings and practices of the *alumbrados*. Inigo does not record this. Instead, he says they asked him about the Trinity and the Blessed Sacrament. They found him innocent and released him and his companions after some three weeks of imprisonment, saying only that he must steer clear of discussing mortal and venial sin until he had studied for four more years. Inigo rather indicates that the friendliness that was shown to him had something to do with a curious event that occurred. All the prisoners in the town's jail escaped—he does not say how—leaving only Inigo and his four companions still in the cells with the doors open, a fact that caused considerable comment. So impressed were the authorities that they transferred them to a nearby palace.

Notwithstanding the friendliness that had been shown him, Inigo believed that, without being able to discuss the distinction between mortal and venial sin, he was limited in what he could do in Salamanca. It was also by now clear to him that he needed a more thorough grounding in theology, and he therefore decided to make his way to the University of Paris. He went by way of Barcelona, with books laden on a donkey. But he went alone. The disciples he had made he now left behind in Salamanca, though there is a hint in the *Reminiscences* that he thought they might all meet up again. It did not happen.

Inigo, his donkey, and his books arrived in Paris on February 2, 1528. He had in some sense attended two universities already, those of Alcalá and Salamanca, but had never registered for any courses. This time, however, registering first at the Collège de Montaigu, which had a reputation for strict discipline, including corporal punishment, and for hospitality toward the poor. Erasmus had been a student, though he did not like the place, and so had John Calvin and, later, John Knox. During 1528 and 1529 Inigo was, he says, "studying with the boys, following the structure and method of Paris." He was studying Latin, essential if he were to move on to theology, and at this time he "Latinized" his name: he began calling himself Ignatius, apparently under the mistaken, but understandable, impression that this was the equivalent in Latin of the name Inigo.

His years in Paris were crucial in the history of the Society of Jesus, but Ignatius says remarkably little about them. He mentions that he attempted to give rather more attention to his studies, though without entirely, as will be seen, refraining from talking about spiritual matters. He tells us too about the problems of providing a living for himself by begging—mainly, apparently, in Flanders but once in England where he "brought back more than he normally did in other years."[22] It was a significant experience. When the Constitutions of the Society came to be written, Jesuits were expected to live on alms, but not those engaged in studies: begging, as Ignatius had discovered the hard way, could get in the way of learning.

After a year at the Collège de Montaigu he moved to the nearby Collège de Sainte-Barbe,[23] founded in 1460. It is unclear why he did so. Jean Lacouture[24] suggests as one possible reason that he "was opting for the Renaissance over the Middle Ages," but, he adds, it was also more academically ambitious than Montaigu with a rather less brutal regime. But it is also possible that Ignatius chose it because there were a number of Spaniards already there, one of them being Francisco de Iassu de Apilcueta y Xavier, known more simply to future generations as Francis Xavier. When he moved to Sainte-Barbe, Ignatius came to share a room with Xavier and his friend, the Savoyard Pierre Favre, as well as with their tutor.

Soon after his arrival at Sainte-Barbe Ignatius took, and passed, his first examination. He passed it reasonably well: there were a hundred candidates, and he came thirtieth.[25] He could progress to the next stage. In 1534 he became a master of arts of the University of Paris and now, at last, could turn his mind toward theology, which for eighteen months he studied under the Dominicans in the rue St. Jacques as well as possibly attending lectures at the Franciscan house.[26]

During this time he gathered more followers. He met, seemingly by chance, two former students at Alcalá, Diego Laínez and his

---

[22] Munitiz and Endean, *Saint Ignatius of Loyola*, 50. He was in London in 1531 (ibid., 372n114).

[23] It survived until 1999, the longest existing—by far—medieval college of the University of Paris. It is now a university library.

[24] Lacouture, *Jesuits*, 46–48, at 47.

[25] Ibid., 55.

[26] "Martial Mazurier, a learned Doctor of the Sorbonne . . . said of him that never had he heard any man speak of theological matters with such mastery and power." Quoted in Hugo Rahner, *Ignatius the Theologian* (London: Geoffrey Chapman, 1968), 1. Rahner adds that Ignatius was aware that "his knowledge came mystically 'from above'" (ibid.).

younger friend Alfonso Salmerón. Possibly, however, it was not an entirely chance encounter. Although Laínez and Salmerón had not been at Alcalá at the same time as Ignatius, it is quite likely that they had heard about him and in Paris may have sought him out. They were joined the following year by Nicolás Bobadilla, who had also studied at Alcalá, and by the Portuguese Simâo Rodriguez, who had already been in Paris when Ignatius arrived. What bound them all together was the experience of making the *Spiritual Exercises* under the guidance of Ignatius.

The *Exercises* more or less as they exist at the present day date from the 1530s. In 1535 someone, either Ignatius himself or, more likely, Pierre Favre, guided an English priest, John Helyar, through them, and Helyar left a written record. There is a Latin version in manuscript dating from 1541, and there is a Spanish version three years later. This manuscript is generally referred to as "The Autograph" because there are corrections to the text clearly made by Ignatius himself, possibly as late as 1550. The first printed edition, in 1548, was a Latin translation of "The Autograph" and was produced to be presented to the pope: "Most scholars are agreed that its preoccupation with elegance exacts a certain lack of fidelity."[27]

Versions of the *Exercises* are now widely available, including, of course, English translations.[28] Ignatius was hesitant about getting it into people's hands, not because it is an esoteric text, but because the short book is meant for the person guiding a retreat rather than for the retreatants themselves, as is made clear in the second of the "Annotations," or guidelines, with which the received text begins. It is then divided into four "weeks" of differing lengths—"weeks" is not meant to be taken literally. The First Week opens with the statement "The *Spiritual Exercises* having as their purpose the overcoming of self and the ordering of one's life on the basis of a decision made in freedom from any ill-ordered attachment."[29] The aim, therefore, is clearly stated: it is to enable the exercitant to make a life-changing

---

[27] Munitiz and Endean, *Saint Ignatius of Loyola*, 281. A particularly interesting study, "The Development of the Exercises" by Santiago Arzubialde, SJ, appeared in *The Way* 50, no. 4 (October 2011): 78–96.

[28] That used here is in Munitiz and Endean, *Saint Ignatius of Loyola*, 283–358.

[29] Ibid., 289. The sections of the *Exercises* are conventionally numbered: what is quoted above is §21.

choice or, in Jesuit parlance, an "election." There are steps to be gone through, in particular an examination of conscience and a number of meditations, including one on Hell in which the exercitant is asked "to see with the eyes of the imagination the length, breadth and depth of hell" (§65).

Preliminary to the Second Week is a reflection on the call of a great king "to whom all Christian leaders and their followers give their homage and obedience" (§92). The week is for the most part a series of meditations on the life of Christ, though in the middle of it there is a meditation on "The Two Standards," one being "that of Christ our Commander in Chief," the other that of the devil, Lucifer (§136), all clearly leading up to the election. The Third Week consists of meditations on the passion and death of Christ; the Fourth, on the resurrection, which closes with "Contemplation for Attaining Love"— in other words, a commitment to the service of Christ (§230).

This is the bare outline. There is advice on methods of prayer and, as has been mentioned,[30] on how to deal with scruples. There are numerous "points" for meditation. The "Annotations" provide guidance for the person giving the *Exercises*, especially on how to tailor them to different types of individuals: "The Exercises are to be adapted to the capabilities of those who want to engage in them" (§18).[31]

At the very end there are what is conventionally known as "Rules for Thinking with the Church" (§352–70).[32] Given that aspects of the *Spiritual Exercises*, the emphasis on consolation and desolation, for example, and the "Contemplation for Attaining Love," might easily have given rise to the accusation that Ignatius was an *alumbrado*, the "rules" drew attention to the *Exercises'* strict orthodoxy. In his *Reminiscences* Ignatius makes no mention of the considerable impact made in Paris during his time there of the Lutheran reform, but a number of the Rules undoubtedly reflect the challenges faced by the Church

---

[30] See above, p. 12.

[31] Munitiz and Endean, *Saint Ignatius of Loyola*, 287.

[32] Ibid., 356, translate the Spanish "Para el sentido verdadero que en la Iglesia Militante debemos tener, se guarden la reglas siguientes" as "Rules to follow in view of the true attitude of mind that we ought to maintain [as members] within the Church militant," which seems a bit long-winded: "The following rule should be observed to have a correct understanding of what we ought to believe in the Church militant."

because of the Reformation, sometimes in a manner that would now be considered inappropriate, as, for instance, Rule 4: "We should praise greatly religious life, virginity and continence, and we should not praise matrimony to the same extent as any of these" (§356).[33]

The penultimate Rule, Rule 17 (§369), is especially significant in the context of the Jesuit approach to Christian life in general and theology in particular. It was clearly aimed at the Lutheran doctrine that free will in men and women had been overwhelmed by sin and only God's grace would enable them to achieve salvation, to such an extent that a person's good works were of no avail, only his or her faith. As has been remarked, the whole point of the *Exercises* was to enable those making them to make a free choice: "We must not talk of grace at such length and with such insistence as to poison people's attitude to free will," wrote Ignatius.

As the *Spiritual Exercises* were geared to bringing the exercitant to the point of making a fundamental decision about his or her relationship with God, making an "election," the whole thing lasting, conventionally, for thirty days should in theory be undergone only once, and that was the practice under the first four general superiors of the Society. During the generalate of Claudio Acquaviva (1581–1615), however, it was decreed that the Thirty Days retreat should be undergone twice, first shortly after entering the Society, that is in the noviceship, and then in the final period of spiritual training known as the tertianship. Jesuits were from then on also expected to make a shortened, eight-day version of the *Exercises* every year, as well as using the techniques for meditation described by Ignatius as their form of daily prayer. Even more so than by the Constitutions of the Society, therefore, Jesuits are formed by a constant return to the *Spiritual Exercises*.

Ignatius and his Paris companions had made their election, even Francis Xavier who was at first reluctant and had not yet undergone the *Exercises*, and they determined to give, as it were, concrete evidence of the fact. On August 15, 1534, the Feast of the Assumption of the Virgin, they made their way to a small chapel dedicated to St. Denis (Dionysius), the patron saint of the city who was reputed to have been martyred on this spot on the side of Montmartre about

---

[33] Ibid.

the year 250. The chapel was kept locked but the key was obtained from the Benedictine nuns to whom the building belonged. Mass was said there[34] by the recently ordained Pierre Favre, the only one of the group who had so far been ordained. Before receiving the host, each of the companions took vows of chastity and of poverty—though Favre was, of course, already bound to chastity through his ordination to the priesthood. They did not take a vow of obedience because they had no one to whom they could make it: they were not a religious order, though it seems that Ignatius himself had begun around this time to consider the foundation of an order as a possible next step. The nearest thing to a vow of obedience was a commitment to go to the Holy Land and either to work among Muslims or, if that were to prove impossible, as Ignatius from his own experience must have expected, go to Rome and put themselves at the disposition of the pope.

In April the following year, after a bout of ill health, Ignatius left for Spain to visit his family, though he did not stay in Castle Loyola. He also called on the families of Xavier, Laínez, and Salmerón and settled some outstanding business. He then left for Venice, where he arrived at the end of 1535. Venice was the port of departure for the Holy Land, and it had been agreed that the other companions— during the absence of Ignatius from Paris their number had been increased by three (Claude Jay from the Savoy, Paschase Broët from Picardy, and Jean Codure from Provence), largely through the zeal of Pierre Favre—would all meet up again in Venice in January 1537.

Ignatius spent the whole of 1536 alone in Venice. Or not quite alone, because in Venice he recruited a new disciple, Diego Hoces, a young man from Málaga, who seemingly could not at first choose between Ignatius as his spiritual guide and Gian Pietro Carafa, bishop of Chieti and cofounder of the Theatines,[35] a religious order of priests. He eventually chose Ignatius. For whatever reason, Carafa came to harbor an intense dislike for Ignatius, which was unfortunate at the time, but even more so when he became Pope Paul IV. To balance, as it were, Carafa's hostility, Ignatius became a friend of the papal legate

---

[34] The chapel, much renovated after being destroyed in the French Revolution, can still be visited.

[35] The name "Theatines" comes from the Latin name of Chieti. Hoces died, possibly of the plague, in 1538.

Girolamo Veralli (1497–1555),[36] a consummate papal diplomat who, a decade or so later (1540), was to become a cardinal.

The companions all met up again in Venice in January 1537, still determined to travel to the Holy Land, but as priests. Leaving Ignatius in Venice they set off for Rome to seek papal approval for their pilgrimage and for permission to be ordained. They were received warmly and were invited to conduct a theological debate before Pope Paul III. They were rewarded by the pope with both permissions and with money for their journey: cardinals and other prelates, taking a lead from the pontiff, substantially added to their funds so they returned to Venice with the wherewithal to pay for their passage to the Holy Land.

The first of these, ordination to the priesthood, was readily arranged: the ceremony was conducted on June 24. "They offered us two bishops," wrote Ignatius in a letter dated a month later,[37] but two bishops performing the ordination would have been impossible so in the end they were ordained by a Bishop Vincenzo Negusanti. It is usually presumed that the other one mentioned was the legate Girolamo Veralli, but it is not known when he was consecrated bishop, and he was formally appointed to a bishopric only in 1540. Whatever his ecclesiastical status, he was able to use his legatine powers to grant Ignatius and his companions authority to teach and to preach and to interpret Scripture throughout the Republic of Venice, a remarkable change in fortunes after so many brushes with the Inquisition.

At the time of their ordination the companions had formally pronounced their vows of perpetual poverty in the presence of the papal legate. By this time they were calling themselves "the company" of Jesus, or, in Italian, "la Compagnia di Gesù." While in Ribadeneira's interpretation of Ignatius as a soldier[38] "compagnia" translated into a squadron of horse, it simply meant to those early not-yet-Jesuits a "society." By their vow they were edging ever closer to defining themselves as a religious order, but they were as yet not quite ready

---

[36] Sometimes Verallo.

[37] Munitiz and Endean, *Saint Ignatius of Loyola*, 145–46. Salmerón was too young to be ordained priest, despite a dispensation he had been granted, and was only ordained to the deaconate.

[38] See above, p. 11.

to do so. First, they were still hoping to make their way to Jerusalem. The newly ordained priests delayed saying their first Mass for month, possibly, Brodrick speculates, because they were hoping to do so in the Holy Land.[39]

That was not to be. In 1537 no pilgrim ship sailed because of the likelihood of war between Venice and the Ottoman Turks. There were skirmishes, and Pope Paul III persuaded Emperor Charles V to join with Venice and himself in a Holy League against the threat to Venice and indeed to the whole coastline of Italy. Unable to travel across the Mediterranean, the companions split up into groups, the groups decided by lot, and went out preaching to towns lying within the Republic of Venice, where the legate's authority was acknowledged. But still no pilgrim ship materialized. They had agreed to wait until June 1538 for a ship, so they again separated, some of them this time going further afield than before, and Ignatius with Favre and Laínez traveling to Rome. About eight miles north of Rome, at the village of La Storta, Ignatius had a vision of God the Father and the Son. He says little of this in his *Reminiscences*, and it was left to Laínez, to whom a good few years later he recounted the episode, to fill in the details. En route to Rome, the companions had no clear idea of what their reception might be, but the vision at La Storta encouraged Ignatius. "I will be propitious to you in Rome," were the words Ignatius recalled. He also recalled being set by the Father beside the Son.

The three continued their short journey into Rome, where they were offered accommodation near the church of Santissima Trinità dei Monti: Ignatius in the *Reminiscences* describes it as a vineyard. While Laínez and Salmerón, both, of course, as indeed was Ignatius, masters of the University of Paris, were sent by the pope to teach at La Sapienza, the University of Rome, Ignatius continued to preach and give the *Exercises*. Chief among those who made the *Exercises* was the Venetian nobleman and diplomat Gasparo Contarini, who had recently (1535) been made a cardinal although he was at the time still a layman. As cardinal, he was one of the "Spirituali"—along with his friend, the Englishman Cardinal Reginald Pole—and dedicated to the reform of the Church. Pope Paul put Contarini in charge of a commission to propose Church reform: the subsequent document,

---

[39] Brodrick, *Saint Ignatius Loyola*, 347. Ignatius, however, put off saying his first Mass for eighteen months.

Consilium de Emendanda Ecclesia, "Advice of Reforming the Church," although at the pope's instruction circulated to all the cardinals, was never implemented. Contarini was, then, a significant figure in the papal court and therefore a particularly useful friend for the nascent Society of Jesus.

For that is what the companions had decided to become, perhaps spurred to do so by the renewal of criticism within the Spanish community in Rome, who had heard rumours of their being branded in Spain as *alumbrados* or even Lutherans. They were exonerated, but for Ignatius that was not enough. He demanded that they be formally and publicly cleared, a demand that was unwelcome even to some of their supporters in the city but was eventually agreed by the pope himself, who had been out of the city when the trouble started. If they were formally constituted as a religious order with papal approval, the companions, who were now drifting into Rome to be reunited with Ignatius, would be, they hoped, safe in the future from all such persecution.

They moved from their small house among the vines to a larger one in the center of the city. Though there was still a hankering after Jerusalem, the pope told them, so Bobadilla later reported, that "Rome could be their Jerusalem." There was a series of daily meetings stretching from mid-March 1539 to June 24. On April 15 Pierre Favre celebrated Mass, as he had done on Montmartre nearly five years before, and asked each of those gathered whether it was their will to create a religious order, and if so would they join it. All agreed that this was their intention, and then each received the Eucharist. More debate followed on what should be the structure of this new order. At a meeting on May 3, they decided (1) to take a special vow of obedience to the pope, (2) to put themselves under a religious superior, (3) to go anywhere the pope sent them, (4) to teach catechism, and (5) that each one's work would be determined by the religious superior.

All this was put down in five "chapters," in reality little more than five paragraphs, which were then passed on to Cardinal Contarini to be presented to the pope. Contarini was naturally in favor of establishing the Society of Jesus without more ado, and he read the chapters to the pope, who seemed ready to give his approval. Others among the cardinals were not so certain. One expressed alarm at the fact that there was to be no saying (or singing) of the Divine Office in choir, hitherto a staple of religious life but which had been omitted because such a commitment would have adversely affected the freedom of the Society's members to engage in pastoral work. One thought that the proposal of a special vow of obedience to the pope was unnecessary, and another pointed out that Popes Innocent III and Gregory X had issued instructions that no new religious orders were to be formed—instructions that had not in fact been observed. This last cardinal waived his objections if the number of members were to be restricted. And so it was. When Pope Paul III issued the bull *Regimini militantis ecclesiae* on September 27, 1540, approving the Society of Jesus, the number of members was limited to sixty: the limit was removed four years later by the bull, also of Paul III, *Injunctus vobis*.

The five chapters became the "Formula of the Institute," the basic rule of Jesuit life. It was revised and reproduced once again in the bull of Julius III, *Exposcit debitum*, dated July 21, 1550. The two versions reflect the experience of a decade of Jesuit life, and though the differences were slight, they are significant and will be noted below:

> Whoever wishes to serve as a soldier of God beneath the banner of the cross in our Society, which we desire to be designated by the name of Jesus, and to serve the Lord alone and his vicar on earth, should keep in mind that once he has made a solemn vow of perpetual chastity he is a member of a community founded chiefly for this purpose: to strive especially for the progress of souls in Christian life and doctrine and for the propagation of the faith by the ministry of the word, by spiritual exercises and works of charity, and specifically by the education of children and unlettered persons in Christianity. He should further take care to keep always before his eyes first God, and the nature of this Institute which is his pathway to God; and let him strive with all his effort to achieve this end set before him by God—each one, however, according to the grace which the Holy Spirit has given to him and according to the particular grade of his own vocation, lest anyone should perhaps show zeal, but a zeal which is not according to knowledge.
>
> The selection of each one's grade as well as the entire distribution of employments shall be in the power of the superior or prelate who is to be elected by us, so that the proper order necessary in every well-organized community may be preserved. This superior, with the advice of his associates, shall possess in the council, where the majority of votes always has the right to prevail, the authority to

establish constitutions leading to the achievement of this end which we have set for ourselves. In matters that are more serious and lasting, the council should be understood to be the greater part of the whole Society which can conveniently be summoned by the superior; but in matters less important and more temporary it will be all those who happen to be present in the place where our superior will reside. All right to execute and command, however, will be in the power of the superior.

All the members should know not only when they make their first profession but daily, as long as they live, that this entire Society and each one individually are campaigning for God under [the pope] and the other Roman Pontiffs who will succeed him. And although the Gospel teaches us, we know from orthodox faith, and we firmly profess that all the faithful in Christ are subject to the Roman Pontiff as to their head and the vicar of Jesus Christ, still, for the greater humility of our Society and the perfect mortification of each one of us and the abnegation of our own wills, we have judged that it is of the greatest profit to us to go beyond the ordinary obligations and bind ourselves by a special vow, so that whatever the present Roman Pontiff and others to come will wish to command us with regard to the progress of souls and the propagation of the faith, or wherever he may be pleased to send us to any regions whatsoever, we will obey at once, without subterfuge or excuse, as far as in us lies. We pledge to do this whether he sends us among the Turks or to other infidels, even to the land they call India, or to any heretics or schismatics, or to any of the faithful.

Therefore, those who will come to us should, before they take this burden upon their shoulders, ponder long and seriously, as the Lord has counselled, whether they possess among their resources enough spiritual capital to complete this tower; that is, whether the Holy Spirit who moves them is offering them so much grace that with his aid they have hope of bearing the weight of this vocation. Then, after they have enlisted through the inspiration of the Lord in this militia of Christ, they ought to be prompt in carrying out this obligation which is so great, being clad for battle day and night.

However, to forestall among us any ambition for such missions or provinces, or any refusal of them, let each one promise never to carry on negotiations with the Roman Pontiff about such missions directly or indirectly, but to leave all this care to God and to his vicar and to the superior of the Society. This superior, too, just like the rest, shall also promise not to approach the Pontiff in one way or another about being sent on some mission, except with the advice of the Society.

All should likewise vow that in all matters that concern the observance of this Rule they will obey the superior of the Society. The superior, however, should issue the commands which he knows to be opportune for achieving the end set before him by God and by the Society. In his superiorship he should be ever mindful of the kindness, meekness, and charity of Christ and of the pattern set by Peter and Paul, a norm which both he and the council should keep constantly in view. Particularly let them hold in esteem the instruction of children and the unlettered in the Christian doctrine of the Ten Commandments and other similar elementary principles, whatever will seem suitable to them in accordance with the circumstances of persons, places, and times. For it is very necessary that the superior and the council watch this ministry with diligent attention, since the edifice of faith cannot arise among our fellowmen without a foundation, and also since in our own members there is danger that as one becomes more learned he may tend to decline this occupation, less prestigious at first-glance, although no other is in fact more fruitful either for the edification of the neighbour or for the exercise by our own members of activities that combine both humility and charity. Assuredly, too, both because of the great value of good order and for the sake of the constant practice of humility (never sufficiently praised), the subjects should always be obliged to obey the superior in all matters pertaining to the Society's Institute, and to recognize and properly venerate Christ as present in him.

From experience we have learned that a life removed as far as possible from all contagion of avarice and as like as possible to evangelical poverty is more gratifying, more undefiled, and more suitable for the edification of our neighbours. We likewise know that our Lord Jesus Christ will supply to his servants who are seeking only the kingdom of God what is necessary for food and clothing. Therefore one and all should vow perpetual poverty, declaring that they cannot, either individually or in common, acquire any civil right to any stable goods or to any annually recurring produce or fixed income for the sustenance or use of the Society. Rather, let them be content with only the use of necessary things, when the owners permit it, and to receive money and the sale price of things given them that they may buy what is necessary for themselves.

They may, however, set up a college or colleges in universities capable of having fixed revenues, annuities, or possessions which are to be applied to the uses and needs of students. The general or the Society retains the full government or superintendency over the aforementioned colleges and students; and this pertains to the choice of the rectors or governors and of the scholastics; the admission, dismissal, reception, and exclusion of the same; the enactment of statutes; the arrangement, instruction, edification, and correction of the scholastics; the manner of supplying them with food, clothing, and all the other necessary materials; and every other kind of government, control, and care. All this should be managed in such a way that neither may the students be able to abuse the aforementioned goods nor may the professed Society be able to convert them to its own uses, but may use them to provide for the needs of the scholastics. At length, after their progress in spirit and learning has become manifest and after sufficient testing, they can be admitted into our Society. All those who are in holy orders, even though they can acquire no right to benefices and fixed revenues, should nonetheless be obliged to recite the office according to the rite of the Church.

These are the matters which we have been able to explain about our profession in a kind of sketch, which we are now doing that by this written document we may give succinct information, both to those who are asking us about our Rule of Life and also to those who will later on follow us if, God willing, we shall ever have imitators along this path. By experience we have learned that the path has many and great difficulties connected with it, so we have considered it appropriate to prescribe that no one should be received into this Society who has not been carefully tested and shown himself prudent in Christ and noteworthy for either his learning or the purity of his Christian life. Only in this case should he be admitted into the militia of Jesus Christ. May Christ deign to be favourable to these our tender beginnings, to the glory of God the Father, to whom alone be glory and honour forever.

Amen.[40]

In the later version of the Formula the phrase "for the progress of souls in Christian life and doctrine and for the propagation of the faith" had become "for the progress of souls in Christian life and doctrine and for the *defence* and propagation of the faith," an acknowledgment that Jesuits were already engaged in disputes with Lutherans.[41] There

---

[40] "Formula the Institute (1540)," https://jesuitportal.bc.edu/research/documents/1540_formula/. From *The Constitutions of the Society of Jesus and Their Complementary Norms* (St. Louis: The Institute of Jesuit Sources, 1996), 3–13.

[41] But see Ignatius to Peter Canisius in August 1554: "Seeing the progress that heretics have made in so short a time . . . it seems that our Society has been accepted

was also included a statement about different ranks—"grades," Jesuits called them—in the Society. In neither version, however, is there any mention of schools, the running of which became a major activity: the colleges referred to were those for the education of members of the Society. And above all, what is missing from this brief outline (detailed Constitutions were to come later) is any mention of prayer in common, distinctive dress, and such minutiae of religious life as hitherto embodied in Benedictines, Dominicans, Franciscans, and others.) how important was that??

The Formula speaks of "the superior" of the Society, but when it was drawn up and approved by the pope in his bull, the Society did not have one. On April 9, 1541, Ignatius was unanimously elected to that office. This choice was, perhaps, a foregone conclusion, but Ignatius was not ready to accept the office. He insisted on another vote, held four days later. Again he was elected. He consulted his confessor, who told him to accept, and this time he did so. The companions had all been living together in a large house on the Piazza Frangipani. Now Ignatius moved to a smaller house near the church of Santa Maria della Strada where he was joined, as his secretary, by Juan Alfonso de Polanco. The residence soon proved too small, and one was built beside the church, which, by the time of Ignatius's death, housed eighty Jesuits. It was called the Gesù.

Polanco (1517–1576) had been a papal notary before becoming a Jesuit in 1547 and was an obvious candidate for the role assigned him. Ignatius continued his pastoral work as best he could, among prostitutes and to convert Jews—the latter apostolate meeting with some considerable success.[42] But his main activity in his last years was, with Polanco's assistance, to draw up the Constitutions of the Society and to write letters—letters to friends and benefactors but, above all, letters to members of the Society now around the world. But he also insisted that members of the Society, and by his death on July 31, 1556, there were some seven hundred or more (Polanco reckoned a thousand: many more were recruited, not all stayed, and some were dismissed), should write regularly to Rome to give a detailed

---

by divine providence as one of the efficacious means to repair so immense and evil." Quoted by Harro Höpfl, *Jesuit Political Thought: The Society of Jesus and the State, c. 1540–1630* (Cambridge: Cambridge University Press, 2004), 67.

[42] Meissner, *Ignatius of Loyola*, 212.

account of their activity. Though Ignatius's Constitutions[43] have sub-sequently been copied by other religious orders, they departed from what had hitherto been the norm in many ways, freeing members of the Society from religious duties common in the traditional religious orders so that they might dedicate themselves without hindrance to apostolic work. In asking what was distinctive about the Jesuits, the commitment imposed on members to send to Rome regular accounts of their activities was a very significant element. When in the second half of the eighteenth century the Society came under pressure from hostile governments, the very close links between individual Jesuits and the Society's Generalate were one of the aspects of the Society that most aroused their enemies' ire.

[43] The Constitutions were promulgated in December 1551, and Jerónimo Nadal (1507–1580) was given the task of explaining them to members of the Society through-out Europe. They received formal approval at the first general congregation, sum-moned in 1558 to elect a successor to Ignatius.

Chapter 2

Trent and Its Aftermath

As a new kind of religious order, it was easy to misunderstand the Society of Jesus. As has been seen,[1] Ribadeneira understood the vocation in somewhat militaristic terms, as did Nadal when commenting on the *Spiritual Exercises*.[2] Ignatius, however, had not been a soldier, and the "military" language can be explained away as the common idiom of the period. The founder had, after all, rejected the life and dress of a knight for the life and dress of a pilgrim. But misunderstandings can readily give rise to hostility, and a "black legend" of the Society was soon in circulation.[3] One misunderstanding is, however, still in circulation: that the Society of Jesus was created to oppose the rise of Protestantism.

It is an easy mistake to make. It was shared by many members of the Society. Ambroise Matignon, for instance, wrote in *Études* that "At the time of which we speak [the Council of Trent] the Society had only just been born. God had brought it into being to confront heresy and, as has often been remarked, its founder seem to have been by Providence opposed to Luther, as Saint Augustine had once been to Pelagius."[4] Inigo de Loyola and Martin Luther were roughly contemporaries, and Jesuits very soon found themselves actively opposing the advance of Protestantism in Europe. But that had not been Ignatius's original vision as encapsulated in the Formula of the

---

[1] Above, p. 11.

[2] John W. O'Malley, *The First Jesuits* (Cambridge, MA: Harvard University Press, 1993), 45.

[3] Cf. pp. 291–95.

[4] *Études*, 1867, 326. This rather suggests that in Matignon's view Ignatius was on a par theologically with Augustine of Hippo!

Institute.[5] What was it, then, that made them among the foremost agents of the Counter-Reformation? They were, of course, "reformed" clergy, but then, so were others such as the Theatines, mentioned in the previous chapter. As has also been seen, they were close to one of the leading advocates of Church reform, Cardinal Contarini, but none of this necessarily committed them to a campaign against Protestantism. Although Protestantism appeared to be making inroads in Paris while Ignatius was attending the university there, he does not seem to have reacted to it at the time, at least, in any way that has been recorded. It was only in the 1550 version of the Formula of the Institute that the word "defense" was added to "the propagation of the faith."[6] What had happened between the first and second versions of the Formula was the opening of the Council of Trent.

Trent (Trento) was—is—a town in northern Italy, but while geographically it lay south of the mountains that separate Italy from Germany, it was nonetheless part of the Holy Roman Empire and therefore satisfied Emperor Charles V's demand that a council of the Church to settle the dispute between Rome and the Protestants should be held within the territory of the empire. Charles was eager for such an event. The empire was not, as its name might suggest, a centrally organized political entity. It had come together haphazardly over centuries and was a mix of various types of duchies, bishoprics, and other regimes whose rulers, known as princes, were "electors" of the emperor. Not that, at the time of Charles V, "election" meant anything, if it ever did: from the mid-fifteenth century to the mid-eighteenth the emperor came from the Habsburg family.[7] The rulers of the con-

---

[5] "Luther appears only once in Ignatius's letters; it is regarded as certain that he had read none of Luther's books, and not even an inclination to engage in controversial theology is evident." Hubert Jedin in *History of the Church*, ed. Hubert Jedin, vol. 5 (London: Burns and Oates, 1980), 450. See, however, Ignatius writing to Peter Canisius in August 1554: "Seeing the progress the heretics have made in so short a time, spreading the poison of their evil doctrine through so many peoples and regions . . . it seems that our Society has been accepted by divine providence as one of the efficacious means to repair so immense an evil. It must therefore be solicitous in preparing good remedies to preserve those who remain healthy and to cure those already sick with the heretical plague." Quoted in Harro Höpfl, *Jesuit Political Thought: The Society of Jesus and the State, c. 1540–1630* (Cambridge: Cambridge University Press, 2004), 67.

[6] See above, p. 28.

[7] Charles was also the hereditary king of Spain. His son, Philip II of Spain, did not, however, succeed him as emperor.

stituent states of the empire were independent-minded, not always willing to follow the imperial, that is to say, Habsburg, policies. In particular some had, at the time of Luther's revolt, remained Catholic while others, to the consternation of Charles, had adopted Lutheranism. Charles, threatened to the west by Francis I of France and to the east by the advance of the Turks under Suleiman the Magnificent, was in desperate need of unity among the states of the Holy Roman Empire. He hoped, in vain as it was to turn out, that a council might reconcile Catholics and Protestants within his dominion. To do so two things were needed from the churchmen, namely, the settlement of doctrinal issues dividing Catholics and Protestants and the reform of much that Protestants regarded as corrupt within Catholicism. When the council eventually met, after long delays occasioned, largely, by political factors, especially the conflict between Charles and Francis, it was decided that theological issues and questions of reform should be addressed together.[8]

Both of these issues arose from the teachings of Martin Luther, an Augustinian friar who had been lecturing on biblical exegesis, especially the exegesis of St. Paul, at the University of Wittenberg. He seems to have developed his radical theological opinions around 1515, and these will be discussed in a moment, but the Lutheran "revolt" sprang more immediately from his posting Ninety-Five Theses on the door of Wittenberg Cathedral. If indeed he did so: it is disputed whether the theses were actually "posted" on the cathedral door, but they were undoubtedly published one way or another and quickly achieved a wide circulation. The theses arose from Luther's indignation at the preaching of the Dominican Johann Tetzel, who was attempting to persuade people to buy indulgences to help pay for the rebuilding in Rome of St. Peter's basilica. This Luther regarded as an outrageous abuse, indicative of the corruption of the Church and its officials.

Though now marginal to current Catholic devotion, indulgences remain part of the Church's practice despite the complexity of the theology and the controversy surrounding them. Obtaining an indulgence, to put it in its crudest form, was thought to release from purgatory the soul of those to whom the indulgence was applied, the

---

[8] Pope Paul III wanted doctrinal issues to be discussed first and afterward matters concerning reform, and he agreed only reluctantly that the two should be discussed *pari passu*.

"time off" being determined by the type of indulgence: a plenary indulgence remitting all the time that a soul might otherwise have spent in the next life being punished for their sins. One obvious problem with this explanation, and one that recurs in other contexts, is that in the next life, whatever it may be, there can be no "time," though this was not Luther's objection. Nor was it that the Church, or at least Tetzel, was selling holy things for cash, which amounts to simony. His problem sprang from the theory of justification by faith alone, which he developed during his lectures on St. Paul and from his reading of St. Augustine, especially Augustine in his controversy with the Pelagians. They had held, or were thought to have held, that because human nature was created by God it was capable of itself to choose the good, thus denying, at least by implication, the need for God's grace.[9] Indulgences, which amounted to good works on behalf of oneself or on behalf of others, could not, in Luther's eyes, contribute anything to the salvation of the soul: men and women could only be saved ("justified") by faith alone.

There was much, of course, on which Catholics and Lutherans could agree.[10] They agreed with the doctrine of original sin, as formulated by St. Augustine, that the guilt of the sin of Adam had been passed on from generation to generation. Again according to Augustine, one of the consequences of original sin to be found in every human being, even after baptism when the guilt of original sin had been expunged, was concupiscence, a disordered or irrational desire for material things that could override the rational desire for things of God. Catholics and Lutherans also agreed that concupiscence led to sinfulness, but for Lutherans that remaining concupiscence was itself a sin despite baptism—in other words, that human nature itself was totally corrupt, thus preventing humankind seeking salvation. Only by the grace of God, therefore, could a person be saved, a doctrine that inevitably led to the doctrine of predestination, that some were destined by God for salvation and others for damnation—a

[9] What exactly was taught by Pelagius himself, a British-born theologian (c. 360–418), is unclear: the version of his teaching that Augustine set out to refute was mainly propounded by his disciples, in particular by Julian of Eclanum (386–455).

[10] By the time justification was being debated at Trent, early in 1546, there were even more radical ideas about it in circulation, in particular those of the Geneva-based Reformer Jean Calvin (1509–1564).

teaching that was more prominent in Calvinism, it should be said, than in Lutheranism.

The topic was further complicated because, although Catholics could not deny the necessity of God's grace, they were nonetheless unwilling to accept the Lutheran doctrine that sinfulness, in the form of concupiscence, remained even after baptism. Hence, they also rejected the conviction, to be found in Luther and Calvin, that original sin had in effect destroyed free will. It was this that the Jesuits attending the Council of Trent seized upon, schooled as they were in the *Spiritual Exercises*, where the freedom to make a free choice for God was central. As the late Michael Buckley, SJ, has put it, "Freedom constitutes a presupposition of the *Exercises*, the condition of their possibility."[11]

There were four Jesuits present at the council, though only Diego Laínez and Alfonso Salmerón were there for all three sessions. They came as papal theologians at the request, in the first instance, of Pope Paul III, though Laínez, perhaps the most academically gifted of Ignatius's first followers, attended the final session in his own right as the general superior of the Society, elected in July 1558 after the death of Ignatius on July 31, 1556. The other two present were the Savoyard Claude Jay and the Nijmegen-born Peter Canisius, both there at the request of the reform-minded prince-bishop of Augsburg, Count Otto Truchsess von Waldburg.

All played some part in the proceedings. Canisius, who had taken part in several debates in Germany with Lutherans, proposed that the chalice be extended to the laity, thus responding to one of the Lutherans' major grievances, but nothing came of it. Jay, whose experience in Germany had driven home to him the generally poor state of the clergy's grasp of theology, was active in promoting the need for priestly formation, and the council eventually mandated seminaries that, after they had been established by bishops, Jesuits frequently found themselves running. Toward the end of the council

---

[11] Michael J. Buckley, "Freedom, Election and Self-Transcendence," in *Ignatian Spirituality in a Secular Age*, ed. George P. Schmer (Waterloo, Ontario: Wilfrid Laurier University Press, 1984), 67. Buckley goes on, "This understanding of human freedom as the potentiality for self-determination must be sharply distinguished from other meanings that this word has enjoyed in the history of Western thought. Liberty, for example, in Locke and Hume is not located in choice, but in the unimpeded power to execute choice" (ibid., 69).

Laínez and Salmerón were very active defending the prerogatives of the papacy, especially perhaps in the debate over the requirement for bishops to reside within their dioceses, a particularly important aspect of Church reform.

It was in the debate over justification, however, that Laínez made his mark, thanks largely to a speech by the very learned Girolamo Seripando (1493–1563), from 1539 to 1551 the prior general of the Augustinians, the religious order to which Martin Luther had belonged. In October 1546 Seripando proposed a theory of double justification in an effort to reach some sort of accommodation with the Lutherans. Ignatius had sent the Jesuits at Trent a letter laying down how he expected them to behave: they were to engage in their customary apostolic work, to advance their views modestly, and to live together simply. Juan de Polanco, Ignatius's secretary and secretary to the generals who succeeded him, added that Ignatius did not want the Jesuits he sent to Trent to side with opinions held by "the heretics."[12] In Seripando's intervention Laínez thought he saw elements of Lutheranism, and he launched an attack on the unfortunate Augustinian in which he laid out at length what he understood to be the Catholic doctrine concerning the relation of nature and grace and in defense of human freedom. He would not, he said, quote any authority that he had not thoroughly read. The fathers of the council were impressed at the Jesuit's tour de force: they requested that his disquisition be entered into the proceedings of the council of which the Jesuit, though a papal theologian, was not technically a member. His views carried the day, and Seripando's much more conciliatory approach was rejected. If Emperor Charles V, who had died by the time the council had ended, had wanted the council to bring about some reconciliation between Catholics and Lutherans, his hopes were to be dashed.

Laínez and Salmerón may have been distinguished theologians, but there were others at Trent, such as Girolamo Seripando and the Dominican friar Domingo de Soto, with a far longer established reputation for learning. And then there arrived in Trent another Dominican, Melchior Cano (1509–1560), who not only did not share the

---

[12] O'Malley, *The First Jesuits*, 325. Polanco went on to say that Ignatius was thinking at one time of removing Laínez from Trent as the council did not, or so it seemed to him, appear to be making any progress.

Jesuits' views on grace and free will but was hostile to the Society itself and to Ignatius Loyola personally.[13] He had met Ignatius several times and thought him arrogant and prone to laying claim to divine revelation—something that, in Cano's view, put him on par with the *alumbrados*.

In 1552 the two Jesuit theologians, in an attempt to settle their differences, paid Cano a visit. The meeting did not go well. It ended with Laínez swearing at the Dominican, using words Cano, it would seem, rather relished referring to but not revealing.[14] Laínez, on the other hand, was deeply embarrassed by his behavior—which he reported to Ignatius and asked for a penance—and immediately returned to Cano's residence to ask forgiveness, but forgiveness was not forthcoming. It was the very worst time to be making more enemies. As essentially "the pope's men," the Jesuits had enjoyed excellent relations with the papacy, but with the election of Ignatius's old enemy from his Venice days,[15] Gian Pietro Carafa, as Paul IV in May 1555, that changed: Ignatius visibly shook at the news, reported an eyewitness. He already had troubles enough. Some Dominicans in Spain had been campaigning against the Society. In 1549 Ignatius persuaded the master general of the Dominicans to send out a letter forbidding members of his order from attacking the Jesuits. The letter was briefly effective, but then the Spanish campaign broke out anew, with Melchior Cano to the fore.

Ignatius died on July 31, 1556, while the hostility to the Society was at its height. It was almost two years before Laínez could be elected as his successor. There were a number of reasons for the delay, not least the antipathy to all things Spanish manifested by the pope, who entered into a foolish war with Philip II of Spain in which the papal forces were fairly swiftly and comprehensively defeated.[16] It did not help that some leading Jesuits had originally wanted the

---

[13] O'Malley (ibid., 292) suggests Cano had met Ignatius in Rome in 1542 when the Dominican was attending a general chapter of his order, but he had also been in the Dominican house in Salamanca when Ignatius ran into trouble with the Inquisition; cf. above, pp. 15–16.

[14] Jeronimo Nadal, on the other hand, had no such inhibitions: "This is shit," said Laínez (O'Malley, ibid., 293n29).

[15] Cf. above, p. 21.

[16] The Carafa family were proud of their Neapolitan heritage and resented that city falling under Spanish rule, governed as it was at this time by Castilian viceroys.

election of a new general to take place in Spain. Even when the election took place, Paul IV sent a cardinal to preside, rather than leave it all to the Jesuits themselves. His presence almost certainly did not affect the outcome; Laínez had always been the most likely candidate, but the pope then demanded that the general's term of office should be limited to three years, in contradiction to the life term Ignatius had written into the Constitutions. He also insisted that one of Cano's complaints, that members of the Society did not pray the Divine Office together in choir, should be met. This too the new general had to concede, but when Paul IV died in August 1559, much excoriated by the people of Rome, Jesuits reverted to saying the Office individually, as mandated by the Constitutions.

To understand what happened next in the conflict between the Society and (some, certainly not all) Dominicans it is necessary to recall the various degrees of being a Jesuit. There were the new entrants, novices, some of them already ordained priests. After they had taken their first vows, they were known as scholastics until they took, after their ordination to the priesthood, final vows either as spiritual coadjutors or as professed fathers—these last the only ones who took the fourth vow binding them to serve the pope of the day. There were, and are, also "lay brothers" who go through the noviceship but who are not seeking, for whatever reason, to become priests. Significant canonical differences exist between the "simple" first vows and the final solemn vows, not least the fact that those in simple vows, which for Jesuits were permanent and did not have to be renewed annually, could be readily dismissed from the Society by their superiors, something that became significant in the controversy with the Jansenists,[17] whereas those in solemn vows could not. At a time of rapid growth in numbers, which the sixteenth century certainly was, the number of those in simple but permanent vows far outstripped those in final vows, so when a Spanish Dominican named Peredo started to claim that those in simple vows were not properly members of a religious order, the Jesuit general, by this time Everard Mercurian from the prince-bishopric of Liège, had to ask the pope, Gregory XII, to intervene. Gregory condemned this opinion in two bulls in consecutive years, 1583 and 1584.

---

[17] Cf. below, p. 217.

The papal bulls failed to halt the controversy, and it was joined by Domingo Bañez, OP, the leading theologian in the University of Salamanca, who, in December 1589, approved the public defense by a young Dominican of the thesis that those in simple vows were not properly members of a religious order. The Jesuits in Salamanca could not let this pass and appealed to the pope's ambassador, or papal nuncio, to have it banned. During the unfortunate young man's defense of the thesis a lawyer strode in and read out the nuncio's instruction that the discussion must stop immediately.[18] Not surprisingly, such a public humiliation made Bañez even more critical of the Society, criticisms that he listed in a book of 1590 titled *Relectio de merito*. Chief among his allegations was the charge that Jesuits had departed from the teaching of St. Thomas to which they were committed by their Constitution and later and more explicitly by their own plan of studies, the *Ratio Studiorum*.[19] The controversy, largely confined to Spain—even Philip II became involved as a supporter of the Dominicans—became fairly rancorous, and the authorities in Spain, both of the Order of Preachers and of the Society of Jesus, attempted to put an end to it, which might have succeeded had it not been for the Spanish Inquisition. Not that the Inquisition was concerned with the niceties of the debate. It simply wanted to revise the index of forbidden books and set up a commission to do so. Domingo Bañez was a leading member of the commission, giving him the opportunity to denounce recent Jesuit writings on theology.

That was the opinion of Luis de Molina (1535–1600), the first Jesuit to write a commentary on Thomas Aquinas's *Summa Theologica*, the "set book" for Jesuits beginning their course of theology according to the *Ratio Studiorum*; one of the Jesuit books denounced to the Inquisition in 1591 was the *Ratio Studiorum* itself. More significant in this conflict between Jesuits and Dominicans, however, was one of

[18] This account, and much of what follows, is drawn from James Brodrick's two-volume work *Robert Bellarmine* (London: Longmans, 1950). Although the book was published by Longmans, the chapter being used here was not: it was removed at the behest of the diocesan censor. Nonetheless, a copy of the complete, uncensored version is to be found in the Jesuit Library currently at Senate House, University of London. The excised chapter was intended to be the first chapter in volume 2.

[19] George E. Ganss, *The Constitutions of the Society of Jesus* (St. Louis: Institute of Jesuit Sources, 1970), 219. The *Ratio Studiorum* is much more explicit, and will be discussed below, pp. 151ff.

Molina's own books in which he engaged with one of the major issues at the Council of Trent, human freedom and its relationship to divine grace, described by Ambroise Matignon as "the most complicated of all the difficulties that one encounters in trying to establish a perfect accord between God's foreknowledge and human liberty," that is to say, how "the will of the Creator and our own [can] operate simultaneously, yet remain distinct."[20] Molina's book was titled "The concord [agreement] of free will with the gifts of grace, and with [God's] foreknowledge, providence, predestination and condemnation," commonly known simply as the *Concordia*, and originally published in 1589. Molina's argument, however, which he developed while lecturing at the University of Evora, was already well known before it appeared in print.[21]

As a contemporary philosopher has pointed out, "This discussion concerning divine omniscience and its harmony with human freedom is given in a theological context in which the arguments are incomprehensible when posited from the perspective of a philosophy that does not share the dogmas of revelation."[22] But for both Molina and Bañez it was the theological context that mattered, the relationship between grace and free will, the major issue left unresolved by the Council of Trent: the Council fathers, while rejecting the Lutheran doctrine, refused to adjudicate between competing Catholic interpretations. The "solutions" proposed by both Molina and Bañez had, of course, not been discussed because they were not yet formulated.

Or, more accurately perhaps, Molina's version had not yet been formulated whereas that of Bañez was, the Dominicans claimed, nothing other than the teaching of St. Thomas Aquinas, which the Jesuits were obliged to follow, according to their Constitutions' *Ratio Studiorum*. That was not the case with Molina, whose theory of the relationship between grace and free will departed from Aquinas. In volume 3 of his monumental *History of Philosophy*, Frederick Copleston explains Molina's position as follows:

---

[20] For Matignon, cf. above, p. 31, n. 4.

[21] The full Latin title is *Liberi Arbitrii cum Gratia Donis, divina praescentia, providentia, praedestinatione et reprobatione, Concordia*.

[22] David Alvargonzález, "Relevance of the Metaphysical Discussion Concerning Divine Sciences in Molina's *Concordia* and Bañez's *Apology*," *International Journal of Philosophy and Theology* 3, no. 1 (June 2015): 91.

Molina affirmed that "efficacious grace," which includes in its concept the free consent of the human will, is not intrinsically different in nature from merely "sufficient grace." Grace which is merely sufficient is grace which is sufficient to enable the human will to elicit a salutary act, if the will were to consent to it and co-operate with it. It becomes "efficacious" if the will does in fact consent to it. Efficacious grace is thus the grace with which the human will does in fact freely co-operate.[23]

But in any understanding of God's omniscience, God must know how an individual will act, in which case is not an individual predetermined (predestined) to act one way rather than another? Not so, says Molina, because God knows all possible actions, one of which the individual freely chooses. This knowledge of all possible actions, which possible actions are sometimes called "futurabilia," is "scientia media," and it is by using this concept of "scientia media" that Molina seems most obviously to depart from Aquinas.

Copleston suggests that whereas Molina began with what is best known to us, namely, human freedom, Bañez began with first principles, namely, that God must be the first cause of all human action: "His view was that God moves non-free agents to act necessarily and free agents, when they act as free agents, to act freely. In other words, God moves every contingent agent to act in a manner conformable to its nature,"[24] an argument that in the view of Molina and his supporters explained nothing and could, if followed to its logical conclusion, make God responsible for sin. Molina accused Bañez before the Inquisition of Lutheran and Calvinist sympathies and sent the Inquisition extracts from the Dominican's writings alongside extracts from Luther and Calvin. Meanwhile, Dominicans across Spain preached against the theory of the Jesuit. There followed public debates in Valladolid, the first held in the Jesuit house, the second a few weeks later in the Dominican, both of which succeeded in inflaming feelings

[23] Frederick Copelston, *History of Philosophy*, vol. 3 (London: Burns and Oates, 1953), 342. Copleston was professor of the history of philosophy at the University of London. He was himself a Jesuit, but his multivolume history from Greek philosophy down to modern times is nonetheless generally regarded as a remarkably objective account.

[24] Ibid., 343. Copleston comments, "One might perhaps suggest that the general humanistic movement of the Renaissance was reflected to some extent in Molinism."

rather than reaching agreement. In May 1594 Rodrigo de Castro, the cardinal archbishop of Seville, referred the whole affair to Pope Clement VIII. The pope passed on the case to his theologian.

While that was the natural thing to do, there was a problem: the pope's theologian was a member of the Society of Jesus, Robert Bellarmine (1542–1621). With the issue of scientia media, which the Dominicans had attacked as being an innovation—a potent criticism at the time—Bellarmine had no problem. The term may be new, he said, but the idea behind it was quite traditional. Though he criticized Molina, sometimes arguing that the censures launched against him, though they were justifiable, were nonetheless too harsh, for the most part he defended the theories of his fellow Jesuit.

Next, the Dominicans presented a memorial, dated October 1597, to the pope asking that the "law of silence" imposed on both parties in Spain should be removed from their order because they were only teaching long-held doctrines whereas the Jesuits were innovators and had therefore had rightly been told to keep quiet. The memorial was again passed on to Bellarmine, who this time had much less sympathy with the position of Bañez, who had translated the document from Spanish into Latin for the benefit of the pope—though he went on to say he had added some things and suppressed others, about which Bellarmine took a dim view. In his final report to Pope Clement, Bellarmine acknowledged that both sides were convinced that their arguments were correct and that it was going to be a long time before the issue of grace and free will could be resolved. Meanwhile, he suggested even-handedly, let each side teach and defend their own position, and criticize the other, but neither side was to call their opponents heretics.

That was not the plan pursued by Clement. Instead he set up a seven-member commission to examine Molina's *Concordia*. They reported with surprising speed, given the complexity of the issue, and declared that the book should be banned. Clement was not impressed. He ordered that more evidence be gathered in Spain and sent to Rome, where the commission was set to work again. This time they took eight months rather than three but came to the same conclusion. There was something of an outcry against the potential condemnation of Molina, and not just from Jesuits, so Clement decided on a new tack: the different theories were to be debated before the Inquisition in Rome. There were two inconclusive debates in February 1599, then a third in March. For the March debate Clement added to the cardinal in charge of the Inquisition two other cardinals, one Dominican and one Jesuit—the Jesuit being Robert Bellarmine, created a cardinal just before the debate began.

It was hardly a debate. The two sides, when they were not criticizing each other, were starting from different premises. The Dominicans wanted Luis de Molina's *Concordia* to be examined line by line—and then condemned. The Jesuits, on the other hand, said they were not prepared to defend every word of the *Concordia* but instead insisted that the real issue to be discussed was the relationship between grace and free will, not necessarily Molina's interpretation of it. Then in April 1600 the cardinal in charge of the Inquisition died, and the process came to an end; Pope Clement reinstated the earlier commission of enquiry, increasing its numbers to eleven. Once more this enlarged commission took surprisingly little time to reach its conclusion, presenting its report at the end of August 1600. It censured twenty propositions taken from the *Concordia*.

It was clear by this time that Clement VIII was more sympathetic to the Dominican point of view than that of the Jesuits. It is possible he was considering a general council to decide the matter, but according to Bellarmine's own account he was thinking of making a decision himself, defining, in other words, what Catholics ought to believe on grace and free will. Bellarmine rather boldly pointed out that he, the pope, was no theologian and should do no such thing—Clement was in fact a lawyer by training. There was a rumor in Spain that an effigy of Molina had been publicly burned in Rome, or so a Spanish Jesuit wrote to Bellarmine in some alarm. Bellarmine said in reply that the rumor was not true and added that the subject of grace and free will was not at the time being discussed but, "When it comes up for debate, we hope in the Lord that the theory which affirms it [the predetermination by grace of the will] and so destroys the indifference necessary for freedom of choice will be judged at least very dangerous."[25]

The commissioners met again to hear the twenty condemned propositions from the *Concordia* debated by a Jesuit and a Dominican. Again they came down on the side of the Dominicans and sent their

---

[25] The story is told by Brodrick on what would have been pages 32 and 33 of his second volume, see above, footnote 17.

report and all other papers to the pope, suggesting (a) that he did not need to show them to the Jesuits and (b) he did not really need to study them, just to accept the commissioners' findings. Pope Clement was clearly jaded by the prolonged impasse, and Bellarmine was seriously alarmed that he would indeed decide for himself. The cardinal therefore wrote another letter to the pope pointing out that the matter needed to be decided either by a council of the Church or by learned theologians, and he reminded Clement with sundry examples that only confusion had resulted when pontiffs went their own way in such matters.

Whether or not Clement was moved by Bellarmine's letter, he now decided on a different strategy, namely, to hold discussions in his presence, beginning in March 1602. These became known as the *Congregationes* [meetings] *de Auxiliis* ["about help," "auxilium" means assistance/help/aid, i.e., the aid of grace], when Jesuit and Dominican theologians once again came before the pope who fairly clearly favored the Dominican position, despite the fact that his personal theologian was a Jesuit. An opportunity presented itself to solve the problem when the archbishopric of Capua became vacant: Robert Bellarmine was appointed and speedily withdrew from Rome to take up residence in his new see. As he himself commented, his sudden disappearance came as a surprise to many, because it was usually difficult to winkle people out of the papal court.

Bellarmine's departure occurred after the first of the *Congregationes*. There were, in all, sixty-eight sessions over the years from 1602 to 1605. Molina died just before they began; Bañez shortly before they ended.[26] Clement VIII died in March 1605, and his successor, Innocent XI, elected on April 1, died on the twenty-seventh of that month. Innocent's successor, Paul V, was much friendlier to the Jesuits, not least, perhaps, because in the clash between the Paul and the Republic of Venice over papal prerogatives the Society backed the papacy and, as a consequence, were expelled from Venice, a ban that remained in force even after the pope had conceded defeat. One sign of Paul's leanings toward the Jesuits was his summoning Bellarmine back from Capua to take part in the debates over grace and free will and his adding to the tribunal a French cardinal, du Perron, who had told Clement that French and German Calvinists and Lutherans held

[26] Brodrick, *Robert Bellarmine*, 42–43.

similar views to those espoused by the Dominicans and were delighted the debate seemed to be going their way.

Hitherto the debate had fundamentally been about Molina's *Concordia*, Pope Paul tried to change the direction of the discussions by focusing on Bañez. One of the central planks of his theory of grace was *praedeterminatio* or *praemotio physica*, a phrase that his opponents believed committed the Dominican to denying the freedom of the will. In his book *When Great Theologians Feuded: Thomas Lemos and Leonardus Lessius on Grace and Predestination*, Guido Stucco remarks:

> [The] term was first coined and amply used by Dominican theologian Bañez, who claimed that although it does not appear in Scripture and Tradition (just as the term 'Trinity' did not either prior to the Council of Nicaea), it fittingly conveyed what Augustine and Aquinas taught concerning the way God operates in the human heart and will, by causing and determining a person to physically move and perform certain deeds even before (pre) he/she arrives at the moment of exercising the choice of doing or not doing a certain deed. Disputed questions include: does PP [*praemotio physica*] consist of an irresistible physical movement or in moral exhortations and suasions? Can PP be resisted and opposed? Does PP really differ from Luther's and Calvin's views of how God operates on the human will? Is it a heretical or an orthodox view? Does it apply to evil deeds as well, meaning: does God predetermine human beings to commit sins?[27]

One of those who thought that *praemotio physica* verged on the heretical was Robert Bellarmine. In 1576 he had been appointed to the newly created professorship of controversy at the Jesuits' Roman College, and his lectures had appeared in two volumes in 1586 and 1588 under the title of *Disputationes de controversiis Christianae fidei adversus huius temporis haeretici*, which were commonly known simply as Bellarmine's *Controversies* and much admired. As one of the commissioners appointed by the pope to debate grace and free will pointed out, Bellarmine in these much acclaimed volumes had already rejected Bañez's position, and no one had complained about

---

[27] This book, which appears to have been privately printed, was published in 2017. The quotation is on p. 4.

it. This argument effectively counteracted the other commissioners' efforts to have Molina's *Concordia* put on the list of banned books.

Something had to be done to break the impasse. Pope Paul called together the cardinals from the commission and asked their views, at the end of which he made a decision: the Jesuits were to be allowed to continue teaching Molina's theory, the Dominicans that of Bañez. And neither side was to claim their opponents as heretics. This was precisely the solution, it should be recalled, that had been proposed by Bellarmine a decade earlier.[28]

That should have been the end of the debate over grace and free will, but it was not. In 1610 Leonard Lessius (1554–1623), a Jesuit professor of theology at the University of Leuven (Louvain), published a book titled *On Efficacious Grace and Predestination*. Bellarmine was alarmed and criticized the book, arguing that Lessius's position was contrary to that of St. Augustine and therefore risked embroiling the Jesuits once more in a theological controversy with the Dominicans, contrary to the pope's explicit instruction. Lessius, who as a student in Rome had studied under Bellarmine, was rather taken aback to find himself apparently at odds with his former professor and wrote a book defending himself, which he sent to the Jesuit general, Claudio Acquaviva. He did not receive the response he had hoped for. Instead, in December 1613 Acquaviva issued an instruction to members of the Society imposing on them Bellarmine's understanding of the relationship of free will and grace, which was contrary to that of Lessius, though Brodrick claims that he did not mean to impose it in every detail, that Acquaviva's successor as general, Muzio Vitelleschi, who governed the Society from 1615 to 1645, made that clear, and, he added, that in any case many Jesuit theologians in practice did after all follow the teaching on grace as expounded by Leonard Lessius.[29] Lessius was something of a firebrand. A few years later Vitelleschi banned one of his books attacking King James VI and I's *Basilikon Doron*, a defense of the divine right of kings, because the Jesuits were hoping for a more sympathetic attitude to English Catho-

---

[28] See above, p. 44.

[29] Brodrick, *Robert Bellarmine*, 49, citing the seventeen-column article "Congruisme" in volume 3 of the *Dictionnaire de Théologie Catholique*.

lics from the new king—in vain as it turned out.[30] Bellarmine wrote to Lessius in May 1614, "I approve and am glad that you have given up writing and turned your mind to reading and contemplation, for it is almost impossible to write anything at present, without laying oneself open to the cavils of either enemies or friends. Your Reverence has published quite enough already."[31] The cardinal went on to tell him that two books by Spanish Dominicans on grace had been banned by Rome and that in his opinion only a general council of the Church could settle the matter.

So soon after the Council of Trent, however, it was highly unlikely that another would be called. Rather than a council, Pope Paul had instead promised a papal decree. It has never been written. In the meantime, the pope forbade the publication of any further books on grace and free will, a prohibition that came into force in December 1611 and was twice renewed.

The *De Auxiliis* controversy, pitting upstart Jesuits against well-established Dominicans, is not commonly an expansive topic in histories of the Society of Jesus, and it is far from contemporary concerns. Having a common, if not enemy, at least adversary—some of the language employed being distinctly unfriendly—fostered a sense of community in a Society that, as will be seen in the next chapter, was rapidly becoming spread across the globe. But more significant, perhaps, is the emergence of Francisco Suarez (1548–1617), whom Pope Paul V labelled the *doctor eximius* [= "outstanding"] *et pius*. As a young Jesuit Suarez studied at the University of Salamanca where, as a layman, he had already studied law. After completing his studies,[32] he taught in various places in Spain and then, for a short time, in Rome (1580–1585), where Lessius was among his pupils: it was Suarez's terminology in the grace and free will debate that Lessius used rather than that of Molina. Suarez presented his writings on philosophy and theology as a commentary on Thomas Aquinas, though he did not hesitate to distance himself from Thomas on occasion, especially

---

[30] Despite it being banned, a copy of the book, printed by the Jesuits at St. Omer, found its way into the library of George Abbot, archbishop of Canterbury from 1611 to 1633, thence into the library of Lambeth Palace, the archbishop's London residence, and a refutation published.

[31] Quoted by Brodrick, *Robert Bellarmine*, 49.

[32] Or almost—he did not take a doctorate until late in life.

in his teaching on metaphysics, the nature of being.[33] Although they were not obliged to do so, Jesuit lecturers tended until late in the twentieth century to follow Suarez rather than Thomas—the present writer was, in the late 1950s, taught epistemology, the theory of knowledge, by someone who was a Suarezian. By that date, however, he was an exception among his colleagues, but for some three centuries there was a common body of teaching within the Society, even if not every Jesuit philosopher or theologian fully adhered to it.

Possibly Suarez's most important work was not in theology or philosophy but in political theory. His *De Legibus*, "On Law," was written while he was teaching at the University of Coimbra, a post to which he was appointed in 1596 by Spain's Philip II and that he held until his death: the book itself appeared in 1612. It may seem odd to bring in legal theory under the mantle of theology, but everyone agreed that law ultimately came from God: the question at issue was how it was mediated. But in any case the Jesuit Constitutions forbade members from entering faculties of law (Suarez, as has been noted above, studied law before entering the Society), so it was only under the aegis of theology that legal issues could be discussed. And it was inevitable that they should be discussed. As Harro Höpfl puts it, "The Society's rooted belief was that order [in the community] presupposes orders [from a ruler]."[34] Which is all well and good—and not particularly controversial—but it leaves all sorts of difficult questions unanswered, the most obvious being what happens when there is an unjust ruler.

One Spanish Jesuit, Juan de Mariana (1536–1624), had a simple solution. In his *De rege et regis institutione* ("On the King and the Institution of Kingship") of 1598 he argued that in the case of political oppression it was morally legitimate to remove the monarch, if necessary by tyrannicide. Mariana, who during a fairly brief professorship in Rome had taught Robert Bellarmine, was a somewhat problematic character who apparently wrote a book, unpublished at his death but found among his effects, on the errors of government in the Society (*Discursus de erroribus qui in forma gubernationis Societatis Jesu occur-*

---

[33] For a summary of Suarez's views, see Copleston, *History of Philosophy*, 356–79.
[34] Höpfl, *Jesuit Political Thought*, 209.

runt):[35] it was later to be used against the Society when the Jesuits were suppressed in Spain. As will be seen below (p. 52), Mariana's views on tyrannicide caused considerable problems for Jesuits in France, despite the fact that the general of the Society almost immediately after *De rege et regis institutione* had been published forbade its members from teaching it, a ban that was reasserted in 1610 and again in 1614—and by the pope in 1625.[36]

An alternative to tyrannicide would have been the right of a pope to depose a monarch—as Pope Pius V attempted to do in 1570 to Elizabeth I of England with unfortunate consequences for her Catholic subjects and, of course, to the Jesuits, priests and brothers, who were later to work there. The conviction that a pope could depose a monarch for heresy—and in the view of Catholics the English monarch was undoubtedly a heretic—was commonplace, but it was not straightforward and in any case was becoming much less of an issue by the early seventeenth century.[37] More significant in England was the doctrine of the divine right of kings espoused by James I and VI, which, as has been seen, was attacked by Lessius (cf. above, pp. 46ff.). In the form of political theory advanced by Suarez, and later by Bellarmine likewise, while all authority comes from God, a standard Catholic doctrine, the authority of a prince came by way of the community over which he ruled. Authority was given by God to the community, which then passed it on to the ruler; it did not come directly from God to the prince. There was, in other words, a contract between the people, on whom God had bestowed authority, and the ruler who was called on to exercise it for the good of the community—for the common good, in other words. This was not original to Suarez; similar views had been expressed in the Middle Ages, but no one had developed it so fully as did the Jesuit theologian in his *Defense of the Catholic Faith*: not surprisingly, King James I had the book burned.

---

[35] There is no entry for him in the otherwise pretty comprehensive *Cambridge Encyclopedia of the Jesuits* edited by Thomas Worcester, SJ (Cambridge: Cambridge University Press, 2017). He is not even in the index.

[36] Höpfl, *Jesuit Political Thought*, 337. The book was condemned to be burned by the Parlement of Paris in 1610 (ibid., 321).

[37] Ibid., 346.

The authority of a pope, on the other hand, came directly from God. As Copleston remarks,

> What better way of taking the wind out of the sails of the royalists could be devised than that of maintaining that though the monarch's power does not come directly from the pope it does not come directly from God either, but from the people? What better way of exalting the spiritual power could be found than that of asserting that it is the pope alone who receives his authority directly from God?[38]

Once again, there was nothing original in these arguments. The superiority of the spiritual power over the temporal was a constant of Church teaching from the (very) early Middle Ages. But there was a twist to the approach of Suarez and more particularly Bellarmine: while they both certainly believed in the authority of a pope to depose, in certain circumstances, a wayward monarch, to the displeasure of the papacy, Bellarmine argued that a pope's authority over a monarch was only indirect, in as much as, where there was a clash between the temporal and the spiritual, the former must make way for the latter, the traditional teaching that was reasserted by Suarez in his *Defense of the Catholic Faith*.

For a Society whose fifth general congregation, which took place from November 1593 to January 1594, told its members in no uncertain terms to avoid meddling in the secular affairs of princes—a prohibition that was a decade later repeated by Acquaviva—its theologians seemed to spend a great deal of time discussing political issues.[39] The difficulty lay with the word "secular." From the perspective of a Jesuit, there was not much that a prince could do when drawing up laws for his subjects that did not have some bearing or other on their eternal well-being. They believed, along with almost everybody else, that religion was necessary for the well-being of the state and

---

[38] Copleston, *History of Philosophy*, 347.

[39] "Over all, Jesuits accepted political involvement related to concrete goals of the Society such as the establishment of colleges, approved limited activity in support of more general goals such as the struggle against heresy, and rejected any action that could harm the Society's reputation." A. Lynn Martin, *The Jesuit Mind* (Ithaca: Cornell University Press, 1988), 225. Persons's activity in relation to a possible Spanish invasion of England to restore the Catholic faith rather stretches the meaning of the word "limited."

that the religion in question was Catholicism: heresy undermined the state. Jesuit commitment to freedom did not go so far as embracing the right of heretics to pursue their own version of religion. The most they would accept was that heretics should be allowed to exist when there was no alternative. Again, this was not a Jesuit position; it remained the formal view of the Catholic Church down to the publication of the Declaration on Religious Freedom by the Second Vatican Council in December 1965, a document that owed much to the theology of an American Jesuit, John Courtney Murray. Of the document, Murray wrote, "It can hardly be maintained that the Declaration is a milestone in human history—moral, political or intellectual. The principle of religious freedom has long been recognised in constitutional law, to the point where even Marxist-Leninist political ideology is obliged to pay lip-service to it. In all honesty it must be admitted that the Church is late in acknowledging the validity of the principle."[40] It has, however, been fully embraced by Pope Francis, including showing reverence for the indigenous religions of Latin America, as demonstrated, controversially, at the synod on the Amazon of 2019.

But this was a long way in the future. For Jesuits and most other Catholic theologians in the sixteenth and seventeenth centuries, becoming a Christian or, more specifically after the Reformation, becoming a Catholic was necessary for salvation, and the state was, or ought to have been, a means to that end. As Höpfl puts it, "Much of the enmity that the Society aroused was due to its unflinching insistence that the secular commonwealth of citizens under certain circumstances becomes an instrument for the supernatural ends of the Church, whose custodian is the Vicar of Christ."[41] Or as Suarez himself put it in his *Defense of the Catholic Faith*:

> The Supreme Pontiff, by virtue of his spiritual authority, is superior to kings and temporal rulers, so that he may direct them in the exercise of their temporal authority in order to the spiritual end, by reason of this he can command or forbid any such use of this

[40] Walter Abbott, *The Documents of Vatican II* (London: Geoffrey Chapman, 1967), 673. For a short discussion of the issues, see Michael Walsh, "Religious Freedom: The Limits of Progress," in *Unfinished Journey*, ed. Austen Ivereigh (London: Continuum, 2003), 134–48.

[41] Höpfl, *Jesuit Political Thought*, 286.

[temporal] authority, demand it or prevent it, to the extent that it is expedient for the spiritual good of the Church.[42]

This has to be read carefully, especially the final clause quoted: it was no carte blanche for papal interference in secular affairs. But it was certainly a live issue at the time when Suarez was writing. But as John Bossy has pointed out in an article about the most "Jesuitical" of Jesuits, Robert Persons, "The burning question in Catholic politics during the 1580s was whether Catholics were entitled, or perhaps obliged, to organize, collaborate in or encourage civil or military action aimed at the overthrowing of Protestant governments or of Catholic government thought to be in collusion with them."[43] Persons was certainly not the only Jesuit—though perhaps the most (in)famous—who was engaged in such political conspiracy, with or without the knowledge, or at least explicit approval, of the Jesuit general. It was particularly difficult for Jesuits who had come to be confessors to monarchs and thus in some ways their advisers. They found it difficult to remove themselves from politics. As has been seen, the fifth general congregation warned against "meddling" in the secular affairs of princes, and in 1602 Acquaviva issued an "Instruction for all Confessors of Princes," which urged them as far as was possible to stay away from the court. But even if they did so, it proved impossible to maintain a nonpolitical stance, at least as their opponents saw it. As will be discussed below (p. 182), they were blamed for the attempted assassination of Henry IV of France by Jean Châtel in December 1594 simply because he had been educated by them: one of his Jesuit teachers was executed, and most of the remaining Jesuits in France exiled.[44] They were readmitted in September 1603 by the Edict of Rouen. Fifteen years after the unsuccessful assassination attempt of the life of Henry IV, a successful one in 1610 by François Ravaillac was also laid at the Jesuits' door, this time because of the tyrannicide argument in Juan de Mariana's *De rege et regis institutione* (cf. above, p. 48). The death of Henry left his nine-year-old

---

[42] Quoted in ibid., 351.

[43] John Bossy, "The Heart of Robert Persons," in *The Reckoned Expense*, ed. Thomas M. McCoog (Woodbridge: The Boydell Press, 1996), 143.

[44] The edict to exile members of the Society, promptly passed in 1595 by the Paris Parlement, was not in the end endorsed by all the other regional parlements.

son Louis XIII as king of France with his mother, Marie de' Medici, as the queen regent. Despite the charges of regicide against the Society, Marie appointed Henry IV's Jesuit confessor, Pierre Coton, as confessor to the young king.

Marie de' Medici's confidence in the Society was not widely shared by the French political class. Jesuit protestations of innocence over the assassination were regarded with skepticism. There was an unwillingness to grant that they might be telling the truth. Harro Höpfl comments that Jesuits "could not bring themselves to say straightforwardly that deceit and lying are sometimes permissible";[45] on the other hand, there were many situations—especially at this period in England—where it was dangerous to tell the truth. Hence the Jesuit practice of equivocation and mental reservation. These could be practiced, the theory went, if the questioner had no right to the truth, particularly if telling the truth might put oneself or others in imminent danger. Perhaps a more pertinent example: a priest could legitimately say that he did not know when questioned about something he had learned in the confessional—there being an absolute prohibition against breaking what was called the "seal" of the confessional. So, for example, were a priest to be asked whether a particular person had committed a murder, if he had learned this fact through that person's confession, he was permitted, indeed, in the Church's view, morally obliged, to say that he had no knowledge of that person's guilt.

This is perhaps not quite as odd as it might seem at first sight. In a court of law, for example, moral theologians would not regard it as a lie if a person who had committed a crime pleaded not guilty. A clearer example of equivocation—at least when households had servants to answer the door—is a caller being told that a person is "not at home" when what is really meant is that he or she is not receiving visitors. In sixteenth- and early seventeenth-century England a Jesuit who was asked if he was indeed a member of the Society could legitimately deny it on the grounds that what was in effect being asked was whether he was a traitor, a crime punishable by death: the Jesuit missionaries in Britain would certainly not have considered themselves to be treacherous. The English Jesuit martyr (St.) Robert

---

[45] Höpfl, *Jesuit Political Thought*, 153.

Southwell (1561–1595) himself wrote a treatise on equivocation that the prosecutor at his trial made much of. It never appeared in print.[46]

Equivocation was not a specifically Jesuit doctrine. Indeed, the roots of it can be found in Thomas Aquinas, who wrote that it was "licit to hide the truth prudently by some sort of dissimulation."[47] This was a simple form where the person questioned used an ambiguous sentence to hide his or her real meaning. In the sixteenth century there developed a more radical form where the individual under interrogation might say something under their breath, or as an aside, or in some way that the questioner could not detect to change the meaning of what they were saying. For instance, to take an English example, if asked to take the oath of allegiance to the monarch (which, for various reasons, it was generally thought a Catholic could not do), they might reply, "I will *not* take the oath," where the word "not" was said in such a way that the questioner was not able to hear it.

This form of equivocation or mental reservation was not the brainchild of some duplicitous Jesuit but came from the writings of a distinguished canon lawyer, Martin Azpilcueta (1492–1586), also known from the place of his birth as "the Navarrese doctor." Azpilcueta's argument was taken up by Suarez and even expanded upon by the important Jesuit moral theologian Tomás Sánchez (1550–1610). Though it is true there were other Jesuit moralists who rejected this form of "strict mental reservation," as it came to be called, the doctrine of equivocation became associated with the Society, somewhat to its detriment. The doctrine as such was in the end condemned by (the Blessed) Pope Innocent XI in 1679, in his general opposition to probabilism (see below, pp. 187ff.).[48]

---

[46] His companion on the English mission, Henry Garnett, looked for a copy and could not find one. Consequently he compiled a similar treatise. That too went unpublished.

[47] *Summa Theologiae* I.II.q.110.a.3, ad 4, quoted by James Keenan, s.v. "Mental Reservation," in *The Cambridge Encyclopedia of the Jesuits*, ed. Thomas Worcester (Cambridge: Cambridge University Press, 2017), 513.

[48] While this may nowadays seem a very remote debate, it is perhaps worth commenting that the present author, when in the late 1960s sitting his final (oral) examination as a student of moral theology, was interrogated by his Jesuit inquisitors on lying and equivocation.

It is possible that the readiness of some Jesuit moral theologians to embrace and defend mental reservation arose from their concern about the difficult, not to say dangerous, situation in which their confreres in England found themselves. It was not long before similar problems assailed the Jesuit missionaries in Japan.

Chapter 3

Journey to the East

At 9:13 in the morning on November 23, 2019, Pope Francis arrived in Japan. "Over time, I felt the desire to go as a missionary to Japan, where the Jesuits have always carried out a very important work," he had said in *El Jesuita*, published in 2010.[1] As was required of any member of the Society wanting to go on the foreign missions—an ambiguous term, about which see below—he had written to Pedro Arrupe, then the superior general, to be assigned there, but his request was refused on the grounds of his ill health: from his teenage years he suffered from a collapsed lung. By the time he came to write his letter, Bergoglio was a solemnly professed member of the Society, a "professed father,"[2] and as such had taken the fourth vow. In the vernacular this says, "I further promise a special obedience to the Sovereign Pontiff in regard to the missions."[3] The Society of Jesus, as a consequence, sounds like a missionary order, one whose members mainly work in the "foreign" missions, overseas, away from their home country. In that sense, the Jesuits do indeed constitute the largest missionary order in the Catholic Church, but that is not what the vow really means. In the Latin version of the Constitutions it reads, "Insuper, promitto specialem obedientiam Summo Pontifici circa missiones," which seems clear enough and is certainly compatible with the English translation cited a moment ago. But in Latin there is no definite or, for that matter, no indefinite article. "Circa missiones" can undoubtedly be translated as "in regard to *the* missions," but it can equally correctly be translated as "in regard to

---

[1] *Vatican News*, November 24, 2019.

[2] For the "grades" in the Society, see above, pp. 29, 38.

[3] "Further," because he will have already taken the traditional vows of any religious: poverty, chastity, and obedience.

missions," that is to say, in regard to any task, or mission, that the pope has asked someone to undertake—as, for example, the role of Laínez and Salmerón as the pontiff's theologians at the Council of Trent, described in the second chapter.[4]

The fourth vow, therefore, cannot necessarily be understood as a commitment to "foreign" missions. Nonetheless, "foreign" missions were a major undertaking of the Society from the very beginning. They came eventually to be under the management of the Vatican's Congregation de Propaganda Fide, which was permanently established in 1622, though before that there had been formed a nine-man commission of cardinals, including the Jesuit Cardinal Bellarmine. The congregation was the brainchild of a Jesuit, Antonio Possevino (1533–1611). Possevino had been sent more as a diplomat than a missionary to Sweden, to Poland, and to Tsar Ivan IV's Muscovy, though without notable success. He had himself, however, never been on a "foreign" mission, though he was able in Rome to talk to Jesuits who had been: Michele Ruggieri in China, José de Acosta who had worked in Peru and Mexico, and the controversial Alonso Sanchez from the Philippines.[5] Drawing on a proposal originally made by Jean de Vanderville, a professor of law in Louvain and later bishop of Tournai, Possevino recommended that the congregation should have five secretaries with a knowledge of languages, each concerning himself with the Church's outreach to different parts of the globe: first, the British Isles and Scandinavia; second, Saxony and Poland, Russia, and Hungary; third, Greece, Constantinople, and Hungary; fourth, the Levant and Algeria; and finally, the East and West Indies. He also suggested that the religious orders be required to send some of their best men to study under the aegis of the congregation in what became in 1627 the Collegium Urbanum, named after Pope Urban VIII who founded it, for training missionary clergy.[6]

The clergy who attended the Urbanum were eventually, though not initially, drawn from around the world. Some aspects of the train-

---

[4] See above, pp. 35ff.

[5] The work of these Jesuit missionaries will be discussed below: Ruggieri, pp. 80ff.; de Acosta, pp. 82 passim; and Sanchez, pp. 81ff.

[6] For these proposals, see John Patrick Donnelly, "Antonio Possevino's Plan for World Evangelization," *The Catholic Historical Review* 74 (August 1988): 179–98. "Success in the missions played a considerable role in restoring Catholic morale in the late sixteenth century," remarks Donnelly (ibid., 197).

ing, especially the emphasis on languages, reflected Jesuit experience, but Jesuits themselves did not attend the college. Nonetheless, the Society's missionary activity developed remarkably rapidly: "In practice, this [fourth] vow makes a Jesuit a cosmopolitan being at home in the world—anywhere in the world," one modern Jesuit author has remarked.[7] As Camilla Russell puts it in her study of the petitions from young Italian Jesuits to the general at the turn of the seventeenth century:

> It was to Asia that one of the founding members of the Society of Jesus, Francis Xavier and his three companions, travelled in 1541, shortly after the Society's official establishment in 1540. The Jesuit missionary enterprise in Asia got under way at the same time as the order itself was expanding, arriving in Goa in 1542, in Malacca in 1545, and the Moluccas in 1547; they followed Portuguese trade routes to Japan in 1549, to Portuguese Macao in 1563, entering China proper in 1580. The speed of Jesuit movement through Asia is brought into relief if we consider that, in Naples, the first Jesuit college was set up in 1552, a full ten years after Xavier's arrival in Goa, while the order's legal entrance into French territories was as late as 1562.[8]

Such rapid expansion brought problems, not least that of manpower.

In 1540, when the Society came formally into existence, there were ten members; by the time of Ignatius's death, sixteen years later, there were approximately a thousand.[9] The growth may have been impressive, but so were the number, and the variety, of missions these sixteenth-century Jesuits were being asked to undertake, including foreign missions. Commitment to missions in Asia is underlined by

---

[7] Thomas M. Lucas, *Landmarking: City, Church and Jesuit Urban Strategy* (Chicago: Loyola Press, 1997), 108. Perhaps not at home quite everywhere, as the missionary journeys of Francis Xavier seem to indicate.

[8] Camilla Russell, "Imagining the 'Indies': Italian Jesuit Petitions for the Overseas Missions at the Turn of the Seventeenth Century," in *L'Europa divisae i nuovi mondi*, vol. 2, ed. Massimo Donattini, Giuseppe Marcocci, and Stefania Pastore (Pisa: Edizioni Normale, 2011), 179–90, at 179.

[9] William V. Bangert, *A History of the Society of Jesus* (St. Louis: Institute of Jesuit Sources, 1986), 25. Bangert's book, while not exactly an official English-language history, is perhaps the one most commonly put in the hands of new entrants into the Society.

the numbers sent. During the 1540s twenty-six arrived in Goa, and the numbers steadily increased, reaching an all-time high for the sixteenth century in 1575 when forty-three arrived, though that number was surpassed in 1602 when sixty-two made the journey. There were 559 by 1607, twice as many as there had been at the beginning of the century.[10] But why Asia as the first locus of Jesuit evangelization?

The answer is the colonial ambitions of King John (Jão) III (1502–1557) of Portugal, known to Portuguese historians as John the Colonizer. The 1494 Treaty of Tordesillas between Spain and Portugal constrained the latter's westward expansion to the Americas but did not limit its ambitions in the East, and the devoutly Catholic monarch wanted priests to evangelize in the recently acquired territories. He had heard of the Jesuits through the man who had headed the College de Sainte Barbe while Ignatius was there as a student and was eager to recruit them—by way of the pope, to whom, of course, they had pledged their service. Further pressure was brought on Ignatius to grant King John's request by the king's ambassador in Rome. This was problematic for Ignatius: he was the ambassador's father confessor, and Ignatius eventually gave way. Francis Xavier and Simão Rodrigues were sent.[11]

What instructions they were given is not known, but it is reasonable to assume that they would have acted, once they arrived in Lisbon, in the manner established by their companions in Italy—hearing confessions, attending the sick, giving the *Spiritual Exercises*. They did indeed perform all those ministries, but for the most part in the royal court. While they were remarkably successful within this limited compass, this was not the purpose for which they had traveled across Europe. They had come with the intention of going to the

---

[10] Dauril Alden, *The Making of an Enterprise* (Stanford, CA: Stanford University Press, 1996), 47; Camilla Russell, "Imagining the 'Indies,'" 180. Russell makes the point that recruitment for the "Indies" came increasingly from Italy partly, she suggests, to obviate tension between Spaniards and Portuguese after Portugal had in effect been annexed by Spain in 1581 (until 1640), and partly to mitigate "the dubious Iberian track record of imperial expansion, conquest and forced conversion in which missionaries were so often implicated" (ibid.).

[11] Xavier had not been Ignatius's first choice of companion for Rodrigues. He had first selected the Spaniard Nicolas Bobadilla, but Bobadilla could not go because of illness. Rodrigues, as his name indicates, was Portuguese.

Indies. The pious monarch was reluctant to let them go, wanting their services inside his kingdom, but eventually he agreed to let one of them travel East. It was Xavier who was chosen to go, leaving Rodrigues to become, eventually, the first superior of the province of Portugal.

India

On April 7, 1541, his thirty-fifth birthday, Xavier left Lisbon on a warship going to Goa, the center of the Portuguese Indian Empire, and, traveling by way of Mozambique, he arrived at Goa in May the following year, a journey of thirteen months: the ship was also carrying the newly appointed governor of Goa. Xavier, who was destined never to return to Europe, was not alone. Though not accompanied by Rodrigues, there were another priest and a lay brother with him. They were not the first priests, not even the first members of a religious order, to arrive in Portuguese India. Quite apart from the indigenous priests serving the "Thomas" Christians, a Syrian rite that claimed descent from the apostle Thomas himself,[12] there had been Franciscans in Goa from 1500. The mission entrusted to Francis Xavier by John III was quite specific: he was to evangelize the Pearl Fishery Coast, the coastline of Tamil Nadu in the extreme south of the subcontinent.

That the local inhabitants should be properly instructed in the Catholic faith was the king's responsibility. The "Padroado" was the agreement between the crown of Portugal and the papacy that allowed the Portuguese monarch to control the Church overseas by appointing bishops, taking charge of religious buildings, and collecting Church taxes. In return, the monarch undertook to support the Church in the mission territories. There was a similar arrangement between the papacy and the Spanish crown, in this instance called the "Patronato." The precise details of the Padroado and the Patronato varied over time, but the principle was the same: the colonial powers of Spain and Portugal were permitted by the papacy to supervise the Church in their overseas dominions. In sending Francis

---

[12] Once when visiting a museum in Kochi, the present author, engaged in conversation with the museum director, questioned the historicity of Thomas the Apostle's visit to India. It turned out this was a mistake!

Xavier to the Pearl Fishery Coast—a particularly profitable part of Portugal's overseas territories—King John was simply exercising his responsibilities under the terms of the Padroado.

The Portuguese had occupied the region in 1525, but when in 1532 the indigenous people of the area, the Paravas, were attacked by Arabs they turned to the Portuguese for support. Three years later a Portuguese army drove out the Arabs, and in gratitude the Paravas en masse embraced Christianity. They had not, however, been adequately instructed in their new faith, and it was to do this that Xavier was despatched to India by King John III. On his arrival, however, he found he could not immediately make his way to the Fishery Coast because of the monsoon, and he stayed in Goa, acting as his erstwhile companions did in the cities of Italy and elsewhere, teaching the catechism to children and to slaves, as well as fostering the faith of adult Christians. There was already a college, the College of St. Paul, founded in 1541 as a seminary for training indigenous clergy. As more Jesuits arrived, Xavier was asked if they could assist in the college and eventually, in 1548, to run it: it formally became a Jesuit institution when it was given to the Society by King John in 1551. Although it was a Jesuit-run training college for both indigenous and Portuguese clergy, as well as for Jesuits, Xavier did not believe that clergy drawn from the local population would make satisfactory members of the Society of Jesus, a view with which, in far-away Rome, Ignatius profoundly disagreed.[13]

The college became the largest of its kind in southeast Asia and continued to be administered by Jesuits until they were expelled from all of Portugal's dominions, but at the time Xavier was in India education had not yet become a major work of the Society. Xavier had been sent to evangelize along the Fishery Coast, and when, after a year in Goa, he was able to travel there, this is what he did with quite extraordinary energy, baptizing, it is claimed, many thousands. He did not speak the local language, Tamil, but had some basic texts and prayers translated into it, and, although he traveled with an interpreter, he committed to memory a sermon in Tamil. While instruction

---

[13] Given Xavier's negative opinion, it is perhaps ironic that the Society is flourishing in modern India. As this chapter was being written, it was announced that a new province of Madurai (for Madurai, see below, pp. 66ff.) was to be established, carved out of the province of Chennai because of the number of Jesuits in the latter.

in the doctrines of Catholicism might have been extremely basic, if
the teachings were at all comprehended by his hearers, he could
console himself with the thought that the people had been baptized:
in common with most of his contemporaries, he believed in the doctrine enunciated over a thousand years earlier by St. Augustine of
Hippo that without baptism there was no hope of salvation, no hope
of going to heaven. Not that he was happy with the situation. He
insisted that those who were to follow him should be proficient in
the local tongue.

His inability to communicate easily with the people of the Fishery
Coast may well have hindered his appreciation, or lack of it, of their
culture and religion. He was, however, moved by their destitution
and by the oppression from which they suffered. He wrote to King
John to complain about the way the colonizers were exploiting the
Indian population, an extraordinarily rash thing to do, given that the
king was the patron of his missionary activity, which at this point
embraced not just the Fishery Coast but extended to Malacca and to
what is now Sri Lanka. While in Malacca he had heard from a samurai
of a country that seemed to him—on the basis of very little evidence—
a rather more advanced civilization than he had found in India: in
1549 he set sail for Japan.

Given their humanistic education, the concept of "civilization"
was an important one for the sixteenth- and seventeenth-century
Jesuits, especially perhaps to those from Italy and the Iberian Peninsula, by far the largest group within the Society at this time. They
were men of the city. They set themselves up in churches "unencum-
bered by parish obligations where the Jesuits could preach, teach,
and celebrate the sacraments; a convenient location that was easily
accessible to large number of citizens. . . . Proximity to the local
court was a decided advantage."[14] They wanted churches, in other
words, to be in the center of towns—though the buildings, wherever
possible with gardens, to house members of the community were
generally located in rather more salubrious surroundings.[15] These
were not particularly the conditions in which Xavier found himself
preaching, especially along the Fishery Coast, so the attraction of
what he understood to be a more "civilized" nation to be evangelized

[14] Lucas, *Landmarking*, 137.
[15] Ibid., 141.

he found irresistible. Crucially, he judged it to be a nation more suited to the call of the Gospel. "We shall never find among heathens another race equal to the Japanese," he wrote. "They are a people of excellent morals—good in general and not malicious."[16]

Xavier's successor as superior on the Fishery Coast was Antonio Criminale, who had the dubious distinction of becoming the first Jesuit martyr, dying in 1549 in defense of his converts in an uprising stirred up by Brahmins but occasioned by the rapacious behavior of a Portuguese sea captain. He was replaced as head of the mission by Henrique Henriques. Henriques had been born in Portugal and had entered the Franciscans, but he had been forced to leave the order when it was discovered that his family were *conversos*; in other words, he was, though a Christian, of either Muslim or Jewish ancestry. This, however, did not prevent him being recruited into the Society while he was studying at the University of Coimbra and sent first to Goa and then to the Fishery Coast.[17]

Xavier had wanted those who worked on the mission to be able to speak the local language. Henriques went further. Not only did he learn Tamil, but he produced the first Tamil-Portuguese dictionary as well as other works. Perhaps even more significant, he acquired from Italy a printing press that he established at St. Paul's College. Though his dictionary was apparently never printed—it circulated widely in manuscript form—other works written or translated by him, including a catechism written by Xavier, were produced on the press using the Tamil script.[18] His work on the Konkani language— the language spoken on the west coast of India—also remained in manuscript form and was probably used by Thomas Stephens to produce the first grammar of Konkani.

While the Jesuits in India were either Italian or from the Iberian Peninsula, Stephens was a remarkable exception. He was born in

[16] Quoted in John W. O'Malley, *The First Jesuits*, 76.

[17] "*Converso*" was a term used in both Spain and Portugal of converts from Judaism to Christianity—the equivalent for Muslim converts, who were treated more severely, was "*morisco*." The *conversos* were suspected of retaining some of their Jewish traditions and rituals. For the treatment of *conversos* in the Society, see below, p. 140, and O'Malley, 188–89.

[18] The first Tamil book was printed in Lisbon in 1554, transliterated into Roman script.

1549 in (Royal) Wootton Bassett, the son of a merchant. In 1575 he traveled to Rome where he joined the Society with a number of other Englishmen, most of whom aspired to work in their home country. Stephens, however, much taken by the accounts of Xavier's exploits, asked to be sent to India, arriving in Goa in October 1579. He undertook a fairly brief period of theological study before being sent to the mission of Salcete, south of Goa, an area with a combined population of about eighty thousand and temples dedicated to the cobra goddess. He remained for forty years. One of his first tasks was to find the bodies of four Jesuits—one of them being Rudolfo Acquaviva, about whom more below, together with someone who had been with Stephens in the novitiate in Rome—who had been slaughtered with a large group of indigenous Christians in 1583: the massacre had been brought about by the destruction of a local temple by overzealous Christians.[19]

Stephens showed a great deal more sympathy for the culture of the local population. In the style of a Hindu epic or *purana* he wrote *Kristapurana*, three editions of which were published, in 1616, 1649, and 1654. It is an imaginative form of catechesis. As Barnes remarks,

> If the content is very much the Gospel story, the form or style in which it is recounted comes from the cultural world of Stephens' brahmin converts. The word *purana*, literally "old" or "ancient," may be translated as "account of past history." It refers to a genre of Hindu literature which in its classical form is held to deal with topics such as creation, destruction and re-creation, the genealogy of gods and ancient sages, and the rule of kings and heroes. . . . Stephens used the form to exhort his audience to lead good and honest lives in imitation of Jesus Christ. But it would not have escaped his attention that the ritual which is inseparable from myths and legends has a certain political or social dimension. *Sutas* were often employed at court to celebrate ancient lineages and trace royal descent by linking the deeds of ancestors and heroes to the world

---

[19] Much of this section is taken from an article on the life of Stephens by Michael Barnes, SJ, "The First English Jesuit in India: The Remarkable Story of Thomas Stephens SJ," published in the online Jesuit magazine *Thinking Faith* (October 29, 2019): www.thinkingfaith.org/articles/first-english-jesuit-india-remarkable-story -thomas-stephens-sj. Stephens also has a fairly substantial entry in the *Oxford Dictionary of National Biography*.

of the gods. In terms of form the *Kristapurana* has such a religious and political purpose: the validation of the religious pedigree of the Christian community. The story proclaims who these people are.[20]

The *Kristapurana* is obviously an accommodation of the Christian message to a culture far different from that in which Christianity had originally been taught. It is, in other words, a form of inculturation that was not without its contemporary critics, as the Madurai Rites controversy demonstrated.

Madurai is an ancient city in the center of Tamil Nadu and the cultural center for Tamil speakers. It had only fairly recently (1559) reasserted its independence from the Delhi sultanate when the first Jesuit arrived there in 1595 at the request of its ruler. The man who was sent to Madurai was Gonçalo Fernandes Trancoso, who had arrived in India in 1560 as a soldier but who had, the following year, joined the Society of Jesus, was trained, ordained, and sent to work on the Fishery Coast. He was chosen for the new—for Jesuit evangelism—territory because of his thorough knowledge of the Tamil language and culture. He was, however, a singularly unsuccessful missionary, failing in a decade in Madurai to convert a single Hindu to Christianity. In 1606 the mission received a new recruit in the person of Robert de Nobili (1577–1656). The Rome-born de Nobili came from an aristocratic family and, when he arrived in Madurai, he had been a Jesuit for just a decade. Conscious of Fernandes's failure, he adopted an entirely new approach to spreading the Gospel. He moved from the Jesuit residence and went to live in an area of the city that contained the residences of Brahmins and began to adopt their practices: the sacred thread, the tuft of hair, and the sandalwood paste mark on the forehead. He also followed their habit of purification and of dietary rules, and he dressed in the yellow robes of sanyasi, or the Hindu holy man. He made a friend of a young Brahmin who translated for him the Hindu scriptures—at great risk to his own life because to make them known to foreigners was forbidden—and who eventually himself became a Christian, taking the name Boniface.

Xavier had been particularly hostile to the Brahmins, regarding them as a form of Hindu priesthood and therefore idolaters, a view shared by Fernandes and other Jesuits on the Madurai mission. On

---

[20] Ibid. The online article does not have page or paragraph numbers.

the other hand, it was understandable for de Nobili, from a noble Italian family and a member of a religious order, to see the sanyasi as simply "upper class" Hindus, a professional caste to whom he could more easily relate. He argued that the symbols of their status— the thread, the mark on the forehead, the tuft of hair—were purely social and had no religious significance. There was a theory behind this convenient and pragmatic approach:

> Jesuits and other early-modern missionaries operated with the idea of three revelations. To begin with there was a natural revelation, shared by all human beings because they were born rational. The unity of mankind was guaranteed by the fact that all men were descendants of Adam and Noah . . ., and in this respect this natural revelation was a historical event as well as an anthropological reality. These assumptions supported monotheism, and monotheism was, from that perspective, understood to be natural. That is to say, the existence of a supreme creator God was not something that some people arbitrarily believed and others did not, but rather something that all rational beings originally knew to be the case. If they failed to believe so at a later historical stage, this was because they had degenerated into irrationality.[21]

De Nobili presented Christianity as the natural culmination of the fifth, and now lost, Veda, which contained the outline of the original monotheism common to all peoples but which had been overtaken by idolatry. For him, idolatry seems to have been "a natural enough minor error which became major, a kind of forgetfulness which got out of hand and led to intellectual confusion and moral depravity. Idolatry is primarily a problem of ignorance, and persuasive and instructive words, not fear or force, are the appropriate response."[22] His approach rested on Aquinas's defense of human rationality that— unlike the conviction of many of the Reformers—had not been entirely

[21] Joan-Pau Rubiés, "Reassessing 'the Discovery of Hinduism': Jesuit Discourse on Gentile Idolatry and the European Republic of Letters," in *Intercultural Encounter and the Jesuit Mission in South Asia (16th–18th centuries)*, ed. Anand Amaldass and Ines Županov (Bangalore: ATC, 2014), 5.

[22] Francis X. Clooney, "De Nobili's *Dialogue* and Religion in South India," in *The Jesuits: Cultures, Sciences and the Arts, 1540–1773*, ed. John W. O'Malley, Gauvin Alexander Bailey, Steven J. Harris, and T. Frank Kennedy (Toronto: University of Toronto Press, 1999), 406.

corrupted by the sin of Adam and was therefore able to attain some natural knowledge of God. It was this belief that the Jesuit theologians had defended at Trent.

De Nobili's approach worked. Converts were at last made. For religious services they came together, from their different castes, in the one church building; sensitive to the structures of Indian society, though, within the church there was separate seating for the Brahmins and others. As will be seen below, in the end it was this implicit acceptance of the caste system that proved to be the biggest problem for the Jesuit mission, but meanwhile de Nobili had the full support of his provincial in Goa and in 1619 the backing of a commission of theologians who had been appointed to examine the question of his living and dressing as a Brahmin even though members of the Goan Inquisition were divided on the issue.[23] In his constitution *Romanae Sedis Antistes*, dated January 31, 1623, Pope Gregory XV, the first Jesuit-educated pontiff,[24] appeared to settle the Madurai dispute in favor of de Nobili.

There were, however, serious limitations to de Nobili's approach. If the idea had been that conversion of the "upper class" Brahmins would lead to a trickle-down effect with the conversion of those lower in the social order, in the highly stratified society of India that was unlikely to happen. Moreover, as Brahmins the Jesuits would have been unable to work with the lowest class of all, the "pariahs" or untouchables, the Dalits in modern parlance. In that regard, de Nobili's model was bound to have a limited legacy. Instead, new missionaries adopted the lifestyle of "pantarams," a class of Hindu holy men who associated with the pariahs: the first to do so was Baltasar da Costa who, even during a visit to Europe between 1670 and 1673, maintained his pantaram dress and lifestyle, never eating fish or meat or drinking wine, and sleeping on hard boards.[25]

The missions were not, of course, without their troubles. There was rarely enough money or manpower. And the missionaries were

---

[23] On the inquisition in Goa, see José Pedro Pavia, "The Impact of Luther and the Reformation in the Portuguese Seaborne Empire," *Journal of Ecclesiastical History* 70, no. 2 (2019): 287–91.

[24] It was Gregory XV who canonized both Ignatius Loyola and Francis Xavier.

[25] Paolo Aranha, "Discrimination and Integration of the Dalits in Early Modern South Indian Missions," *The Journal of World Christianity* 6, no. 1 (2016): 184.

not always welcome. John de Brito, once a member of the Portuguese royal court, joined the Society of Jesus and traveled to India in 1673 to follow in the footsteps of de Nobili, though, in de Brito's case, as a roving holy man. In 1686 he was expelled from one Indian kingdom and went back to Europe, only to return in 1690 to become a singularly successful evangelist. When, however, he converted one of the wives of a nobleman who promptly separated from her husband, the husband complained to the king and de Brito was executed.[26]

The most severe threat to the survival of the mission came not from outside but from within the Catholic Church. In 1703 French Capuchins in Pondicherry complained to Rome about the steps the Jesuits had taken to accommodate Catholicism to Indian society, despite the approval of Gregory XV eighty years earlier. They had the support of Bishop Carlo Tomasso Maillard de Tournon, patriarch of Antioch, who was despatched by Clement XI as papal legate to the Indies and—more especially—to China. De Tournon made a very leisurely journey eastward via Manila and Pondicherry, where he stayed for eight months. Just before he departed he produced a list of demands related to the practices of accommodation, insisting that, as papal legate, his decisions should be respected under pain of ecclesiastical penalty.

He cannot have had much first-hand knowledge of the Jesuit missions and may very well have been influenced by the Capuchin community in Pondicherry—none of whom had mastered Tamil—which was already at odds with the Jesuit bishop of the (no longer existing) Diocese of St. Thomas of Mylapore, but his intervention gave rise to the Malabar Rites controversy, which lasted from 1704 until 1744.

There were two main strands to de Tournon's complaints against the Jesuit missionaries. One concerned changes to the liturgy, changes that made the ceremonies more acceptable to converts. "Insufflation," that is to say, blowing or breathing on those being baptized, which was then, but in the western Church is no longer, part of the ritual of baptism, was omitted by the Jesuits on the grounds that in Indian society it was regarded as offensive. The other strand was the fact that Jesuits would not enter the houses of the pariahs. As was remarked above, many had adopted the lifestyle of the pantarams, which had

[26] He was canonized as a martyr in 1947.

at one time made it possible to associate with the pariahs, but mores had changed. The Jesuits appealed to Rome against the legate's decree, and although the pope, Clement XI, granted a stay of execution, in his brief *Non sine gravi* of 1712 he made it clear that de Tournon's instructions had to be followed. The matter continued to be debated between Rome and India until September 1744 when Benedict XIV issued *Omnium Sollicitudinum*. The pope was ready to tolerate, at least for a period of time, many of the aspects of Jesuit accommodation to Indian society in matters of dress, for example, and liturgical practices, but what he was not prepared to tolerate was the Jesuits' apparent acceptance of the rigid divisions of the caste system.[27] As this was not something possible to change, the proposal of the Jesuit general, who had urged obedience to the Holy See's ruling, was the creation of a special class of "pariah" Jesuits, but as Bangert remarks, if up to the mid-seventeenth century the number of Catholics continued to grow, in the latter part of the century, after *Omnium Sollicitudinum*, the number of conversions went into decline.[28]

Much less controversial than the Madurai mission was the presence of Jesuit missionaries at the court of the third Mughal emperor Akbar, who ruled from 1556 to 1605. The Mughals were fairly recent arrivals on the Indian subcontinent, after being driven out of their ancestral lands in central Asia: the first Mughal emperor, Babur (1526–1530), established himself first in Kabul, then drove south to occupy much of northern India. The Mughals, therefore, were arriving in India at more or less the same time as the Portuguese and were to some degree competing with them for power, so when Akbar requested that Jesuits visit his court, the provincial was careful to send priests who were not Portuguese. Their leader was Rudolfo Acquaviva (mentioned above, p. 65), an Italian nobleman and nephew

---

[27] "Capuchin missionaries had informed Rome that the native elites converted by the Jesuits believed that Parreas [pariahs] were not only socially unworthy but even incapable of attaining eternal salvation. The logical consequence of such an alleged belief, constantly denied by the Jesuit missionaries, was that Parreas should not even be baptized. The Roman Inquisition—with the approval of Pope Benedict XIV—decided to write an instruction to the Capuchins (but not to the Jesuits) urging them to persuade high-caste catechumens on the falsity of such an opinion, while not calling into question the validity of strict hierarchies in the social and political domain" (Aranha, "Discrimination and Integration," 189).

[28] Bangert, *A History of the Society of Jesus*, 334.

of the fifth general of the Society. He was accompanied by a Catalan and a Persian convert, chosen for his knowledge of the language: the Mughal court had for five years—1540 to 1545—been forced to flee India for Persia, and Akbar's mother was a Persian princess. The Jesuit emissaries—they were more ambassadors than missionaries—arrived at Akbar's new, and soon to be abandoned, capital of Fatehpur Sikri at the end of 1579.

The contingent of Jesuits had been brought to the Mughal capital in order to debate with Muslims, Jains, and Hindus in an elaborately decorated hall. Akbar had no intention of converting to Christianity, but he was interested in religion as such, and the debating skills of the Jesuits impressed him: he seems to have forged a personal friendship with Acquaviva. As one commentator has remarked, "The Mughal mission of the Society of Jesus was—pastorally speaking—a fantastic and extravagant failure."[29] That is rather harsh. Successive Mughal emperors, who were tolerant of religious diversity in their domain, helped the Jesuits to open churches and, with a couple of short breaks, they remained in and around the court and served two small congregations of converts in Lahore and Agra. They also provided information to the Portuguese authorities in Goa about troop movements and other such matters of interest, "often in rivalry with the English ambassador Sir Thomas Roe."[30]

But perhaps the most significant contribution to the Mughal court was the introduction of European art, "a representative collection of European engravings, paintings and statues" through which "the Mughal artists were able quickly to master the Late Renaissance style."[31] And then there were the catechisms compiled in Persian, in one of which, appropriately, a chapter was devoted to the use of images. The author was Jerome Xavier, to whose writing in Persian Sir Edward Maclagan devotes a whole chapter in his *The Jesuits and*

[29] Gauvin Alexander Bailey, "*The Truth-Showing Mirror*: Jesuit Catechism and the Arts in Mughal India," in O'Malley et al., *The Jesuits*, 381.

[30] Joan-Pau Rubiés, "Ethnography and Cultural Translation in the Early Modern Missions," *Studies in Church History* 53 (2017): 273.

[31] Bailey, "*The Truth-Showing Mirror*," 381, though Bailey argues that the devotional art was employed by the emperor as royal propaganda, "bestowing celestial approval on imperial rule" (ibid., 383).

the Great Mogul, still regarded despite being written nearly a century ago, as one of the best accounts of this somewhat exotic mission.[32]

Japan

Jerome Xavier was, as his name suggests, a relative—though a distant one—of the founder the Jesuit mission in India. But the responsibilities of Francis Xavier under the Padroado extended further than India, to all the Portuguese territories in the East, including the trading post of Malacca with it small Portuguese community. He went there toward the end of 1545 and conceived the idea, eventually realized but only long after his death, of establishing a Jesuit college. From Malacca he went on to the Moluccas, the "Spice Islands," but returned to Malacca where he met a Japanese fugitive—he had apparently committed a murder in his youth—variously called Anjiro or Yajiro who wanted to become a Christian (when eventually baptized he was given the name Paul of the Holy Faith). It would not be easy to convert his fellow countrymen, he told Xavier, but they were reasonable people and open to persuasion. Xavier was himself persuaded. On April 15, 1549, Palm Sunday, together with Cosme de Torres and a lay brother, Juan Fernández left for Japan and on August 15 stepped ashore from a Chinese junk at Kagoshima on the south coast of the island of Kyushu, Anjiro's home town. It was the fifteenth anniversary of the vows the first companions had taken on Montmartre.

Xavier's first letter to Rome from Japan, written in Kagoshima that November, claimed "that the Japanese were 'the best people discovered so far,' because they refrained from stealing and valued honour over wealth, something that appealed to Xavier's own aristocratic values." They "enjoy listening to things according to reason," he reported.[33] He was not, however, as complimentary about the Buddhist monks, though he held long conversations with them. They practiced sodomy, he reported, which they did not regard as wrong—

---

[32] Edward Maclagan, *The Jesuits and the Great Mogul* (London: Burns, Oates & Washbourne, 1932).

[33] Joan-Paul Rubiés, "Real and Imaginary Dialogues in the Jesuit Mission of Sixteenth-Century Japan," *Journal of the Economic and Social History of the Orient* 55 (2012): 450.

although, he added, some of the Japanese "laity" certainly did so.[34] Nonetheless, he established a close relationship, even friendship, with the abbot of one monastery, and his criticism of the morals of the monks did not prevent him having extensive discussions with them. To describe these as "dialogues" would be a mistake, because it would imply that there was openness to learn on both sides, whereas Francis and his successors in Japan—Cosme de Torres became the superior of the mission after Francis departed—were certain of the superiority of their own convictions. What Francis did indeed, to some extent, learn, and attempted to explain to his fellow Jesuits after he had returned to Goa, was the sectarian divisions within Japanese Buddhism. Rather than rejecting outright this alien creed, as he had with Hinduism on the Fishery Coast, he was ready to attempt at the very least to understand it.

In Kagoshima, reading from a written text, Francis explained the Christian faith to anyone who would listen. He made a few converts and in the process aroused the anger of the Buddhist monks with the result that the local daimyo, or warlord, forbade further proselytizing. The Jesuits had arrived in Japan after a series of civil wars and general political upheaval that had left the "emperor" as a mere figurehead with real power being in the hands of the daimyos. Francis was, however, not aware of the politics, and after the local warlord had stopped his preaching in Kagoshima he decided to travel to Miyako, the modern Kyoto, to seek permission of the emperor; he was also attracted there by the existence of a university with which he hoped to make contact. He went by way of Yamaguchi, the chief city of Satsuma province in Southern Kyushu, where there was a particularly powerful warlord, so when, in Miyako, he found he could neither meet the emperor nor even enter the grounds of the university, he returned to Yamaguchi.

As he had been rebuffed in his first attempt to meet the daimyo Ouchi Yoshitaka, Francis decided to change tack. Before leaving Goa he had been given documents establishing him as a Portuguese ambassador to Japan, and with the aid of Portuguese friends he therefore dressed as such. Equipped with his elaborate ambassadorial credentials, and attired in elegant robes, he presented himself at Yoshitaka's

[34] Ibid.

court and this time was cordially received. He was even given an unused temple in which to live and in which he preached, making numerous converts. The generous welcome was not surprising. Yoshitaka had established his rule by force of arms only a decade before the arrival of Francis. Seemingly tired of warfare, his policy by this time was to foster foreign trade for the benefit of Yamaguchi, and someone presenting himself as a representative of Portugal and bringing gifts, opening up further possibilities of trade—he already dominated trade with China and Korea[35]—not to mention acquiring Portuguese weaponry, was not going to be turned away.

Unfortunately for the Jesuits, however, they had arrived at the end of Yoshitaka's rule. In attempting to move the imperial capital from Kyoto to Yamaguchi he had overreached himself.[36] Toward the end of 1551 there was an uprising against him, and he was forced to commit suicide, putting the missionaries in danger, though by the time the revolt broke out, Francis had already left for Bungo on the north coast of Kyushu where, he had heard, a Portuguese ship had just arrived. The two Jesuits remaining in Yamaguchi, Cosme de Torres and Juan Fernández, were given sanctuary by the wife of Yoshitaka's secretary.

In Bungo Francis learned that the behavior of the Jesuit left in charge in India was causing problems for his subjects, and he decided to return to India. He was back in Goa in February 1552 and a few weeks later sailed for Canton to attempt to expand his mission into China. He never got there: there was a ship promised, but it failed to arrive. He died on the island of Sancien some thirty miles from Canton, though only a couple from the coast of China, on December 3, 1552. He was forty-six years old. In 1554 his body was brought back to Goa, where it has been venerated ever since.

Francis had left Cosme de Torres in charge of the mission to Japan. One of the attractions of that country for Jesuit evangelists was that, unlike India, there was a single language to be mastered. Cosme never managed to do so himself, but over time Fernández became reasonably fluent. Yet despite this linguistic barrier, Cosme was remarkably successful, converting the lord of Bungo and getting permission to

---

[35] Thomas D. Conlan, "The Failed Attempt to Move the Emperor to Yamaguchi and the Fall of the Ouchi," *Japanese Studies* (September 2015): 3.

[36] The story is told in detail in the article by Thomas Conlan cited above.

open a hospital. Though it occurred only after his death in 1570, he started the process that led to the Society's headquarters in Japan being established in Nagasaki, which became something of a Christian enclave—and also a trading post, especially in silk, for the benefit of, and administered by, the Jesuit missionaries.[37] By the time Cosme had died, there were believed to be around thirty thousand Christians, a quite remarkable achievement. He was followed as mission superior by Francisco Cabral, whose strategy was to win over the warring daimyos, including the lord of Bungo, something he did with surprising success—so much so that with the fervor of recent converts the warlords in some instances destroyed the Buddhist temples and required their subjects either to embrace Christianity or to go into exile.

Despite the efforts of the daimyo of Bungo to centralize authority, Japan was not a peaceful region. In the midst of a civil war, there arrived Alessandro Valignano (1539–1606) from Chieti in the Kingdom of Naples who, after a distinctly riotous youth, had joined the Society of Jesus in 1566 and was ordained priest in 1571. The general of the Society, Everard Mercurian, in 1573 appointed him "visitor" with authority exceeding that of the local superiors to all the Jesuit missions in the East Indies. In 1580 Mercurian was followed as general by Acquaviva, and he made Valignano provincial superior of the East Indies. After Francis Xavier himself, Valignano must rank as perhaps the most significant figure in the development and ethos of the missions, especially, perhaps, as an advocate of the ordination to the priesthood of indigenous clergy, about which superiors in India, his first port of call, and in Japan had been opposed. He became associated with the conviction that the Catholic Church must seek as far as possible an "accommodation" with local cultures so as not to appear too much of a foreign import—despite the fact that in Goa, the provincial headquarters, he tried without success to impose the Latin rite liturgy on the Syro-Malabar Church.

The territories, such as Goa, over which Valignano had jurisdiction all fell under the Portuguese Padroado Real: Mercurian, in appointing him, seems to have wished to diminish slightly the influence of

---

[37] The income generated by the trade was essential for the survival of the mission, but it was incongruous—and also gave rise to envy—that priests vowed to poverty should engage in such an activity.

Portugal without antagonizing its monarch by selecting a Spaniard; when the appointment was made Spain and Portugal were still two separate monarchies. Valignano was careful of the Padroado, but he was also aware that Spanish missionaries, coming from Manila, were seen by the daimyos as a possible bridgehead for an invasion by Spain, which was certainly not beyond the bounds of possibility.[38] He therefore struggled to keep Japan as a Jesuit monopoly, as guaranteed by Pope Gregory XIII's brief in 1585, though this decree, already ignored by some Franciscans who made their way to the court of Hideyoshi in Kyoto, was overturned by Pope Paul V in 1608.

The notion of accommodation to the Japanese manner of life was not without its problems, as the missionaries had discovered even before the arrival of Valignano. The hospital they had opened in Bungo 1556, for example, included a section for lepers, but lepers could be cared for only by outcasts, which in the eyes of the Japanese lowered the all-important social status of the Jesuits.[39] Valignano, at odds with the Jesuit provincial in Japan, wrote that since the Japanese "will not change their things, we are the ones to accommodate to them as seems necessary in Japan, and this means a lot of effort for us. . . . [H]aving to change our nature, the difficulty is on our side to try whatever it takes to reach them, and it is not on their side."[40] These ideas were not without critics, both in Rome, where there was anxiety about the mercantile activities of the Jesuits in Nagasaki, and within the Society in Japan. The practice of present-giving, for instance, which Valignano believed to be essential, troubled many because it gave the impression to potential converts that the missionaries, who espoused poverty, were on the contrary really quite wealthy. Another example of his eagerness that Jesuits should learn from and, as far as possible, accommodate themselves to Japanese culture was his attempt to structure the mission along the lines of a particular form of Zen Buddhism, based on a leading temple in Kyoto. But by the late sixteenth century that sect was in decline, and Valignano himself seems to have had second thoughts—though the

---

[38] See below, p. 81.

[39] The interpretation here of Valignano's role in Japan depends heavily on J. F. Moran, *The Japanese and the Jesuits* (London: Routledge, 1993).

[40] Valignano, *Sumario de las cosas be Japón* (1583), quoted in A. C. Hosne, *The Jesuit Missions to China and Peru* (London: Routledge, 2013), 51.

structures he introduced, which were not wholly approved of in Rome, helped the "hidden Christians" to survive the long centuries of persecution that followed the eventual expulsion of the Jesuits.

Even the literature Valignano commissioned, some of which was printed on a press he had brought to Japan, was regarded by his critics as problematic. Although it set out to explain Christian doctrine, it avoided some of the more controversial issues and ones that Buddhists would find difficult to understand or to believe. The printing press, the first in Japan, left the country with the expulsion of the Jesuits and was set up instead in Macau, and it continued to produce books in Japanese and on Japanese grammar in the hope that the Society would return: they did not do so until 1908, almost forty years after the ban on Christianity had been lifted.

Valignano himself must bear some of the blame for the ban. The Jesuits had come to rely on the goodwill of several leading daimyos, including Oda Nobunaga, the daimyo of a small province who set out to unify Japan, successfully relying on his military skills to do so and capturing the capital, Kyoto, in 1568. Though several of the daimyos had themselves become Christian, Nobunaga did not, but he was very well disposed to the Jesuits whose connection to the trade with Portugal, and especially access to gunpowder, he needed for his campaigns. His leading general, Toyotomi Hideyoshi, who took over after the 1582 assassination of Nobunaga by another of his officers, was far less sympathetic to Christianity, especially after he learned that Nagasaki had been fortified, a decision approved by Valignano, and that some of the Christian daimyos were forcibly converting their subjects and destroying Buddhist shrines. When in 1587 Hideyoshi seized control of Nagasaki, and of the lucrative trade that flowed through it, some Jesuits tried to call on the Catholic daimyos to defend their interests by force of arms: the daimyos, however, were unwilling to do so, and Valignano was steadfastly against. In July Hideyoshi, perhaps concerned to preserve the hegemony of Buddhism within the newly united Japan, ordered the Jesuit priests to leave the country and banned the practice of Christianity, but his decree remained for the most part dormant, and life continued much as before. The number of converts grew, as did the number of Japanese Jesuits. A noviceship had been opened in Usuki in 1580, and, despite Hideyoshi's ban, by the end of the century there were some seventy Japanese Jesuits educated both in Japan—in a former

Buddhist monastery where the students, even those of Portuguese origin, were required to dress in Japanese-style clothing and eat Japanese-style food—and in the College of St. Paul that Valignano had opened in Macau and that survived until the suppression of the Society in Portuguese territories. There were two colleges in Japan that, at their height, were training some three hundred students who, as in Macau, were expected to immerse themselves equally in the Eastern and Western classics.

Hideyoshi's tolerance of Christianity was put to the test when a Spanish ship, the San Felipe, en route from Manila to Acapulco laden with extremely valuable cargo, was wrecked on a sandbar on the Japanese coast in July 1596. The cargo was seized—some of it helped to finance the Japanese invasion of Korea—but in the discussions about the shipwreck, the Spanish pilot on board the San Felipe, which was also carrying Franciscan friars, claimed that missionaries were the forerunners of conquest. Hideyoshi apparently also learned for the first time that Spain and Portugal were now under one monarch, something that, it seems, the Jesuits had been keeping from him. The shogun was furious. He ordered the execution, at Nagasaki and by crucifixion, of six Franciscan friars, seventeen of their Japanese Christian coworkers, and three Japanese Jesuit scholastics.[41]

They died on February 5, 1597. Hideyoshi died eighteen months later, in September the following year. He was succeeded, eventually, as shogun by Tokugawa Ieyasu, Hideyoshi's son-in-law, who had been one of the regents for Hideyoshi's young heir and who at first showed himself just as tolerant of Catholicism as had Hideyoshi himself. The Jesuits were encouraged when he chose one of their number, João Rodrigues, as his interpreter. The early years of the sixteenth century under Ieyasu marked the pinnacle of Jesuit achievement in Japan. There were 122 priests and brothers, a large number of Christian assistants known as dojuku, and well over two hundred thousand Christians: one Jesuit chronicler claimed as many as 750,000, although among the converts were no more than seven or eight

---

[41] Students for the priesthood in the society of Jesus are called scholastics: Paul Miki was already a scholastic when arrested; the other two took vows as scholastics on their way to execution. Why the Jesuits were included is a puzzle: it may have been an accident. Hideyoshi remained friendly toward the Society.

daimyos, a small proportion of the more than two hundred in the whole of the country.[42]

To describe the Jesuit missionary activity in Japan as fragile would be unfair. After members of the society had been banished from the country in and around Nagasaki there remained a large group, perhaps some thirty thousand, of "hidden Christians" who survived without clergy, service books, or Bibles. They kept statues of saints, but in the form of figurines resembling Buddhas or Buddhist "saints" so as not to attract attention during the centuries when Christianity was proscribed. When religious toleration was granted in 1873 most, though not all, of this community with their—by now—heterodox beliefs and practices re-joined the Catholic Church: an unusual testimony to the depths of faith inculcated by the Jesuit missionaries.

But the collapse of the formal Jesuit presence in Japan was sudden. Ieyasu became suspicious of the influence wielded by members of the Society and suspected them of a lack of respect toward the traditional religions of Buddhism and Shinto. In 1609 Rodrigues was replaced as official interpreter by William Adams, an English, and Protestant, mariner who arrived on a Dutch merchantman in 1600. He became an influential figure at Ieyasu's court, even being raised to the rank of samurai, and was suspected by the Jesuits of arousing hostility toward them. Certainly Ieyasu began once again to think that the missionaries were forerunners of conquest by Spain and, now that he knew Spain and Portugal had been united under one monarch, by Portugal as well. The Portuguese were replaced as trading partners by the Dutch, and in 1614 Ieyasu ordered the expulsion of the missionaries and commanded that all Japanese Christians return to their traditional faith. Together with a few Franciscans, eighty-eight Jesuits left for Macau or Manila in November of that year.

Some stayed behind and remained in hiding.[43] Over the next three decades or so a number of Jesuits entered Japan, perhaps in the expectation of martyrdom. Many were caught and executed; others were caught and, under torture, apostatized.[44] In 1639 the link between

---

[42] Alden, *The Making of an Enterprise*, 131.

[43] Bangert, *A History of the Society of Jesus*, 157, says twenty-seven stayed behind.

[44] Shusaku Endo's novel, *Silence*, which in 2016 was turned into a film with the same name by Martin Scorsese, tells the highly fictionalized story of these final years of the Jesuit mission.

Macau and Nagasaki ceased. The vice province of Japan survived, but in name only, its members working elsewhere in Asia, in Laos, Cambodia, or Siam.

China

Francis Xavier had died on the island of Sancien in December 1552 as he waited hopefully, but in vain, for a ship to take him to China. The desire to evangelize in China was similar to that which had taken him to Japan: he had heard the Chinese were a cultured and literate people, not unlike the society in which he had grown up and therefore, he believed, ready to respond to the message of the Gospel. He had also discovered that the Japanese were not a little in awe of their neighbors. "If yours is the true faith, why have not the Chinese . . . heard of it?" he was asked.[45] He was impressed by what he had heard: "People from China," he wrote not long before he died, "they are wise, wiser than the Japanese, and extremely learned."[46] In the racial taxonomy, therefore, that is implicit in much of Jesuit missionary writing, the Japanese and the Chinese were on a par with Europeans, which meant they were ranked above the indigenous inhabitants of South America, who in turn were ranked above the indigenous inhabitants of the continent of Africa.

China, then, was the great prize, but entry to the Middle Kingdom was extremely difficult. A large number of would-be missionaries to the country, including thirty-two Jesuits and twenty-four Franciscans, had attempted to gain access, but all had been turned back.[47] Valignano, after his experience in Japan, surmised that one of the major problems was the lack of Chinese language skills, and he set two young men to tackle what was undoubtedly a challenging task. The first was Michele Ruggieri (1543–1607), who arrived in Macau in July 1579 and traveled frequently to Canton (Guangzhou) and to Zhaoqing, the administrative center of Guangdong. After a number of failed attempts to obtain permission to establish a permanent house within China, such a permission finally came in 1582, not so much because of Ruggieri's efforts but because the governor of Guangdong

---

[45] Quoted in Alden, *The Making of an Enterprise*, 67.
[46] Quoted in Hosne, *The Jesuit Missions*, 49.
[47] Alden, *The Making of an Enterprise*, 67.

had heard about the clock Matteo Ricci (1552–1610) had brought with him to Macau as a present for the emperor. Ruggieri was invited to take the clock to the governor, which he did, and Ricci joined him in Zhaoqing the following year.

In the meantime, however, while still in Macau, Ruggieri had been visited by the Spaniard Alonso Sánchez, who had been a missionary in the Philippines and regarded by some, though not the Jesuit general, as a particularly holy member of the Society: the general thought his devotional practices too extreme. Sánchez eventually proved himself to be more of a Spaniard than a Jesuit, an agent for the commercial ambitions of the Manila-based Spanish merchants. In 1584 Sánchez was back in Canton in the company of a Spanish royal official, though this time he was imprisoned and, he later claimed, threatened with beheading,[48] an outcome that did not endear this particular Jesuit to the Chinese: to the consternation of the general and the outrage of José Acosta (1540–1600, about whom much more later[49]) he proposed taking China by force and imposing Catholicism on its people. It would, in his view, be a simple operation. The invasion force

> was to cross the Strait of Magellan with 10,000 or 12,000 Italian and Spanish soldiers, together with a smaller number of Japanese and Filipinos. The Society of Jesus was called on to perform two strategic roles: to help the army during the conquest and then defend and disseminate the reasons for the conquest. It was to say that the invasion had been necessary and appropriate to free the Chinese from the "tiranias de sus mandarinas" and thus give them "libertad del cuerpo y de anima." Finally, the report explained the advantages Spain would obtain from the conquest, which would help increase the wealth of the church and the religious orders, as well as of the settlers and the crown.[50]

[48] A. C. Hosne, "Gateways to China," in *Missioni, Saperi e Adattamento tra Europa e Imperi non Cristiani*, ed. V. Lavenia and S. Pavone (Macerata: EUM, 2015), 63.

[49] See below, p. 110.

[50] Girolamo Imbruglia, "The Jesuit 'Made in China': A Meeting of Empires—Spain, China, and the Society of Jesus, 1586–1588," 6; accessed online at https://www.academia.edu/19703108/. There is no further source given. Imbruglia is professor of modern history at the University of Naples and the author of numerous studies, especially on the Jesuits.

Acosta, whose writings on the conversion of the indigenous inhabitants of the Americas took an entirely different line, could cite
in his defense the most distinguished of the Jesuit theologians of his
age and, indeed, possibly of any age, Francisco Suarez (1548–1617),
who had written

> This view is certain and absolutely true . . . to attract men to reli-
> gion by coercion would be unbecoming to the Church; it would be
> much better for the faith to be accepted and professed with complete
> spontaneity. And this is primarily desirable in order that the power
> of the divine word and the grace of God may be displayed in the
> act of conversion.

Suarez goes on to add that the authority of the state is concerned with
"natural ends" whereas "the sin of unbelief is remote from that purpose and that end, so to punish it does not come within that sphere."[51]

Sánchez's harebrained scheme came to nothing, and the Jesuit
missionaries in China went peacefully about their business. Ruggieri
was the pioneer, though it has been the brilliant mathematician Ricci
who has attracted by far the most attention, not least, perhaps, because Ruggieri's stay in the Middle Kingdom was relatively short.
He traveled back to Europe in 1588, ostensibly to persuade the pope
to send an ambassador to the emperor, but possibly because he had
lost the confidence of Valignano. He never returned to China. It is
sometimes suggested that his grasp of Chinese was inadequate, and
it was certainly less than that of Ricci, but nonetheless he had produced the very first Chinese catechism and, in collaboration with
Ricci and a Chinese lay brother, the first Portuguese-Chinese dictionary (despite the fact that he was, of course, Italian), the first Chinese
dictionary in any European language, and in the process invented a
method for transcribing Chinese characters into Roman script. He
brought back to Italy manuscript maps of China and continued translating classic Chinese texts into Latin, so it can hardly have been his
linguistic skills, or lack of them, that ended his missionary career.

---

[51] Quoted in Bernice Hamilton, *Political Thought in Sixteenth-Century Spain* (Oxford:
Clarendon Press, 1963), 112–13. Although to the best of my knowledge it was not
alluded to at the time, it is a similar argument to that crucially employed by John
Courtney Murray, SJ, when arguing for religious liberty during the Second Vatican
Council; see below, p. 274.

Michele Ruggieri was the first Jesuit missionary in China, yet he does not get an entry in Thomas Worcester's *Cambridge Encyclopedia of the Jesuits*[52] whereas Matteo Ricci, whose sojourn in China was very much longer and who died there, is granted almost two pages, and, of course, he has been the subject of many individual monographs. Ruggieri's contribution was significant to the start of the mission and its early years. He realized that, as in Japan, present giving was an important means of gaining influence, whether through the all-important clocks or the much-prized ostrich feathers.[53]

Was there tension between the two Jesuits? Ruggieri had arrived in China first, and, conscious to adapt to Chinese ways, he had taken on the dress of a Buddhist monk, but Ricci came to regard this as a mistake. Though he never set foot in the Middle Kingdom, Valignano shared Ricci's view, and after Ruggieri's return to Europe he persuaded the Jesuit General Claudio Acquaviva that Ruggieri was too old to make the journey back. After his exposure to Chinese Buddhism with its myriad venerated statues, Ricci had come to regard Buddhism as idolatrous and not something on which a Chinese version of Catholicism could be built, despite Catholicism's rather similar proclivity for statues. It was Ricci's decision to depart from the humbler role of Buddhist monks, who were not highly regarded, and to take up the role of someone versed in the culture not of Buddhism but of Confucius to become, in other words, a scholar. It was, he concluded, the only way to reach out to the emperor.

Not that he ever met the emperor, though in 1601 he was appointed to the imperial court because of his skill in astronomy and was allowed to settle in Beijing, his final home in China. His life had set a pattern. There followed generations of Jesuits living in the Middle Kingdom who survived occasional persecutions—never really very threatening—though their survival depended very largely on the good relations established between the Society and the imperial court through a succession of very able mathematicians and astronomers.

---

[52] Thomas Worcester, *Cambridge Encyclopedia of the Jesuits* (Cambridge: Cambridge University Press, 2017). Ruggieri is not even mentioned in the index, though his name occurs in the text.

[53] He even investigated the possibility of importing into the country a live ostrich; cf., Jonathan D. Spence, *The Memory Palace of Matteo Ricci* (London: Faber and Faber, 1985), 189.

Occasionally they were helped by a piece of good fortune. The discovery near Xi'an sometime around 1623 of a stele in Chinese and Syriac demonstrated that there had been Christians in China in the eighth century: Jesuits translated the text and made it known in Europe where it caused a minor sensation.[54] A few years earlier, in 1615, a collection of Ricci's writings in Italian was translated into Latin and published as *De Christiana Expeditione apvd Sinas svscepta ab Societate Jesv* (The Christian Mission among the Chinese undertaken by the Society of Jesus). This too caused a stir and was swiftly translated into various languages, making Jesuits for a time the primary source for knowledge of the Middle Kingdom. This was further enhanced by the appearance, for the first time in 1703, but they appeared sporadically until 1776 in thirty-four volumes, of the *Lettres Édifiantes et Curieuses*. The letters were drawn from the reports that Jesuits in China, but also elsewhere, including the Americas, sent to Rome primarily to account for their apostleship but including information about the flora, fauna, geography, and customs of the countries in which they were working. The publication was intended to foster goodwill toward the Society as well as to solicit donations. They contributed importantly to the growing fashion in Europe for chinoiserie and to the general knowledge of the Middle Kingdom and were eagerly read by the great literary figures of the day. And not only literary figures. A fifteen-year-old Josiah Wedgewood, then working in his brother's pottery in Burslem, copied into his commonplace book an account of the making of porcelain written by a Père d'Entrecolles, a Jesuit running a parish and a school in Jingdezhen, then the center for that craft.[55]

---

[54] Though there was an early attempt to claim it as a Catholic text, it was soon agreed that it was a Nestorian (Church of the East) monument. It can still be seen in the museum in Xi'an.

[55] Edmund de Waal, *The White Road* (London: Chatto and Windus, 2015), 240. In 1685 Louis XIV, equally entranced by the vision of the Chinese Empire, sent a group of French Jesuits to Beijing, where they arrived in 1688, with total disregard for the rights of the Portuguese Padroado. For the impact of Jesuit writings on European culture, see Carmen Lícia Palazzo, "Jesuits: Favored Agents of Image Transfer from China to Europe, 16th to 18th Centuries." This is an English translation, accessed online March 28, 2020, of an article in Portuguese that appeared in *Tuiutí: Ciência e Cultura* 48 (Curitiba, 2014): 13–31.

If Jesuits mediated Chinese culture to Europeans, they also brought European culture to the Chinese, especially, but not only, in mathematics and astronomy.[56] More will be said about astronomy below, but among the other skills they brought with them was medicine, in the person of the Swiss-born Johannes Schreck (1576–1630), who arrived in China in 1621. Schreck had, however, also studied astronomy under Galileo and found himself in competition with Chinese astronomers predicting the solar eclipse of 1629. The Jesuits won, and they found themselves in charge of rewriting the imperial calendar. After Schreck's death he was replaced by Adam Schall (1591–1666), who was born in Cologne and who found himself organizing the import into China of canon to defend the Ming dynasty against the invading Manchus, who became in turn the Qing dynasty, even eventually to making canons.

When the Manchus captured Beijing Schall stayed behind in the capital. In the chaos several Jesuits lost their lives and the Society in China was divided in its loyalties between the new dynasty and the old. But not Schall. Having taken part in the defense of Beijing, he was nonetheless ready to abandon his old allegiance and switch to the incoming Manchus, under whom he served as imperial chamberlain. After the death of the emperor Shun-chih there was again an outbreak of persecution fomented by Buddhist monks and by those in Beijing who were hostile to, and jealous of, the influence that they had been exercising at court: Schall himself had become a close friend of the old emperor and had recommended that his third son, K'ang-hsi, succeed him. Not surprisingly, therefore, the persecution ceased soon after 1668, when K'ang-hsi at the age of fourteen took over the imperial government.

By this time the Flemish Ferdinand Verbiest (1623–1688) was the leading Jesuit in Beijing, and, after errors were found in the official calendar, like Schall, he became the head of the calendar bureau and was appointed to the highest rank of Mandarin. Schall is described by Dauril Alden as "remarkably talented both linguistically and technically, [he] could be choleric, blunt, and morose, but he was also

---

[56] Mention should also be made of European art. See Harrie Vanderstappen, "Chinese Art and the Jesuits in Peking," in *East Meets West: The Jesuits in China, 1582–1773*, ed. Charles E. Ronan and Bonnie B. C. Oh (Chicago: Loyola University Press, 1988), 103–26.

opportunistic, urbane and unconventional."[57] He was also very aware of his own importance. Verbiest, who, again like Schall, also established a close personal relationship with the reigning emperor, seems a much more attractive figure and one, moreover, who never forgot the primary reason the Society had come to China: through his influence Jesuits were permitted to preach Christianity anywhere in the Middle Kingdom. To take advantage of that permission, more manpower was needed. He appealed to his confreres in Europe, and it was in part this request that led Louis XIV, jealous of England's growing commercial ties with the East, to send the party of French Jesuits mentioned above.[58] Verbiest was something of a polymath, publishing a number of books in Chinese, including translations of Euclid and Thomas Aquinas. But perhaps his most enduring legacy is the one that can still be seen, and visited, on the roof of Beijing's Old Observatory: a collection of astronomical instruments he designed and had made, some of them inscribed with the date and the name of the individual Jesuit responsible for their construction.

There were occasional persecutions, as has been seen, and especially after the death of the Society's great defender, Emperor K'ang-hsi, but a perhaps greater challenge came not from Beijing but from Rome itself. As in Japan, Jesuits had at first enjoyed a monopoly in the Chinese mission but, again as in Japan, the monopoly was gradually broken by the arrival in China of the mendicant religious orders, especially Franciscans and Dominicans, in the 1630s. They were unhappy at the degree of "accommodation" to Chinese culture that had been espoused by Matteo Ricci and had become the way of proceeding for subsequent Jesuit missionaries, though not all were entirely sympathetic. Ricci's successor as superior in China, Niccolò Longobardo, was one of the doubters. He expressed his hesitations in a book—which the Jesuit vice-provincial ordered to be burned.[59] It was the beginning of a century of conflict over what has become known as the Chinese Rite controversy, a controversy similar in many ways to that over the Malabar Rites at the time of Robert de Nobili, but one with far greater resonance back in Europe.

---

[57] Alden, *The Making of an Enterprise*, 145.

[58] On the French Jesuits, see John W. Witek, "Understanding the Chinese: A Comparison of Matteo Ricci and the French Jesuit Mathematicians sent by Louis XIV," in Ronan and Oh, *East Meets West*, 62–102.

[59] Bangert, *A History of the Society of Jesus*, 247.

There were a number of distinct, though related, issues. As remarked about teaching Catholic doctrine in Japan,[60] problematic issues were sidestepped. As Joan-Pau Rubiés remarks, "Authors working with the abundant Franciscan and Dominican sources for the rites controversy have emphasized the fact that the Jesuits' presentation in China of European realities and of the fundamental beliefs of Christianity was highly selective. For example, the crucifixion and resurrection of Christ, intellectually repugnant to many Confucian scholar-officials, were often (albeit not always) kept as a private teaching."[61] Indeed, according to Longobardo, the Chinese scholars or men of letters, the literati, were not interested in Christian dogmas.[62]

Unlike in Japan, where it was decided to use transliterations of European Christian terms, in China Chinese terms were adopted for Christian concepts with varying degrees of accuracy: the Franciscans and Dominicans—and some Jesuits—believed this had damaged the integrity of the faith.[63] In this there was ample room for doubt. Jacques Gernet, for instance, has argued that the Jesuits were wholly mistaken: "The whole programme of accommodation was bound to fail because it was based on cultural mistranslations, and that the attempt to bridge between incompatible philosophical languages—like those of China and Europe—was futile."[64] As Gernet puts it, "Just as some missionaries thought that the Chinese men of letters possessed a suitable disposition to receive their faith, there were some men of letters who judged that, once rid of their false notions, such as the belief in a creator God, the missionaries might have made quite good Confucians."[65]

Ricci's approach to understanding Chinese culture was based on classic Confucian texts—though these lacked any notion of heaven or hell, and for these he had to fall back on Buddhism, which, as

[60] Above, p. 77.

[61] Joan-Pau Rubiés "The Concept of Cultural Dialogue and the Jesuit Method of Accommodation: Between Idolatry and Civilization," *Archivum Historicum Societatis Iesu* (2005): 240.

[62] Jacques Gernet, *China and the Christian Impact* (Cambridge: Cambridge University Press, 1985), 32.

[63] A. C. Hosne, *The Jesuit Missions*, 154.

[64] Rubiés, "The Concept of Cultural Dialogue," 240–41. As Rubiés argues, however, Gernet proves too much: in his thesis, it would become almost impossible for one culture to understand another.

[65] Gernet, *China and the Christian Impact*, 40.

noted above, had been Ruggieri's first recourse.[66] It made a difference. In Ruggieri's presentation of the Christian message, for example, Christ himself was spoken of as "Savior," which would have been unintelligible to the Confucian literati; Ricci's solution, on the other hand, was to speak of him as "Master."[67] Both Ricci and de Nobili argued that Brahmin customs (in the case of de Nobili) and Confucian veneration of one's ancestors, to take one example in Ricci's case, had no religious significance in themselves: after all, as Ricci pointed out, nobody actually prayed to Confucius, nor, indeed, did they pray to their ancestors. As Rubiés puts it, "Ricci succeeded in interpreting Confucianism as a non-idolatrous ethical system which was in conformity with natural law, raising the possibility that the virtuous pagan might be saved."[68] The problem with this interpretation, however, is that it was not simply applicable to Confucianism (or Brahminism, as has been seen with de Nobili) but also to atheists in general. A second issue was whether Ricci had correctly interpreted the Confucianism of his day. Schooled in Europe in classical humanism, it was only natural that he would look to classical texts in Chinese in order to present the philosophy of the Chinese literati to the European world. It was the question whether Confucianism was a philosophy or a religion that gave rise to the Chinese Rites controversy in the seventeenth and eighteenth centuries.

The issue was first brought to Rome by a Dominican friar from the Philippines, Juan Baptista Morales. Though there were in China Jesuits of various nationalities, until the arrival of French Jesuits sent by Louis XIV, they were all well aware that they were operating under the Portuguese Padroado. Morales, however, owed allegiance to the king of Spain. There was, in other words, an element of nationalism, as well as rivalry between religious orders, at the root of the controversy. Unlike the Philippines, which had been conquered by Spaniards—though many of them coming not directly from Spain but from Mexico—there was no military conquest by Portugal of either Japan or China, no occupying army to enforce religious conformity.

---

[66] See above, p. 83.
[67] Hosne, *The Jesuit Missions*, 156.
[68] Rubiés, "The Concept of Cultural Dialogue," 246.

Morales cast his critique of Jesuit methods in seventeen propositions that were put before theologians appointed by the Congregation for the Propagation of the Faith, usually known simply as Propaganda, the Vatican department created in 1622 to oversee the Catholic Church's missionary activity.[69] He put the "rites" evolved by the Jesuits to accommodate Chinese sensitivities about ancestors and about Confucius into an uncompromising liturgical context. When the theologians reported to the congregation, their verdict was negative, and the congregation ruled against the Jesuits in a decree, approved by Pope Innocent X, on September 12, 1645. All missionaries were to obey, the decree stated firmly, "even those of the Society of Jesus."

For Jesuits on the missions this was a major setback. They reacted by sending to Rome Martino Martini (1614–1661), who had been in China from 1643. Martini is another missionary in the Middle Kingdom who is too often overlooked, though there is a statue of him in his native Trent (Trento). Like several of his better-known predecessors his chief interest before he went to China was astronomy, but he became much more famous as a cartographer: his *Novus Atlas Sinensis* ("A New Atlas of China"), a work with seventeen maps and nearly two hundred pages of text, was published in Amsterdam in 1655. He also wrote for a European audience a history of China and a grammar of the language, as well as several religious works in Chinese, not all of which—including a translation of Suarez—have survived.

Martini set off for Rome in 1651 but did not arrive there until the spring of 1655, at which point he presented his defense of the Jesuits' accommodation to Propaganda and to the Holy Office.[70] He was persuasive: the "Chinese Rites" were approved by the Holy Office, and Pope Alexander VII confirmed this in a decree of March 23, 1656. Martini then returned to China and died from cholera in Hangzhou where he ministered, having in the meantime constructed there the cathedral of the Immaculate Conception, which still stands.

[69] "Propaganda" is derived from a Latin verb that simply means to extend or maintain. "Propaganda" has, however, clearly come to have a pejorative meaning, and in 1967 the congregation or department overseeing missionary activity was renamed the Congregation for the Evangelization of Peoples.

[70] Now called the Congregation for the Doctrine of the Faith, it is the Vatican's doctrinal watchdog.

Three years after Pope Alexander's decree Propaganda appointed three bishops for China, partly, it seems, in an attempt to break the hold of the Padroado.[71] The bishops were issued with instructions that further endorsed the Jesuits' approach:

> Make no endeavour and in no way persuade thee people [in the missions] to change their rites, habits and mores as long as these are not manifestly contrary to religion and good mores. Indeed what would be more absurd than to introduce Gaul [i.e., France], Spain, Italy or some other part of Europe to China? Bring not these things but the faith, which neither rejects nor harms the rites and customs of any nation provided they are not perverse but which rather desires them to remain intact.[72]

In 1665, during one of the occasional outbreaks of persecution, a large group of missionaries, Jesuits, Dominicans, and a lone Franciscan, found themselves detained together in Canton (Guangzhou). They took the opportunity to try to find common ground on the matter of Chinese Rites and Alexander VII's decree, the details of which are described as "a very probable opinion."[73] All signed up to the conclusions of this ad hoc conference, though some, including the Franciscan, with reluctance. One who was also reluctant to sign, and after he returned to Europe repudiated the agreement, was the Dominican Domingo Fernández de Navarrete whose anti-Jesuit treatise, *Tratados históricos, políticos, éticos y religiosos de la monarquia de China*, was published in Madrid in1676 and enjoyed substantial success, being translated into several European languages and feeding the anti-Jesuit sentiment already widespread, especially in France. France became further drawn into the controversy when Charles Maigrot, the vicar apostolic, that is, a quasi-bishop though without episcopal orders, forbade priests in his vicariate of Fukien to follow the decree of Alexander VII, claiming that Martini had given an inaccurate account to Propaganda Fide. When Propaganda took no action, it was referred to the archbishop of Paris, who in turn referred it to

---

[71] According to George Minamiki's *The Chinese Rites Controversy from Its Beginnings to Modern Times* (Chicago: Loyola University Press, 1985), 31. It is Minamiki's clear presentation of the controversy that is followed here.

[72] Ibid.

[73] On probable opinions, see below, pp. 187ff.

the theologians of the Sorbonne who were already deeply embroiled in controversy with the Society.

Meanwhile there were developments in China. The emperor K'ang-hsi who was, as has been seen, very friendly toward a number of Jesuit priests, issued a rescript approving of the Chinese Rites—an encouraging endorsement as far as the Jesuits were concerned but an unwelcome interference by the state in religious issues in the view of Rome. But Rome also had come at last to a conclusion about Maigrot's instruction to his clergy. Although it studiously avoided Maigrot's contention that Martini had misrepresented the facts, after a thorough examination it fundamentally rejected the accommodation to Chinese customs that Ricci had developed. A decree to that effect received Clement XI's approval in November 1704, but it was not made public immediately. Instead it was put in the hands of Carlo Tomasso Maillard de Tournon, sent as papal legate to K'ang-hsi's court.[74] Tournon arrived in Beijing in December 1705, had an audience with the emperor at the end of the month, and had two more six months later.

They did not go well. During the first audience Tournon asked for a permanent representative of the pope to be established at the imperial court. K'ang-hsi was perfectly ready to accept this—as long as the representative was a Jesuit. Tournon did not immediately reveal his intention to impose on missionaries the papal decree of 1704, but the emperor, suspicious of his intentions, withdrew his blanket approval of missionaries and said only those who followed the terms of the accommodation designed by Ricci, and who took an oath to that effect, would be allowed to stay in the Middle Kingdom, and even then they were not to proselytize. He also summoned Maigrot and the two other vicars apostolic and banished them. When Tournon tried to insist that the Jesuits and other clergy abide by the 1704 decree, he was imprisoned in Macau.

Clement XI did not make the 1704 decree public until 1709, and then in March 1715 he issued an apostolic constitution titled *Ex Illa Die*,[75] which reasserted previous papal prohibitions, listed the ways in which the missionaries had tried to avoid the ban, and imposed

---

[74] For Tournon, see above, p. 69.

[75] "From that day forth": papal documents take their name—usually in Latin—from their opening words.

an oath to observe the papal directives. When this new directive arrived at the Chinese imperial court—it was promulgated by the vicar general of Beijing in November 1716—it aroused considerable hostility that this time K'ang-hsi made no effort to moderate. The vicar general was packed off to Canton and ordered to collect all copies of *Ex Illa Die* and send them back to Rome. Rome then made another attempt to establish diplomatic relations with Beijing, sending a new papal legate, one far less controversial than Tournon, but he in the end only added to the confusion. In 1735 Clement XII issued yet another decree, in this instance insisting that only Rome had the authority to decide the question.

Then, in July 1742, Pope Benedict XIV did just that, in a bull titled *Ex Quo Singulari*. The bull summarized the history of the controversy, then reprimanded all those who had found ways of circumventing the papal prohibitions of the Chinese Rites. It not only reimposed an oath to be taken by missionaries against the rites but threatened religious superiors with deprivation of their office if they failed to demand of their subjects obedience to the papal decrees. But the missionaries were not to worry, Benedict XIV insisted, because God would provide as long as the Catholic religion was taught with "that purity with which it has been handed down to them by the Holy See."[76]

It is an illuminating phrase. In the seventeenth and eighteenth centuries Catholicism was being taught in countries whose culture was alien to the European culture in which had been nurtured. As will be seen in the next chapter, the divergence in Central and South America, where there was an army of conquest, was less problematic than in India or Japan or China, where there was a highly developed civilization, in Japan and China especially, at least as old as that in Europe. But, the pope demanded, the framework within which the Gospel was to be proclaimed was that dictated by Rome. Jesuit tolerance of diverse cultures, Jesuit attempts to recast Christianity, and especially liturgical worship, in ways that made sense to potential converts, was, on orders from Rome, to be abandoned in favor of a one-size-fits-all model of Roman Catholicism.

Rubiés has suggested that

---

[76] Quoted in Minamiki, *Chinese Rites*, 74.

As the case of Valignano has illustrated, the Jesuits' key assumption was not that religious conversion had nothing to do with civility, but rather that civilization should make conversions more easy. They thus adopted the Thomistic assumption that rationality, the pre-requisite for an orderly, sophisticated and prosperous social life in Renaissance thinking, was the best basis upon which Christianity could rest. The Jesuit strategy (although with variations within the order) involved a shift from the Augustinian emphasis on faith as the key to the Christian religion to a more rationalist emphasis on a dialogue across civilizations as the basis for the historical transformation of the civilized gentile into a Christian gentile—or so they thought. In effect, I would like to argue, the Jesuits helped transfer the universalistic impulse of Christianity onto a secular field which, as the Enlightenment was to prove, ultimately lay outside their control.[77]

It was the conviction implied in this approach that faith was not necessary for salvation that eventually made the papacy turn against the Jesuit experiment in China. Or so Rubiés has argued. One may doubt if the papal thought processes were quite that sophisticated. Papal policies may well have been dictated more by the hostility against the Society of Jesus among the Catholic monarchs of Europe.[78]

Jesuits, some themselves Chinese, remained in China until the Society was suppressed. They, and other clergy, continued to minister to a Catholic population of some three hundred thousand. The story of the Society of Jesus in the Middle Kingdom has tended to concentrate on Ricci, Schall, Verbiest, and the other learned astronomers and mathematicians, those who came to be known as "court Jesuits" and whose concern, in preaching the Gospel, was to win converts among the elite, if not the emperor himself, at least some of the high-ranking mandarins of the imperial entourage. While they had some, though modest, success, "A rather rare and very specific statistic of 1636 shows that the elite represented only 1.33 per cent of the total Catholic population, while the number of literate persons probably did not exceed 10 per cent of the of the total Catholic population."[79]

[77] Rubiés, "The Concept of Cultural Dialogue," 263–64.

[78] See below, chapter 8 passim.

[79] Nicholas Standaert, "Jesuits in China," in Worcester, *The Cambridge Companion to the Jesuits*, 175.

Most, though not all, of the Jesuits in China were priests,[80] many of them with a vow of special obedience to the pope. They therefore obediently accepted the bull of Benedict XIV, but they could be forgiven if they felt they had been betrayed.

---

[80] Some were, of course, lay brothers, among whom was Giuseppe Castiglione (1688–1766), the talented court painter who taught the Chinese the use of perspective.

Chapter 4

The New World

In 1493, soon after Christopher Columbus had returned from the Americas, *los reyes Catolicos*, Ferdinand and Isabella, turned to the Spanish Pope Alexander VI, Rodrigo Borja, or, in the Italian spelling, Borgia. With the overseas expansion of both Spain and Portugal the conflict between the two seaborne powers over control of the Atlantic had been settled by the 1480 Treaty of Alcaçovas—the treaty that, incidentally, bestowed the Canary Islands on the kingdom of Castile.[1] But with the discovery of new lands on the far side of the ocean a new agreement had to be reached, hence the appeal to the pope as mediator. Alexander issued five bulls, the first of them, dated May 3, 1493, was titled, as was—and still is—customary, after its opening words: *Inter Caetera*. This bull granted:

> To all and singular the aforesaid countries and islands thus unknown and hitherto discovered by your envoys and to be discovered hereafter, provided however they at no time have been in the actual temporal possession of any Christian owner, together with all their dominions, cities, camps, places, and villages, and all rights, jurisdictions, and appurtenances of the same. . . . Moreover we command you . . . you should appoint to the aforesaid countries and islands worthy and God-fearing, learned, skilled, and experienced men to instruct the aforesaid inhabitants and residents in the Catholic faith.

The following day a second bull, with the same name, was issued, demarcating what we might now call "spheres of influence." It

---

[1] The chief purpose of the treaty was to bring an end to the war of Castilian succession, but "spheres of influence" in the Atlantic was an important, if secondary, outcome.

divided the new world—Africa as well as America—between Spain and Portugal along a line one hundred leagues west of the Azores and Cape Verde Islands in a north-south direction. The Catholic monarchs were to own land west of the line; the Portuguese, to the east of it, apart from the Canary Islands, which remained Spanish. Anyone crossing or entering the territories of the Spanish monarchy without permission would incur instant excommunication.

As it was originally framed, the papal bull gave the Portuguese very little leeway, and it was conceded by both Spain and Portugal that the agreement had to be amended. *Inter Caetera* was therefore replaced by the Treaty of Tordesillas, signed in the town of that name, not far from Salamanca, on June 7, 1494. There were various provisions, but the most significant was the new line of demarcation, 370 leagues west of the Cape Verde Islands, thus in effect handing some of what is now Brazil to the Portuguese while Spain kept the remainder, the greater part, in other words, of what is now known as Latin America. Hedged in as they now were, the Portuguese turned then, as has been seen, to the Far East while maintaining a presence in Brazil. The measurements in the Treaty of Tordesillas, such as they were, were imprecise. They did not coincide except by accident with features such as rivers or mountain ranges that might naturally mark off one territory from another. The Portuguese, for example, claimed that their territory reached the Rio de la Plata, and the Spanish that theirs included Rio de Janeiro. It was a recipe for conflict, though that, as will be seen, came much later.[2]

Alexander VI's bull gave the right to Catholic monarchs to assert ownership of newly discovered lands, provided they were not already under the dominion of some other Catholic monarchs. The papal decree is the foundation of what has become known as the much-debated "doctrine of discovery," which the indigenous people of the Americas wish to have repudiated. More to the point here, however, is the teaching of Jesuit theologians, and in particular of Francisco Suarez (1548–1617), on the rights of conquest as they are portrayed in the document. According to Suarez, the pope has the authority to

---

[2] See below, pp. 120ff.

divide pagan provinces and kingdoms among secular kings and princes, not so much that they may do what they like with them, which would be tyranny . . . but so that they may arrange for preachers of the gospel to be sent to the infidels and may have power to protect the preachers, even (if reason and a just cause demand) so far as declaring a just war.

The purpose of conquest, in other words, was to spread the Gospel, as *Inter Caetera* demanded.[3]

The conquistadores had landed in the New World both with chaplains and with soldiers. Suarez doubted whether the missionaries should be backed up by the use of the military. This, he argued, would cause the indigenous population to defend themselves and therefore lead to war—and not simply to war, but, on the part of the local population, to a just war. It also implied that Catholicism might be imposed by force, and that would not in the end be a true conversion to the faith. On the whole Suarez does not spend much time discussing the morality of the Spanish conquest of the Americas, perhaps because, Bernice Hamilton suggests, it had already been treated at some length by the Dominican theologian Francisco de Vitoria. It had, however, also been dwelt on by Suarez's slightly older confrere, Luis de Molina (1535–1600). He, like Vitoria, believed the right of conquest to be strictly limited: Spain had no jurisdiction over the indigenous peoples of the Americas, not even to stop them behaving in a manner that European Christians found immoral, provided that no innocent person was suffering as a consequence, as they might, for example, in the practice of cannibalism or human sacrifice; people ought to be saved from being unjustly killed even if they did not want to be saved.

Not, says Molina, that even this concession gives the invaders carte blanche. The conquest must be of limited duration, though they can charge for their expenses:

---

[3] The quotation is from Suarez, *On Faith, Hope, and Charity*, disputation 18, section 1, cited by Hamilton, *Political Thought*, 111. According to Hamilton, among other theologians holding the same view was the Scot John Mair or Major (c. 1467–1550) who was for a time principal of the University of Glasgow and, toward the end of his life, provost of St. Salvator's College in the University of St. Andrews.

> The invaders are not obliged to risk their lives and expend their
> energies without reward: the enemy who by their unjust acts gave
> cause for a just war are obliged to defray these expenses themselves.
> Any possessions left over are the rightful due of the innocent people
> for whose sake the fighting was started.[4]

According to Molina, then, an invaded people could be charged for
being invaded.

On the question of what constituted a "just" war, little had changed
since St. Augustine of Hippo had, early in the fifth century, discussed
the notion in his *The City of God*. The criteria for a just war were long
established and agreed upon by the sixteenth-century authors discussing the conquest of the Americas. One could not argue, says
Suarez, that the people being invaded were somehow inferior, because there is no evidence for that, or that they had sinned against
God, in which case it was up to God to punish them, not anyone else.
The only valid reason for going to war was if some serious wrong
had been perpetrated on the aggressor, because then the wrong might
justly be redressed. In the New World, this was patently not the case.

As a recently founded religious order the Society of Jesus was fairly
late in arriving in the Americas. Other religious orders had been there
before them, and it was one member of the Order of Preachers, the
Dominicans, who above all others had protested at the treatment of
the native population, the brutal behavior of the conquistadors
toward the Indians, and their virtual enslavement. Bartolomé de las
Casas (c. 1484–1566) had arrived on the island of Hispaniola at the
beginning of the sixteenth century as a colonist and slave owner. He
became a priest in 1510, soon afterward taking part in the Spanish
invasion of Cuba. But shortly thereafter he came to think that the
encomienda system from which he had himself benefited was unjust,
the equivalent of slavery, and ought to be abolished.

An encomienda was a grant by the Spanish monarch to a colonist—the encomendero—of the work of a number of the indigenous
inhabitants of the conquered territory. The encomendero was put
under an obligation to teach his workers Spanish and the rudiments
of Christian doctrine. They were not exactly slaves, though very close
to it: when de las Casas proposed doing away with the encomienda

---

[4] Molina, *Commentaries*, vol. 6, appendix 2, quoted in Hamilton, *Political Thought*,
130.

system because of the harsh conditions to which the colonists subjected their workers, he advocated bringing in African slaves to fill their places, something for which he later repented.

He twice traveled back to Spain to attempt to persuade the king of his views, but without success. In 1522 he entered the Dominican Order, and two decades later he was appointed bishop of Chiapas in Mexico, taking possession of his diocese in 1545. Such was the opposition to him from the colonists—he had refused them absolution unless they freed their slaves—and from the bishop of Guatemala that the following year he returned to Spain to continue his campaign on behalf of the Indians. He never again set foot in the New World, staying for the most part in the royal court to advise on matters concerning the Indians. In 1550 and 1551 he took part in the debate in Valladolid, called by Emperor Charles V, about the status of the native inhabitants of the conquered territories. His opponent, Juan Ginés de Sepúlveda, a canon lawyer and theologian, argued that the Indians were natural slaves, as Aristotle had defined it, and needed to be saved from their barbaric practices by the civilizing mission of the conquistadores. It was the duty of Spain, he claimed, that the Indians be converted to Catholicism, by force if necessary. De las Casas responded that the Indians were perfectly capable of logical reasoning and could embrace Catholicism of their own free will. It was, moreover, the duty of Spain to ensure that people were treated justly, which he knew from personal experience the Indians certainly were not. In any case, Sepúlveda's arguments were in flat contradiction to the 1537 encyclical *Sublimis Deus* of Pope Paul III, in which the pope insisted that the indigenous inhabitants of the New World were perfectly rational human beings with rights to private property. It was only the enemy of the human race—the devil, in other words—who could deny this, declared the pope.

No members of the Society of Jesus were directly involved in the Valladolid debate, though, as has been seen, the issues there discussed were addressed by Suarez and Molina. It was this febrile milieu that the Jesuit missionaries entered when they started to evangelize the New World. They accompanied the expedition sent to Brazil in 1549 by João III, king of Portugal, three priests and two lay brothers together with Manuel da Nobrega (1517–1570) as the superior (and eventually provincial) of the new mission: he had joined the Society only five years earlier.

The king's purpose for the expedition, which included the first governor general and a force of a thousand soldiers, was to bring order to the colonists. Unlike elsewhere in South America, there were no deposits of silver or gold to attract adventurers: the colonists engaged in agriculture, the cultivation of sugar cane in particular; in enslaving the indigenous inhabitants; and in multiple concubinage. The clergy, the early Jesuits discovered, were little better.

The governors sent from Portugal wanted an improvement in the moral standards of the settlers, or some of the early ones did; the missionaries, on the other hand, were more concerned with converting the local inhabitants, the Tupi. Even in their mission to the Tupi they were, in the beginning, obstructed by the first governor of Brazil, who would not allow them to venture into the interior. Language was always going to be a problem. Although José de Anchieta (1534–1597),[5] who arrived in Brazil in 1553, produced the first grammar of the language in a remarkably short time (*The Art of the Language Most Used on the Coast of Brazil*), the Jesuits also invented a form of lingua franca: learning the language of every one of the groups to whom they ministered would have been impossible.[6]

The natives were as resistant to giving up their traditional manner of life as were the settlers to give up theirs. The Tupi were not only a warlike people, given to polygamy and reliance on magic, but also cannibals who ate those they conquered in battle.[7]

> This round of drinking feasts occurred on an appointed date following successful war campaigns to honor kin lost in battles, something only possible when survivors enacted the ultimate defeat on the enemy. The feasts culminated when prisoners-of-war were bashed on the head, quartered and roasted. Then, "everything that can be found in the bodies of such prisoners, from the tips of the

[5] He was canonized by Pope Francis in 2014.

[6] That this lingua franca, known as the lingua geral, was a Jesuit invention is challenged by M. Kittiya Lee in "Cannibal Theologies in Colonial Portuguese America (1549–1759): Translating the Christian Eucharist as the Tupinambá Pledge of Vengeance," *The Journal of Modern History* 21 (2017): 71.

[7] In 1556 they are said to have consumed Pedro Fernandes Sardinha, bishop of Bahia, when he was shipwrecked on his way back to Portugal. While there is some debate over the prevalence, and meaning, of cannibalism in general, the Jesuit missionaries in Brazil did not doubt it was practiced by the Tupi.

toes up to the nose, ears and scalp [except the brain] is entirely eaten by them." United in song and revelry, the Tupinambá gnawed on barbecued bones and gulped cauim.[8]

The missionaries' first impressions of the Tupi were that they seemed ready enough to embrace Christianity. "These heathens do not have idols for whom they would lay down their lives," wrote Nobrega to Simão Rodrigues back in Lisbon, "and they believe everything that they are told. The only difficulty lies in eliminating their evil customs by transforming them into good deeds that are pleasing to Christ."[9] Unfortunately for the missionaries, the Natives regarded the "evil customs" such as polygamy as perfectly natural, and, moreover, they rapidly forgot what they had been taught and proved reluctant to abandon their shamans. Forced conversions were forbidden by the Church, but Anchieta and Nobrega came to the conclusion that there was no other way. For, as Nicholas Cushner puts it, "The European Jesuit who had been educated to believe that the forces of evil waged a continual struggle against the forces of good, easily translated Native American opposition into Satan's handiwork."[10]

The Tupi were herded into self-governing *aldeias* (townships) in an attempt to create a more stable environment in which the faith might be taught. At first these townships were located close to settlements of the colonists, on the grounds that, by observing the customs of the settlers, they might learn civilized living. As the settlers were, especially in the early years, a dissolute conglomeration, this was clearly not going to work. Moreover, it made it easier for the colonists to raid them for slaves, and as a consequence the *aldeias* were moved further away. This did not stop the enslavement, and the settlers blamed the Jesuits for hindering their various enterprises. Nor did it stop the governors, when need arose, from calling on those living in the *aldeias* to defend the colony and providing them with the weapons to do so—though this arming of the Tupi had the approval of the missionaries.

---

[8] Lee, "Cannibal Theologies," 81. Cauim was the local form of alcohol.

[9] Stuart B. Schwartz, ed., *Early Brazil: A Documentary Collection to 1700* (Cambridge: Cambridge University Press, 2010), 143.

[10] Nicholas R. Cushner, *Why Have You Come?* (New York: Oxford University Press, 2006), 11.

A further complaint of the settlers was that the Jesuits, by teaching the native population in their own language, or in the lingua franca, rather than in Portuguese, were making it difficult for the settlers to communicate with their workers. Only in the eighteenth century were the Jesuits, and also other religious orders by this time working in Brazil, instructed to teach the Tupi Portuguese.

In the early years of the mission the colonists were not the only opponents to be confronted by the Portuguese authorities and the missionaries. In the south of the colony, around Guanabara Bay, there was a settlement of French Protestants, Huguenots, which Governor Mem da Sa succeeded in driving out with the help of the Jesuits. Mem da Sa's struggle against the Huguenot's was the occasion for Anchieta's epic poem in praise of the governor, *De Gestis Mendi da Sa*, "the first epic poem written in the Americas" written in 1560, though the final French garrison did not surrender until 1567.[11] The French were to wreak their revenge in 1570, when two ships carrying in all seventy-five Jesuits were seized by Huguenot corsairs, and a total of fifty-two Jesuits, together with their superior, were thrown overboard.[12]

When the *aldeias* had become more firmly established, the policy of forcing Christianity on the Tupi gave way to a policy of accommodation. Anchieta's epic poem had "justified imperialism by dehumanizing the Indians. Cannibalism was an offence against natural law and so deprived practitioners of natural law's protection. For Anchieta, cannibalism justified military intervention."[13] Once they had been well settled in the *aldeias*, however, Anchieta, who came to be revered as a worker of miracles, employed his literary skills to win them over, in particular through his plays, building on their practices—even their (former) cannibalism: one of his plays concerns in particular Saints Lawrence and Sebastian, the former, of course, having died upon a grill, the latter pierced by arrows, both manners

---

[11] Entry for Anchieta by Danilo Mondoni, SJ, in *The Cambridge Encyclopedia of the Jesuits*, ed. Thomas Worcester (Cambridge: Cambridge University Press, 2008), 27. It is hard to imagine how there might have been an earlier one.

[12] Forty of them from the first ship to be captured were declared "Blessed" in 1854.

[13] Anne B. McGinness, "Between Subjection and Accommodation: The Development of José de Anchieta's Missionary Project in Colonial Brazil," *Journal of Jesuit Studies* 1 (2014): 234.

of death being something to which, especially in their pre-*aldeias* lives, the Tupi could relate.[14]

The beginning of the Jesuit mission in Brazil, like those in China and elsewhere, was the "heroic" period. As the years went by the pattern of settler attempts to effectively enslave the indigenous inhabitants and the missionaries' attempts to prevent it became a constantly repeated battle: the Jesuits bolstered by the intermittent support of the Portuguese crown; the settlers resisting the laws the crown had tried to impose for the benefit of the Tupi. Their resistance sometimes became outright rebellion with, occasionally, the missionaries being forced to leave their houses and take refuge elsewhere. In 1640, for instance, Pope Urban VII issued a brief that reiterated Paul III's *Sublimis Deus* and threatened excommunication on those who enslaved the Indians. When it arrived in Brazil in 1641 and was promulgated by the priests, they were attacked and were menaced with death. This conflict was never ending—at least, not until the Society of Jesus was banished from all Portuguese territories.[15] Against the settlers "the Jesuits' weapons consisted of spiritual devices such as excommunication, moral suasion, and vigorously argued remonstrances," remarks Dauril Alden. "Those of the settlers included anti-Jesuit diatribes filled with lurid but unproven charges and blatant physical intimidation."[16] And this, despite the Society having opened colleges in the major centers that served the settler population and not the Indians—nor, indeed, those of mixed race.

One of the more remarkable figures in the evangelization of Brazil was the long-lived Antonio Vieira (1608–1697), who, though born in Lisbon, had been brought up in Salvador Bahia where he studied in the Jesuit college. He entered the Society in 1623 and was ordained a priest eleven years later. He was an indefatigable missionary and held a variety of roles, particularly in the provinces of Pará and Maranhão: a brief biography by Danilo Mondoni in *The Cambridge Encyclopedia of the Jesuits* describes him as "diplomat, social reformer, apostle and protector of Indians, administrator, preacher and literate"

---

[14] Ibid., 241. Sebastian was the patron saint of Rio de Janeiro.

[15] See below, p. 210.

[16] Alden, *The Making of an Enterprise*, 499.

(*sic*, "man of letters"?).[17] But he was also a controversial character, once dismissed from the Society by the general though fairly swiftly reinstated, and occasionally in trouble with the Inquisition and, through his defense of the Indians, with the settler population. His preaching and writing exemplify the ambivalent attitude toward slavery within the Society of Jesus.

In 1455, at the behest of the king of Portugal, Pope Nicholas V issued *Romanus Pontifex*, which gave Portugal a monopoly of the slave trade as a form of compensation for the expenses it would incur in spreading the Catholic faith in its newly acquired dominions overseas. Granting a license to engage in the exporting of slaves from Angola to South America became an important source of revenue to the crown.[18] The Jesuit moral theologian Luis de Molina (1535–1600), of whom much more later, discussed slavery in his *De Justicia et Jure* ("On Justice and Law"), which appeared in six volumes from 1593 to 1609. While Molina condemned the way slaves were treated and thought slavery ought to be brought to an end, he did not regard it as either illegal or immoral in itself. There were Jesuits who thought otherwise, both in Lisbon and in Brazil. The superior in Lisbon wrote to the general of the Society in 1586 denouncing slavery, but the Jesuits continued to be not just slave owners but also slave traders, sending captive Africans from Angola to Brazil, each one physically branded by a hot iron with the royal seal.

For the settlers it must have been confusing. The Jesuits were trading in slaves from Africa while at the same time vigorously opposing the enslavement of the indigenous inhabitants of South America. Antonio Vieira had an explanation. For him, it was a great miracle that the Africans had been saved from death as pagans and transported to Brazil where they could live in a Christian environment— that the environment was not Christian enough because of the immoral behavior of the settlers was a constant Jesuit complaint—and thereby save their souls. This was, as Luiz Felipe de Alencastro has remarked in the chapter cited above, much the same argument as

---

[17] *Cambridge Encyclopedia of the Jesuits*, 828.

[18] This section on slavery draws heavily on Luiz Felipe de Alencastro, "The African Slave Trade and the Construction of the Iberian Atlantic," in *The Global South Atlantic*, ed. Kerry Bystrom and Joseph R. Slaughter (New York: Fordham University Press, 2018), 33–45.

that contained in *Romanus Pontifex*, but Vieira's writings and his published sermons had a far longer, and longer-lasting, reach in the New World than the papal bull.

Just as Brazil was part of the Portuguese overseas empire, New Spain was, as the name implies, part of the Spanish Empire. The viceroyalty, as it was denominated, roughly coincided with present-day Mexico. It did, however, include Florida, which is where the first Jesuits landed and began evangelizing in March 1567. Like Nobrega in Brazil, the superior, Juan Rogel—who had trained as a doctor before entering the Society—at first reported enthusiastically about the possibilities of converting the local tribes, but, again like Nobrega, he was faced with Indian practices such as polygamy that ran contrary to the Christianity he and his companions were attempting to inculcate: if the Indians seemed interested it was largely because they saw in the Spanish troops who were accompanying the missionaries a defense against hostile tribes. An additional problem was the general poverty of the area, which produced scarcely enough to feed the Indians and was unable to support both soldiers and missionaries: Rogel and others made forays to Havana to bring back food, which they shared with the Indians. In this difficult environment the missionaries found themselves working very closely with the soldiers, using the forts that had been established along the coast as their bases. Rogel in particular, because of his medical knowledge, was much in demand by the troops. It was an uncomfortable position for the Jesuits, which, together with their obvious lack of success in converting the natives, led the general in Rome, Francis Borgia (Borja), to close down the mission in 1572.

It was nearly two decades before the Spanish Jesuits began a new mission station among the native peoples. In the meantime they undertook the traditional—if the word "traditional" can be used in the context of an order not half a century old—apostolates: they opened colleges. The first of these began in Mexico City in 1573, financed by the donation of a hacienda. The course of instruction was also traditional, the pupils in the New World studying the classical authors of the old in Latin and Greek, from texts printed at a Jesuit printing press.[19] There was a separate college for the sons of the native

---

[19] Jesuit education will be discussed in the next chapter.

elite, established in 1586, where the local languages were taught. Similar institutions were opened in other major centers of New Spain, including in the mining areas as well as cities, and there was even one opened in 1751 for native women, a remarkable venture for the Society.

Missions to the Indians began again in 1591 when two priests were sent to Sinaloa, which the Spaniards had been attempting to colonize because of the silver to be mined there, but they had more than once been wiped out by the indigenous population. The governor asked for Jesuits, and two were sent to begin evangelizing a territory that eventually extended into what is now Arizona: San Xavier de Bac, a few miles south of Tucson, was founded by Kino in 1692 and is still in use by Yaqui and other tribe members.[20] Kino, a Spanish version of the original Italian Eusebio Chini (1645–1711), was one of the more remarkable of the missionaries working with numerous different tribes, began to evangelize in Baja California, but had to abandon this mission because of drought. When he began again it was in Sonora, traveling widely along ancient pathways, mapping and noting, and even naming, geographical features that he encountered. Like his confreres elsewhere, he established villages for the Indians, teaching them agriculture and cattle rearing.

Gathering the local population into the villages—though it made them easier to teach, to treat during epidemics brought by the Europeans, and to feed in times of famine—was not easy, and the Indians often had to be bribed to enter the new settlements. There were several Indian uprisings, mainly because of exploitation by the Spanish colonists, especially those in search of silver in the Sierra Madre, but also because of the brutal way in which Spaniards attempted to root out what seemed to them idolatry and to make the Indians conform to European ways.

There were differences of opinion on how to regard traditional Indian worship, and nowhere more so than in the viceroyalty of Peru, where eight Jesuits arrived in March 1568. They came, the first of the order in South America, at the direct request of the newly appointed viceroy, Francisco de Toledo, a friend of the Jesuit general of the day,

---

[20] The present church and compound is slightly distant from that established by Kino and is no longer in the charge of Jesuits. Kino is represented by a statue in the US Capitol's Hall of Statuary and even has a mineral named after him.

Francis Borja (1510–1572), the fourth duke of Gandia.[21] So many years after the conquest, the eight were not the first missionaries in the viceroyalty: there were already in the country Franciscans, Augustinians, Mercedarians, and Dominicans, and it was in a Dominican house in Lima that the Jesuits lodged on their arrival. A few months later the viceroy arrived, accompanied by more Jesuits.

The apostolate they expected to undertake was similar to that to which they had been accustomed in Europe, to preach, hear confessions, give the spiritual exercises and instruction in Christian doctrine, and, above all, to open colleges.[22] One of the first things they did, therefore, on arrival in Lima, was to open the College of San Pablo: by the time they were expelled from the Spanish dominions, just two centuries later, there were fifteen colleges in Peru. The colleges accepted boys both of Spanish and of mestizo origin, that is to say, with a Spanish father, generally an encomendero, and an Indian mother. Indeed, at first the Jesuits in Peru accepted mestizos into the order as well as those of purely Spanish ancestry—they needed their knowledge of the local languages—but in 1582 they stopped doing so on the grounds, it was claimed, that the mestizos would not entirely abandon their traditional practices. The first mestizo to become a Jesuit priest, ordained in 1573, was Blas Valera (1544–1597), who later in life made a spirited defense of Inca religion (see below, p. 117), views that might be seen as giving credence to the 1582 decision. Valera's approach was much at odds with the attitude of José de Acosta (1540–1600), last seen arguing against a Spanish invasion of China (see above, p. 81), and similar to the tension over the language to be used in Catholic catechesis when translated into local languages.[23]

Though favorable to the Jesuits, the viceroy wanted more from them than colleges. He wanted the indigenous population, Quechua

---

[21] Borja, or Borgia, entered the Society of Jesus in June 1546, his wife having died the previous March. He was elected the third general of the Society in July 1565. A great grandson of the dissolute Pope Alexander VI, he was declared a saint by Pope Clement X in 1670.

[22] Jesuits and education will be discussed in the next chapter.

[23] See Ana Carolina Hosne, "*Dios, Dio, Viracocha, Tianzhu*: 'Finding' and 'Translating' the Christian God in the Overseas Jesuit Missions (16th–18th Centuries)," in *The Rites Controversies in the Early Modern World*, ed. Ines G. Županov and Pierre Antoine Fabre (Leiden: Brill, 2018), 322–44.

and Aymara, instructed in Catholicism: he wanted them to take charge of villages, known as *doctrinas*. For the Jesuit clergy that was a problem: it would in effect turn them into parish priests, something that was strictly against the Constitutions of the Society. Yielding to pressure from the viceroy, however, in 1570 they agreed to take charge of the *doctrina* of Huarochiri, east of Lima, an extensive and demanding region rather than a modest township that had been abandoned by other clergy and religious because of the difficulty of working there. One of those who was sent was Valera, not yet ordained priest, chosen no doubt because of his knowledge of the local languages.

The Jesuits reported initial success. Corpus Christi was celebrated in 1570, as elsewhere in the Catholic world, with processions, but the processions in Huarochiri incorporated native dances and costumes that reflected traditional Indian practices—there was, in other words, a degree of accommodation to the mores of the indigenous tribes. Yet after only a couple of years, the Jesuits withdrew. Two of those who had been sent to Huarochiri had died, which may be one of the reasons for the sudden reversal, but as Sabine Hyland puts it,

> The Jesuit missionaries eventually came to believe that although the natives may have professed to be Christians, they still retained many of their native beliefs. The Jesuit emphasis on interiority made the fathers question native sincerity in faith, even when the indigenous people complied with all of the external requirements of sixteenth-century Spanish Christianity.[24]

The priests and brothers displaced from Huarochiri went next to El Cercado, an Indian settlement close to Lima, and they also accepted the *doctrina* of Juli, on Lake Titicaca, which had first been established by the Dominicans.[25] They retained Juli, a village now in Bolivia in-

[24] Sabine Hyland, *The Jesuits and the Incas* (Ann Arbor: University of Michigan Press, 2003), 46.

[25] De Toledo banned the works of de las Casas from Peru, despite them having royal approval, and was hostile to any Dominican who promoted them. In his *Memorial de Yucay* (1571) the viceroy "insisted that the writings of the Dominican were 'a most subtle work of the devil' to persuade the world that the Incas had not been idolatrous tyrants but 'perfect kings' and 'legitimate lords.'" "Toledo also took care to politicise the famous inquisitorial process against the Dominican Fray Francisco de la Cruz, prior of the convent of St Dominic in Lima and rector of the budding University of San Marcos. . . . Despite his many disagreements with Las Casas, Fray

habited by some fifteen thousand Aymara, until in 1767 they were driven from Peru at the suppression of the Society in the Spanish dominions. No Spaniards were allowed to live there, and the Indians were preserved from the burden of the encomienda system. For the Jesuits it served as a center for teaching languages to, and generally acclimatizing, new recruits to the Peruvian mission.

Though in the first instance, and reluctantly, they had agreed to the viceroy's request to take over a couple of *doctrinas*, they quickly learned just how problematic it was to be close to de Toledo. He wanted them, for example, to teach at the University of San Marcos, which the viceroy had seized from the Dominicans. They did not want to do so, perhaps not so much out of a wish not to upset members of another religious order as from a concern that at San Marcos, unlike in their own College of San Pablo, they would only be instructors without further responsibility for the governance of the institution and the spiritual welfare of its students. But what most aroused their hostility was the public execution in 1572 of Tupac Amaru, the last Inca, ruling a remnant of the Inca Empire in the upper Amazon, northeast of Cusco. After Jesuit pleas for his life were rejected by the viceroy, one of their number attended the Inca on the scaffold, while another, Luís Lopez, declared the viceroy to be "the most hated man in the world." Lopez, a rather troublesome character, was later arraigned before the Inquisition, charged with improper behavior with a woman. Apparently the charge was unproven, because he was not punished at the time, but he was imprudent enough to commit to writing his thoughts on de Toledo, the Inquisition, and even the Spanish king. Though he did not intend them for publication his notes became known. He had to be packed off to Spain where he spent the rest of his life confined to a Jesuit college.[26]

Criticism by Jesuits of the regime imposed by the State on the native inhabitants of Peru and surrounding regions was common. The

---

Francisco was a firm believer in the imminent transplantation of the European Church to the Indies. There, he was convinced, Lima would be declared the new spiritual capital of the world just before the soon-to-be-expected Final Judgment." Ramón Mujica Pinilla, "Angels and Demons in the Conquest of Peru," in *Angels, Demons and the New World*, ed. F. Cervantes and A. Redden (Cambridge: Cambridge University Press, 2013), 198.

[26] Jeffrey L. Klaiber, *The Jesuits in Latin America, 1540–2000* (St. Louis: Institute of Jesuit Sources, 2009), 71.

mines were a particular problem, especially labor in the silver mines at Potosi and the mercury mine at Hunacavelica. The work was hard and dangerous, the workers forced to walk great distances to reach them. The miners no doubt produced considerable wealth, argued Pedro Oñate, SJ, but it was quite wrong that this wealth should then be exported to support another kingdom, Spain, rather than the one in which it was produced, Peru. And workers should not be forced to labor in the mines; they ought to be induced to do so by the terms under which they worked. As it was, they were earning more for themselves by working on their farms than they ever could in the mines.[27] Most criticism, however, was aimed at the encomendero system, not for the most part at the system itself, but because of the abuses of it by the Spanish settlers.

The encomendero structure was, however, defended by many because it enabled the Quechua and the Aymara to be instructed in the Christian faith. The most appropriate method of evangelization was a particular concern of José de Acosta, who arrived from Spain in 1572. He was formidably learned: as one French historian has commented, "Jesuits can be distinguished from other missionaries by their investment in scholarly knowledge."[28] Acosta had expected to spend his time in Peru as he had spent it in Spain, teaching theology and preaching, and that was indeed the way he began his sojourn in the Americas. But a year or so after his arrival the provincial sent him on a fifteen-month tour of the province, and he was to make two other lengthy journeys through the viceroyalty, becoming familiar not just with the geography of the region but with the languages, Quechua and Aymara, and the beliefs of it peoples: as Jeffrey Klaiber has put it, these tours constituted "Acosta's discovery of America."[29] In 1575 he became rector of the Jesuit college in Lima and the following year the provincial of Peru at the remarkably young age of thirty-six, serving in that office until 1581. He was also an adviser to Toribio Alfonso de Mogrovejo, who was, from 1579 to his death in 1606, the archbishop of Lima.[30] In particular Acosta was a significant presence

---

[27] Ibid., 76.

[28] Charlotte de Castelnau-Estoile, "Jesuit Anthropology," in *The Oxford Handbook of the Jesuits*, ed. Ines G. Županov (Oxford: Oxford University Press, 2019), 812.

[29] Klaiber, *The Jesuits in Latin America*, 29.

[30] Toribio did not arrive in Lima until 1581. He was declared a saint in 1726.

as an official theologian at the Third Council of Lima held from August 1582 to October 1583.

This provincial council implemented in the viceroyalty the decrees of the Council of Trent—of which, of course, the Jesuits were considerable protagonists—but, more important, it attempted to ensure that the local Church was adapted to the local culture. At least, up to a point. It demanded that the indigenous population be treated with dignity, "not as slaves but as free men," that the local languages be used, together with Spanish, but not Latin. Seminaries were to be established to train local clergy, and the council laid down rules for their conduct. In the debates Acosta argued for the ordination to the priesthood of indigenous men, a view in which he was opposed at the council by one of his own Jesuit brethren and indeed by royal decree, even though he had come to believe that they should not be allowed to join the Society. He was also tasked with preparing a catechism in three languages, Quechua, Aymara, and Spanish; it was later to be translated into Guaraní for use in Paraguay.

It was here, in the drawing up of the catechism, that there emerged one of the most important differences between Acosta's approach and that of the mestizo Jesuit—he had entered before the prohibition—Blas Valera.[31] Valera thought that the local language should be used for specifically Christian terms, in other words, that Inca concepts, for instance, that there was a creator deity who sometimes walked on earth, could be translated into Christian ones or that there was even in Inca tradition a status not unlike that of nuns. As Sabine Hyland puts it, "Valera was an unabashed apologist for the Incas. His praise for his mother's people emphasised, in particular, the civil order, learning and high moral standards" of the Incas.[32] Acosta, on the other hand, was convinced that Inca religion, though originally "natural" and therefore compatible with Christianity, had been degraded by the devil and needed to be entirely eliminated before Catholicism could take root. In the *Catechism of the Third Council of Toledo*, the first book to be printed in South America, he insisted on using

---

[31] Valera had a brother, Jerónimo, also educated by the Jesuits. He too entered the Society but left after observing the harsh treatment meted out to Blas. He became a Franciscan and a professor of theology in Lima, specializing in Duns Scotus. He was also a judge of the Inquisition. cf. Hyland, *The Jesuit and the Incas*, 23.

[32] Ibid., 104.

Spanish terms for Christian concepts—God, for example—rather than Quechua equivalents. He also believed, something Valera vehemently denied, that before the coming of the Spaniards the Incas had practiced human sacrifice: Acosta's source had misinterpreted the chronicles, said Valera.[33] Although Acosta saw in their religion the work of Satan, hence it had to be extirpated, he also believed, along with Toribio and contrary to the civil authorities, that the work of conversion had to be gradual rather than imposed by the sword, even if sometimes coercion was needed. As he wrote:

> Experience has abundantly taught us that the nature of the barbarians is completely subservient. In practice, if they are not frightened and if they are not forced like children, they will not fall under obedience. What to do, then? Should only people of a free condition and mature judgement have hope of salvation? Should not the children be given a teacher in Christ? Undoubtedly. We will have to employ a more prudent procedure and surveillance; we must sometimes use the stick, but for God's sake; we must urge them to come to dinner for the love of the Lord.

This quotation is taken from Acosta's *De procuranda indorum salute*, which, together with his *Historia natural y moral de las Indias*, was published only after he had returned to Spain in 1587, possibly on the grounds of ill health. The *De procuranda*, however, had been written in 1576, only a few years after his arrival in Peru. Through his writings a great deal is known about what Acosta thought: he was a prolific author, producing theological treatises as well as giving an account of his experiences of the New World in general and more particularly about Peru and Mexico.[34]

He prefaces the *De procuranda* by warning missionaries that in their approach to their work they should adapt their approach to the different sort of societies they would encounter. He provides a crude taxonomy of societies, dividing them into three distinct types. First

---

[33] Ibid., 173. However, "no one doubts today that the Incas had human sacrifices" (Klaiber, *The Jesuits in Latin America*, 44).

[34] On his journey back to Spain Acosta visited his brother, a Jesuit superior in Mexico, and spent a year there. The above quotation from *De Procuranda* is taken from Carlos Zeron, "Political Theories and Jesuit Politics," in Županov, *The Oxford Handbook*, 206.

of all, there are those communities that are very like the European society the missionaries had left behind. These communities would be properly governed, engage in trade, and, above all, be literate. They are, in other words, "civilized." He included in this group the Chinese, whom he claims to have seen even though he can have known very little about them: *De procuranda* was written, though not yet published, before Ruggieri and Ricci had set foot in the Middle Kingdom. After this class comes the people among whom he had worked, the Mexicans and especially the Peruvians. They had, he granted, a form of government, but they lacked literacy. He was honest enough, however, to mention the system of colored strings and knots, the *quipu*, that enabled the Incas to keep accounts and a form of record.[35] The lowest class had neither government nor literacy, were given to cannibalism, and lived like wild animals.

Obviously the Peruvians did not fall into this last class, so why had the spreading of Christianity proved so difficult? There were, he wrote, three reasons. The first was the violence of the conquistadores; the second was the immorality of many of the Spaniards, including the missionaries, whose moral teaching was contradicted by their style of life; and only in the third place was the tenacity with which the indigenous population held on to their—in his eyes—demonically inspired religious beliefs. He was also critical of the encomienda system, but the Jesuit General Acquaviva told him to cut that from the text, and Everard Mercurian, Acquaviva's successor, instructed him to remove the first two reasons: they were impolitic, the Society being too close to the Spanish monarchy.[36] Despite such criticisms of the way the conquest had been carried out, Acosta never doubted that it should have occurred. It was, in his eyes, providential because it had brought Christianity to the Incas. This did not alter his conviction, however, that a prerequisite for the conversion of the Indians of Peru—if it was to be more than a superficial adherence to the outward observances of Catholicism—was a higher moral standard from the Spanish colonizers. Apart from that, he argued, what was

---

[35] It was later recommended for examining one's conscience before confession. For the use of the quipu, see Ana Carolina Hosne, "The 'Art of Memory' in the Jesuit Missions in China and Peru in the Late Sixteenth Century," *Material Culture Review* 76 (Fall 2013): 30–40, esp. 32–35.

[36] Hyland, *The Jesuit and the Incas*, 177–79.

needed was education in general and not just education in the faith, important though the latter was. It was all the more important because for Acosta and his Jesuit colleagues basic knowledge of Christianity was not enough to ensure salvation: to be saved the Indians had to have, he believed, explicit belief in Christ, a maximalist position that departed from the attitude of earlier missionary priests in Peru. In 1578 he was involved in the trial of a Dominican priest by the Inquisition. The Dominican was found guilty of adhering to the Lutheran doctrine of justification by faith alone, for which he was burned at the stake. That same year a Jesuit was accused of the same heresy but was only imprisoned, not executed. What was at issue was not Lutheranism as such, but what degree of knowledge of Christ was needed by the Indians if they were to achieve salvation. Though Acosta was something of maximalist in this regard, he had an imaginative approach as to how to achieve it: education not simply by book learning but also through music, dance, and the theater.

While José de Acosta was the most significant of the missionary Jesuits in Peru, perhaps in South America, his subsequent career proved more problematic. Even before leaving Peru he appears to have alienated some of his fellow Jesuits by joining the Inquisition—and especially so after condemning one of his own brethren. Back in Spain he became associated with dissident Jesuits, backed by Philip II, uneasy with the apparent loss of control of the Society by Spain after the election of two successive non-Spanish generals, Mercurian and Acquaviva, the first three, of course, Ignatius himself, Laínez, and Francis Borgia, all having been born in Spain. Initially Acosta had been appointed by Acquaviva as one of the three visitors to look into the unrest both in Spain and in Portugal, but he had eventually sided with the dissidents and in 1593 persuaded Clement VII to make the Rome-based Jesuit theologian Francisco de Toledo a cardinal[37] so that he might preside at the general congregation Philip II had succeeded in forcing on the Society. A general congregation did indeed meet, from November 1593 to the following January, but without de Toledo presiding. The outcome was solid endorsement of the Society's Constitution, and of Acquaviva's generalate.

---

[37] He was the first of many Jesuit cardinals, despite the society's Constitutions requiring the solemnly professed to vow not to seek high office unless ordered to do so under obedience. Jesuit cardinals have become especially numerous under Pope Francis.

The Society's troubles were not yet over. It had been saved from having to adopt a new name in 1590 only by the death of the pope, Sixtus V, who had ordered the change. Sixtus's successor, Clement VIII, then decided that the—admittedly unusual—practice of electing a general for life should be abandoned. This time it was Cardinal de Toledo who, for reasons of his own, managed to persuade him otherwise. Then Philip III of Spain, at the prompting of a disgruntled Jesuit, asked Pope Clement to instruct Acquaviva to come to Spain: this time the general's health failed, he was ordered by his doctors not to travel, and the crisis passed.

Surprisingly, perhaps, Acosta managed to rehabilitate himself with the Society. He became rector of the college in Salamanca, where he died in 1600. His one-time colleague at the Third Council of Lima, Blas Valera, was much less fortunate. In April 1583 he was accused of a crime the nature of which has never been revealed. For three years he was imprisoned in the basement of the Jesuit house in Lima and, Hyland reports, flogged weekly.[38] This was followed by eight years of house arrest before he was allowed to leave Peru for Spain—at the instigation of Acosta, it seems, who was sympathetic to his plight. He arrived in Cadiz in 1596, just in time to be badly injured in an English raid on the port. He died of his wounds in Malaga a year later.

There is a further mystery about Valera. Documents discovered in a private collection in Naples tell a different story. They claim that Valera recovered from his injuries and returned to Peru, where he wrote a book hitherto believed to have been authored by someone else. While there is considerable doubt about the authenticity of these new papers, Valera is known to have written at least one book, *Historia Occidentalis*, though it survives only as it was extensively quoted by another mestizo author, not himself a Jesuit, called Garcilaso de la Vega. De la Vega's book was in turn read by, and greatly influenced, a Jesuit missionary, Giovanni Anello Oliva, who arrived in Peru in 1597 and died in 1642. Oliva's own book, *Historia del Reino y Provincias*

---

[38] Hyland, *The Jesuit and the Incas*, 69–71. The weekly flogging may be a misunderstanding: until the mid-twentieth century Jesuits, like most if not all religious orders, were accustomed to beat themselves once a week as a form of mortification. Nonetheless, the punishment seems excessive. As Hyland points out (187), Miguel de Fuentes, who had taught the young Valera, was not punished as harshly even though found guilty of seducing a whole convent of nuns.

del Peru, was, like Valera's, very sympathetic to the Incas and, again like Valera, highly critical of the Spanish conquest. Probably because of his criticism of Spain, which he no doubt found easier to make because he was an Italian by birth, Muzio Vitelleschi, general of the Society from 1615 to 1645, banned its publication: it appeared only in 1895.[39]

After all the controversy that accompanied the Jesuits' first decades in Peru, the subsequent 150 years or so was less fraught. Though it retained the *doctrinas* of Juli and Cercado, the main work was in the colleges that were established in Lima (San Pablo), Cusco, Arequipa, Potosi, and La Paz, the last two, of course, located nowadays not in Peru but in modern-day Bolivia.

It was from Peru that Jesuits spread out into other parts of South America apart from, as has been seen, Brazil, and the first expeditions were to what was the viceroyalty of Paraguay. In his *The Jesuits in Latin America*, Jeffrey Klaiber wrote, "Much has been written about the famous Paraguay reductions, or missions, but little comparative analysis has been undertaken."[40] If that were true in 2009 it is no longer the case: a good deal of detailed study of the reductions has since been done. Cunningham Graham's picture of a "vanished arcadia"[41] has been modified but not entirely rejected. The system of townships that was set up by the Jesuit missionaries, thirty of them in all, was not a new idea. They were similar to the *aldeias* of Brazil[42] and, indeed, were not uniquely Jesuit: Juli, which was one such, had been founded by Dominicans, and in Paraguay a Franciscan missionary, Luis de Bolaños, had not only established eighteen townships for the indigenous inhabitants, the Guaraní, but also written the first grammar of the Guaraní language.[43] It is, however, the network of Jesuit reductions that have received most attention and were the subject of *The Mission*, the 1986 film starring Robert De Niro and Jeremy Irons.

[39] Klaiber, *The Jesuits in Latin America*, 46.

[40] Ibid., 127.

[41] R. B. Cunningham Graham, *A Vanished Arcadia* (London: Heineman, 1901).

[42] Cf. above, p. 101.

[43] Klaiber, *The Jesuits in Latin America*, 129. The name "Guaraní" means "warrior" in their own language: they did not use it of themselves, though they did not object to the title; cf. Barbara Ganson, *The Guaraní under Spanish Rule* (Stanford, CA: Stanford University Press, 2003), 18.

When the Franciscans first arrived among the Guaraní they learned that the Indians believed that the world would be destroyed by a great flood, which gave the friars the conviction that they already had some knowledge of Christianity. When the Jesuits arrived—the first of the reductions was established in 1610—they were told by a shaman that someone had long ago come across the sea to teach them agriculture and how to behave morally. This, said the Jesuits, was undoubtedly St. Thomas the Apostle, and one of the mission stations was dedicated to him.

Unlike some of the fiercer tribes in the region, the Guaraní for the most part welcomed the Jesuits, who not only learned their language but also lived among them. They had good reason to turn to the missionaries. The fathers of the Society offered them better living conditions—the encomienda system was waived for those living in the reductions—but also protection against those Spanish and Portuguese settlers who raided the townships in the hope of carrying off slaves. The Jesuits moved their first reductions further away from the colonial settlements, but that did not end the practice. In 1637 permission was sought to arm the Guaraní, though even before permission was received from Spain the missionaries had gone ahead: a Guaraní force defeated a Paulista (i.e., from São Paulo) force at the battle of Mbororé, which included a river battle depicted, though anachronistically, in *The Mission*. The defeat did not put an end to Paulista incursions, and the Jesuits wanted the Guaraní to be able to keep their arms in the reductions. The settlers opposed this suggestion, fearing a possible Guaraní uprising against them, but this never happened, despite occasional flare-ups, and in the end keeping all weapons in Asunción proved impracticable.

Not that there wasn't a degree of hostility toward the Jesuit regime, especially at first and especially from the shamans who feared losing their authority among the Indians. As one shaman said, addressing the Jesuits, "Our ancestors lived in freedom, having as many women as they wanted . . . with whom they lived and spent a happy life, and you want to destroy our traditions and want to burden us by tying us to only one wife."[44] According to Klaiber, the missions "responded to the felt needs of a semi-nomadic people for whom

---

[44] Quoted Ganson, *The Guaraní*, 37.

sedentary urban life based upon agriculture and the tending of herds constituted the next step up in their evolution."[45] Perhaps, but the establishment of the reductions brought about an enormous change in the Guaraní lifestyle and traditions, as the shaman quite correctly claimed. The practice of polygamy, prohibited within Christianity, was important to the Indians as a means of establishing tribal networks—which is why, when the Spanish settlers took Indian concubines, the expectation of the Guaraní was very different from the reality they encountered, a status little different from slavery. The coming of the Jesuits also changed interfamily relationships. Before the arrival of the reductions, the men had been hunters in the forest while the women grew such crops as there were. But with the settlements, men also engaged in agriculture, for the Guaraní men a nontraditional occupation. They also became herdsmen, though the herds of cattle were often at some distance from the reductions, with the result that those engaged in herding were often away from their families for long periods of time. During these absences wives, and indeed any young women, were given separate and highly regulated accommodation. The Jesuits were, not surprisingly, eager to maintain Christian moral standards. As a result they insisted that young men in the reductions married at seventeen years of age and young women at fifteen. Such early marriages led to a high birth rate: Julia Sarreal quotes a study that shows the average Guaraní woman had 7.7 children during her lifetime.[46]

For the Guaraní in the reductions the working year was in two unequal parts. From June until December they worked partly on their own and partly on communal plots, but for the first part of the year the men spent their time herding cattle, gathering yerba maté, or in other activities such as brickmaking for the sturdy buildings, individual for family units and communal, in the reductions. Communal buildings included, of course, the church, often a very splendid construction in what has, perhaps inaccurately, become known as the

[45] Klaiber, *The Jesuits in Latin America*, 131.
[46] Julia J. S. Sarreal, *The Guaraní and Their Missions: A Socioeconomic History* (Stanford, CA: Stanford University Press, 2014), 50.

"Jesuit style,"[47] as well workshops and the "hostels" for unmarried women and young girls.

Cattle were not native to South America, but once introduced they flourished. The Guaraní men looked after large herds of them for part of the year, and beef, obviously a nontraditional food for the Indians, became very popular. Sarreal claims that mission-based Guaraní consumed more beef per head in the eighteenth century than do United States citizens do in the twenty-first.[48] Nevertheless, the main product of the reductions was the yerba maté or "Jesuit tea": the maté was the gourd from which it was traditionally drunk. The Indians foraged for the plant in the forests until, well into the eighteenth century, the Jesuits discovered how to cultivate it. The yerba, however, was a further cause of friction with the settlers. They also produced it, but that which was manufactured on the mission stations was acknowledged to be of a much better quality than that of the settlers and commanded a much higher price. It accounted for 70 percent of mission income, far outstripping income from textiles and from tea.[49] The missions prospered under the Jesuits but, according to Sarreal, were not efficient, and their prosperity depended on Jesuit subsidy, special privileges granted by the crown, and a lack of competition.[50]

There were, of course, Jesuits, usually two of them, allotted to each township, but they were for the most part self-governing. Each had an Indian headman and a Guaraní-staffed cabildo, or council, members of which constituted a kind of aristocracy within a reduction, wearing special dress, carrying symbols of office, and seated in the front rows of the church. Discipline was strict, and strictly enforced, though there was no capital punishment. The Jesuits' concern was the well-being of the Guaraní, but above all their instruction in

---

[47] "Recent literature on Jesuit architecture has pointed out that contrary to previous assumptions, no uniform set of stylistic norms has ever been issued. There simply was no single 'Jesuit style,' and, more important, neither the Roman curia nor anyone else really ever tried to create one." Markus Friedrich, "Jesuit Organization and Legislation," in Županov, *The Oxford Handbook*, 32. Nevertheless, the "Jesuit" variant of the baroque style of architecture is often easily recognizable, not least by its "IHS" symbol.

[48] Sarreal, *The Guaraní*, 75.

[49] Ibid., 89.

[50] Ibid., 7.

Christianity. This was carried out in the native language, which was one of the factors that attracted the Indians: most entered the reductions willingly, and by the end of the Jesuit period some 85 percent of the Guaraní lived in these Jesuit-run settlements. In 1743 the policy of the Spanish government changed, and instruction was to be in Castilian. This proved to be impossible to implement as Guaraní had become something of a lingua franca, but in 1760 Charles III reiterated the demand that they learn Spanish "in order to improve administration and the well-being of the natural ones [i.e., the Indians] and so they can understand their superiors, love the conquering nation, rid themselves of idolatry, and become civilised."[51]

The biggest threat to the future of the reductions—before, that is, Charles III ordered in February 1767 the expulsion of the Jesuits from all Spanish dominions—came from the Treaty of Madrid, signed by Ferdinand VI of Spain and John V of Portugal on January 13, 1750.[52] The purpose of this treaty was to establish a firm border between Spanish and Portuguese possessions in South America. Spain ceded quite a lot of territory to Portugal, including land on which there were seven reductions. The Jesuits tried to oppose the terms of the treaty, not just because of the loss of the reductions and also a very considerable economic loss, but because conditions for the Guaraní under Portuguese rule would be far worse than those negotiated by the Jesuits with the Spanish authorities. To try to bring the Jesuits into line the general despatched Lope Luis Altamirano, whose approach is described by the usually mild-mannered William Bangert as "abrasive."[53] He was detested and distrusted by the Guaraní, especially after he ordered the Jesuits to leave the seven reductions transferred to Portuguese control, and most of them, in accordance with their vow of obedience, did so. The superior of the mission sent out scouts to see if other locations could be found, but without success. In 1754 Spanish troops were sent to move the Guaraní, but they failed. There were skirmishes over the next two years, the Guaraní War or the War of the Seven Reductions, but in February 1756 the Guaraní army was decisively defeated after their leader had been killed in an ambush.

[51] Quoted by Ganson, *The Guaraní*, 81.

[52] It is the aftermath of this treaty that is the theme of *The Mission*, mentioned above.

[53] Bangert, *A History of the Society of Jesus*, 353.

The war, in which no Jesuits were directly involved—though they had over many years trained the Guaraní militia—brought to an end the Society's "experiment" in Paraguay.

The same effort to keep settlers and Indians apart in Peru and Paraguay was repeated again in Chile, which Jesuits setting off from Peru reached in February 1593. The indigenous population, the Mapuche—though the Spanish named them the Araucanians—was considerably more warlike than the Guaraní, and a major uprising in 1598 destroyed Spanish settlements. One of those to die, along with forty-eight soldiers, was the governor of the region, Martín García Oñez de Loyola, a nephew of Ignatius Loyola. The Jesuits, under the leadership of Luís de Valdivia, proposed a policy of "defensive war," a misleading name because the aim of the policy was to keep Spaniards and Mapuche apart. The colonists and their troops were restricted to certain forts and not allowed to go beyond them. The first implementation of the program, which eventually received the approval of the Spanish monarch, was simply to keep the two sides separate because the Jesuits were convinced that the hostility of the Indians arose from their mistreatment, and virtual enslavement, by the settlers. While attempting to implement the arrangement three Jesuits, one of them a novice, died at the hands of the Mapuche, who had not at first understood the policy.

Though the idea of the "defensive war" was abandoned in 1625, the Jesuits remained, and, as they had done elsewhere in South America, they established colleges and mission stations, including missions on the inhospitable islands of the Chiloé archipelago where, because the indigenous communities were so scattered, they had to become itinerants, traveling by canoe from one group to the next for that part of the year when the weather made it possible.

Colleges were, in South America, both for the sons of settler families and for those of the Indians, at least those of a higher status, as much a part of Jesuit life as they were in Europe. And the Jesuits themselves, or at least those who were so inclined, were able to engage in scientific research, in map making, in recording the flora of the New World, and even in astronomy. Though Jesuits could hardly be said to have "discovered" quinine, it was they who brought it to Europe. It was a Spanish Jesuit prelate in Rome, Cardinal de Lugo, who was among the first to be cured by it of the malaria that was rife in Rome, and he subsequently distributed the remedy to the poor of the city. It became available from the pharmacy in the Society's Roman College, the precursor of the Gregorian University.[54]

In writing about the mission of the Jesuits in the New World it is impossible to avoid the topic of slavery. The slave trade had been condemned by Pope Paul III just three years before he granted the new Society of Jesus its foundational bull; it might therefore have been expected that this would have been a sensitive issue, and indeed in 1569 Francis Borgia, as general of the Society, forbade Jesuit involvement with slavery.[55] Nonetheless, as has been seen (above, p. 104), in Brazil Antonio Vieira welcomed the arrival of slaves from Africa as an alternative to the enslavement of the Amerindians he was evangelizing.

There was some unease among Jesuits. One, who had traveled from Africa to New Granada (Colombia) on a slave ship, expressed his anger at the way the slaves were being treated—and there is little evidence that Jesuits treated their slaves much better than lay owners.[56] Antonio Sandoval enquired of the superior in Luanda whether the slaves had been properly obtained. He need have no worries on that score, he was assured; they had for the most part been legitimately acquired and once acquired there was no reason why they should not be sold on: he quoted in support of his argument the Jesuit moral theologian Tomás Sanchez.[57]

In 1627 Alonso Sandoval published in Sevilla a lengthy study of the slave trade with an appropriately lengthy title that was, in the 1647 edition, shortened to *De Instauranda Aethiopum Salute* ("On bringing about the salvation of the Ethiopians"). Sandoval had been born in Sevilla in 1576 but had been taken to Peru as a small child. After he joined the Society he was sent in 1605 to Cartagena, the main port for the arrival of slaves from Africa, and remained there for most of the time up to his death in 1652. His experience in Cartagena per-

---

[54] Miguel de Asúa, *Science in the Vanished Arcadia* (Leiden: Brill, 2014), 96. The subtitle of the book is *Knowledge of Nature in the Jesuit Missions of Paraguay and the Rio de la Plata*.

[55] When Hideyoshi questioned the Jesuits in Japan about their involvement in the slave trade, the provincial responded that the shogun was in a position to ban it. The missionaries came to the conclusion, however, that it was an obstacle to evangelization, and the trade came to an end around the beginning of the seventeenth century, and in China a couple of decade later, cf. Alden, *The Making of an Enterprise*, 509.

[56] Ibid., 518.

[57] Ibid., 510.

suaded him that the African slaves he encountered were no less intelligent, or less capable of rational thought, than non-slaves, and the fact that they were condemned to servitude (a fact which in itself he had no difficulty in accepting) was a matter of bad luck. All individuals, he believed, were born equal, but circumstances had condemned some to the status of slaves. In the spiritual realm, however, they were still equal and free to accept baptism. However, some who had been baptised on the ship bringing them to the New World had not understood what was happening because they did not understand Spanish: he considered that there had to be a particular apostolate to explain to them the faith to which they had been unwittingly committed. This was a duty on their owners who were, moreover, duty bound not to mistreat them. Manuel Méndez Alonzo argues that "no matter how limited it may seem, [Sandoval's book] was very important with the context of the expansion within America of the slave economy, for it recognised the humanity of the Africans and their equality with the Spaniards, at least within defined and partial context."[58]

Jesuits were not alone in possessing slaves: "Excepting the Franciscans, most of the other [religious orders] who served in Portugal and its empire became slaveholders, but none on a scale to match the Jesuits."[59] Though the context was very different, the same proved to be as true in North America as it was in Central and South America.

The apostolate of the Society of Jesus in North America began not in what is now the United States but in New France, now Canada. Quebec was established in 1609 and Catholics there—there were also Huguenots among the early settlers—were served at first by secular clergy who set out to convert the local native population by "a long-term plan of gentle assimilation through good-neighbourly relations."[60] Two Jesuits arrived in 1611, bringing with them a rather brisker Christianity as endorsed by the Council of Trent. This was

---

[58] Manuel Méndez Alonzo, "El derecho a la vida y la salvación en los subyugados," *Bulletin de la Sociètè d'Étude de la Philosophie Médiévale* (2020): 1–11; the citation (my translation) is on 10. See also Andrea Guerrero Mosquera, "Los jesuitas en Cartagena de Indias y la evangelización de africanos. Una aproximación," *Montalbán: Revista de Humanidades y Educación* (2018): 1:27.

[59] Alden, *The Making of an Enterprise*, 525.

[60] Dominique Deslandres, "New France," in *A Companion to Early Modern Catholic Global Missions*, ed. Ronnie Po-Chia Hsia (Leiden: Brill, 2018), 127.

itself unpopular, but, perhaps more significant, they were opposed to the Gallicanism (on Gallicanism, see below, pp. 179ff.) that was the version of Catholicism favored by not only the clergy already in New France but also the governor. Together with the hostility of the Huguenots it proved to be an impossible situation, and the two missionaries moved south to Maine, where they encountered opposition from Protestant English settlers. In 1613 their mission was destroyed, one Jesuit killed, the other taken as a prisoner to Jamestown though he was eventually released and returned to France.

A dozen years later the Jesuits returned to minister in particular to the Hurons, but again the mission was destroyed when the British captured Quebec in 1629. The colony was, however, soon afterward returned to the French, and in 1632 missionary work began again along the valley of the St. Lawrence River though they also served the colonists and opened a college in Quebec in 1635.

Their work with the indigenous population mirrored that which had seemed so successful in Spanish America. Like their confreres in the viceroyalty of Paraguay, the Jesuit missionaries in New France believed that evangelization might best be achieved if the potential converts were living in stable communities. Such communities would have the additional advantage of keeping the neophytes away from the detrimental influence of the French settlers and particularly away from readily available alcohol. These aims proved to be next to impossible to achieve. The Hurons, traditionally a seminomadic tribe, tended to abandon the settlements during the hunting season, and, moreover, they continued to be prey to alcohol. The French were also unhappy about the establishment of stable Huron communities; they relied on the indigenous population for hunting for furs, a major part of the trade in this part of North America. There was an additional benefit for France: the Jesuits who sometimes traveled with the Hurons on their treks into the interior slowly opened up more territory for French expansion.

Living embedded within a Huron village proved to be a successful means of proselytizing, but it carried considerable risks—both to the Native Americans themselves, who carried no immunity to European diseases, and to the missionaries. In 1642 Isaac Jogues, a Jesuit priest, was traveling with René Goupil, a lay missionary, and a group of Christian Hurons when they were captured by Mohawks and savagely tortured. Goupil was killed—he made his profession as a Jesuit before he died—but Jogues was eventually released and made his way back to France, his hands so badly mutilated that he had to have special permission from the pope to use them while saying Mass. Despite his sufferings he chose to return to the mission among the Hurons. In 1645 the French attempted to broker a truce between themselves and the warring tribes. When it appeared to break down the following spring Jogues offered his expertise in the languages of the indigenous tribes. He paddled to the meeting place across Lake George, the first European to see this stretch of water, but he was again captured and this time beheaded. In all, seven Jesuits lost their lives in the Canadian mission, eight if Goupil is included.

In 1659, however, the Jesuit-educated François Montmorency de Laval arrived in Quebec as vicar apostolic and not only put the administration of the Church in New France on a much more structured footing but also, to the delight of the Jesuits, banned the sale of alcohol to the native peoples and threatened excommunication to those who engaged in this trade. Not surprisingly, his actions were unpopular with the French settlers, meeting with such a degree of opposition that in 1663 he appealed for help to King Louis XV, and New France became a royal colony.[61]

The Jesuits in North America may have been remarkable for their tenacity, to the point of martyrdom, in seeking to convert the indigenous peoples, but they were also remarkable as explorers of the region, as has been remarked, opening up the territory for the would-be settlers. René Ménard, having traveled with a group of Chippewa in 1660 across Lake Superior, simply disappeared when he went in search of a band of Catholic Hurons. Jean Claude Allouez replaced him, establishing a mission near what is now Ashland in Wisconsin and traveling widely around Wisconsin and Illinois.[62] Between 1646 and 1652 Gabriel Druillettes, who had an extraordinary grasp of the local languages, went, at their request, to the Abenaki tribe on the Kennebec River in Maine, creating "what was unique among the Indians, a people entirely Catholic."[63] Traveling around Maine he encountered, and made friends with, English settlers and later went

---

[61] Robert Handy, *A History of the Church in the United States and Canada* (Oxford: Clarendon Press, 1976), 40.

[62] Ibid., 41.

[63] Bangert, *A History of the Society of Jesus*, 263.

to Boston to negotiate a commercial treaty for the Quebec government with the Massachusetts Bay Colony; a year or so later he went to New Haven for talks with the United Colonies of New England.

Druillettes served for a time as mentor to perhaps the best-known of this generation of French Jesuits, Jacques Marquette. Marquette arrived in Quebec in September 1666 and was assigned to the Trois-Rivières mission on the St. Lawrence River, with Druillettes in charge, and started to learn the local languages. In 1668 he was again with Druillettes as they founded the mission of Sault Ste. Marie, and three years later Marquette founded the Michilimackinac mission. From the tribesmen he had heard about a great river along which they traded, and he asked permission, which was granted, to explore it. At Michilimackinac he was joined by the Jesuit-educated (in a college in Quebec) Louis Jolliet, a fur trader and explorer, and they set off in May 1673 along the shore of Lake Michigan, down to what is now Green Bay, then along the Fox River to the Wisconsin River and finally to the Mississippi, which they followed as far as Louisiana. They learned that the Mississippi emptied into the Gulf of Mexico, but when they had reached the Arkansas River they turned back, fearing to enter what was Spanish-held territory. Marquette stayed at a mission station near Green Bay, but Jolliet returned to Quebec to report their discoveries. Unfortunately his canoe overturned, and though he himself survived, his diaries were lost. Marquette, however, spent the months after his return putting his diaries and maps in order, but the journey had taken its toll. Although he still found strength to establish yet another mission, his health gave way, and he died in May 1675 and was buried near the mouth of what is now the Marquette River. Jolliet, on the other hand, continued exploring and is presumed to have died in the late summer of 1700, though nothing is known of how or where, simply that in Quebec in September that year a Mass was said for the repose of his soul. Both Jolliet and Marquette are remembered in the names of geographical features and in monuments, the latter especially, with a statue of him in the US Capitol's National Statuary Hall and another in the Parliament Building in Quebec.

So much is known about these early exploits of the Jesuit missionaries because, like their confreres in Asia with their *Lettres édifiantes et curieuses*, the French missionaries in North America recounted their exploits and their explorations from 1632 to 1673 in a series of publications known, in their English translation, as *The Jesuit Relations*, so called because they were drawn from the reports, or *relations*, sent to the Jesuit superiors in France. Unfortunately publication of the *Relations* stopped in 1673 when, during the controversy over Chinese Rites, they were banned.

Chapter 5
In Search of Prester John

When Jorge Bergoglio was elected pope in March 2013 he was seventy-six years of age.[1] Despite his length of days he has managed to maintain a punishing program of overseas visits. He has twice been to Africa south of the Sahara: the first time to Kenya, Uganda, and the Central African Republic, November 25–30, 2015; the second time to Mozambique, along with Madagascar and Mauritius, September 4–10, 2019. At the time of writing, he has not yet visited the African country, apart from Ethiopia, most closely associated with the early history of the Society of Jesus—the Portuguese settlement of what is now Angola.[2]

The presence of Jesuits in Angola's capital, Luanda, has already been mentioned (cf. above, p. 129) in the unfortunate context of the slave trade. It was, however, not there but further north, in what was then the Kingdom of Kongo, that the Society first ventured into Africa. They were invited there by King Diogo I (1545–1561), arriving at the capital of Kongo, M'banza, in 1545. Diogo needed more priests for the Catholic Church already existing in his territory, hence the invitation, but it was a Church like no other the Jesuits had hitherto encountered, one that was thoroughly indigenized and governed by an African bishop in accordance with local customs, though a Portuguese-appointed bishop in São Tomé claimed to be in charge.

---

[1] He was born on December 17, 1936.

[2] The historiography of early Jesuit missions in Africa, again with the exception of Ethiopia, is sparse. In the *Cambridge Encyclopedia of the Jesuits* Angola does not, apparently, even merit an entry. The *Oxford Handbook of the Jesuits* fares rather better, as does *Companion to Early Modern Catholic Global Missions* published by Brill, but neither of these accounts is particularly extensive.

It was an uncomfortable situation for the Jesuits, but nonetheless they managed to establish a school, in accordance with the king's wishes.

But if Kongo was uncomfortable, some of its smaller satellite kingdoms proved to be even more of a problem. The king of Kakongo twice asked for Jesuit missionaries, the first time in 1605, the second time some two decades later: the fathers made some progress in converting the elites, but only modest progress outside the local nobility. Missionaries, including Jesuits, went to the Kingdom of Ndongo in 1560, where all of them were imprisoned. One of the Jesuits, Francisco de Gouveia, was kept in prison until his death in 1575, yet even from his jail he became a major figure in the kingdom, apparently much admired and consulted by the king. This harsh treatment of the missionaries brought retaliation from Portugal, whose troops invaded and gradually dominated the country, subjecting it to the Portuguese base at Luanda. If what the king of Ndongo had wanted by inviting missionaries into his territory was the greater possibility of trading with the Portuguese, he may have achieved this, but ultimately only at the cost of his independence.

The fate of Mutapa was very similar. Mutapa was a powerful kingdom, sometimes even described as an empire, on the south bank of the Zambesi River and embracing what are now the countries of Zimbabwe, Zambia, Mozambique, and South Africa, an alliance of several different tribes ruled over by the "mwene" or king. As it stretched to the east coast of Africa it was, at least on its periphery, open to the influence of the Portuguese, and in 1559 the son of the chief of Inhambane, a port town, asked for missionaries to be sent to his people. The request was sent to Goa, and the person chosen to lead the mission was the provincial of Goa himself, Gonçalo da Silveira. Silveira's arrival was met with almost immediate success. The mwene was fairly promptly converted to Catholicism and in 1561 was baptized with the name "Constantino." Some two hundred and fifty to three hundred others also became Catholics.

But only a few nights after the baptism Silveira was murdered in the hut in which he was sleeping. What happened is known in detail from an account written very shortly afterward by Silveira's translator, Antonio Caiado: the priest was held down and strangled by ribbons, and his body was very probably thrown into a lake to be eaten by crocodiles. It is usually suggested that the mwene's change of heart came about because of the influence of Muslims, often said to be Muslim traders, concerned that Silveira was the spearhead of a Portuguese takeover of the country, in other words, a spy.

A close reading of Caiado's text in the light of what is known of the customs and traditions of the people of Mutapa suggests that this account is an accurate description of what happened, though the Muslims mentioned were not themselves traders but the mwene's spiritual advisers.[3] Gai Roufe's article shows that Silveira was killed because he was taken to be a traitor, possessed by a hostile spirit, and sent by an enemy tribe. "Both in early documents and in modern scholarship the murder of Gonçalo da Silveira is regarded as a key moment in the history of the Portuguese presence in Africa and of the political and social system along the Southern bank of the Zambesi."[4] It was key because after the death of the missionary the Portuguese invaded the kingdom of Mutapa. They met stiff resistance and had to withdraw, but then came back later and stayed, incorporating its extensive territory into their overseas empire.

What is striking in the strategy of the Jesuits working in Africa south of the Sahara is that there was much less sympathy—indeed none—for the spiritual beliefs of the indigenous inhabitants than they had shown toward the Chinese and Japanese and even in the India from which Silveira had come. As one historian of the region has commented, "Given that later in the 16th century the Jesuits were famously associated with an intellectual form of accommodation in Asia, [it] is an irony to savour that in Kongo of the 1540s and 50s the Jesuits appear to be appalled critics of the local and organic forms of religious rapprochement, or that in Mutapa and Angola it was Jesuit failures to convert kings which helped provide ideological cover for Portuguese aggression."[5]

Further north on the African continent, however, the situation was very different. There had long been a story circulating in Europe of "Prester [= Presbyter] John," a priest-king who ruled over a Christian nation that was surrounded by pagans. The location of Prester John's kingdom was variously thought to be in the Middle East or possibly

[3] Gai Roufe, "The Reasons for Murder," *Cahiers d'Études Africaines* 55, no. 3 (2015): 467–87.

[4] Ibid., 482.

[5] Alan Strathern, "Catholic Missions and Local Rulers in Sub-Saharan Africa," in *A Companion to Early Modern Catholic Global Missions*, 177.

in India, but Portuguese exploration, having failed to find it in India, eventually decided on Ethiopia. While little was known of the Church in Ethiopia it was not entirely mysterious. There had long been Ethiopian monks in Jerusalem, and Pope Eugenius IV had invited the Ethiopians to attend the Council of Florence, called to bring about reunion between the Orthodox and Roman Churches, and four of the Jerusalem monks turned up in 1441. A bull of union between the Ethiopian and Roman Church, optimistically titled *Cantate Domino* (Sing to the Lord), was promulgated in February 1442, but the attempt to bring about a lasting reunion remained only on paper.

Just over a century later King Galawdewos, also known by his Latinized name of Claudius, was indeed beset, as the legend of Prester John described, not, however, by pagans but by Muslims. He turned to the king of Portugal, João III, for military assistance. João rather misunderstood the plea for help and took it to include the possibility that the Ethiopian Church was prepared, as part of the alliance, to submit to the authority of the Roman pontiff. The Portuguese monarch in turn approached the founder of the Society of Jesus, Ignatius Loyola, who in 1554 gave his permission for the episcopal ordination of three members of the Society and designated them, and twelve others, as missionaries to Ethiopia.[6]

To understand what happened, it is important to know a little of the history of Christianity in that country. Sometime around 330 a Christian, Frumentius from Tyre in Palestine, landed, apparently by chance rather than design, on the coast of Ethiopia where he and a companion were taken captive and brought to the court of the king in Axum where they became servants in the king's household. They stayed in the country even after they had been given their liberty and began to proselytize. Frumentius's companion eventually went back home, but he himself journeyed to Alexandria to ask the bishop, Athanasius, to send missionaries. Instead, Athanasius made Frumentius a bishop and sent him back. By his death, around 380, many in the country had converted to Christianity: he was known as "Abuna," Father, a title still borne by the head of the Ethiopian Church. The

---

[6] O'Malley, *The First Jesuits*, 327–28. As O'Malley points out, Ignatius was opposed to Jesuits being ordained bishops, or being given any other ecclesiastical rank beyond that of priest, but gave his permission in this instance because there was no benefit to be had by the appointments.

conversion to Christianity was continued by the "Nine Saints" who arrived from Syria in the late fifth century. The Church they helped to create—which Rome regarded as heretical because of the Ethiopian understanding of the nature of Christ—was therefore closely linked to that of the Copts in Egypt, and it was the patriarch of Alexandria, since the mid-eleventh century a resident not of Alexandria but of Cairo, who had until 1959 appointed the abuna, usually, though not always, a Copt.

The abuna was not, therefore, a patriarch himself but a bishop. When choosing his priests for Ethiopia Ignatius nominated one of them, João Nunes Barreto, to be the future patriarch of a Church reunited to Rome. The missionaries, Ignatius insisted, were to tread carefully and only very slowly to introduce any changes they believed to be necessary. The omens, however, were not good. There was already a Jesuit at the king's court, living there for a month in early 1555, and on his return to Goa he wrote a book listing all the errors he had found in the faith of the Ethiopians, hardly the approach Ignatius had been commending.

Barreto, the patriarch-in-waiting, sailed from Lisbon in March 1556 together with an ambassador from King João to King Claudius. The Portuguese viceroy in Goa, who had in the meantime received a report from the Jesuit who had been at the court of Claudius, had apparently realized that Lisbon had read the situation incorrectly, and would let neither Barreto nor the ambassador proceed any further. Instead only a small group of Jesuits together with one bishop, André de Oviedo, all of whom had set off for Goa almost two years before Barreto, were allowed to continue their journey to the court of Claudius/Galawdewos where they arrived in March 1557. They stayed there for three years discussing religion, including with the king himself, but failing to make any headway, and Oviedo decided to abandon the court and wrote a letter to the Portuguese who had settled in the country to have no further dealings with the Ethiopians. It was a tactless letter to write. Galawdewos had treated his uninvited guests courteously and engaged with them in debate, but he was himself killed in battle with the Turks who by this time were blockading Ethiopia. He was succeeded by his brother who was much more hostile to the Jesuits and to the Portuguese in general. Oviedo was imprisoned for six months, then expelled from court: he and a lay brother—all the other Jesuits had left—settled on the country's northern frontier at a place they named Fremona in honor of St. Frumentius. By this time Oviedo was nominally the patriarch, Barreto having died in 1562.

The two Jesuits stayed at Fremona, ministering to such Portuguese who remained in the country, until Oviedo himself died in 1577. Before his death he had ordained the lay brother, Francisco Lopes, a priest. Lopes himself died at Fremona in 1596, however, without a replacement, and consequently the first Jesuit mission to Ethiopia ended.[7] But that was, in a manner of speaking, accidental. Philip II of Spain—and, from 1580 with the union of the two crowns, at the same time Philip I of Portugal—was eager to keep open the Society's presence in Ethiopia and asked for more clergy to be sent: he wanted to foster relations with the king as an ally against the Turks. Two Jesuits in Goa were chosen for the mission, both from Spain, Pedro Páez and Antonio Monserrate, setting sail in February 1589. What happened subsequently is known in detail because it was reported by Páez in a series of letters written to a Jesuit friend back in Spain, Tomas Iturén. They were taken prisoner by Muslims and spent seven years in captivity, including some time as galley slaves before eventually being ransomed and returned to Goa. During their time as captives they found themselves in places rarely if ever before visited by Europeans: Páez was one of the first Europeans to mention drinking coffee. They were held for three years in relative comfort in Sana'a, where Monserrate wrote three books and revised his account of the time he had spent at the court of Akbar, while Páez studied Arabic, Persian, and Hebrew. In November 1596 they were returned to Goa.[8]

For the next few years Páez worked just south of Goa, alongside the Englishman Thomas Stephens,[9] before setting out again for

---

[7] This account, and what follows, depends heavily on Philip Caraman, *The Lost Empire* (London: Sidgwick and Jackson, 1985). The accuracy of Fr. Caraman's book has been questioned by Leonardo Cohen and Andreu Martínez d'Alòs-Moner in their article, "The Jesuit Mission in Ethiopia: An Analytical Bibliography," *Aethiopica* 9 (2006): 190–212. They describe it as "of little historiographic value" (ibid., 194); to the best of my knowledge, however, I have not used any of Caraman's claims that are open to criticism.

[8] Their (mis)adventures deserve a book of their own, but a shorten version can be read in Caraman, *The Lost Empire*, 25–39. Of the three books Monserrate wrote in Sana'a, only his account of his time at Akbar's court, strictly speaking a revision of a work he had begun in Goa before he left, has survived.

[9] Cf. above, pp. 64ff., and Caraman, *The Lost Empire*, 40.

Ethiopia in January 1601. It took him over two years to get there, but in May 1603 he made his way finally to Fremona. The Portuguese residents in the country had not been left without any religious support after the death of Lopes, and Páez found a small compound with a hut, a school, and a chapel dedicated to St. George. He now set about learning the local language, Amharic, and the hieratic language of the Ethiopia Church, Ge'ez, so it was a year before he felt himself ready to visit the royal court of the emperor, Za Dengel. Za Dengel made him welcome but announced, to Páez's consternation, that he had decided to recognize the religious supremacy of the pope and to change the holy day of the Ethiopian Church, which was much influenced by Jewish customs, from the Saturday sabbath to the Sunday. He then proceeded to write in praise of Páez to the pope and to ask for aid against the Turks, a request he repeated in a letter to the king of Spain, now Philip III.

Whether Za Dengel's conversion was motivated solely, or even mainly, by religious considerations is an open question, but whatever the case, Páez had cause to be alarmed. Ignatius had advised the first missionaries to proceed with caution and introduce changes only gradually. In his short time in Ethiopia the Jesuit missionary had already been given good reason to think that any sudden alteration in the religious customs of the country might give rise to unrest. He had read the situation correctly: the conversion of the king led to a period of civil war in the course of which he was killed in battle, as indeed three years later was his successor and the abuna Peter. From all the unrest there emerged a thirty-two-year-old, deeply religious monarch, Susenyos, who ruled from 1607 (though he was crowned in 1608) until his death in 1632. He, too, promptly declared his desire to become a Roman Catholic, though again, like his predecessor, his decision may well have been influenced by his need for military assistance, especially against the militant Galla tribesmen. Páez gave Susenyos the same advice that he had given Za Dengel, to delay his conversion, and for the same reason: the hostility this might engender in the country, a hostility fomented by Ethiopian monks in particular, though the Jesuit achieved something of a coup when, in 1612, a leading abbot converted along with a group of the nobility and courtiers.

Páez's activities were not, however, limited to religion. He organized the building of a new palace for the king, or, rather, the very first palace, for hitherto the king had been nomadic, living in different compounds dotted around the country. The palace was an unusual building for Ethiopia in that it had two stories, and it also had a flat roof to which, as extra security, only Susenyos had access. Susenyos also decided to make a permanent capital, and Páez helped him to choose the location, almost certainly Gondar. Work on a new church, paid for by the king, began at the end of 1617, with the foundation stone being laid by Susenyos himself: it was not finished until 1622 with Páez overseeing the building works. He was at the time writing his *History of Ethiopia*, a work of serious scholarship, Páez being careful wherever possible to provide sources.[10] He died at the beginning of May 1622, shortly after Susenyos had publicly announced that he was a Roman Catholic, something the Jesuit had discouraged him from doing for fear of countrywide unrest.

While Páez was in charge of the mission there had never been more than half a dozen Jesuits in Ethiopia.[11] Before he died Susenyos had asked for more to be sent to his kingdom, and the Jesuit general responded by appointing Manuel de Almeida, who set out from Goa in November 1622 with two other priests and reached the country just over twelve months later; others were sent by separate routes, dressed as Turks or Arabs, to minimize risks. They arrived safely and made their way to Fremona and were later hospitably received by Susenyos for whom they had brought imposing gifts, including an organ.

Since the death of Oviedo in 1577 there had been no bishop in the country, and certainly no patriarch. In 1621, however, Alfonso Mendes was appointed to that role, appointed not by the pope or by the Jesuit general but by King Philip IV before whom he had preached an elaborate sermon that appealed to the king. Mendes then asked for two assistant bishops, one of whom was his secretary: they were all ordained bishops in March 1623 and left for Ethiopia—though they did not arrive at Fremona for another two years. Mendes had with him one bishop—the other had died on his way to Goa—and Jerónimo Lobo, who later wrote an important account of his and Mendes's years in the country. Mendes proved to be the wrong man for the role

---

[10] It has been fairly recently (2011) published in two volumes in an English translation by the Hakluyt Society of London.

[11] Caraman, *The Lost Empire*, 121.

he had readily accepted. He had none of the flexibility of Páez and certainly none of the sympathy for the faith of the Ethiopians that had been shown by Páez. He wanted laypeople to be rebaptised and the local clergy to be reordained (though he allowed at least some of them to keep their wives), and he attempted to impose Tridentine Catholicism on a reluctant people. To overcome their reluctance, Mendes asked Susenyos to impose the faith by force, something Páez had opposed: it did not help that the campaign was overshadowed by a plague of locusts. Forced conversions led to an uprising against the king, who, despite Mendes's protests, in June 1632 decided that his subjects might choose for themselves which form of Christianity to embrace.

Susenyos died in September of that year, having written a letter proclaiming his Catholic faith and criticizing the succession of abunas who had governed the Ethiopian Orthodox Church. He was succeeded by his eldest son, Fasilides, no friend of the Jesuits or of the new version of Christianity they were propagating, and he ordered them all to return to their base at Fremona. Mendes's response was to ask for Portuguese troops. There was indeed an incursion of Portuguese soldiers on the East African coast, but they were outside Ethiopia's admittedly rather vague borders. It was, however, enough to spur the king to order all Jesuits out of the country. Mendes refused to go, and Fasilides sent soldiers to remove him by force if necessary. Instead he escaped and took refuge with the governor of one of the seaports hoping to make it a base for a Portuguese invasion. The governor was tempted to rebel against Fasilides but was offered a free pardon if he handed Mendes over. Instead he passed him on to the Turkish governor of the port at Suakin, from which they—Mendes was accompanied by nine priests—were ransomed and returned to India. The would-be patriarch died in Goa in 1656. The assistant bishop who had traveled with him to Ethiopia in 1625 had, together with seven other Jesuits, ignored Fasilides's order to leave the country. He and five priests were hanged in 1640, the other two priests already having been killed. The Jesuit mission to Ethiopia was at an end.[12]

---

[12] Ibid., 155–56. In Caraman's judgment, the achievements of Páez were "thrown away by the blundering arrogance of Mendes" (156).

It must have been particularly galling for Mendes to hear, from his imprisonment in Suakin, of the arrival through that port of a new abuna coming from Cairo. The Society had made some tentative approaches to the Copts of Egypt, beginning in 1561 when Cristófero Rodrígues was sent from Rome to Alexandria, accompanied by a lay brother, by a Coptic deacon who had been living in Rome for some years, and by Giovani Battista Eliano, a Jesuit priest and a convert from Judaism who knew some Arabic. The small party arrived at Alexandria in November and were welcomed by the Patriarch Gabriel VII who at first seemed not unwilling to accept papal authority, though he refused to commit this to writing. They then traveled with the patriarch to St. Anthony's Monastery where discussions took place on the theological differences between the Churches of Alexandria and of Rome, discussions made more problematic for the Jesuits because of their lack of a translator, Eliano finding it difficult to deal with the intricacies of the debates and the Coptic texts. After nineteen days they decided to return to Cairo, and Rodrígues, who was a theologian by training, as one historian has put it, "acquired an irreversible detestation of the Copts."[13] They set sail for Rome toward the end of November.

There was a particular problem for Eliano. As a convert from Judaism he risked death by breaching the Ottoman law against changing one's religion, and as far as possible he had to remain in hiding. Nonetheless, toward the end of the Jesuits' stay he was recognized and arrested but managed to leave on the ship for Rome. Not wholly deterred, however, in 1582 Eliano made a second visit to Egypt to meet the new patriarch, John XIV. He was once again received in a friendly fashion by the patriarch. He was much more conciliatory than Rodrígues had been, and managed to persuade John to write a letter to the pope, but it was no more than a restatement of the Coptic Church's theological position on the nature of Christ, one completely at odds with that of the Church of Rome.

In the end no more was achieved in Eliano's second visit than had been in the one from 1561 to 1562, and it was not until 1697 that the

---

[13] Alastair Hamilton, *The Copts and the West* (Oxford: Oxford University Press, 2006). Modern Jesuit texts seem remarkably reticent about Egypt: neither "Egypt" nor "Copt," for instance, are to be found in Bangert's standard history.

Society established a residence in Cairo. The purpose of this new venture was not to convert, or even dialogue with, the Copts but to serve as a base for a renewed foray into Ethiopia. The first Jesuit who made the journey died in 1698 outside Gondar. A second mission in 1700 managed to make it as far as Gondar, but they were promptly expelled. Guillaume Dubernat arrived in Cairo in 1702 at the age of twenty-five. He too intended to continue on to Ethiopia, but in 1704 his expedition to do so collapsed, and instead he decided to dedicate his apostolate to the Egyptian Copts. It was, however, a carefully nuanced apostolate. He was conscious of the difficulties of making converts, not least the Turkish prohibition against changing religion. There were also problems of theological terminology, made more complicated by the lack of education of the clergy in whose bailiwick, as in Europe, the study of religion fell.[14]

Only a couple of years after he had arrived in Cairo Dubernat wrote to Rome complaining of the attitude of the Franciscans who were critical of the Jesuits' conciliatory approach to the Coptic Church,[15] of which one remarkable example was that of Claude Sicard. He arrived in Cairo in 1707 and became superior of the Jesuit residence five years later. Before being sent to Egypt he had worked in Aleppo in Syria where he had acquired working knowledge of Arabic. He traveled widely in the country, producing the first map of Egypt and visiting Coptic monasteries but also the forgotten monuments, including Luxor and the Valley of the Kings. These he carefully recorded, sending the details back to France for the attention of his patron (at least in this regard), the dauphin, and for publication. He lived like a Copt, feasting and fasting as they did, and by 1718 he had made enough converts to create the first Catholic Coptic Church in the services of which, during the administration of the sacraments, he made no distinction between Catholic and Orthodox. He died in 1726, ministering to plague victims in Cairo. He was only forty-nine years of age.[16]

[14] There was a better educated laity, but, Dubernat noted, they had little interest in religion. Cf. Hamilton, *The Copts and the West*, 161.

[15] Ibid., 91.

[16] Sicard has an entry in Worcester's *Cambridge Companion to the Jesuits*, while Dubernat, whom Hamilton regards as the more important, does not.

It has just been mentioned that Claude Sicard had traveled to Cairo from Aleppo in Syria, both, in the course of the sixteenth century, had come to be within the Ottoman Empire. But in both cases the Jesuit mission had not been, at least in the first instance, to Muslims but to Christians, to Copts, as has just been seen, and in the case of Syria, to Maronites. In 1578 the Maronite patriarch, residing in what is now Lebanon, had made contact with the pope to reaffirm his Church's unity with the Church of Rome. Eliano and Giovanni Bruno went to Syria to study the beliefs and rituals of the Maronite Church, then returned two years later to take part in a synod, held in August at the monastery of Quannobin, where they presented the Tridentine faith—and a pallium for the patriarch. After the synod Bruno and Eliano traveled to Damascus and Jerusalem before returning to Rome. Elated by the success of the mission, Gregory XIII established a Maronite College in Rome, of which Bruno became the rector in 1590.

Ignatius himself had, of course, visited Jerusalem and, until dissuaded by the Franciscan Guardian of the Holy Places, had wished to stay there to convert Muslims (cf. above, pp. 13ff.; of his encounter with a Muslim, see p. 10). His followers were rather more circumspect.[17] Antonio Possevino (see above, pp. 58ff.), though he had originally attacked Islam, later pointed out shared beliefs, insisted on the importance of learning Arabic, and praised Arab thinkers. He was convinced that Muslim converts would be attracted not so much by the Christian faith itself as by the example of Christian society—so those Jesuits working among Muslims had to be unimpeachable role models.[18] Muslim respect for the Virgin Mary was an obvious starting point for building bridges between the two faiths.

The Ottoman advance into central Europe, reaching its apogee with the siege of Vienna in 1529 (a battle to be repeated again in 1683), was seen as an existential threat to Christendom, and in October 1571

---

[17] Ignatius had been happy to admit convert Jews and Muslims into the Society. Some members in the sixteenth century opposed this policy, and entry into the novitiate was banned at the fifth general congregation (November 1593 to January 1594) to all who had Jewish or Muslim ancestry. Though the absolute prohibition was modified a decade later, it remained substantially in force until 1946. Dispensations from the provision were, however, fairly readily granted.

[18] Emanuele Colombo, "Jesuits and Islam in Early Modern Europe," in *The Oxford Handbook of the Jesuits*, ed. Ines G. Županov (Oxford: Oxford University Press, 2019), 351.

there were Jesuits serving as chaplains on the galleys of the Holy League, which defeated the Ottoman armada at Lepanto. Despite this apparently militant stance, "Jesuits made attempts to build bridges, trying to understand what was acceptable in Muslim culture and accommodating their approach accordingly."[19] Up to a point. Antonio Monserrato gave a somewhat sour account of life at the Islamic Mughal court, a jaundiced view that may well have been colored by the fact that he was writing it while being held prisoner in Sana'a (see above, p. 134).[20] It was a Jesuit, Ignazio Lomellini (1564–1644), who published in 1622 the first Latin translation of the Qur'an. Jesuit controversialists drew attention to the contradictions to be found in that Islamic sacred text and criticized Muslim practices of polygamy and divorce and their unwillingness, so the Jesuits claimed, to engage in debate about the Qur'an and Islamic law. Especially problematic for them was the belief that Muslims were "living according to a sort of fatalism that devalued human liberty."[21]

On the whole, however, Jesuit studies of Islam, such as *Confutatio alcorani* (1610) by István Szántó of the Austrian province or *Manuductio ad conversionem Mahumetanorum* (1687) by the controversial thirteenth general of the Society, Tirso González (1624–1705; see below, pp. 194ff.), while pointing out what were, from a Christian point of view, theological errors, were not unsympathetic to Islam. González had spent many years in Spain preaching to domestic or galley slaves or other Muslims in an attempt to convert them, and his book became something of a guide to Jesuits working as missionaries. Someone who also worked among galley slaves, in his case in Genoa and Naples, was Baldassare Loyola (1631–1667). He deserves a mention because he had been born in Fez, Morocco, as Mohammed Attazi and had become a Catholic and then a Jesuit after spending some time in Malta: he died in Madrid while on his way to the Mughal court.[22]

---

[19] Ibid., 358.

[20] Daniel Madigan, "Global Visions in Contestation," in *The Jesuits and Globalization*, ed. Thomas Bouchoff and José Casanovas (Washington, DC: Georgetown University Press, 2016), 72.

[21] Colombo, "Jesuits and Islam," 355.

[22] Emanuele Colombo, "A Muslim Turned Jesuit: Baldassarre Loyola Mandes (1631–1667)," *The Journal of Early Modern History* 17 (2013): 479–504, and also Emanuele Colombo, "Conversioni Religiose in Calderón de la Barca: El Gran Príncipe de Fez (1669)," *Drammaturgia* 16 (2019): 49–79.

Conversions were, however, rare: for the most part, missionary activity was devoted to winning back Christian converts to Islam; converting from Islam to Christianity in a Muslim country could be a life-threatening decision both for the reborn Christian and for the missionary.

That is, of course, if Jesuit evangelism was taking place within Muslim—Ottoman—territory among Christians such as Maronites or Copts. In one instance, however, it was undertaken with a Roman Catholic context, Poland, to which in 1564 they were invited by Cardinal Stanislaw Hosius. Antonio Possevino had served as a papal emissary to attempt a reconciliation between Grand Prince Ivan of Moscow and Stephen Bathory, from 1575 the king of Poland—though the ultimate aim was the reunion of the Russian Church with that of Rome. Possevino managed to arrange a truce, but his religious quest remained unfulfilled. Jesuit interest in Poland had been sparked by a visit there by the Nijmegen-born[23] Peter Canisius (1521–1597). Canisius is rather better known for his work in countering the spread of Protestantism in what is now Germany than in Poland, but he was instrumental in establishing the Society in Poland first under the active patronage of the very religious Stephen Bathory and then from 1587 that of the equally devout King Sigismund. Sigismund appointed, in 1588, as his court preacher Piotr Skarga, a post he held for over two decades. Skarga had enjoyed a distinguished career in Poland but spent 1569 to 1571 in Rome, where he joined the Society of Jesus, serving first in the Jesuit academy in Vilnius, Lithuania, then part of the Polish-Lithuanian Commonwealth, before moving to Krakow. His sermons and his lives of the saints were both widely read, and he became something of a legendary figure[24] despite being criticized in his lifetime for the close association of Church and State advocated in his writings. "The Jesuits contributed to the construction of a theological justification for the concept of the state and its structure held by the majority of the *szlachta* (Polish gentry)."[25]

---

[23] Was then part of what was then the Austrian, or Habsburg, Netherlands. He was canonized in 1925.

[24] He is a main character in *Jeremiah*, one of the plays written by Karol Wojtyła, Pope John Paul II.

[25] Stanisław Obirek, "Jesuits in Poland and Eastern Europe," in Worcester, *The Cambridge Companion to the Jesuits*, 145.

Among Skarga's writings was *The Unity of the Church of God*, published in 1577. As has just been seen, Possevino had failed in his efforts to reunite the Russian Orthodox Church—the patriarchate of Moscow was only established in 1589—with Rome. Skarga was one of the theologians pressing for a reunion with Rome of the Orthodox[26] Christians in, mainly, what is now Ukraine. This was eventually achieved at the Union Brest—hence the churches in this union came to be called "Uniate"—in a ceremony December 1595 at which Skarga and other Jesuits were present. Not all those who signed up to the Union remained within it, with the result that there is a Ukrainian and a Catholic Orthodox Church, with very similar liturgies. Jesuits opened colleges in Poland, Ukraine, and Russia. Paul Shore comments that Orthodox scholars often attended Jesuit educational institutions, some even going to Rome, and some converted to Catholicism, though they tended to revert to Orthodoxy once they were back in Ukraine. They had, however, in the meantime acquired something of the Western theological tradition.[27]

A similar policy to that pursued in Ukraine was followed further east. In Bohemia, now part of the Czech Republic, an important college was opened at Olomouc in 1573, and there was a considerable Jesuit presence in Prague. There were Jesuits in Hungary from 1553 and in Romania from shortly afterward. The first Jesuits in Romania were Hungarians, a fact that did not endear them to the locals; later, their perceived association with the Habsburgs also made them unpopular across Slavic lands. Their apostolate was seen as being to some degree tied to the ambitions of Austria in these territories. When Austria was not the dominant political presence in Eastern Europe, then it was the Ottomans, for the priests of the Society an even more complicated environment in which to work. To add to the complications, much of the region was Orthodox rather than Catholic, though the Republic of Dubrovnik, independent though strictly speaking under the overlordship of Serbia and hence the Ottomans, was firmly Roman Catholic: a Jesuit school was founded there in 1634. A schoolboy there was one of the most famous of Jesuit scientists, famous

---

[26] The term "Orthodox" was a problematic one for the Society's members, for it could also mean fidelity to Rome. Cf. Paul Shore, "Jesuits in the Orthodox World," in Županov, *The Oxford Handbook*, 315.

[27] Ibid., 320.

enough to be made a Fellow of London's Royal Society, Roger Boscovich (1711–1787),[28] who was, unlike many of his brethren, sympathetic to the Orthodox Church.

The Orthodox Church, or Churches, had in theory been reconciled to Rome at the Council of Florence (1438–1445)[29] by the decree *Laetentur Caeli* ("Let the heavens rejoice"), which was signed on July 6, 1439. The Byzantine emperor, John VIII Palaiologus, was hoping that reunion with Rome would bring him allies from western Europe against the Turks who were threatening Constantinople, but this did not happen. Nor indeed did the act of reunion, which was promptly repudiated by the majority of the monks and laity of the Eastern Churches and remained a dead letter. The decree did, however, provide a basis for Jesuits working in Orthodox areas, and they had some success in reconciling a number of Armenians to Rome, creating a small Armenian Catholic Church that still survives.

The center of Orthodoxy was, of course, the ancient Byzantine capital of Constantinople, now Istanbul. French Jesuits went there to establish a residence in 1583, but all died of plague. It was not easy to survive in the Ottoman city, but a group returned early in the seventeenth century to minister to the Venetian community: they were, however, expelled in 1628, being acceptable neither to the Orthodox nor to the Muslims. Ignatius himself had considered opening a college in Cyprus as a seminary for Ethiopians,[30] and colleges were begun on other Greek islands, as well as a college for Greeks in Rome.

There were, of course, small Christian communities scattered in what was predominantly Muslim territory. At the request of Pope Urban VIII Jesuits were sent to Aleppo. They were promptly expelled but then traveled to Constantinople to seek the permission of the sultan and the backing of the French consul, both of which they received. They returned to Aleppo where they settled with the aid of the Greek Catholic bishop, established a school, and ministered to several varieties of Christians, including Armenians and Maronites, from the cha-

[28] On Boscovich, see Lancelot Law Whyte, ed., *Roger Joseph Boscovich* (London: George Allen and Unwin, 1961). Dubrovnik was then known as Ragusa, and the college was known as the Ragusinum.

[29] Strictly speaking a continuation of the Council of Basel, it had opened in Ferrara but moved to Florence when Ferrara was hit by the plague, hence is sometimes known as Ferrara-Florence.

[30] Shore, "Jesuits in the Orthodox World," 321.

pel of the French consulate. From there members of the Society went to Damascus and to Palestine and even to Persia where they were close to the shah. As so often, this association with the ruling house proved a dangerous tactic, and when Nadir Shah was assassinated in 1747, the Jesuits had to leave the country, the victims, however, not of the hostility of Muslims but of Armenian Christians.[31]

---

[31] John Donohue, "Middle East" in Worcester, *The Cambridge Companion to the Jesuits*, 520–21.

Chapter 6
Schoolmasters and Politicians

As has been seen, where there were Jesuit missions, there followed, and usually sooner rather than later, Jesuit colleges. It has been remarked earlier (pp. 57ff.) that "mission," though an ambiguous term, was to be found in the Constitutions of the Society of Jesus as drafted by St. Ignatius. A similar ambiguity is also true of colleges. The very first Jesuits were all graduates of the University of Paris, and so it was natural that some should be immediately put to work lecturing in theology. The Formula of the Institute had indeed envisaged colleges run by the Society, but these were not to be teaching institutions as such, despite the fact that a papal bull of 1547 gave them permission to teach anywhere—an exceptional privilege—and to teach anything. They were more like residences than colleges in the modern sense of the word, establishments where student Jesuits (scholastics) could live while attending classes at nearby universities. The earliest scholastics were sent to a college attached to the University of Paris, but in 1542 the outbreak of war between France and the Holy Roman Empire meant that subjects of the empire had to leave Paris. They went instead to Louvain.

By 1544 there were seven of these "colleges," at the universities of Paris, Louvain, Cologne, Padua, Alcalá, Valencia in Spain, and Coimbra in Portugal. Unlike other houses of the Society, the colleges were to be endowed: Ignatius did not want the students to be so concerned with raising money to pay for their board and lodging and their tuition that they could not simply concentrate on their studies. There was some teaching, above all, in a large college of St. Paul in Goa (see above, p. 62), but at the start that was the exception. The catalyst for a major change of direction was Francisco de Borja, the duke of Gandía. After founding a college attached to the

147

University of Valencia, he decided he should have one in Gandía itself, despite the fact that Gandía did not have a university. In his newly founded Jesuit college, Jesuit scholastics were students while Jesuit professors did the teaching. The difference was that it was not only Jesuits who attended the classes; laymen did so as well. This model of Jesuit students studying alongside young laymen inspired the viceroy of Sicily to petition for a similar institution in Messina, to be funded by the authorities of the city, which would provide the Jesuits sent there with food and lodging. This was a major departure, for though scholastics would study—and other Jesuits would teach—at Messina, its primary purpose was to serve the young men of the city who could study there every discipline up to what we would now call tertiary level, everything, that is, except law and medicine. Other colleges swiftly followed along the same lines. In February 1551 the Roman College, renamed the Gregorian University in 1584 after its patron Pope Gregory XIII, started taking students. "Over its door hung the inscription 'School of Grammar, Humanities, and Christian Doctrine, Free.'"[1]

No doubt that final word "free" contributed to the success of the Jesuit schools and their rapid, perhaps over-rapid, expansion. As Paul Grendler puts it, "When Ignatius died on July 20, 1556, his educational legacies to the Society were forty-six schools and a desperate teacher shortage."[2] Nonetheless the network continued to expand so that by the suppression of the Society in 1773 there were some eight hundred of them: seven hundred in Europe, and the remainder scattered around the world. The teacher shortage was to some extent solved by Laínez when in August 1560 he ordered that all Jesuits, or, more correctly, all those preparing for ordination, should spend some time in the classroom, even though, according to John O'Malley, some left the Society because of the pressure of teaching,[3] and others may not have been particularly competent. As Fulvio Carduto commented, writing

---

[1] This account has been lightly adapted from Michael J. Walsh, *Heythrop College, 1614–2014: A Commemorative History* (Heythrop College, University of London, 2014). The section was, however, very dependent on O'Malley, *The First Jesuits*; the quotation is on p. 205 of that excellent book, but see also, and especially, pp. 32 and 200–205. For Rome's Gregorian University, see Philip Caraman, *The University of the Nations* (New York: Paulist Press, 1981).

[2] Paul Grendler, "The Culture of the Jesuit Teacher, 1548–1773," *Journal of Jesuit Studies* 3 (2016): 19.

[3] O'Malley, *The First Jesuits*, 228.

sometime between 1584 and 1590, "We seem to be tricking people with promises to give the young a good education in letters then failing to fulfil the obligation when we assign teachers who are inadequate and inept," a criticism that was, apparently, not uncommon.[4]

The ruling that every Jesuit should teach survives to this day, as the life of Pope Francis can testify.[5] Some would then, as today, spend the rest of their lives in the classroom, in either schools or universities, though most would move on to other things. The schools were not, however, in remote locations but generally in the middle of towns, with a Jesuit church attached, so that the pastoral activity of the clergy was not limited to teaching but could include peaching, hearing confessions, instructing children—and adults—in the catechism, and even, perhaps, engaging in controversy with non-Catholic pastors in the locality. So no Jesuit was completely tied to the classroom, which may account for the lack of opposition to Laínez's decree, a remarkable consensus about the importance of colleges, a consensus that, as Grendler points out, could not be taken for granted.[6]

There were, however, important downsides to the establishment of schools. Ignatius had envisaged his followers as itinerant preachers. Some continued in the mold, but schools tied many Jesuits down to a particular place. Even more problematic was finance. The Society of Jesus was, according to its Constitution, a mendicant religious order, one that relied on alms in order to survive. With the creation of colleges, this could no longer be the case: the schools might be free to attend, but the schoolmasters still needed to eat and somewhere to live, and the college buildings had to be erected and maintained. Colleges, therefore, could not be opened unless there was an appropriate endowment, whether from the municipality, as in the case of Messina, or by some wealthy patron, as in the case of the English

[4] Cristiano Casalini and Claude Pavur, eds., *Jesuit Pedagogy, 1540–1616: A Reader* (Boston: Boston College, Institute of Jesuit Sources, 2016), 218. *Plus ça change*: the present author has heard a Jesuit remark, "No, I don't know any Greek. I haven't even taught it."

[5] Pope Francis, as Fr. Jorge Bergoglio, SJ, proved to be a particularly successful schoolmaster, a fact his biographers regularly attest; see, for example, Jimmy Burns, *Francis, Pope of Good Promise* (London: Constable, 2015), 122–24.

[6] Grendler, "The Culture of the Jesuit Teacher," 22: "Anyone who has read the documents knows that the sixteenth-century Jesuits were not docile, cadaver-like supinely obedient. . . . There were controversies which elicited full discussions and some open rebellions."

Jesuit college at Liège, which in 1627 was handsomely endowed by the Archduke Maximilian I of Bavaria and his wife Elizabeth of Lorraine—so generously indeed that the Jesuit general told the rector of the college to keep the amount secret. It must have helped that the archduke's brother, Ferdinand, was the prince bishop of Liège (and archbishop elector of Cologne) when the Jesuits purchased the property and that he was still there when they moved in, some years later: the two brothers had both been educated by the Society.[7] The problem with this manner of finance by municipality or by individual donor was its reliability. Colleges needed to be stable institutions, and too often they were not. Several simply had to close because of a shortage of funds.

The colleges being free of charge attracted not only the sons of the rich but also those further down the scale of wealth, so there was a degree of mixing of social classes that seems very progressive. But as John O'Malley has observed, the Society was socially conservative,[8] with no desire to overturn the social order, and in any case Jesuits depended on the wealthy for the endowments of their colleges. In return, the wealthy were well served by the education their sons received. As Jaska Kainulainen remarks, "By offering students instruction in the *studia humanitatis*, a daily mass and frequent confession and Communion, the Jesuit ministry of secondary education aimed to produce Christian citizens capable of administering civic affairs for the greater glory of God,"[9] which is exactly what urban elites required for their sons. They were prepared, especially perhaps through the study of rhetoric, to take their places in the administration of the municipality or, for that matter, in the Church in order to serve the common good. The text most frequently turned to in the classroom, John O'Malley has pointed out, was Cicero's *De Officiis*, which he translates as "On Public Responsibility."[10]

---

[7] See Walsh, *Heythrop College*, 13–14. The college in Liège was originally only for the education of Jesuits, but it gradually opened its doors to others.

[8] O'Malley, *The First Jesuits*, 205.

[9] Jaska Kainulainen, "Virtue and Civic Values in Early Modern Jesuit Education," *Journal of Jesuit Studies* 5 (2018): 531.

[10] In his introduction to *The Jesuits II: Cultures, Sciences and the Arts, 1540–1773*, ed. John W. O'Malley, Gauvin Alexander Bailey, Steven J. Harris, and T. Frank Kennedy (Toronto: University of Toronto Press, 2006), xxxii.

When writing of the Jesuit system of education—and, as will be seen, there was a system—historians generally discount the creation of the college in Gandía, while the college at Messina, on the other hand, inspired by what had occurred in Gandía, holds a particularly important place. *De ratione studiorum Messanae*, or "On the system of study at Messina," a program for study in each of the different year groups, was perhaps produced as an example of best practice to be shared among the growing network of Jesuit educational institutions. But this was a program based on a single institution and the work of a small group of educators. What was needed, it was decided, was a plan of study for Jesuit schools that took into account diverse experiences in various localities. Committees were set up and drafts made, one of which was issued in 1586 and another in 1591, before the definitive version of what is known as the *Ratio atque Institutio Studiorum Societatis Iesu* or, more simply, the *Ratio Studiorum* was issued by General Claudio Acquaviva in 1599, though it had been printed in Naples a year earlier. After a letter from Acquaviva, it begins with "Rules for the Provincial," the first of which reads:

> Since one of the leading ministries of our Society is teaching our neighbour all the disciplines in keeping with our Institute in such a way that they are thereby aroused to a knowledge and love of our Maker and Redeemer, the provincial should consider himself obliged to do his utmost to ensure that our diverse and complex educational labour meets with the abundant results that the grace of our calling demands of us.[11]

So rapidly did the Jesuit network of schools expand that it is easy to forget that education, other than teaching the catechism to the poor, had not been part of the Society's original agenda.

The curriculum at Messina for the year 1550 was described by Hannibal du Coudret (1525–1599). His account makes instructive reading.[12] As Kainulainen remarks, the Christian writers whose works were to be studied were of doubtful orthodoxy: Erasmus, for example, about whom Ignatius himself was wary though not entirely

---

[11] In the translation of Claude Pavur, *The Ratio Studiorum* (St. Louis: The Institute of Jesuit Sources, 2005), 7.

[12] See Kainulainen, "Virtue and Civic Values," 541–43.

condemnatory, was placed on the Roman Index of Prohibited Books published in 1559. The majority of texts were those of pagan authors, with Cicero at the forefront. "I do not hold that profit will be derived only from Cicero's volumes," wrote the English Jesuit martyr, Edmund Campion, "but I believe that in reading other authors one should be a critic, in reading Cicero a disciple."[13] The *Ratio* itself had many more references to Christian authors but, unlike that of Messina, it covered the study of not just grammar and rhetoric but also philosophy, Aristotle being the favored author, and theology, where Thomas Aquinas was to be the major text—as insisted on by Ignatius in the Constitutions. It was, however, possible to deviate from Aristotle with good cause, especially if his teaching seemed to contradict the faith. The rules governing Aquinas were less generous, but even in this case some distancing was permissible, provided, it seems, that Jesuit theologians did not strike out on their own just to be different. In the end it was the interpretation of Aquinas to be found in Francisco Suarez that tended to become the norm in the Society, at least until the revival of Thomism toward the end of the nineteenth century (see below, pp. 250ff.).

Compared with a modern school curriculum, there are some very obvious lacunae. Although there was great emphasis on knowledge of Latin and Greek, there was no teaching of "modern languages." But at the time all serious scholarly, and much formal civil, discourse took place in Latin, and in that Jesuits would have been proficient— and as the story of missionary journeys testifies, members of the Society proved remarkably adept at learning the languages of, say, China or India. But also missing from the *Ratio* was any science as it is now understood, apart, that is, from mathematics. That mathematics was included can be attributed to the influence of the German Jesuit Christopher Clavius (1538–1612). Clavius, who has a crater on the moon named after him and was one of those advising on the preparation of the Gregorian calendar, managed to establish within the Roman College an institute of higher mathematics, to which each province was expected to send one young Jesuit. For him, however, and generally at the time, mathematics was a generous term, embracing sundials and even astrology, as well as calendars, astrolabes, and,

---

[13] Quoted in R. A. Maryks, *Saint Cicero and the Jesuits* (Farnham: Ashgate, 2008), 90.

of course, astronomy: Matteo Ricci was one of those who had attended Clavius's classes in the Roman College and translated into Chinese two of his books, one on Euclid's *Elements* and the other on geometry, texts that were widely used in schools, and not just Jesuit ones, throughout Europe.

In 1587 Clavius, as the foremost mathematician of his day, was visited in Rome by a twenty-three-year-old budding mathematician, an unemployed Galileo, and the two remained in contact: two years later, on the recommendation of the Jesuit, Galileo was appointed professor of mathematics at the University of Pisa, though he moved in 1589 to a much more lucrative post at the University of Padua. The "Galileo Affair" is an acknowledged watershed both in the development of science and in the often fraught relationship between science and religion, and it is something in which Jesuits found themselves entangled.[14]

Galileo, in his astronomical observations, had been persuaded of the truth of the theory of Nicolaus Copernicus that the sun, rather than the earth, was the center of the planetary system. Using a telescope, which he falsely claimed to have invented, though he certainly developed it, he discovered the moons of Jupiter, which he called the Medicean Stars, after his patron the Medici family of Florence. These, he believed, confirmed the heliocentric system advanced by Copernicus. He published an account of his discoveries in a small book, scarcely more than a pamphlet, titled *Siderius Nuncius* or "Starry Messenger," which appeared in 1610. Clavius wrote to congratulate him, saying that the astronomers at the Roman College tended to agree with him. This endorsement encouraged Galileo to return to Rome in 1611, where he again met Clavius and was enthusiastically welcomed by the students of the Roman College.

Clavius's support was not surprising. He had observed, and had written about, the fact that the movement of the planets could not be explained, as Aristotle had claimed, by one simple circular motion around the earth. He had put forward an alternative version in his

---

[14] That the Galileo affair became such a *cause célèbre* was due in part to the fate of the records taken from the Vatican archives on the orders of Napoleon and transferred to Paris, where they vanished—though they were eventually recovered, in Vienna, three decades later. See Owen Chadwick, *Catholicism and History* (Cambridge: Cambridge University Press, 1978), 14–45.

Commentarius in sphaerem Ioannis de Sacro Bosco suggesting there was not one spherical motion in the observable universe but several, and not all of them were spherical, in a clear departure from the Aristotelian cosmology.[15] This was problematic: the Constitutions of the Society laid down that Aristotle had to be followed, and the Greek philosopher also has pride of place in the *Ratio*. But there was an even greater problem: the heliocentric theory appeared to contradict the Bible, and in Counter-Reformation Rome, questioning a traditional interpretation of Scripture was a dangerous game. Perhaps conscious that his scientific colleagues at the Roman College had endorsed the *Siderius Nuncius*, in 1611 the theologian Cardinal Robert Bellarmine (1542–1621), who was for a period rector of the Roman College, asked their opinion, which was favorable—indeed that year the Roman College bestowed on Galileo what has been described as "an honorary doctorate."[16]

Unfortunately, the Roman Inquisition did not share this view. The heliocentric theory of the heavens appeared to be explicitly contradicted by Scripture, in particular, in the book of Joshua when Joshua commands the sun to stay still over Gibeon and, according to the Bible, it delayed its setting for a whole day (Josh 10:12-14). Bellarmine, who was a member of the tribunal of the Inquisition, was required by Pope Paul V to warn Galileo not to hold or to teach the Copernican system, which the cardinal did on February 26, 1616, and just over a week later, on March 5, the Congregation of the Index, on which Bellarmine also sat, banned Nicolaus Copernicus's magnum opus, *De revolutionibus orbium coelestium* ("On the Revolution of the Heavenly Spheres"), the source for Galileo's theories.[17] He was, of course, well aware of the problem posed by Scripture, and in 1615 he had written his *Letter to the Grand Duchess Christina of Tuscany*, in which he explained his understanding of the relationship of Scripture to science, an explanation remarkably in keeping with modern biblical exegesis.

---

[15] Very little is known about Ioannis de Sacro Bosco. He is presumed to have been a monk, and was quite likely born in England or possibly Ireland. His *Tractatus de Sphaera* ("On the Sphere of the World") appeared c. 1230.

[16] William R. Shea and Mariano Artigas, *Galileo in Rome* (Oxford: Oxford University Press, 2003), 43.

[17] Copernicus (1473–1543) was a priest and a member of the chapter, i.e., a canon, of the cathedral of Warmia in what is now Poland. He seems to have anticipated that his theories would give rise to controversy and was hesitant to publish his book, which appeared only just before his death.

Meanwhile relations with the Jesuits had soured, and not because he had been admonished by a Jesuit cardinal. Claudio Acquaviva, the superior general, set up a board of censors or revisors in Rome and in every province of the Society to ensure that a common doctrine was taught. "It does not seem to be either proper or useful for the books of our members to contain the ideas of Galileo," wrote one of the revisors in February 1615, "especially when they are contrary to Aristotle."[18] In 1612 Christoph Scheiner at the Roman College published a series of letters on sunspots, which he believed to have been caused by moons crossing the face of the sun. Galileo disputed this— quite rightly, as Scheiner eventually acknowledged—but in doing so claimed it was he, not the Jesuit, who had first discovered them. More crucially, however, was the intervention of Orazio Grassi, also at the Roman College, who observed the passage of comets and proposed an explanation that undermined the heliocentric theory promoted by Galileo. A pamphlet war broke out, in which Galileo easily proved himself the better polemicist, and when in 1633 the astronomer was at last formally tried and condemned to house arrest by the Inquisition, he blamed, quite unfairly, the machinations of the Jesuits. The sentence of the Inquisition read in part:

> That the Sun is the centre of the universe and does not move from its place is a proposition absurd and false in philosophy, and formerly heretical; being expressly contrary to Holy Writ: That the Earth is not the centre of the universe nor immoveable, but that it moves, even with a diurnal motion, is likewise a proposition absurd and false in philosophy, and considered in theology at least erroneous in faith.

Despite the constraints imposed by the *Ratio* as well as by the Inquisition, the condemnation of the heliocentric account of the cosmos presented problems to Jesuit scientists, whether lecturing in universities or teaching in schools. A way had to be found to deal with the problem. In 1651 Giovanni Battista Riccioli, SJ, wrote of the condemnation in his *Almagestum Novum*, "As there has been no definition on this matter by the Sovereign Pontiff or by a General Council directed and approved by him, it is in no way of faith that the sun

---

[18] Cf. Richard Blackwell, *Galileo, Bellarmine and the Bible* (Notre Dame, IN: University of Notre Dame Press, 1991), 150.

moves and the earth is motionless. . . . Still, all Catholics are obliged . . . at least not to firmly teach the opposite of what the decree lays down." Not surprisingly, Riccioli regularly had problems with the Inquisition, despite over time hardening his attitude toward the Copernican system itself.[19] There were various solutions in use up to the time the Inquisition's ban was removed, toward the end of the eighteenth century, though "by 1633 Jesuit scientists had abandoned strict Aristotelian and Ptolemaic cosmologies. They recognised that the choice lay between the Tychonian system (or some variant of it) and the Copernican. While leaving open the possibility that the true system might be neither of these but some other not yet thought of,"[20] some Jesuits argued that Galileo's version might be taught as hypothetical, one among several competing cosmologies, an approach that found its way into many school textbooks, or alternatively Jesuit astronomers could content themselves with gathering data, an outcome that proved itself scientifically very productive.[21]

The assimilation of modern science by members of the Society was not a straightforward linear progression. There were setbacks. In an attempt to impose uniformity, in 1651 the general Francesco Piccolomini issued a list of teachings that Jesuits were forbidden to propagate, and this was used by some to condemn new scientific theories. The Copernican cosmology was not the only challenge to the Aristotelian understanding of the world. The theory of gravity advanced by Isaac Newton in his *Philosophiae Naturalis Principia Mathematica*, which appeared in 1687, was another such. It was cautiously, then fully, embraced by the Dubrovnik-born polymath Roger Boscovich (1711–1787)—described by one biographer as an "astronomer, mathe-

---

[19] On Riccioli, see Alfredo Dinis, "Giovanni Battista Riccioli and the Science of His Time," in *Jesuit Science and the Republic of Letters*, ed. Mordechai Feingold (Cambridge, MA: MIT Press, 2003), 195–234.

[20] John L. Russell, "Catholic Astronomers and the Copernican System after the Condemnation of Galileo," *Annales of Science* 46 (1989): 376. Russell (himself a Jesuit) added a footnote that teachers in Jesuit schools were slower to abandon Aristotelianism. He goes on to cite a Jesuit teaching mathematics in Marseilles who wrote in 1679, "Copernicus gives the simplest explanation of all these motions [of planets, etc.], so much so that if his hypothesis was not contrary to scripture it could almost be called divine" (379).

[21] Cf. Luis Caruana, "The Jesuits and the Scientific Revolution," in *The Cambridge Companion to the Jesuits*, ed. Thomas Worcester (Cambridge: Cambridge University Press, 2008), 243–60. The quotation from Riccioli is on p. 247.

matician, physicist, geodesist, hydrographer, philosopher and poet"[22]—despite opposition from some of his Roman confreres. Among Boscovich's major achievements was a map of the Papal States, in the production of which he was aided by the English Jesuit Christopher Maire. But his most ambitious work was his *Theoria Philosophiae Naturalis* (1758), in which, directly inspired by Newton, he advanced what was in effect a "theory of everything." Hostility toward him at the Roman College contributed to his 1759 self-imposed exile in France, shortly after he had persuaded the pope to remove Copernicus's book from the *Index*: the prohibition on Jesuits teaching the heliocentric system had been abrogated in 1757. He remained for nine years in France, though the country proved no more congenial, possibly because of the general hostility there toward the Society of Jesus (see below, chapter 7 passim). On the other hand, his "triumphal tour"[23] of England from 1761 to 1762, where he was elected a member of London's Royal Society, was something of a consolation.

The Jesuit contribution to astronomy—and they still staff the Vatican Observatory based in Castel Gandolfo[24]—has attracted the most attention, perhaps because of its importance in the Jesuit mission to China, but they were involved in many other branches of scientific research. José Acosta's 1590 *Historia Natural y Moral de las Indias*, for example, was a pioneering work in natural history. Athanasius Kircher (1602–1680) made an attempt to understand Egyptian hieroglyphics and claimed, wrongly, to have produced a translation. He made use of the newly invented microscope to study the blood of plague victims, thereby making a modest contribution to epidemiology, and he worked around the ban on promoting Copernicus's heliocentric system by the imaginative use of science fiction, describing the journey of someone who might now be called an astronaut through the cosmos. His curiosity extended to a remarkably wide

---

[22] Elizabeth Hill, "Roger Boscovich: A Biographical Essay," in *Roger Joseph Boscovich*, ed. Lancelot Law Whyte (London: Allen and Unwin, 1961), 17–111, quotation at p. 17.

[23] Paul Shore in *The Cambridge Encyclopedia of the Jesuits*, ed. Thomas Worcester (Cambridge: Cambridge University Press, 2017), 114.

[24] The former deputy director of the Vatican Observatory, Christopher Corbally, in mid-2020 joined the ranks of Jesuits who have had astronomical phenomena named after them: in Fr. Corbally's case, an asteroid.

range of disciplines, biblical languages as well as hieroglyphics, magnetism as well as astronomy, though his contemporary fame, which was considerable, rested most, perhaps, on the extraordinary museum he set up in the Roman College containing objects sent to him from Jesuits around the world. He "had such a variety of intellectual interests that Carlos de Sigüenza y Góngora, Cosmographer of New Spain and chair of mathematics at the Royal University of Mexico, referred to Kircher as 'el monstro de la sabiadura' (the behemoth of learning)."[25]

Kirchner did not move from the Roman College, but other Jesuits, trained there or elsewhere, took their learning, in the sciences as well as the humanities, into schools, of which, by the end of the sixteenth century, there were 245; in 1615, at the death of Claudio Acquaviva, the fifth general of the Society, there were 372.[26] In these mathematics was firmly on the syllabus, but as has been seen in the case of Clavius, mathematics had a far wider connotation—clocks, for instance, proved to be of particular interest. Individual Jesuits teaching in the schools, as well as in the universities, engaged in what could certainly be described as scientific research, producing school textbooks as well as learned papers, while others had rather more unexpected occupations: the role of Jesuit mathematicians in training naval officers has recently been studied by Marcelo Aranda.[27]

Just as schools had not been part of Ignatius's original vision for his Society, neither had combatting Protestantism. Nonetheless, in 1554 the founder wrote to the Nijmegen-born Peter Canisius:

> Seeing the progress that heretics have made in so short a time, spreading the poison of their evil doctrines through so many peoples and regions . . . it seems that our Society has been accepted by divine providence as one of the efficacious means to repair so immense an evil. It must therefore be solicitous in preparing good

---

[25] Quoted by Marcelo Aranda in "Deciphering the Ignatian Tree: The Catholic Horoscope of the Society of Jesus," in *Empires of Knowledge*, ed. Paula Findlen (London: Routledge, 2018), 109.

[26] Bangert, *A History of the Society of Jesus*, 105. Problems consequent upon this rapid expansion have been touched on above, pp. 148ff.

[27] "The Jesuit Roots of Spanish Naval Education," *Journal of Jesuit Studies* 7 (2020): 185–203.

remedies . . . to preserve those who remain healthy and to cure those already sick with the heretical plague.[28]

To stem the tide of heresy, quite early on Jesuits were sent to northern Italy for fear that the Reformation would be carried across the mountains from Germany into Italy. Germany as such did not, of course, then exist: the Holy Roman Empire with the capital, in so far as it had one, in Vienna was a loose federation of separate states ruled by princes, dukes, or bishops, each of whom rejoiced in the title of "elector" from their role in choosing the emperor, although in the sixteenth century the title had become an effectively hereditary title of the Habsburg family, archdukes of Austria.

The first Jesuit in Germany was the Savoyard Peter Faber (or Pierre Favre, 1506–1564), one of Ignatius's first companions. In 1543 in Mainz he encountered Canisius (1521–1597) whom he guided through the *Spiritual Exercises* and who promptly entered the Society. The impact of Canisius on the Counter-Reformation in Germany can hardly be overestimated, to the extent that he is sometimes called the "second apostle" of Germany.[29] His first undertaking as a Jesuit, however, was to the college at Messina, where he taught rhetoric. He was then sent to the University of Bologna to study for a doctorate in theology, which he then taught at Ingolstadt, serving briefly as rector of that city's university before moving in 1552 to Vienna, where again he lectured in theology as well as being court preacher and, rather remarkably for a Jesuit at the time, administrator of the Diocese of Vienna. In 1556 he became the provincial of one of the three German provinces, founding several schools. It was in a school, that of Fribourg in Switzerland, that he died. The success of the schools was remarkable; that at Trier, for example, had 550 students in 1564, and fourteen years later the number had increased to well over a thousand,[30] not all of them Catholics, but all of them subjected to the same curriculum, which included catechesis: Canisius himself produced three catechisms that were widely circulated in Germany as

---

[28] Harro Höpfl, *Jesuit Political Thought: The Society of Jesus and the State, c. 1540–1630* (Cambridge: Cambridge University Press, 2004), 67.

[29] The Anglo-Saxon St. Boniface (Winfrid), martyred 754, being the first.

[30] Bangert, *A History of the Society of Jesus*, 71.

well as elsewhere, being translated into eleven languages before the suppression of the Society in 1773.[31]

The colleges and other residences served as bases for Jesuit catechizing and preaching in a fairly successful effort within the Holy Roman Empire to roll back the Reformation. The preachers were provided with ammunition not just from the catechisms but also from Bellarmine's *Disputationes de Controversiis Christianae Fidei adversus huius temporis Haereticos* ("Debates about the controversies of Christianity against the heretics of the present age," known simply as *De Controversiis*), the first volume of which came out in 1586 and the second two years later. These hefty tomes, which went through many editions, were the outcome of Bellarmine's teaching at the Roman College, where he held the newly established chair of controversial theology from 1576 to 1589. Three years later, after a period in France in the entourage of the papal legate, sent there after the assassination of Henry III, he became rector of the college and then, in 1599, was named a cardinal and appointed to the Inquisition.

Armed with the catechisms and Bellarmine's all-encompassing tomes, Jesuit preachers managed to halt the tide of Protestantism with the empire and to some extent push it back. They frequently served as chaplains/confessors, and in effect as advisers, at the courts of Catholic princes. They were especially influential at the courts of Vienna and Munich, whose princes, who were cousins, the Habsburg Archduke Ferdinand—afterward Holy Roman Emperor Ferdinand II—and the already mentioned (see above, p. 150) Wittelsbach Maximilian, duke, afterward elector, of Bavaria, had been educated by Jesuits at the University of Ingolstadt. The foundation of the university had long predated that of the Society, yet in some ways Ingolstadt became a symbol of Jesuit success. It had almost been won over to the Reformers before the arrival of members of the Society as lecturers, after which it became a bastion of the Catholic Reformation. Progress, however, was severely hindered by the outbreak of the Thirty Years' War between the Protestant and Catholic states of the empire.

---

[31] Though this was far behind Bellarmine's catechism, which was translated into twenty European languages and seventeen non-European ones. Cf. O'Malley et al., *The Jesuits II*, 27.

The conventional date for the outbreak of hostilities is May 23, 1618, the occasion of the Defenestration of Prague, when two imperial officials and their secretary were thrown out of a third-floor window of Hradčany Castle by representatives of the Bohemian Protestants, rebelling against the rule of the Catholic Emperor Ferdinand. They survived their seventy-foot fall, an apparent miracle that the Catholics, not least the Jesuit General Muzio Vitelleschi, seized on as a sign of God's favor on Ferdinand.[32] Not surprisingly, he associated the Society with the imperial cause: Jesuits were already serving as confessors to both Ferdinand and Maximilian, as well as to the young King Louis XIII of France. That they did not play the same role in the Spain of Philip III, Robert Bireley suggests, was because in the country, having been much less impacted by Protestantism, the older religious orders remained more entrenched.[33] Nor can it have helped that Vitelleschi, elected superior general in 1615, was the first to hold that office who was not a subject of the Spanish monarchy.

The war faced the Jesuits with many challenges, not least the danger, feared by Vitelleschi and his successor, that there would be a growing nationalist spirit among members of the Society that would threaten its unity, a threat that proved to be especially severe in France (see below, chapter 7 passim). But an even greater threat to Jesuit cohesion was to what extent, if at all, concessions could be made to Protestants. Though Vitelleschi had himself in effect appointed as confessor to Ferdinand the Dutch Jesuit Martin Becanus (Maarten van Beek), who had been teaching theology in Vienna, he found himself at odds with Becanus when the emperor, with the support of his confessor, conceded a degree of religious freedom to Protestants to secure their allegiance. Nor was the pope best pleased, but the Jesuit, who in 1607 had already published the book *De fide haereticis servanda* ("On keeping faith with heretics"), argued this was the lesser of two evils because Ferdinand simply did not have the resources to impose Catholicism against the will of nobility—and in any case, the Peace of Augsburg, signed between Emperor Charles V and the Protestant Schmalkaldic League, had already enshrined the principle *cuius regio eius religio*, giving the ruler in any region the right to impose

[32] The following account is largely drawn from Robert Bireley, *The Jesuits and the Thirty Years' War* (Cambridge: Cambridge University Press, 2003).
[33] Ibid., 18.

his own version of Christianity on his subjects. Pope Paul IV, not someone given to religious toleration, had been persuaded to accept it by Canisius and other Jesuits.[34] There were exceptions to this principle, one of which, that of "reserved lands," became an important issue toward the end of the Thirty Years' War.

Ferdinand's hand was strengthened when the imperial troops, supported by Maximilian's forces, defeated the Protestants in November 1620 at the Battle of the White Mountain—a location then just outside Prague but now within its boundaries. No fewer than eleven Jesuits had accompanied the victorious army, and, in gratitude, Maximilian petitioned the pope for the canonization of the Society's founder:[35] Ignatius was declared a saint by Pope Gregory XV in March 1622 alongside Francis Xavier.

A complicating factor in the religious wars was the policy of France under Cardinal Richelieu and his successor Cardinal Mazarin, during the reigns of Louis XIII and Louis XIV. The role of Jesuits in France will be discussed at greater length in the next chapter, but they were faced with a strategy that, because of hostility to the Habsburg dynasty, allied France with the Protestant states within the empire and with the Protestant Gustavus Adolphus of Sweden who invaded northern Germany in mid-1630. Under his leadership Protestant forces won remarkable victories over imperial troops at the Battle of Breitenfeld in September 1631 and, fifteen months later, at the Battle of Lützen, though during the latter engagement Gustavus Adolphus was killed after becoming separated from his troops while leading a cavalry charge. This association with Protestants gave Jesuits on the imperial side plenty of ammunition. Adam Contzen, the confessor to Maximilian, wrote two pamphlets critical of Richelieu, arguing that support for Protestants might give rise to an uprising of the French nobility and suggesting that a monarch publicly backing such a policy would run the risk of excommunication: the pamphlets were publicly burned in Paris in October 1625.[36] Despite his anti-French stance, Contzen was sent by Maximilian as an emissary to Paris. This came perilously close to overt political activity, expressly forbidden by the fifth general congregation (1592–1593), which ordered, "Let

---

[34] Höpfl, *Jesuit Political Thought*, 97.
[35] Bireley, *The Jesuits and the Thirty Years' War*, 41–42.
[36] Ibid., 69.

no one at all meddle in any way in the public and secular affairs of princes,"[37] repeated in the "Instruction for the Confessors of Princes" drawn up by Acquaviva in 1602, and endorsed in 1608 by the eighth general congregation. The confessors were also told that they must live in Jesuit houses and attend court only when summoned, an ordinance that was not always followed to the letter and certainly not by Hernando de Salazar, the confessor to Gaspar de Guzman Olivares, the first minister of Spain under Philip IV, whose behavior was so scandalous that his confreres demanded he leave the Jesuit house in Madrid where he was living.[38]

It is clear that on many issues, including political ones, there existed within the Society differences of opinion: it was certainly not the monolithic organization it is sometimes presented to be. On the matter of the Thirty Years' War there were, to use modern parlance, hawks and doves. William Lamormaini, confessor in Vienna to Ferdinand II, was in the former camp, as was Adam Contzen in Munich. Up to 1635 Vitelleschi shared their views, but then he adopted a more moderate stance, as indeed did the successors to Contzen and Lamormaini. The Jesuit community at the University of Dillingen remained hawks, while the provincial congregation of the Upper German province proved dovelike, declaring in 1639, "From so many unhappy events of the war it seems that it does not please God that the Catholic religion be propagated in Germany by arms." Many, including Vitelleschi, had seen the apparently miraculous survival of the imperial officials after their defenestration and the victories at the White Mountain and at Lützen as signs of God's favor. Not half a century earlier Antonio Possevino had written that "Catholic princes who have adhered to God with their whole soul have never failed to triumph over their enemies," and this belief in God's intervention on the side of Catholics seemed to have widely prevailed, despite the fact that Possevino had made the claim not long after the defeat of the Spanish Armada.[39] That God always intervened in war in support of the righteous was not, however, the view of the Jesuits of the Upper German province. They argued that what was needed was better books—and better preaching. They praised the example of the English

[37] Quoted by Höpfl, *Jesuit Political Thought*, 58.
[38] Bireley, *The Jesuits and the Thirty Years' War*, 179.
[39] Höpfl, *Jesuit Political Thought*, 109.

province, which may well have come as a surprise to English Jesuits who went about in constant risk of arrest, imprisonment of exile, even possible execution (for the situation in the British Isles, see below, pp. 165ff.). The Germans even suggested that priests from England be brought to Germany to show them how to spread the Catholic faith.[40]

There were four Jesuits present at the electoral convention of Regensburg in 1630. Reinhardt Ziegler, the confessor to the elector of Mainz who had advocated the repossession of Church property that had fallen into Protestant hands, was pessimistic about prospects for peace; Lamormaini, optimistic—he was hoping that the recovery of the lands might be used to fund the establishment of more Jesuit colleges: an Edict of Restitution had been issued in March 1629. It was highly controversial: not to enforce it would appear to be giving support to the Protestant states that had benefited from the seizure, but insisting that the edict be implemented risked alienating the two Protestant states, Brandenburg and Saxony, that had stayed loyal to the emperor and driving them into an alliance with Gustavus Adolphus.[41] The edict remained contentious, with most Jesuits, including Vitelleschi, opposed to any modification except in the case of absolute necessity, and, as the emperor still hoped for victory, that was not yet the case.

As has just been mentioned, all that changed after the 1635 Peace of Prague when, to quote Bireley, "Ferdinand broke with the myth long upheld by Lamormaini and others, including Vitelleschi, that his mission to restore Catholicism in Germany guaranteed him victory with divine aid and forbade concessions to Protestants beyond what the Peace of Augsburg had granted them."[42] The Jesuit general may have been moved to alter his stance, in part, at least, because of a report in January 1631 from the superior of the house in Vienna that people were beginning to hold the Society accountable for the continuance of the war.[43] When the war finally came to an end with the Peace of Westphalia, signed on October 21, 1648, the ecclesiastical lands in the hands of Protestants were still a contentious issue.

---

[40] Bireley, *The Jesuits and the Thirty Years' War*, 226–27.
[41] Ibid., 105–14.
[42] Ibid., 104.
[43] Ibid., 140.

Vincenzo Carafa, Vitelleschi's successor as general, wrote to the confessors of the emperor and Maximilian that no concession should be made: "A peace which will enslave souls is worse than any war," he said.[44] When, however, the superior of the Jesuit college in Münster, a gathering place especially for the pro-imperial delegates where members of the Jesuit community mingled freely with the plenipotentiaries, was reported to the general as not displaying enough neutrality between the hawks and the doves during the negotiations, Carafa rebuked him. The pope was undoubtedly on the side of the hawks, though at the time he forbore to comment.[45]

Bireley remarks that Vitelleschi had shown "deference to princes and persons of high estate."[46] This was not surprising. As has been remarked, the Society depended on princes, and the wealthy in general, for the funding of their colleges, and it was perhaps particularly important in the context of *cuius regio, eius religio*, when rulers determined the religious practices of their subjects. But Jesuits believed that, unlike Protestantism, which fomented division, Catholicism was beneficial to the unity of the state. In his explicitly anti-Machiavellian *Treatise of Religion and the Virtues That a Christian Prince Needs to Govern and Preserve His States*, Pedro de Ribadeneira (1526–1611), who had been Ignatius's secretary and wrote the first biography of the Society's founder, claimed that "heresies are the cause and the ruin and revolutions of kingdoms."[47] Conversely, Thomas Fitzherbert (1552–1640) argued in *A Treatise Concerning Policy and Religion*, "In what state soever he liveth [the true Christian] is humble, meke, religious and consequentlie a good, and excellent member of the commonwealth, in so much that if the precepts of the Christian religion are sincerely followed and observed, there should need no political laws."[48] Religion, and specifically the Catholic faith, was not only good for the soul, argued Jesuit authors, but also good for the state. Edmund

[44] Ibid., 238.
[45] Ibid., 238.
[46] Ibid., 271.
[47] Quoted by Höpfl, *Jesuit Political Thought*, 120.
[48] Quoted by ibid., 115. Höpfl does not seem to have noticed, or, if so, does not mention, that when Fitzherbert published his two-part *Treatise*—the first part in 1606, the second four years later—he was not yet a Jesuit. He entered the Society in Rome in 1615 and became rector of the English College in Rome (the Venerabile), spending the rest of his life there.

Campion (1540–1581), an English Jesuit martyr, but at the time a member of the Austrian province and teaching in the college in Prague, put on a play, "St Ambrose and the Emperor Theodosius," which was performed at the imperial court. "Its main message is unambiguous: heresy leads to internecine conflict and evil actions, and princes, to rule wisely, must be accountable to the Church."[49]

Jesuits were not, of course, allowed to be politicians or to hold government office, something successive generals insisted on. In their theological writings, however, they frequently considered matters of Church and State, and one such issue was the authority of the papacy to intervene in governance by princes. Theologians such as Bellarmine and Becanus argued that the pope had no direct authority to take overt political action, but he had indirect authority.[50] That is to say, he might intervene where the salvation of souls was at stake, and what was true for the papacy was equally true for the confessors to princes. But for them it was even less of a remote issue as it was for the pope because, as John Bossy has remarked, "The burning question in Catholic politics during the 1580s was, whether Catholics were entitled, or perhaps obliged, to organize, collaborate in or encourage civil or military action aimed at the overthrow of Protestant governments or of Catholic governments thought to be in collusion with them."[51] This, of course, was exactly what France had done in allying itself with Gustavus Adolphus—and also with the Turks, who had their sights set on taking Vienna.

Bossy's "burning question" was a very real one for Jesuits in England. By the time in 1639 that German Jesuits appealed to the example of their English confreres, no fewer than sixteen of them had already been put to death for what was defined as treason (a Scottish Jesuit, John Ogilvie, was executed in Glasgow in 1615), and in 1679 another eight were to be martyred in England and Wales, as well as

[49] Alison Shell, "Campion's Dramas," in *The Reckoned Expense: Edmund Campion and the Early English Jesuits*, ed. Thomas M. McCoog (Woodbridge: The Boydell Press, 1996), 108.

[50] In the first volume of the *De Controversiis* Bellarmine had argued that the pope was not the temporal ruler of the whole world and that temporal rulers did not derive their authority from him, but from God by way of the people: the book was placed on the Index. Cf. Blackwell, *Galileo, Bellarmine and the Bible*, 30.

[51] John Bossy, "The Heart of Robert Persons" in McCoog, *The Reckoned Expense*, 143.

a dozen more who died in prison in the aftermath of the totally ficti-
tious Popish Plot, dreamed up by the nefarious Church of England
clergyman Titus Oates. The alleged plot was to assassinate the king,
and not even the target of the assassination, King Charles II, believed
in it, though it caught the popular imagination. All of those executed
were priests except for two lay brothers, Ralph Ashley, a former cook
in one of the Jesuit colleges, and Nicholas Owen, who had designed
hiding holes—known as priest holes—in the houses of the gentry the
Jesuits served.

Edmund Campion left Prague for Rome unwillingly, but he went
at the behest of Everard Mercurian, the Jesuit general. Mercurian and
Campion were both doubtful about the wisdom of traveling to England. Campion and his companions, Robert Persons (1546–1610)
and Ralph Sherwin (1549/50–1581), were not the first Jesuits to visit
the British Isles. Ignatius had sent Paschase Broët and Alfonso
Salmerón to Ireland for a month in 1542 to report on the situation for
Catholics there—they thought it was dire—and a Dutch Jesuit,
Nikolaas Floris, to Scotland. The instructions to Broët and Salmerón
were clear: they were to assess the future for Catholicism in Ireland;
they were to stay out of politics. That last directive could hardly be
said of Floris's trip to Edinburgh in 1562 because the objective given
to him by Pope Pius IV was to persuade the Catholic Mary Queen of
Scots to emulate her namesake Mary Tudor in England and to make
a stand against the spread of Protestantism in her country, to which
she had only recently returned from France. Though Floris met the
queen at the Palace of Holyrood, his mission failed: to take the drastic
action the pope was demanding would have been impossible, for, as
events were to prove, her hold on the throne of Scotland was shaky.
Nonetheless, a Scottish Jesuit journeyed home to make a similar appeal in 1567, which Mary straightforwardly rejected.

Campion, Persons, and a lay brother, Ralph Emerson, traveled
together as far as Rheims, then Persons went on separately. Campion
and Emerson were arrested at Dover but then freed, and they traveled
to London. In London Persons and Campion again met and attended
a gathering with some of the secular clergy to assure them that they
came for religious reasons, not political ones. This was a difficult issue
for the local clergy who had remained loyal to the papacy. There had
been no members of the Society of Jesus in Britain before the Reformation. They now came as missionaries, with, unlike the secular clergy,

no stake in the country that they might wish to recover. After the meeting in Southwark the Jesuits parted company and went around the country from one house of the recusant gentry to another ministering to Catholics in accordance with Mercurian's instructions.

During this time Campion wrote two tracts, the first, known as *Campion's Brag*, was addressed to the privy council, insisting that his mission was peaceful and nonpolitical but ending with the words, "And touching our Society, be it known to you that we have made a league—all the Jesuits in the world, whose succession and multitude must overreach all the practice of England—cheerfully to carry the cross you shall lay upon us, and never to despair your recovery, while we have a man left to enjoy your Tyburn, or to be racked with your torments, or consumed with your prisons. The expense is reckoned, the enterprise is begun; it is of God; it cannot be withstood. So the faith was planted: So it must be restored."[52] The second, *Rationes Decem* ("Ten Reasons"), was written in 1581 and printed on a secret press hidden in the attic of Stonor Park, a recusant household in Oxfordshire. It was a much more academic work—there are over 150 footnotes—and addressed to "the learned members of the Universities of Oxford and Cambridge,"[53] setting out to uphold the claims of Catholicism against the Protestant Reformers. In a considerable public relations coup, copies of the *Rationes Decem* were left on the chairs of the university church in Oxford, just before it was to be used for a university ceremony.

From mid-May until July 11, Campion was at Stonor. From there he went to Lyford Grange, another recusant household, now within the county of Oxfordshire but before boundary changes located in Berkshire. It was while leaving there on July 17 that he was arrested: a proclamation in January had ordered the capture of all Jesuits in the kingdom. He was taken to London astride a horse and on his hat a label read, "The Seditious Jesuit." He was imprisoned in the Tower of London, interrogated and tortured, and then put to debate with Protestant theologians—as he had asked to do in his *Brag*—but with no choice of topics, no time to prepare, and no books of reference available to him except the Bible. Despite these handicaps Campion

---

[52] "Campion's 'Brag': St. Edmund Campion (1581)," The Catholic Thing, February 10, 2022, https://www.thecatholicthing.org/2022/02/10/campions-brag/.

[53] Edmund Campion, *Ten Reasons* (London: Manresa Press, 1914), 89.

held his own, so much so that one observer, Philip Howard Earl of Arundel, converted to Catholicism, though conversion had been banned by Act of Parliament, and was himself later executed in the Tower. In November Campion, together with other priests and a layman, was put on trial in Westminster Hall. The original charge was one of persuading people to convert to Rome and to the obedience of the pope, but this was changed to supporting invasion and assassinating the queen, all of which amounted to treason according to the Act of 1351. The accused were found guilty and sentenced to be hanged, cut down while still alive, and then dismembered ("quartered"). The sentence was carried out on Campion, and on two other Jesuit priests, on December 1, 1581. After the arrest of Campion his two traveling companions from Rome, Emerson and Persons, both avoided capture and went abroad, though Emerson later returned and was arrested while smuggling books by Persons into the country. He spent nineteen years in the Clink, a prison in Southwark, after which he was exiled.

That the Jesuits had come to England with no political agenda— Campion, after all, prayed for Queen Elizabeth on the scaffold—was constantly insisted on by Campion and his successors. After Pius V's bull of 1570, *Regnans in Excelsis*, which excommunicated the queen and ordered English Catholics not to obey her under pain of their own excommunication, it was problematic to maintain there was no political intention behind the Jesuit mission even though the pope at the time had temporarily suspended the bull—which in any case had never been promulgated in England and so, strictly speaking, was not binding. However much Campion insisted that the mission had no political agenda, the same could hardly be said for Persons. John Bossy, in the article cited above (p. 166), makes a very convincing case that in exile he was supporting a plot to assassinate Elizabeth, an idea that was firmly ruled out by Mercurian, and then planning for a Spanish invasion. Had Elizabeth died—or, in any case, when she died—there was obviously, because she had no children, a question about who would succeed to the throne. This was another, and very controversial, topic Persons addressed directly, albeit pseudonymously, in *A Conference about the Next Succession to the Crowne of Ingland*, published in Antwerp in 1594.

The argument, and significance, of Persons's book has been extensively discussed by M. J. Innes, who firmly attributes the book to

Persons, though that has been questioned.[54] The argument that is advanced by the author, Persons or not, is, however, common Jesuit, indeed common scholastic, political thought, namely, that while all authority does, of course, come from God, sovereignty is mediated via the people. While it may have been a standard political theory, it was not one held by Elizabeth's successor, James I (of England, James VI of Scotland) who believed firmly in the divine right of kings, setting out his views, ostensibly for the benefit of his son, in *The Trve Lawe of Free Monarchies: Or, The Reciprock and Mvtvall Dvtie Betwixt a Free King, and His Naturall Subiectes*, published in 1598, and then in *Basilikon Doron* (= "Royal Gift"), first printed in Edinburgh in 1599 and republished in London after he had become king in 1603.

While James's views may have been antipathetic to Persons and other Jesuits, they were hopeful that this son of the Catholic Mary Queen of Scots—who had, Bellarmine revealed, approached the pope suggesting that Catholics might support his claim to the English throne—would ameliorate the anti-Catholic laws enacted under Elizabeth. In that they were deeply disappointed, a disappointment that led to the plot to blow up Parliament, and the king with it, in November 1605. The plot was discovered, somewhat mysteriously, and the conspirators arrested. In the aftermath a number of Jesuits were executed for having had knowledge of the attempt on the king's life, among them Henry Garnet, the superior of the Jesuits in England: he had learned of it in the confessional. It has been argued that the plot had been set up by Robert Cecil, James's chief minister, in order to discredit Catholics but, as one Jesuit historian has remarked, "It is not a view that has gained much traction with historians."[55]

One of the consequences of the Gunpowder Plot was the imposition of a new oath of allegiance for recusants. They were asked to "abhor, detest, and abjure, as impious and heretical this damnable doctrine and position,—that princes which be excommunicated by the pope may be deposed or murdered by their subjects."[56] The doctrine of regicide will be discussed below (pp. 182ff.), but that a ruler

---

[54] M. J. Innes, "Robert Persons, Popular Sovereignty, and the Late Elizabethan Succession Debate," *The Historical Journal* 62, no. 1 (2010): 57–76.

[55] Oliver Rafferty, s.v. "Gunpowder Plot," in *The Cambridge Encyclopedia of the Jesuits*, 354.

[56] "Oath of Allegiance of James I of England," https://en.wikipedia.org/wiki/Oath_of_Allegiance_of_James_I_of_England.

who did not serve the good of his subjects could be legitimately overthrown was one of the themes of Persons's *A Conference about the Next Succession*, and no Jesuit was going to recommend taking an oath that had, in any case, been condemned by Pope Paul V. But opposition to the oath lead the Jesuits into even more conflict, not so much with the State as with other secular clergy in England.

Some thirty Catholic clergy, Jesuit and non-Jesuit, had been imprisoned at Wisbech Castle on the Isle of Ely in Cambridgeshire. It seems that the Jesuits, led by William Weston (c. 1550–1615),[57] and most of the others wanted not just a more structured community life but one that reflected the changes in Church discipline brought about by the Council of Trent. This disagreement gave rise to what came to be called "the Wisbech Stirs," dissension among the prisoners, which came to a head with Rome's appointment of an "archpriest" in the absence in the country of any bishop and of any obvious leader in exile: the leader hitherto, Cardinal William Allen, who was closely associated with Persons, had just died. The person chosen, George Blackwell, was, however, regarded by many of the secular clergy as being too close to the Jesuits. This was, perhaps a perfectly fair appraisal: he had, for example, helped Persons in the writing of *A Brief Discours Contayning Certayne Reasons why Catholiques Refuse to Goe to Church* of 1580. Blackwell's close association with the Society did not last. He later expressed the view, and wrote to the clergy to say so, that Catholics might take the oath of allegiance, a stance for which he was roundly rebuked by no less a figure than Cardinal Bellarmine, who then entered into the controversy surrounding the oath, though under the name of his chaplain, Matteo Torti.

A considerable body of literature was published by both sides of the argument,[58] some of the Jesuit material being printed on the secret press that in 1608 Robert Persons established within the school he had opened for the sons of recusant families in St. Omer in the Spanish Netherlands in 1593.[59] A good number of the boys who attended

---

[57] It was Weston who received Philip Howard into the Church; see above, p. 169.

[58] This can be followed in two volumes by Peter Milward, *Religious Controversies of the Elizabethan Age* (London: The Scolar Press, 1977) and *Religious Controversies of the Jacobean Age* (London: The Scolar Press, 1978).

[59] For the history of the school, see Hubert Chadwick, *St Omers to Stonyhurst* (London: Burns and Oates, 1962), and for the printing press, see Michael J. Walsh, "The Publishing Policy of the English College Press at St Omer, 1608–1759," *Studies in Church History* 17 (1981): 239–50.

the school, including in later years some from Maryland, went on to become priests, many of them Jesuits, and although there were established colleges for training clergy in various places around Europe, including in Rome (now the Venerable English College) and in Valladolid, the English Jesuits set up one of their own specifically for the English mission, first in Louvain and then in Liège.[60] The situation in England for Jesuits to permit their ordinary method of proceeding—setting up colleges and using them as a base for evangelizing as has been described for elsewhere in Europe—was not a possibility except for a brief period during the reign of James II, a convert to Catholicism, and his devoutly Catholic wife, Mary of Modena.[61] In June 1687 the Jesuits opened a school in the Savoy, a former hospital beside the Thames. Some 250 boys, Catholic and Protestant, turned up on the first day for a free education, and the number had nearly doubled by the time, slightly over a year later, it was forced to close because of the overthrow of King James. In the meantime the Savoy had become the residence for London Jesuits, including the provincial, and its chapel an important mass center for the Catholics of the city.[62] From then on English Jesuits led a precarious existence, serving mass centers and wealthy families around the country until the suppression of the Society in 1773, at which point the school at St. Omer, which had moved to Bruges, and the college came together at Liège, both moving in 1794 to Stonyhurst, in a remote part of Lancashire.

Unlike England and Scotland, Spain had been left largely untouched by the Protestant Reformation, thanks in no small part to the rigorous surveillance exercised by the Inquisition with, in some instances, members of the Society as members of their tribunals, and it had also remained free from the wars of religion that had so devastated the empire of Charles V. The first Jesuit to arrive in Spain, then ruled by Charles V's son, Philip II, occurred in 1539 even before the Society had been formally approved. Antonio Araoz (1516–1573) came from a family with a long tradition of service to the Spanish monarchy and was a nephew by marriage to Ignatius himself, which

---

[60] For the theological college, see Walsh, *Heythrop College*.

[61] Mary of Modena had for a time as her court preacher in England a future saint, the French Jesuit Claude de la Colombière (1641–1682), who was canonized in May 1992.

[62] There was also a school in Holyrood Palace, Edinburgh.

perhaps partly explains why he was listened to so sympathetically when he suggested that there ought to be a Jesuit—him—at the Spanish court. He was a problematic character. As John O'Malley remarks, "Especially after about 1565 he played his entrée to the Spanish court up to the hilt, gave up his pretense of performing any ministry, and successfully insisted on having two Jesuit temporal coadjutors as his servants. Because he had the full support of Count Rui Gómez, the most powerful person in the kingdom after Philip II himself, his Jesuit contemporaries were forced to write him off as a lost cause."[63]

That is being generous. It is true that he founded, in 1547, the first province of Spain and that, by the time of his death, there were four provinces in that territory. It is also true that, in a piece in a Jesuit-edited journal, it is claimed that "he was considered one of the secondary patriarchs of the Society,"[64] but he wreaked havoc and left the Society—though he was not the only one to blame—with a singularly unfortunate legacy of anti-Semitism. He was apparently angered by the decision to make the headquarters of the Society in Rome rather than in Spain (its capital at the time was Valladolid) and further upset when Francis Borja was promoted above him. He gave vent to his feelings by trying to prevent money from Spain going to help finance the Roman College and by campaigning for Jesuit superiors to be elected locally rather than appointed from Rome. To counteract this divergent tendency among some Spanish members of the Society, Jerónimo Nadal (1507–1580) was despatched to Iberia to inculcate the structures endorsed by the new Constitution.

Though that particular campaign by Araoz did not make a long-lasting impact on the Society, his hostility to *conversos* certainly did. The *conversos* were Spanish Christians of Jewish heritage who were suspected of harboring Jewish beliefs despite their professed faith.[65] There were a number of them in the Society, including Nadal, who has just been mentioned; Pedro de Ribadeneira; and Juan Alfonso de

---

[63] O'Malley, *The First Jesuits*, 62.

[64] *Studies in the Spirituality of the Jesuits* 25, no. 4 (September 1993): 41. It is apparently an editorial addition to the translation of a text of Araoz's.

[65] Shortly after this chapter was written, the *Journal of Jesuit Studies* published a special issue, "Jesuits and Conversos," vol. 8, no. 2 (2021). Of particular interest is the article by Juan Hernández Franco and Pablo Ortega-del-Cerro, "A Jesuit Utopian Project on Behalf of the Conversos: Fernando de Valdés and the Statutes of Purity of Blood (1632)," 214–32.

Polanco (1517–1576), for a long time the secretary of the Society, who had worked with Ignatius on drawing up the Constitutions. Another *converso* was Diego Laínez, Ignatius's successor as superior general, so clearly most of the first Jesuits saw no problem with the background of some of the Order's most prominent members. Not so Araoz. He firmly embraced the *Estatutos de Limpieza de Sangre* ("Statutes of the purity of blood") promulgated by the archbishop of Toledo, Juan Martínez Silíceo, who was also Spain's inquisitor general. The archbishop's hostility arose not only from the *conversos* themselves but also from their association with the *alumbrados* (see above, pp. 14ff.), who were suspected of heresy.

The hostility to *conversos* proved to be not solely a Spanish problem but one that affected the whole Society. The general congregation after the death in 1572 of Borja was expected to elect Polanco as his successor as general. They did not do so, his Jewish heritage apparently being held against him, though the electors were also undoubtedly influenced by the pope, who expressed a wish for a non-Spaniard to succeed Borja. Mercurian, Borja's successor, was sympathetic to the anti-*conversos* lobby and removed any member of Jewish heritage from positions of influence within the Society. In 1593, during the generalate of Acquaviva, a decree of the fifth general congregation ruled against receiving into the Society anyone of Jewish heritage—and also anyone of Islamic heritage—a ruling, it was at first decreed, that not even the general could dispense, though that was eventually modified. Nonetheless, the 1593 regulation remained in force, shamefully, until 1946, when in the aftermath of the Holocaust it was finally revoked.

The situation in Portugal was oddly similar. Simão Rodrigues (1510–1579), who had been one of the group around Ignatius in Paris, arrived there in 1540 with Francis Xavier at the direct request of the king, John III. As has been seen, Xavier went off to Goa, but Rodrigues stayed to found the province and become a troublesome provincial, causing scandal by living at the royal court. Like Araoz, he was opposed to the admission of *conversos* into the Society and, again like Araoz, encouraged a very penitential spirituality to the extent that Ignatius was forced to remove him from office—except that he did not go for two further years and was eventually expelled from the Society, though being afterward readmitted by Mercurian and given the post of visitor of the Portuguese province, a role that, in the end, he handled in an exemplary fashion. The king's patronage was immensely important, not just for the missions in Portuguese overseas territories but within Portugal itself, leading to the establishment of the Jesuit university at Evora and, perhaps even more significant, a prestigious college within the University of Coimbra where they produced an imposing, and much admired, eight-volume edition of Aristotle with commentary. Given the closeness of the Portuguese Jesuits to the royal house, it is hardly surprising that in their preaching they opposed the union, under Habsburg rule, of Spain and Portugal (1580–1640), an opposition that led within Portugal to some hostility to the Society from those who favored the Habsburgs.

Dilemmas were faced by members of the Society who found themselves, not necessarily willingly, entangled in politics. The remarkable career of Johann Eberhard Nithard (1607–1681) is a case in point. Coupling his life story with that of Athanasius Kircher (see above, pp. 157ff.), Markus Friedrich writes that they both "got away with stubbornly independent behaviour that would surely have resulted in severe measures had they been less prominent."[66] Joan-Pau Rubies describes him as being seen as a master of political intrigue and a contributor to the growth of the "black legend" of the Society.[67] Bangert—who spells his name slightly differently—calls him "a modest Jesuit" despite the fact that he became a cardinal contrary to the wishes of the general at the time, Giovanni Paolo Oliva (general 1664–1681).[68] His rise was largely accidental. He had joined the Society in 1631 and was ordained priest eight years later. After teaching at the University of Graz he was proposed by his provincial as a confessor and tutor to the children of Emperor Ferdinand, and when one of the children, Archduchess Maria Ana, was sent to Spain in 1649 to marry Philip IV, he accompanied her to Madrid, where he lived in the Jesuit novitiate. He became close to the king and was given various prestigious positions in government, which taught him about the problems facing Spain, then in a period of decline after the era of overseas expansion. He was therefore well placed to assist

---

[66] *The Oxford Handbook of the Jesuits*, ed. Ines G. Županov (Oxford: Oxford University Press, 2019), 33.

[67] Ibid., 857.

[68] Bangert, *A History of the Society of Jesus*, 197. Prominent though he may have been, his name does not even figure in the index to *The Cambridge Encyclopedia*.

Queen Maria Ana after the death of her husband and her regency during the minority of Philip's heir, Charles II. The queen appointed him inquisitor general, against the wishes of his Jesuit superiors, and he was released from his vow of poverty by the pope, the vow being incompatible with his new role, one that made him even more prominent in the government of Spain. His promotion, however, aroused considerable hostility, not least among the Spanish clergy (including, apparently, some of his fellow Jesuits), and under the threat of a possible civil war he agreed to go against the wishes of Maria Ana and leave the country. So he could do so with dignity, he was appointed ambassador to Rome, while still a priest, but this was thought to be incompatible with the office, and he was made first an archbishop and eventually a cardinal, contrary to the Jesuit Constitution and the express wishes of the general.

Despite his problems with the Society, Nithard always remained, at least in his own mind, a loyal Jesuit. The wealth he had acquired as a cardinal he left to a Jesuit house in Rome, and he was buried in the Society's principal Roman church, the Gesù.[69] The controversies that surrounded him, however, demonstrate the problems the Society often faced when some of its members became too close to the ruling elite, something that was particularly obvious in France during the eighteenth century.

[69] For a recent account of his life, see Miguel Córdoba Salmerón, "A Failed Politician, a Disputed Jesuit: Cardinal Johann Eberhard Nithard," *Journal of Jesuit Studies* 7 (2020): 545–69, on which the above account depends.

Chapter 7

The Problem of France

In his book *The Catholic Church and Argentina's Dirty War* the Jesuit author, Gustavo Morello, makes occasional reference to Jorge Bergoglio, particularly during his time as provincial superior of the Society in Argentina. In a footnote on the arrest and five-month detention of two of Father Bergoglio's subjects, Fathers Francisco Jalics and Orlando Yorio, Morello writes,

> A week before [their arrest] Buenos Aires bishop Juan Carlos Aramburu had removed their licence to practice ministry in Buenos Aires, and Jorge Bergoglio, their religious superior, had publicly criticized the work they were doing. Both attitudes were understood as a signal to the intelligence services.[1]

Pope Francis, who had served as chaplain to the Peronist Iron Guard, a militia modelled distantly on Mussolini's Blackshirts, was therefore no stranger to the problems faced by Jesuits who, during the Thirty Years' War, had been the confidants of, and political advisers to, kings and princes. While France had been only intermittently involved in that prolonged battle for the soul of the empire, it had religious conflicts of its own between Catholics and Huguenots to contend with, a situation made even more complicated by the divisions among Catholics occasioned by the relatively religiously tolerant policy of the Valois King Henry III. Against Henry was ranged the Catholic League, under the leadership of the duke of Guise. The League naturally also opposed Henry III's presumed successor, the Protestant Henry of Navarre. Jesuits in France found themselves, much to the

---

[1] Gustavo Morello, *The Catholic Church and Argentina's Dirty War* (Oxford: Oxford University Press, 2015), 80.

anger of Claudio Acquaviva, ranged on both sides of this divide, with one of the most eminent members, Édmond Auger, a close friend and confessor of Henry III, supporting the Bourbon Henry of Navarre and his provincial backing the League. The situation faced by the Society, therefore, as it attempted to gain a foothold there was at least as much politically charged, if not more so, as its situation within the empire.

It was, of course, to a small chapel in Paris that the origins of the Society could be traced, and all of those making their first vows on Montmartre had been students at the University of Paris. It was not, therefore, surprising that Ignatius sent a small group of new recruits to study there. In 1552 he appointed one of his first companions, Paschase Broët (c. 1500–1562), who came from Picardy, to take charge of a very small province of only eight members. Numbers grew slowly. By 1575 there were two provinces but still only 315 Jesuits, many of them from abroad, such as the Scottish Jesuit William Crichton (c. 1535–1617), who served for a time as vice provincial of Aquitaine and in 1575 was the rector of the college in Lyon.[2] Yet between 1556 and 1575 there were founded no fewer than fourteen colleges and one university,[3] most of them because of requests from important prelates whom it was impolitic to refuse—the university, that of Pont-à-Mousson, for example, at the behest of Charles de Guise, the cardinal of Lorraine, who eventually became the head of the Catholic League. Given the modest number of Jesuits in the country, the pressure on the staff of the colleges was very considerable, and that may well have been one of the factors that caused men to abandon their vocations to the Society, thus adding further to the difficulty of running their many institutions. Not only that, but in several instances some of these insistent prelates, despite their promises, failed to provide adequate endowment to keep them running.

If there was no influx into the Society in France similar to that which was seen elsewhere in Europe, the primary reason, apart from a French suspicion of anything of apparently Spanish origin, was

---

[2] On the intriguing character of Crichton, see Thomas McCoog, "Converting a King: The Jesuit William Crichton and King James VI and I," *Journal of Jesuit Studies* 7, no. 1 (2020): 11–33.

[3] See the list in Martin, *The Jesuit Mind*, 17.

almost certainly Gallicanism, which ran contrary to the Jesuit commitment to the papacy. Though the term came to be used only in the nineteenth century and in a sense was not only to be found in "Gaul" but also in various forms across Europe, the set of notions that lay behind it go back to the early fourteenth century and the conflict between Boniface VIII, pope from 1294 to 1303, and the French King Philip the Fair (1285–1314). At the root of the problem was money: Philip's desire to tax the clergy. This required the consent of the pope, which was not forthcoming until the king threatened to prevent money going from France to Rome, at which point Boniface caved. But then Boniface appointed a bishop without consulting the king, who promptly imprisoned the bishop. The issue had now moved on from clerical taxes to the broader question of the authority of the pope against that of the king. Boniface was preparing to excommunicate Philip when the king attempted to have the pope seized. The plot failed, but the pope, shaken by the experience, died shortly afterward. The king had meanwhile recruited to his cause theologians of the University of Paris, and had it not been for the pope's death, and the fact that his successor, under pressure from Philip, moved the papacy to Avignon, the crisis might have deepened. Now within French territory, even though Avignon was technically part of the Papal States, and with a preponderance of French cardinals in the papal curia, the freedom of the papacy was curtailed, and it was not until 1377 that a pope, by this time Gregory XI, was able to leave Avignon and return the papal court to Rome.

Gregory died the following year, and the chaotic scenes surrounding the election of his successor, Urban VI, led to a schism—the Great Western Schism—which lasted until 1417 and the election, during the Council of Constance, of Pope Martin V. The schism, and its settlement by a general council, underlined papal weakness that was exploited in the 1438 Pragmatic Sanction of Bourges, which allowed the papacy a say in the appointment to benefices in France but insisted that they had to be "received," that is to say, registered, in France. The Pragmatic Sanction was more clearly delineated in the 1516 Concordat of Bologna, negotiated between Pope Leo X and King Francis I, which gave the king the right to nominate to major benefices, though the approval of the papacy still had to be sought. This gave the king enormous influence over the Church in France while weakening the authority of the papacy, but because of the role of the monarchy, which now presented itself as the guarantor of the *Libertés de l'Église gallicane*, the Bologna Concordat was not well received either by the Parlement of Paris or by the University of Paris, setting up, as events were to show, even more obstacles to the establishment of the Society in France.

The problem became evident as soon as Broët attempted to get recognition from the Parlement of Paris. Henry II had issued letters patent recognizing the Society in France, and these had been repeated by Francis II. Parlement procrastinated, despite Francis's insistence and that of his successor, his ten-year-old brother Charles X, whose mother, Catherine de Médici, was acting as regent. It was agreed that a decision be remitted to a meeting in Poissy, not far from Paris, which Catherine had called not to discuss the Society but to attempt to reconcile Catholics and Huguenots. Pope Pius IV sent as his representatives Juan de Polanco and the recently appointed Jesuit general, Diego Laínez, who told the queen regent she had no business involving herself in matters of religion. The 1561 Colloquy of Poissy, as it has become known, brought modest gains for the Huguenots, paving the way for an edict of toleration the following year. It also brought modest gains for the Society, whose problems were tacked on to the end of the discussions.

Behind the Jesuits' call for recognition of their legal status in the French capital were the French cardinals; opposing it was the extremely powerful—and very Gallican—archbishop of Paris. The issue was the establishment of a college in Paris. The funds to do so had come from an admirer of the Society, the bishop of Clermont, Guillaume du Prat, who had already financed the first Jesuit college in France, that at Billom, in 1556 and a second one, posthumously, at Mauriac in 1563. With the money he had bequeathed them, the Jesuits acquired a building close to the University of Paris that, in the late bishop's memory, they called the College de Clermont. The agreement that had been reached at Poissy gave them the right to open the college, but only as a corporation of clerics, to be known as the Society of the College of Clermont, not as a religious order called the Society of Jesus. For the fathers to teach they had to obtain the approval of the university. This was forthcoming, but not full incorporation into the university itself. Nonetheless, the College of Clermont proved a great success in attracting students, so much so that the university protested to the pope, who eventually ordered the removal of the Jesuits' star lecturer, Juan de Maldonado (1533–1583).[4]

Maldonado was also much in demand as a preacher, including at the royal court where he converted some of the nobility from their Protestantism back to Roman Catholicism. As has been remarked, colleges were not only educational institutions but also centers from which preachers went out to convert Huguenots or to instruct the faithful in their catechism. Auger, mentioned above (p. 178), was not only the court preacher[5] to the de Guise cardinal of Lorraine but also the author of a catechism that rather oddly appeared without the permission of his superiors and, even odder, a book printed in 1568 titled *Le Pedagogie d'Armes* that, like some of his more bellicose confreres in Vienna or Munich, called for a crusade against the Protestants. He also served as an army chaplain. It is at least debatable whether force of arms or the power of preaching did more to halt the advance of Protestantism in France. William Bangert has no doubt. "Far more convincing than the military sallies of the League," he writes, "the ardent and colourful words of this Champagnois [Auger] brought back Calvinists by the thousands. In scenes reminiscent of the Acts of the Apostles, whole colonies of Huguenots through central and southern France, such as nearly two thousand in Lyon alone, returned to the [Catholic] faith."[6] It was not only French Jesuits who engaged in this enterprise because the Spaniard Juan de Maldonado just mentioned was also much involved, as was the Italian Antonio Possevino (for Possevino, see above, p. 58).

With all the difficulties that the Society was experiencing with the Parlement of Paris it is easy to overlook the welcome it received within the jurisdictions of other cities' parlements, especially in the Western region of France, some of which were actively seeking the establishment of colleges. But, especially given its proximity to the royal court, it was the Paris Parlement that really mattered, and it remained hostile. When in December 1594 Jean Châtel attempted

---

[4] On this conflict with the archbishop of Paris, see Bangert, *A History of the Society of Jesus*, 67–71.

[5] "Claude de la Tour de Turenne, Countess of Tournon, had complained about the length of [Auger's] sermons. Auger promised Laínez that he would limit them to an hour, thereby satisfying both God and the Countess" (Martin, *The Jesuit Mind*, 128).

[6] Bangert, *A History of the Society of Jesus*, 66.

to assassinate Henry IV, it emerged that he had been a student at the Jesuit-run College of Clermont; the Society was blamed for the assault on the king's life, and its members were expelled from Paris and some other parts, though not regions, of France. The king readmitted them in 1603, though the College of Clermont did not reopen until 1618, took a Jesuit, Pierre Coton, as his confessor, and endowed the College of La Flèche. In May 1610 François Ravaillac succeeded in doing what Châtel had failed to do: Ravaillac, described as a fanatical Catholic, had tried to become a Jesuit but had been rejected. It should be remarked that the assassination of Henry III in 1589 was committed by Jacques Clément, who was a Dominican lay brother, but it was the Society that, much to the embarrassment of the French Jesuits, became associated with the doctrine of tyrannicide. That Jesuits had been behind plots to assassinate Elizabeth I and then her successor on the English throne, James I, was widely believed and not just in England (see above, p. 170).

And then, even more troublesome, there was the problem of the book by the Spanish Jesuit, Juan de Mariana (1535–1624), published in 1599, *De Rege et Regis Institutione* ("On the King and the Institution of Kingship"). He argued, and quite correctly, that the killing of tyrants was commonplace in scholastic textbooks dealing with politics. It was a prince's duty to look after the welfare of his subjects, and if he failed in this, then the commonwealth was justified in removing him by force if other remedies had failed. It was not only Jesuit theologians who believed this, he pointed out, but Dominican ones as well because it was under Dominican masters that Jacques Clément had studied. In the original edition Mariana had praised Clément's actions. On Acquaviva's instructions this was removed from the 1605 edition, as were other hostile comments about Henry III, but this did not prevent the Paris Parlement in 1610 ordering the book to be burned and all discussion of tyrannicide to cease. Conscious of the damage that had been done to the Society in France (and also in England where James I argued correctly that according to Jesuit theory the pope could authorize his assassination), Acquaviva reiterated the ban in 1614—and the pope did so in 1625.

When Henry IV ordered the readmission of the Jesuits it was against protests from the Parlement of Paris. One of the most impassioned speeches against the Society came from Antoine Arnauld, who cited the Portuguese Jesuit Emmanuel Sà as writing in favor of tyrannicide. The controversy gave rise to some of the earliest publications in launching the "Black Legend" of the Society, with Étienne Pasquier's *Catéchisme des Jésuites* of 1603 arguing that the Society had no other aim than its own domination and Caspar Schoppe's *Mysteria Patrum Jesuitarum*, which rehashes—correctly and with references—arguments for tyrannicide in the writings of Mariana and others.[7]

If the controversy about tyrannicide gradually abated, the hostility of the Paris Parlement did not, and it was not long before another major controversy threatened to engulf the Society, and not just in France, though France was the epicentre. It turned on the doctrine of grace, about which Jesuits found themselves to be at odds with the Dominicans, although, rather oddly, it also involved the status of Jesuits' vows.

In 1582 a Dominican, Diego Peredo, advanced the argument publicly that the simple vows taken by Jesuits after completing their noviceship did not make them members of a religious order—only solemn vows could do that. As Jesuits did not, and still do not, commonly pronounce their solemn vows until after ten or more years as members of the Society, had Peredo's argument any validity it would have undermined the Society's structure, and the Dominican could not be allowed to go unchallenged. The pope was appealed to, and he issued a bull, *Quanto Fructuosus*, in February the following year upholding the Jesuit Constitution. This did not silence Peredo, who claimed both that the pope had been misinformed and that the bull had been written in a private capacity rather than as a pope legislating for the whole Church. As a consequence Acquaviva turned to Pope Gregory for a second time, and he issued another bull, *Ascendente Domino*, in May 1584, again supporting a Jesuit's simple vows. Peredo continued his campaign, however, by claiming that the bull had not been issued in proper legal form. Though Peredo was silenced by his provincial, he received unexpected backing from Domingo Bañez (1528–1604), the most famous Dominican theologian of the

---

[7] For Pasquier, see Dale Van Kley, *Reform Catholicism and the International Suppression of the Jesuits* (New Haven, CT: Yale University Press, 2018), 69, and for Schoppe, Harro Höpfl, *Jesuit Political Thought: The Society of Jesus and the State, c. 1540–1630* (Cambridge: Cambridge University Press, 2004), 338. Höpfl says the German publication was anonymous and gives the date as "2nd edition, 1633," though I can find no reference to an earlier edition.

day and from 1580 professor of theology in the University of Salamanca. He gave permission in December 1589 for the thesis to be publicly defended in the university that only those in solemn vows were members of a religious order. The controversy was well known, and as a consequence there was quite a gathering for the public defense of the thesis when, just as the young Dominican who was propounding it was launching into his opening remarks, it was rather dramatically banned on the orders of the papal nuncio in Spain, a *coup de théâtre* engineered by the Spanish Jesuits. All this was accompanied on both sides by what the Jesuit historian James Brodrick described as a "display of vituperative rhetoric when the occasion offered."[8]

Behind all this controversy there was a matter of greater moment, one that had its origins in the debates at the Council of Trent (see above, p. 37). It had been one of the contentions of the Reformers that human beings had been so corrupted by original sin that they were totally unable even to cooperate in their salvation: it was only by faith alone, a free gift from God, that they could be saved. Catholic theologians rejected this view of human nature, but it left undecided just how the faithful could cooperate in their salvation. All were agreed that grace, freely bestowed by God, was a determining factor. But then in this understanding what part did free will play? How could one avoid the trap of predestination, rejected by all Catholic scholars? The Jesuit theologian Luis de Molina proposed a solution in a four-volume commentary on Thomas Aquinas's *Summa Theologiae* titled *De liberi arbitrii cum gratiae donis, divina praescientia, praedestinatione et reprobatione concordia* ("A reconciliation of free will with the gifts of grace, God's foreknowledge, predestination, and condemnation"), published in Lisbon in 1588. As the title indicated, God must have foreknowledge of all human actions, but in which case, how can they be free? Molina's solution was to propose what he called "middle knowledge," *scientia media*. In this explanation, God's knowledge

---

[8] This reference is somewhat problematic. Brodrick wrote *The Life and Work of Blessed Robert Francis Cardinal Bellarmine, S.J., 1542–1621* (London: Burns, Oates and Washbourne, 1928). The above quote is not taken from this text, however, but from a version of the same in the Heythrop Library that was printed but never published because of objections by the Westminster diocesan censors. The controversial chapter, titled "Jesuits and Dominicans," is what would have been the first chapter in the second volume of Brodrick's biography of the saint, and the quotation is on p. 3.

does not extend simply to what a person will do but to all possible choices that he or she might make, leaving the individual to freely choose among them—though still assisted by God's grace. God brings about an individual's acts through "efficacious grace," which involves the free consent of the human will, and is not different from merely "sufficient grace," which enables an individual to carry out a salutary act, if the person consents to and cooperates with it. While this could hardly be described as an elegant solution to a theological conundrum that goes back at least as far as St. Augustine of Hippo (354–430), it was a solution of sorts, and Jesuits rallied to their confrere's side when the *Concordia* was attacked.

And attacked it was. In 1594 the Spanish Inquisition decided to update the index of banned books, and Bañez was included in the commission set up to advise on the revision. There was even a suggestion that he was intent on including many other works by Jesuits, not least the 1591 *Ratio Studiorum*. Molina heard about these proposals and got in a preventive strike. He wrote to the Inquisition with, side-by-side, quotations from Luther and Calvin, suggesting that Bañez was tainted with Lutheranism. There were various debates in Spain that became so bitter that the matter of *Concordia* was referred to the pope, who in turn referred it to Robert Bellarmine, not yet a cardinal (he became one in 1599). In reporting on the issues he was remarkably even-handed, admitting that he found his fellow Jesuit often difficult to follow, while rejecting the claim by Bañez that *scientia media* was a novelty (there was no greater criticism, in the theological jargon of the day, than to say something was a "novelty"): the term itself may have been new; the concept, on the other hand, he argued, was not.

While Bellarmine was considering the issues referred to him, the pope instructed both Jesuits and Dominicans to cease their controversy. The Dominicans were unhappy with this ruling, and Bañez wrote to the pope saying that only the Jesuits should be ordered to keep silent as the Dominicans were only propounding traditional doctrines. Clement VIII handed this petition too over to Bellarmine. He was unpersuaded but suggested a way forward. The two sides were to stop attacking each other and especially stop accusing the other of teaching heresy, though they should remain free to criticize the views of the other party.

Clement did not follow this advice. Instead he set up a seven-member commission to examine the *Concordia*, which managed to decide in three months that it should be condemned. The pope expressed surprise at the speed with which they had reached their decision and told them to give it further thought. This time they took eight months before coming to the same conclusion. Clement was, however, in no hurry to censure Molina, who had written a lengthy defense of himself—and an attack on Bañez. Clement's next proposal was to call the two generals of the orders together, with theological advisers, to debate the matter. They met three times, but the death of the presiding cardinal brought the meetings to an end. The pope then reverted to his earlier proposal of a commission to study Molina's book, and the commissioners, still hostile to the Jesuit theologian, produced twenty propositions from the *Concordia* that they believed ought to be condemned. The Jesuits naturally produced a defense, backed by Bellarmine.

The pile of documents was getting ever higher, and the pope was not in a position to digest them all. Instead, early in 1602 he proposed that there should be a series of debates on the issues conducted in his presence. They took place at intervals between 1602 and 1605, sixty-eight meetings and thirty-seven debates.[9] There is no accurate account of them, according to James Brodrick, but what evidence survives strongly suggests that Clement VIII was more in sympathy with the views of the Dominicans than he was with Molina and the Jesuits.[10] He had, moreover, sent the Society's most able defender, Robert Bellarmine, away from Rome by appointing him bishop of Capua.

Both Molina and Bañez had died while the meetings were still going on. Clement VIII died in 1605, to be succeeded by Leo XI, but Leo survived only a matter of weeks. Paul V, Leo's successor, was much more sympathetic to the Society and brought Bellarmine back to Rome as an adviser. The members of the commission, however, did not change. They once again presented a list of propositions from the *Concordia* that they claimed were worthy of condemnation. The pope, on the other hand, was swayed by Bellarmine's arguments that the Dominican version was too close for comfort to the position of

---

[9] They are known collectively as the Congregationes de Auxiliis, "meetings abut help," where "help" means the assistance of grace. Purists would point out that "Auxiliis" is plural, "helps."

[10] Brodrick, *Bellarmine*, 37.

Calvin and Luther and decided to defer judgment until a later date, after the matter had been given wider airing. No papal judgment ever came, but both sides in the debate were ordered by Pope Paul not to publish books on the controversy, a ban twice repeated by Paul's successor-but-one, Urban VIII.

The above account has skated over most of the theological niceties of the controversy, but they remained seared in Jesuit minds down to fairly recent times. But what should be evident from what has been said is that most Jesuit theologians, when faced with the dilemma of pitting God's grace against human freedom to choose, came down firmly on the side of a person's free choice. This became even more prominent in the next controversy to engulf the Society, an issue that lasted in one form or another for some two centuries: probabilism.

In some ways the debate over probabilism, an issue of individual responsibility for moral choices, was more contentious than that with the Dominicans over grace and free will, because, as will be seen, it threatened to divide the Society. The theory of probabilism was expressed first by a Spanish Dominican, Bartolomé de Medina (1527–1580), who taught first at Valladolid and afterward at Salamanca. Commenting on Thomas Aquinas in a work published in 1577 he wrote that, when making a moral decision, "if an opinion is probable it is licit to follow it, even if the opposite is more probable." This might seem to fly in the face of common sense, but the reasoning behind it is clear enough: if the right course of action is not absolutely clear, then the choice of what to do lies with the individual conscience. In his *The Making of Moral Theology: A Study of the Roman Catholic Tradition*, John Mahoney quotes the *Dictionnaire de Théologie Catholique*:

> The tutiorist would advocate obedience to the law or any other course which was the safer [*tutior*] to follow, the probabiliorist would urge doing what seemed the more likely [*probabilior*] to be right, the equiprobabilist would judge that either of equally balanced alternatives could be followed, and the simple probabilist would reply that any action was morally justified for which a good case could be made.[11]

---

[11] John Mahoney, *The Making of Moral Theology: A Study of the Roman Catholic Tradition* (Oxford: Clarendon Press, 1987), 137.

Most Jesuits opted to be probabilists, while most Dominicans, despite Bartolomé de Medina being the recognized origin of probabilism, became probabiliorists.

It was not a simple free-for-all. A "probable" opinion was not simply one an individual dreamed up for him- or herself: it had to have some authority behind it. This authority might be intrinsic, namely, the strength of the argument, but it was normally taken to be extrinsic.[12] That is to say, some distinguished moral theologian or canon lawyer is believed to have held that such-and-such a course of action was morally permissible. That, at least, was the theory. In practice, however, few individuals faced with moral choices were likely to consult weighty tomes, even were they to be available; a confessor might have more knowledge of the choices available, but he was not likely to be sitting in a confessional balancing on his knee the writings of one moralist against those of a different moralist on the other knee, trying to decide which opinion was more probable than another. It was just not practicable. St. Thomas Aquinas, however, had insisted that in making a moral choice one was obliged to follow the safer (*tutior*) course, and that teaching was to be found in the Society's Constitutions.[13]

Hearing confessions was the preeminent ministry of the fathers of the Society, and several Jesuits produced manuals for confessors, some of which ran to many editions. At first they embraced the "more probable" or "safer" option in making moral choices as recommended in the Constitutions, but when, in 1600, Acquaviva was asked whether there ought to be one author to be followed in these matters so that there would be, among Jesuits, a uniformity of practice, he replied that every confessor should be allowed to follow a probable opinion.[14] What had happened to change the attitude of the Jesuit superior general and most of the members of the Society, though there was no Society-wide instruction that they were to embrace probabilism? According to Robert Maryks, the experience of teaching in colleges, and especially of teaching the corpus of Cicero's letters, had alerted Jesuits to the importance of prudential judgments that turned on probability: they "employed Ciceronian probability in the weekly

---

[12] In defining probabilism, Bartolomé de Medina had prioritized extrinsic authority over intrinsic.

[13] Maryks, *Saint Cicero and the Jesuits*, 72.

[14] Ibid., 87.

lectures on cases of conscience."[15] Emphasis on choosing the safer option, or the more probable one, would inevitably lead to scrupulosity as an individual weighed up the choices, and though Ignatius's Constitutions may have recommended making the "safer" choice, in a section of the *Spiritual Exercises* he warns against the danger of scruples as well as advising the spiritual director in Annotation 7 of the *Exercises* to be "gentle and kind," advice that was readily adaptable to the confessional.

The first Jesuit to adopt the teaching of Bartolomé de Medina was Gabriel Vázquez, who had been lecturing at Alcalá since 1579, in his commentary on Thomas Aquinas published in 1599, and remarkably quickly this became the practice of Jesuit confessors. It may indeed have avoided scrupulosity but was in danger of the opposite problem, being too lax in moral decision making. Some books that appeared to advocate laxism were put on the Index—though this was later, in the 1660s and 1670s. Acquaviva himself, while advocating probabilism, had warned against the danger, and from 1645 the Society attempted to restrict laxist teachings: in 1650 a general congregation of the Society declared that some teachings, especially on sexual morality, were not to be held by Jesuits and imposed a stricter internal censorship. But by this time a much more dangerous controversy was underway.

It began with the publication in 1643 of a book titled *Augustinus* by Cornelius Jansenius (Jansen) (1585–1638), who became rector of the University of Louvain in 1635 and the following year the bishop of Ypres, promoted to that office, it seems, on the recommendation of Philip IV of Spain: Jansen had written a pamphlet, *Mars Gallicus*, criticizing the policy of Cardinal Richelieu, who had linked France with Dutch Protestants in an alliance against Spain. The full title of his magnum opus is *Augustinus Cornelii Jansenii, Episcopi, seu Doctrina Sancti Augustini de Humanae Naturae, Sanitate, Aegritudine, Medicina adversus Pelagianos et Massilienses* ("The Augustine of Cornelius Jansen, Bishop, or the Teaching of St. Augustine about Human Nature, Health, Sickness, and a Remedy against the Pelagians and Massilians").[16] As a student at Louvain Jansen had been much influenced by the writings of Michel du Bay, commonly known in theological circles as

---

[15] Ibid., 105: hence the "Saint Cicero" of his book's title.

[16] The Paris edition of the *Augustinus* contained an appendix, not written by Jansen, claiming that all who died without baptism, including infants, would go to hell.

Baius, who taught that original sin had so corrupted human nature that people's actions were inevitably evil. Redemption had restored the ability to do good because of gratuitous grace, but this grace was given to some and withheld from others. These views, similar to those held by Calvinists, were vigorously attacked by Jesuit theologians at their college in Louvain, and seventy-nine propositions from his writings were condemned by Pius V in his 1567 bull *Ex omnibus afflictionibus*. The condemnation was renewed by Gregory XIII a dozen years later, though Baius himself was not mentioned by name. Despite these censures, Baius, who claimed he had submitted to the papal ruling, retained his professorship and in 1575 even became the university's chancellor.

While a student at Louvain Jansen shared lodging with Jean du Vergier de Hauranne, better known as the Abbé Saint-Cyran (1581–1643),[17] and in many ways he was central to the spread of Jansen's teachings—Jansenism—throughout France. Saint-Cyran was a relatively well-connected and wealthy man and had supported Jansen financially. From 1611 to 1614 the two had studied the fathers of the Church together, concentrating especially on St. Augustine, while living in a house in Bayonne belonging to the family of Vergier de Hauranne. Aware that the views they were formulating were at the very least controversial, given the condemnation of Baius, they used code in their correspondence. It was Vergier de Hauranne who encouraged Jansen to write and to publish the *Augustinus*. In 1633 Saint-Cyran became spiritual director and confessor of the Parisian Abbey of Port Royal, founded in 1625 by the abbess Jacqueline-Marie-Angélique Arnauld, Mère Angélique, whose younger brother Antoine has already been mentioned (see above, p. 182).

It was Antoine Arnauld who led what the Jesuit theologian John Mahoney called "a major spirited attack" on the Society in his 1643 publication *Théologie Morale des Jésuites*, which drew on the writings of Jesuit moralists to show that the probabilism they espoused led

---

[17] He held the title *in commendam* of "Abbot" of the monastery of Saint-Cyran in the town of Saint Michel-en-Brenne. *In commendam* implies that he could draw on the revenue of the abbey as his benefice, but he did not have jurisdiction over the monks. The monastery was suppressed in 1712, but its remaining buildings, renamed St. Michael's Abbey, was acquired by the schismatic Society of St. Pius X, which for a time it gave shelter to the French Nazi collaborator Paul Touvier.

inexorably to a laxity in morals and eventually to a decline in religion itself. In the same year, although it had been written two years before, he published a book attacking the Jesuit promotion of frequent Communion. This was, he claimed, against the practice of the early Church: the sacrament should be received infrequently, and only after an act of pure contrition for one's sins, even for minor peccadillos, "venial sins" in the jargon of Catholic discourse. Nothing else would do. As the Jesuits attacking Arnauld insisted, this degree of contrition was next to impossible to achieve and would lead to the widespread abandonment of the sacrament. "The rigorous and oppressive nature of Jansenist piety," remarks Mahoney, presents "Jesus as a severe and inscrutable redeemer" who died to bring salvation, not to all, but only to the few because God's grace is not available to all to make it possible for them to obey God's commandments.[18]

The Jesuits had attempted to prevent the publication of the *Augustinus* but had failed. The Roman Inquisition condemned it in 1641, as well as several Jesuit books and pamphlets, not because they contained errors, but because they contravened the papal ruling that nothing further should be produced on the grace and free will debate. Jansen's book was explicitly condemned in the bull *In Eminenti* dated June 19, 1643, but there were problems both about the bull's authenticity in general and with the text itself, and Arnauld made the most of them in *Premieres* and *Secondes Observations sur la bulle*, both of which appeared in August 1643. The Parlement of Paris, it may be recalled, had to "register" documents coming from Rome (see above, p. 179), and this it refused to do, so great an impression had been made by Arnauld's attack on the bull. Neither Richelieu nor his successor Cardinal Mazarin were sympathetic to the Jansenists, and Mazarin saw opposition to Jansenism as a means of gaining favor in Rome. Meanwhile, many in France, including Jansenists, were also Gallican in sentiment, which made an appeal to Rome problematic. One anti-Jansenist, the bishop of Vabres, produced five propositions that he described as Jansenist and at the end of 1650 sent them off

---

[18] Mahoney, *The Making of Moral Theology*, 94. Even Voltaire, who, as Mahoney notes, was "no friend of his former schoolmasters, the Jesuits," wrote that "I know of no sect more barbarous and more dangerous than the Jansenists. They are worse than the Scottish Presbyterians" (ibid., 94–95). Mahoney, it is perhaps worth noting, is a Scotsman.

to Pope Innocent X. The pope handed the matter over to two commissions, one of cardinals, the other of theologians. In the bull *Cum occasione* of May 31, 1653, Innocent, who was as anxious to improve relations with France as Mazarin was to improve relations with Rome, condemned the five propositions: four of them were declared heretical, and the other one as simply erroneous.

The French Jesuits now attempted to seize the initiative. In 1654 King Louis XIV's Jesuit confessor, François Annat, published *Chicanes des Jansénistes* in which he claimed that the five propositions could be found in the *Augustinus*. Arnauld responded, claiming that only one of the five was to be found in the controversial book, in a context that made it entirely orthodox, and that, although the other propositions could be found, though not verbatim, in Jansen's text, they too were in context perfectly in keeping with Catholic doctrine. Arnauld's arguments were taken up by the mathematician Blaise Pascal (1623–1662), who had been converted to Jansenism by the doctors who happened to treat his father for a dislocated hip. For a time Pascal became intensely religious, and though his religiosity declined after a while, it revived when his sister entered the convent of Port Royal. In January 1656 there appeared the first—there were eighteen in all—of his highly popular *Lettres Provinciales*, the fifth of which was an explicit attack, by a far more accomplished writer and polemicist than the Jesuit, on the book by François Annat. The main object of his invective was the Jesuits' moral laxism, as a consequence of their embrace of probabilism. He was on safe ground. In France rigorism in morals was in the ascendant, and there was a ready audience for Pascal's *Lettres*. They were widely read, and not just in France. When successive popes, Alexander VII and Innocent XI, came to condemn laxist propositions, fifty of them were drawn from Pascal's writings. Annat made an attempt to respond, but he lacked the skill and popular appeal of Pascal.[19] As William Bangert remarks, too often Jesuit response to Jansenist attacks were written not in French but in Latin. "With formidable learning and vast erudition the Jesuit apolo-

---

[19] For an accessible survey of the controversy, see Louis Cognet, "Ecclesiastical Life in France," in *The Church in the Age of Absolutism and Enlightenment*, ed. Hubert Jedin and John Dolan (London: Burns and Oates, 1981), 24–56. Cognet writes, "By identifying Jesuits with laxism, Pascal discredited the Society of Jesus to such an extent that they could never quite overcome it" (44).

gists endeavoured to correct the false image of the Society, but those qualities of style, verve, sauciness which might have made them a match for Pascal, they did not have."[20]

The Society had many enemies among the clergy, both priests and bishops, who felt that with their many privileges its members had an unfair advantage in their dealings with the faithful. There were some among the episcopacy who sided with the Society, but their most powerful defenders were the successive kings whom they had served as confessors, and in particular Louis XIV, but Louis's support was conditional and had to be fostered. When in 1675 Louis came into conflict with Pope Innocent XI, the royal confessor, de la Chaize, took the side of the king against the pope, writing to the General that he had done so, against the Society's usual pro-papal stance, because of all the benefits that Louis had brought to the Church.

The dispute between king and pontiff was over the right to appoint to bishoprics—and to draw on their revenues. To settle the matter Louis XIV called an assembly to be held in Paris in March 1682, which was attended by thirty-six bishops and thirty-four deputies. In the course of this gathering the bishop of Meaux, Jacques-Benigne Bossuet (1627–1704), a famous preacher and, until the year before, the tutor of the dauphin, presented the bishops and their representatives with what became known as the four Gallican Articles. Bossuet was highly esteemed both for his admirable life and for his zeal for Catholicism, which was no doubt why he was given the task, though the real begetter was the archbishop of Paris, a confidant of the king and a much more doubtful character. The first of Bossuet's articles proclaimed the authority of kings against popes and civil law against ecclesiastical law. The second reiterated the claim by Edmond Richer, a member of theology faculty of the Sorbonne, in his *De ecclesiastica et civili potestate libellus* of 1611 that because what theologians call the "Deposit of Faith" had been entrusted to the whole Church, therefore only the whole Church could make pronouncements about it, that is to say, only a general council consisting of representatives of the Church. This effectively subordinated the pope to such a council, as had indeed been envisaged by the decree *Haec Sancta* approved by the Council of Constance in April 1415. The third of the Gallican

---

[20] Bangert, *A History of the Society of Jesus*, 207.

Articles reasserted the ancient rights and privileges of the French Church,[21] while the fourth claimed that although the pope was the main teaching authority within Catholicism, his teachings were not irreformable until they had been approved by a general council. Three days after this declaration had been adopted by the assembly, Louis ordered that it be taught in the universities and seminaries.

The pope, the austere Innocent XI, immediately rejected the Gallican Articles and refused to issue the bulls of appointment to any bishop who ascribed to them, thereby leaving many bishoprics vacant. Louis retaliated by trying to force Innocent's hand, occupying papal possessions within France, imprisoning the papal nuncio, and forbidding bishops and Jesuits to have any contact with Rome. Not that all French Jesuits were hostile to the king; a good number of them, including the Louis's confessor, were sympathetic to the declaration.

In January 1688 Louis was secretly informed by Rome that he and his ministers had been excommunicated. Though Louis appears not to have been unduly disturbed by these spiritual sanctions, the 1688 invasion of England by his arch rival William of Orange was a different matter, and he was now eager to make his peace with the papacy. Innocent died in August of the following year without the excommunication being lifted or reconciliation being achieved, and while his successor, Alexander VIII, brought about a partial reconciliation he still would not recognize the appointment of any bishop who did not reject the Gallican Articles. The dispute therefore dragged on into the pontificate of the pious Innocent XII. In 1693 Louis agreed to withdraw the declaration of a decade earlier and not to have it taught in the universities and schools. Gallicanism itself, however, remained a powerful force among the clergy, as well as within the University of Paris, and much of the hostility to the Society of Jesus in France in the eighteenth century sprang from its members' commitment to upholding the authority of the papacy.

Meanwhile the Jesuits were having quite separate problems of their own, though they were distantly linked to the situation in France. In July 1687 the Society elected Tirso González de Santalla (1624–1705) as its thirteenth superior general. González had enjoyed an impres-

---

[21] In 1594 a lawyer of the Paris Parlement, Pierre Pithou, had produced a formal list of these "Liberties" of the French Church. He calculated there were eighty-three of them.

sive career, both as a theology professor and as a missionary preacher, especially in rural Spain. Given his reputation, it is not surprising that he was chosen to be a delegate to the general congregation that was called after the death of the Belgian Charles de Noyelle. It is much more surprising, however, that he was elected to succeed Noyelle. It was a curious choice for several reasons. He was a Spaniard and was elected just at the moment when Louis XIV, already in conflict with the French Jesuits over the Gallican Articles, was at his most anti-Spanish. Even worse, González had written a book, published in Rome soon after his election despite de la Chaize's appeal that he not do so, that was a direct attack on Gallicanism and claimed infallibility for the papacy, citing many French Jesuits as writing in defense of the doctrine. And what is more, unlike the vast majority of his fellow Jesuits, but like Innocent XI, which has led to the assumption, possible but still unproven, that the pope had somehow intervened in the election, he was well-known as a probabiliorist. It was González himself who promoted the idea that Innocent, who had condemned sixty-five propositions declared to be "lax," had been responsible for the choice in order to present his election as being providential, a call to rid the Society of the scourge of probabilism.[22]

González was not the only Jesuit who opposed probabilism, but his election as general made him by far the most prominent. He had long campaigned against the doctrine. He had written to the provincial of the Castile province in 1671 trying to bring about a change in policy. The following year he wrote to the general asking him if he might publish his book against the doctrine—and dedicate it to him. He received no reply. In 1674 he again petitioned the provincial of Castile, asking permission to publish his book, and when, two years later, he was appointed to the royal chair of theology at Salamanca, he had a prestigious base from which to conduct his crusade, much to the distress of his Jesuit community. In his *Fundamentum Theologiae Moralis* ("On the foundation of moral theology") he gave as his reason for opposing probabilism the experience of trying to convert his

---

[22] Jean-Pascal Gay, *Jesuit Civil Wars: Theology, Politics and Government under Tirso González* (London: Routledge, 2012), 107. Innocent XI "desired strongly to see me elected General," González claimed in 1687, and Innocent made this clear to the general vicar when he went to the pope to ask for his blessing on the general congregation. He was, however, elected by only forty-six out of eighty-six votes. Ibid., 155.

penitents to a holier way of life: instead of the rigorist choices he put before them, they opted for a probable opinion, which suited them better.[23]

González continued his campaign to get permission to have his book attacking probabilism published, but in June 1674 Jesuit censors turned it down, arguing, among other reasons, that alternative theories undermined the Jesuit vow of obedience. A subject, they said, might disobey his superior on the grounds that his opinion was more probable than that of the superior, and therefore to act in accordance with the superior's wishes—if one adhered to probabiliorism—would be sinful. It often happened, admitted the censors, that the subject was more knowledgeable than the superior, but this was no reason for disobeying.[24]

Even after he had been elected general, González still had to struggle to have his *Fundamentum Theologiae Moralis* published. In 1691 he sent a letter to the Jesuit rector in Dilingen to have some fifteen hundred to two thousand copies printed and sent to Rome, and he later asked if some of the University of Dilingen's theologians would write to the pope in praise of it. Instead of praising it, however, they were strongly critical. The pope's personal theologian, known by the rather grand title of the master of the sacred palace, told González that the book had been denounced for having been printed without the approval of Jesuit censors. As general, he replied, he was not bound by the Society's laws.

A Jesuit general had then—and still has—a number of advisers called "assistants" who represent geographical areas, in other words, a group of contiguous provinces, or in some instances particular forms of the Jesuit apostolate.[25] In a memorandum to the pope the assistants did not simply criticise González's book but his method of governing, his unshakeable conviction that he was right, and his seeking the support of princes. Charles II of Spain had ordered his subjects who were members of the Society to defend González and

[23] Elsewhere, however, he claims that he opposed probabilism because it would bring the Society into disrepute, as was, of course, the case in France (ibid., 106).

[24] Ibid., 148.

[25] These regional groupings are called "assistencies," and though the usual structure is an assistency of adjacent provinces, occasionally there are other reasons for linking them together.

instructed his ambassador in Rome to do likewise, and the Austrian Emperor Leopold, who for reasons of his own wanted to ally himself with Spain, also backed the general. The pope now asked him to select a number of Jesuits to act as censors. They reported in 1693 and when, the following year, the Inquisition gave final approval for its publication, they stipulated it had to be amended in the light of the Jesuit censors' comments. It was promptly printed in Rome, and widely distributed, but the criticism did not stop despite González's attempts to suppress it.

Most important, he had to prevent the calling of a general congregation. While such a gathering could not remove him from his post, it might at the very least inhibit his actions in favor of probabiliorism. The Society was unusual among religious orders of having general congregations only—except in special circumstances—to elect a new superior general. Innocent X had decreed that there should be a meeting of procurators every nine years, and González did his best to hold up such a gathering until he was able to put in places of authority members of the Society he judged to be sympathetic to his views. When provincial congregations were asked whether they thought a general congregation was needed in the current crisis, fourteen of the twenty-six, the slimmest of margins, voted that one was not necessary: those who voted against were the provinces where the members of the Society were subjects of either the king of Spain[26] or the emperor of Austria. They were voting, as Jean-Pascal Gay comments, along geopolitical lines as opponents of France.[27] Louis XIV, however, had a quite different agenda. Although close to the Society through his confessors, he wanted to make its governance French. He insisted that the boundaries of the French assistency should coincide with the territory over which he ruled and was not best pleased when González, a Spaniard, was chosen to replace the Belgian Noyelle. González did indeed agree to some redrawing of assistency boundaries, but he did not agree when Louis demanded that there be a French vicar general to oversee the French provinces. González

---

[26] When de Noyelle was elected general in 1682 he agreed to receive the ambassador of France before that of Charles II of Spain. Charles then broke off all communication between his government and the new general; cf. Bangert, *A History of the Society of Jesus*, 178.

[27] Ibid., 189.

believed he was constitutionally unable to do this, and Louis ordered all French members of the Jesuit headquarters in Rome, the curia, to return to France. He also instructed that members of the French assistency should have no dealings with González. It seemed for a time that there might be a schism in the Society, for a number of French Jesuits appeared as sympathetic to Louis's plans as they were to Gallicanism, but thanks largely to the diplomatic skills of de la Chaize this was avoided in the end.

In November 1700 Pope Clement XI succeeded Innocent XII. This presented González with another chance to impose probabiliorism on the Society, arguing that the Society's enemies used probabilism against it. He praised the 1700 declaration against probabilism of the French clergy, even though this had been an explicit attack on the Society. The pope was unmoved by González's plea to condemn probabilism, and when the fifteenth general congregation was summoned at the beginning of 1706 to elect González's successor, Clement made a point of saying that his choice was the person whom the electors chose, adding that the charge of laxism in moral teaching of which the Jansenists accused the Society was slanderous.[28]

Meanwhile a new Jansenist apologist had joined in the controversy. Pasquier Quesnel (1634–1719) had joined the Congregation of the French Oratory founded by Cardinal Pierre de Berulle. Berulle, an extremely holy man and a notable spiritual writer, shared that "sense of sin and the vastness of the dangers of damnation"[29] typical of Jansenism, and this much influenced Quesnel. So much so, indeed, that he was banished from Paris in 1681, taking refuge with the Cardinal Coislin, bishop of Orléans. His Jansenist sympathies became obvious in his 1671 book of reflections on the four gospels that eventually became—there were several editions with various titles—*Réflexions Morales sur le Nouveau Testament*. In 1685 he went to Brussels where he shared accommodation with Antoine Arnauld, but he was imprisoned in 1703 by order of the archbishop of Malines at the instigation of Philip V of Spain. He managed to escape from prison and fled to Amsterdam where he spent the remaining years of his life.

---

[28] Gay, *Jesuit Civil Wars*, 277.

[29] Michael J. Buckley, "Seventeenth-Century French Spirituality," in *Christian Spirituality Post-Reformation and Modern*, ed. Louis Dupré and Don E. Saliers (London: SCM Press, 1989), 51.

Though his *Réflexions* is not a systematic treatise, it summarizes the main doctrines of Jansenism, for example, that grace is irresistible but is not offered to all, yet without grace no one can do any morally good act, and that even acts that might on the face of it appear to be virtuous are not if they are performed by a sinner. These views were condemned by Pope Clement XI's brief *Universi Dominici Gregis* of 1708, and in true Gallican fashion Quesnel appealed against the pope to a general council of the Church; his Gallicanism had already been evident when he produced a scholarly edition of the works of Pope Leo I, which, because of the Gallicanism displayed in Quesnel's commentary, had been put on the Index. When in 1713 Clement issued his bull *Unigenitus* condemning Jansenism, he was condemning 101 propositions taken from *Réflexions Morales sur le Nouveau Testament*.

The bull, over which there was conflict between Jesuits and Jansenists for the rest of the century leading up to the suppression of the Society, was issued by the pope on the urging of Louis XIV, but the king himself was almost certainly influenced by his devoutly Catholic—although she had been raised as a Protestant—wife, Madame de Maintenon.[30] She was an active opponent of Jansenism and had the nuns of Port Royal dispersed in 1709 and then the convent destroyed, even the graves in its cemetery, two years later. What Louis had perhaps overlooked was that the bull, to become effective in France had, in accordance with the in the 1438 Pragmatic Sanction of Bourges (see above, p. 179), to be registered by the Parlement. *Unigenitus* had been drawn up with special care in the hope of not offending Gallican sympathies, but its critics found other reasons to reject it. They claimed that some of the doctrines condemned could be found in the writings of the fathers of the Church and particularly in the teaching of St. Augustine. These venerable authors could not be condemned, so the fact that Clement had appeared to do so in the bull was evidence, they claimed, that the pope was not infallible. Louis called a special synod to meet in Paris. Some of the bishops attending, including the cardinal of Paris, Louis Antoine Noailles, demanded that, before they could accept the bull, the pope should show how it did not contradict St. Augustine. In the end forty bishops accepted the bull, only nine rejected it, and the pope wrote in praise

---

[30] Mde de Maintenon, it is believed, married Louis XIV in 1685, though there is no documentary evidence of the wedding.

of those who had agreed to it. This proved to be a mistake. The bull may have been drafted in such a way as to avoid upsetting Gallican sensitivities, but Clement's words gave the impression that the bishops were submitting to the papacy. In the end Louis forced acceptance of the bull on the Sorbonne, and it was published in roughly two-thirds of French dioceses.

Louis XIV died on September 1, 1715. His successor was his great grandson, Louis XV, but Louis was only five years old, and Philippe, duke of Orleans, son of Louis XIV's younger brother, became regent.[31] While Philippe had no great interest in religion, he tended to favor Jansenists and appointed a number of Jansenist bishops whom the pope refused to recognize. Cardinal Noailles, who had been opposed to Louis XIV, was now back in favor and said that, apart from the five Jesuits resident at court, he would not renew the licenses to preach or hear confessions in his diocese of any other members of the Society. The Sorbonne, dragooned into approving *Unigenitus* by Louis XIV, now declared it unacceptable, and its professors, together with the cardinal of Paris, called for a general council of the Church, a demand backed by Noailles. In 1716 a canon of Rheims cathedral, who had been exiled for Jansenism, now returned and published in 1716 *Du Renversement des Libertés de l'Église Gallicane*, something of a bestseller, which argued that bishops' decisions are valid only if they reflect the beliefs of the members of their dioceses, and especially those of their clergy, demonstrating that Gallicanism and Jansenism, both of which Jesuits rejected, were becoming fused together. Philippe of Orleans decreed in October 1717 that there should be an end to the public debates: it did not work. In the September of the following year Pope Clement, in *Pastoralis Officiis*, excommunicated anyone who did not accept *Unigenitus*, and that too was ineffectual in stopping the controversy.

Noailles died in May 1729, to be replaced as cardinal archbishop by Charles Gaspard de Vintimille du Lac, who was prepared to accept *Unigenitus*. Many theologians of the Sorbonne who opposed the bull were simply dismissed from their posts, and in 1730 the bull was made part of the laws of the French state, which meant that any clergy who refused to accept it could be deprived of their living. Some went into exile; others were jailed, with the result that the clergy were

---

[31] Louis XV came of age in mid-February 1723.

sidelined, and the lawyers of the Parlement of Paris became the chief opposition. "France was entirely Jansenist, except for the Jesuits and the bishops of the Roman party," wrote Voltaire in his history of the Parlement of Paris.[32]

Louis XV's attempt in 1754 to put an end to the propaganda war by silencing both parties, like earlier similar efforts, failed to make a difference despite the fact that—or perhaps because—it was five years later endorsed by Pope Clement XIII, who was known to be sympathetic to the Society. As Abbé Clément wrote, "He has a brother and a nephew who are Jesuits, and another nephew who is ultra-Jesuit; he is very ignorant, fully devoted to the Society, and given to the minutiae of piety."[33] The quarrel grew increasingly bitter, especially after it was proposed by the bishops that the last sacraments should be denied to dying Jansenists. The members of the Paris Parlement rejected this on the grounds that the condemnation of Jansenism contained in *Unigenitus* was not part of the law of the State as recognized by them. At the end of 1756 Louis issued an edict denying that the Parlement had any jurisdiction over the refusal of the sacraments to Jansenists.

Less than a month later there was an assassination attempt on the French king by Robert-François Damiens. This was part of a Jesuit conspiracy, claimed the Jansenists, on the grounds that the assailant had attended a Jesuit college and then worked in its kitchen—though why the Jesuits should want to kill a monarch who, for the most part, had supported them was not explained. It did not help that, at about the same time, a new edition appeared of the Jesuit Hermann Busenbaum's *Theologia Moralis*, originally published in 1645. In it the author supported the spiritual authority of the pope over the temporal authority of the king and argued, as many Jesuit political theorists had done before him, that a king's subjects had the right to revolt, even to the extent of assassinating the monarch, if he had proved to be a despotic ruler. The French Jesuits naturally denied any involvement in the assassination attempt and also in the publication of this new edition of the *Theologia Moralis*. Jansenists responded with the argument that, because of the doctrine of probabilism, they simply could

---

[32] Quoted by Dale Van Kley, *The Jansenists and the Expulsion of the Jesuits from France* (New Haven, CT: Yale University Press, 1975), 28.

[33] Quoted by Van Kley, *Reform Catholicism*, 113.

not be believed. That the Society had to be destroyed had been often talked about in Jansenist circles; now, in an issue dated June 2, 1759, it made its way into print in their journal, *Nouvelles Ecclésiastiques*.[34] But the story of how they achieved that end began not in France but in Portugal.

<hr/>

[34] See Van Kley *The Jansenists*, 70–79.

Chapter 8

The Path to Suppression

The eighteenth century had started reasonably well for the Society of Jesus with the issuing of the papal bull *Unigenitus* (see above, pp. 199ff.), but it ended disastrously with another bull, *Dominus ac Redemptor* of July 21, 1773, suppressing the Society throughout the world. In between there had been many setbacks, the most significant of which was perhaps the apostolic constitution *Ex quo Singulari* of July 11, 1742, which put an end to the Jesuits' many attempts to avoid condemnation of the Chinese Rites (see above, pp. 92ff.). Just over two years later, on September 13, 1744, came the bull *Omnium Sollicitudinum*, which suspended the Malabar Rites. As William Bangert remarks,

> In 1748 there were about 300,000 Christians in the area affected by *Omnium Sollicitudinum*. By 1840 they had dropped 60,000 to 240,000. What losses can be ascribed to the decision of the Holy See cannot be measured since war, famine, pestilence, and the removal of the Jesuits by the suppression all took their toll. Mid-eighteenth century marks a turning point. Till then the number of Catholics mounted. After that point it declined.[1]

The religious problems of the mid-eighteenth century were not confined to the Society; papal claims themselves also came under fire. The Gallicanism against which the Jesuits had battled in France entered the empire through the writings of Johann Nikolaus von Hontheim, a native of Trier, of which diocese Johann Nikolaus eventually became an assistant bishop. He had studied at Louvain under

[1] Bangert, *A History of the Society of Jesus*, 334.

the canon lawyer Zeger Bernhard Van Espen, a sturdy defender of Gallicanism, as a consequence of which his writings were put on the Index. In 1742 three electors of the empire, all of them archbishops, approached von Hontheim with a request that he study papal claims. He produced the result of his research two decades later with the title *De Statu Ecclesiae et Legitima Potestate Romani Pontificis* ("On the position of the Church and the legitimate authority of the bishop of Rome"). The book, published under the pseudonym of Justinus Febronius—hence his findings are known as "Febronianism"—followed typical Gallican lines, in particular elevating a general council of the Church above the authority of the pope and transferring from Rome to the local bishops many of the powers that, over the centuries, had accrued to the papacy. In 1764, two years after its publication, Febronius's book was put on the Index, and he was required to make a formal retraction of his claims, which to some extent he did in a volume published in 1781, though without damaging his integrity or entirely reneging on his convictions.

A policy similar to that advocated, if not carried through, by Febronius had to some extent already been implemented by the devout Austrian empress, Maria Theresa,[2] but in its more radical form it was the policy followed by Maria Theresa's son, the Holy Roman Emperor Joseph II, both within his Austrian provinces and in Belgium and Lombardy, which he also ruled. In particular he began a program of suppressing monasteries, or, rather, uniting the smaller ones in order to make them more viable, and, in a country where priest members of religious orders vastly outnumbered diocesan clergy, tried to redistribute clerics so that parishes were properly served. But the Society was admired by Joseph and his mother, especially for its commitment to education, and Joseph took no action against it until obliged to do so under pressure from France and Spain.[3]

---

[2] She had a Jesuit confessor, though a non-Jesuit was for the first time appointed in 1760.

[3] There is a sympathetic account of Josephinism in Derek Beale, "Joseph II and the Monasteries of Austria and Hungary," in *Religious Change in Europe, 1650–1914*, ed. Nigel Aston (Oxford: Clarendon Press, 1997), 161–84. On Maria Theresa's attitude to the Jesuits, "In 1775 the Empress gave remarkable testimony of her respect for Jesuit scholarship: she rejected the idea of forming a Vienna Academy on the ground that she would become a laughing stock, since nearly all those who could possibly be appointed to it were ex-Jesuits who, in obedience to the pope, she had just turned out of their houses" (170).

In 1786, under Joseph's brother Leopold, grand duke of Tuscany and himself a future holy Roman emperor, a synod was held at Pistoia that issued decrees imbued with both Gallicanism and Jansenism—decreeing, for example, that the authority of the Church as a whole in a general council was superior to that of the pope, and that bishops exercised their jurisdiction quite independently of Rome. It also recommended that all religious orders be abolished except the Benedictines, a proposal that would not in any case have affected the Society of Jesus, which by then had already been disbanded. The decrees, which also attacked popular devotions such as that to the Sacred Heart, which was very much part of Jesuit religious practice, proved to be unpopular. Eighty-five of the decrees were condemned by Pope Pius VI in *Auctorem Fidei* of 1794, and the bishop of Prato-Pistoia who had presided at the synod, Scipione d' Ricci, who had resigned his see in 1791 and had subsequently lived as a private citizen, submitted to the Holy See.

.None of these movements—Febronianism, Josephism, or the decrees of Pistoia—greatly affected Jesuits, not least because, as has just been remarked, by the date of the synod the fate of the Society had already been settled. But they were indicative of the attitudes within European governments that determined the Society's future. Saint John Henry Newman remarked that the suppression of the Society of Jesus was "one of the most mysterious matters in the history of the Church."[4] What may have seemed mysterious to Newman, writing less than a century after the event, does not seem quite so odd in the context that has just been described. And it has to be remembered that it occurred in what is often called "the age of the enlightened despots," when European governments were attempting, often fairly successfully, to centralize all authority, including that of the Church, into their own hands. There was a variety of forms of government in the many religious orders within Catholicism, but none had such close ties to Rome and the papacy as the Jesuit Order, and it therefore constituted an obvious and distinctive challenge to any policy of centralization that would subordinate the Church to the State. As

---

[4] Quoted by Jonathan Wright, "The Suppression and Restoration," in *The Cambridge Companion to the Jesuits*, ed. Thomas Worcester (Cambridge: Cambridge University Press, 2008), 263.

Emanuele Colombo and Niccolò Guasti remark in their account of the expulsion of Jesuits from Portugal and Spain,

> During and after the Seven Years' War [1756–1763], parts of the aristocracy and the clergy in the Iberian Peninsula had expressed growing opposition to the administrative (usually centralising) economic and religious reforms launched by the Portuguese and Spanish governments. As a result, these two governments chose to sacrifice the Jesuits in order to set a clear example to the privileged groups in society and to ensure that they would only play a subordinate role in the process of reform. During those years, both in the Iberian Peninsula and to a certain extent across Catholic Europe, there was a convergence among Enlightened sovereigns, reformist groups, Jansenists, and Enlightenment thinkers who perceived the fight against the Society of Jesus to be essential to the birth of a new social order.[5]

But if one wanted to disguise the emergence of a despotic regime, how better to hide it than by accusing the Society of being just that? The person behind this systematic denigration was Sebastião José de Carvalho e Melo (1699–1782), the first count of Oeiras, better known to history as the Marquis de Pombal, though he only received the latter title in 1770. He had received it because of his service to the Portuguese crown: under King José I from 1750 to 1777 he was effectively in charge of the Portuguese state. He had started his political career as an envoy to London in 1738 and then in 1745 was posted to Vienna, serving there for four years just as Emperor Joseph II was developing his religious policy (see above, pp. 204ff.). He returned to Lisbon at the time of the Treaty of Madrid, an attempt to sort out problems left over from the Treaty of Tordesillas (see above, pp. 60 and 96).

The boundaries between the territories of Spain and those of Portugal in the New World, such as they were, were imprecise and did not coincide except occasionally and by accident with natural features such as rivers or mountain ranges that might mark off one sovereignty from another. The Portuguese claimed that their territory

---

[5] Emanuele Columbo and Niccolò Guasti, "The Expulsion and Suppression in Portugal and Spain: An Overview," in *The Jesuit Suppression in Global Context*, ed. Jeffrey D. Burson and Jonathan Wright (Cambridge: Cambridge University Press, 2015), 117.

reached the Rio de la Plata, and the Spanish that theirs included Rio de Janeiro. It was a recipe for conflict: the ownership of the town of Colonia del Sacramento across the Rio de la Plata from Buenos Aires was a particular casus belli, and it changed hands several times. In 1750, however, the wife of the king of Spain was the sister of the king of Portugal, and it seemed an appropriate moment to end the disagreement over national boundaries in the Americas, and it is this entente that the Treaty of Madrid was intended to achieve. It laid down that the territory occupied by one side or the other was to remain their dominion, but with two notable exceptions. One formally transferred Colonia de Sacramento from Portugal to Spain, thus giving it command over the estuary of the Rio de la Plata, and in return Spain transferred to Portugal the land between the Rivers Uruguay and Ibicui, thereby establishing natural geographical frontiers to each other's territory.

The transfer may have made sense cartographically, but it did not make sense from the perspective of the Guaraní to whom the Jesuits ministered. It meant that seven of the missions now came under the rule of the king of Portugal, and Portuguese dominion was much less acceptable to the Guaraní than that of Spain; at least that of Spain was brokered by the Jesuits. It also deprived them both of their cattle ranches and of their plantations of yerba maté, the latter being the mainstay of the economy of the Paraguay reductions. The treaty's terms recognized that around thirty thousand Guaraní were affected and that they would not wish to be under Portuguese rule. The terms of the treaty therefore gave them a year to relocate west across the Uruguay river, taking their belongings—and their cattle—with them.

That the Jesuits would object was also recognized. The king of Spain told his representative in Paraguay that, if there was any resistance, the treaty would be enforced by a combined force of Spanish and Portuguese troops. The Portuguese representative, Gomes Freire de Andrada, was equally concerned, expressing surprise that the Jesuits in Madrid had not protested against the treaty. In fact the contrary was the case: the Jesuit confessor to King Ferdinand of Spain had asked the Jesuit superior general to ensure that his confreres in Paraguay obeyed, and as a result the general, Franz Retz, wrote to the Paraguayan provincial requiring him to observe the terms of the treaty. The successor to Franz Retz, Ignacio Visconti, went further. He not only instructed the Jesuits in Paraguay to obey the king and ensure that the Guaraní vacate the seven reductions, but he added that, if the Guaraní resisted, the Jesuits were to abandon the missions, adding that he was prepared to withdraw all his subjects from Latin America if need be. He also sent a representative, Lope Luis Altamirano, a Jesuit priest who in the film *The Mission*[6] becomes a cardinal, to ensure that his instructions were observed.

The Paraguayan Jesuits were divided as to what their response should be, some being ready to obey, others to continue to protest. Similarly, the Guaraní themselves were divided. One mission steadfastly refused to relocate while representatives of others went off to find new sites for their townships, though, as they quickly realized, their options were limited both by the presence of other reductions and by the quality of the land that remained available to them. The inhabitants of one mission in particular, that of San Nicolás, were especially hostile to the order to move, and their unwillingness to comply encouraged others. They prepared to use force. Some six hundred armed Guaraní advanced on Santo Tomé, where Altamirano was lodging, and in February 1753, fearing for his life, he fled. Also in February a group of armed Guaraní turned away the Spanish-Portuguese boundary commission. The Guaraní were led first by José Tiarayú, known as Sepé, from the mission of San Miguel and then, after Sepé's death, by Nicolás Neenguirú from the Concepción mission. Altamirano, by now residing in Buenos Aires, was well aware that the standing of the Society at the Spanish court was in decline, and to bolster the reputation of his confreres in Madrid he wanted above all to demonstrate the Jesuits' loyalty to the monarchy. He decreed that any Jesuit involvement in the rebellion would be a mortal sin.

Nonetheless, the rebellion began in 1754 when the Guaraní, without Jesuit backing, attacked Portuguese settlements. When de Andrada and the governor of Buenos Aires brought troops to try to occupy the missions that same year they were repulsed. The following year a combined force of Spanish and Portuguese soldiers was sent, and in February 1755 there were two battles. Sepé was captured

---

[6] *The Mission* (1986), which was directed by Roland Joffé, produced by David Puttnam, and written by Robert Bolt, starred Robert De Niro, Jeremy Irons, Ray McAnally, and others. It won the Cannes Film Festival Palme d'Or and an Oscar for Best Cinematography as well as a BAFTA for Ennio Morricone's score.

in the first, burned to death, and, once dead, decapitated. Neenguirú then took over, but in the second battle the Guaraní were decisively defeated, very many being killed and others taken prisoner, including Neenguirú. He did not suffer the same fate as Sepé, simply being banished from his own mission and sent to live on another one. There were few repercussions for the rebels, but the same could not be said for the Jesuits: they had lost the confidence of the Guaraní because they had proved unable to protect them. In any case, the situation of the native population had changed, being by this time less dependent on the Society. They no longer lived in fear of being enslaved by the Portuguese, so although the missions gradually revived after the War of the Seven Reductions, as it was called, they never reached the numbers of inhabitants that there had been before the rebellion. Moreover, as the encomienda system was no longer in force, they could now work for money. The inhabitants of the reductions, at least the male ones, frequently had skills that were much in demand, and, though the Guaraní were regularly paid less than other laborers and artisans, the economic development of the Rio de la Plata region meant there was a considerable increase in work for which there was a monetary reward. Although some of the Jesuits, like some of the Spanish administrators who replaced them, considered the Guaraní to be indolent and in need of constant surveillance, there is good evidence they were nothing of the sort and that their perceived lack of productivity in the townships may have arisen because they were unenthusiastic about working simply for communal benefit. When working for wages outside the reductions they were diligent employees, beginning to acquire property of their own, to trade in goods that they produced, and generally less dependent on the communal supplies provided by the missions. Indeed, there is evidence that they began to trade in the items with which the missions supplied them. This naturally led to greater inequality of wealth among the Guaraní and a more pronounced stratification of mission society. The ones who seem to have gained most were members of the cabildo, the town councillors; those who lost most were the widows and orphans, the sick and the disabled, for whom there was no longer a safety net.

Both the Spanish—with some exceptions—and the Portuguese authorities in Latin America blamed the Society for the rebellion, claiming that the Guaraní would never have taken up arms without the Jesuits' support. De Andrada went so far as to claim that the population of the reductions had been held in slavery by the Jesuits and that the missions had constituted a state within a state, owing allegiance not to the crown but to the Society of Jesus. All this was music to the ears of Portugal's chief minister, the Marqués de Pombal, and he, or, rather, the Portuguese government, published a series of pamphlets attacking the Jesuits that were widely circulated in English, French, German, and Italian. Beginning in 1755 Jesuits were expelled from Portuguese territories in South America on the grounds that they had been attempting to frustrate the implementation of the terms of the Treaty of Madrid.

In 1758 there was an attempt on the life of the Portuguese king. Pombal managed to implicate the Jesuits and the following year had them expelled from all remaining Portuguese dominions. Meanwhile in France the campaign against the Society had been joined by Voltaire, who claimed, like Pombal, that the fathers had not only enslaved the Guaraní but usurped royal authority over them for their own benefit—this despite his words of praise in 1733: "The settlement of Paraguay, established by only a few Spanish Jesuits, appears to be the triumph of humanity."[7] Even Voltaire, however, was shocked by the public burning at the stake—he had, it is true, first been strangled—of the seventy-two-year-old Gabriel Malagrida. The Italian-born Jesuit had served some three decades in Brazil and on returning to Europe settled in Lisbon, which in 1755 an earthquake entirely destroyed with the loss of around seventy-five thousand lives. He published a book the following year claiming that the disaster was a punishment for Portugal's manifest sins, a charge that Pombal took as aimed at him. Malagrida and ten other Jesuits were arrested and imprisoned for complicity in the assassination attempt on the extremely tenuous grounds that they had been chaplains or confessors to the aristocrats suspected of plotting to kill the king. Malagrida appears to have lost his mind while in jail and produced a number of fantastical prophecies that led to his being arraigned before the Inquisition, which was, conveniently for Pombal, headed by his brother, and condemned to death. Pombal's family shared his hostility. It was another brother, Mendonça Furtado, the governor of the

---

[7] Quoted by Maurice Whitehead, "On the Road to Suppression," in Burson and Wright, *The Jesuit Suppression*, 99.

Brazilian captaincy of Maranhão, who described "the Jesuit missions as a 'despotism' that had exploited native 'slavery' in the service of an illicit 'commerce' as the economic means toward an 'empire' under a general whose power posed a threat to the papacy no less than the monarchy's. Mendonça even complained about the use of Molinist and probabilistic arguments by Jesuits in defence of their 'independence' and against incorporating the natives into state controlled villages."[8] It was a remarkably brazen argument, given that one of the aims of the reductions had been to safeguard the Guaraní from enslavement by Portuguese colonists. Nonetheless, it was widely circulated, not least through Jansenist sources. The anti-Jesuit polemic did not flow only one way. Though Jansenists made much of Pombal's charges against the Society, Pombal, after the assassination attempt on the Portuguese king, borrowed from Jansenist propaganda the claim that the Jesuits promoted regicide.

The story of the expulsion of the Jesuits from Spain—the second largest concentration of members after Germany—is in many ways similar to that from Spain's next-door neighbor. Once again the Treaty of Madrid played a part, though perhaps not quite such a significant one as in Pombal's Portugal. Some of the Jesuits' troubles arose simply from their dominance in the royal court, which aroused the resentment of Dominicans and Augustinians whom they had displaced, as well as of the diocesan clergy who saw members of the Society as far too privileged in all kinds of ways, not least as far as taxation was concerned. Under Ferdinand VI, king of Spain from 1746 to 1759, Francisco Rávago, SJ, was in effect the prime minister, so powerful had the office of royal confessor become. Jesuits even ran the Spanish Inquisition and put a book on the banned list despite the pope, Benedict XIV, having approved it, as Dale Van Kley remarks, thus pitting "the supposedly ultramontanist Jesuits against the papacy in an issue about Catholic orthodoxy."[9]

Then, in 1756, Rávago fell from favor, and anti-Jesuit ministers began to replace pro-Jesuit ones. At least part of the antipathy toward the Society was, as in Portugal, the supposed Jesuit resistance to the

---

[8] Cited from Van Kley, *Reform Catholicism and the International Suppression of the Jesuits*, 159, but Van Kley is himself quoting from Samuel J. Miller, *Portugal and Rome* (Rome: Università Gregoriana Editrice, 1978).

[9] Van Kley, *Reform Catholicism*, 169.

Treaty of Madrid, and one minister asked the governor of Buenos Aires to send back to Spain for trial a number of Jesuits who, it was claimed, had been fomenting the Guaraní rebellion, but as the governor did not think the priests were guilty, he ignored the demand.

Ferdinand VI was succeeded on the Spanish throne by his half-brother, and former ruler of Naples, Charles III. Although Charles himself was not overtly hostile to the Society, some of the ministers and advisers who came with him from Naples certainly were, as were others whom the king appointed, in particular Pedro Rodríguez de Campomanes y Pérez, first count of Campomanes, who in 1760 was put in charge of Spain's economy. One of his immediate proposals was to impose a limit on the amount of land held by religious orders that was free from taxation and to prohibit them from gaining more, a plan that was at first welcomed by the diocesan clergy, as much in New Spain as in Spain itself, and one that, on the face of it, was not aimed specifically against the Society. But Spanish grandees, many of whom had been educated by the Jesuits and who were already hostile to the new ministers of Charles III who were regarded as being of an inferior class, rallied to the support of the Society. There were other issues. A large number of French Jesuits had taken refuge in Spain in 1764 after they had refused to swear an oath of loyalty to Louis XV and accept the Gallican Articles. Campomanes argued that, as disloyal subjects of the French crown with whom in 1761 Charles had agreed to a Bourbon "Family Pact,"[10] they should not be allowed to stay.

Even more threatening to the Society, however, were the "hat and coat" riots of March 1766. The riots occurred all over Spain, though most particularly in Madrid, and arose from a variety of causes, most important, the rise in food prices brought about by the economic reforms[11] of one of Charles's Neapolitan advisers, Leopoldo di Gregorio, marqués de Squillache. In Spain he was known as Esquilache, and the riots are, as a consequence, sometimes known as the "Motín [uprising] de Esquilache." The minister had banned the wearing of the traditional large hat—the sombrero—on the grounds that it could hide the faces of would-be opponents of the regime, and the

---

[10] There had been two previous "Bourbon family pacts," agreed in 1733 and 1743.

[11] The financial burden of the Seven Years' War (1756–1763) had necessitated tax increases in Spain and elsewhere in Europe.

wearing of long cloaks was forbidden because they might be used to conceal weapons. Not only was Esquilache in the eyes of the Madrileños a foreigner, but the government had attempted, vainly, to put down the riots by using foreign—Walloon—troops from the Spanish Netherlands, which further angered them.

The king first gave in to the demands of the rioters, then rescinded the concessions, reducing the price of essential commodities, allowing the wearing of the traditional capes and hats, promising to rid his government of foreign-born ministers, and then he fled the city. He ordered an investigation into the causes of the Motín, an enquiry that ended up in the hands of Campomanes. It—or he—concluded that those behind the uprising were members of the higher aristocracy who had for the most part been educated by the Jesuits, had Jesuit confessors, or were members of Jesuit-run confraternities so therefore, although there was no direct evidence, Jesuits were obviously to blame. A flurry of anti-government pamphleteering followed the Motín, for which Campomanes also held the Society responsible, especially after the provincial of Navarre, one of those who had sought asylum in Spain, was found to have some of this literature in his possession as well as a French defense of the Society, which violated the terms on which Jesuits had been allowed to remain in the country. The uprising was, Campomanes claimed, a prelude to an attempted tyrannicide of the kind the French Jesuits had long been suspected of (see above, p. 182) and, incredibly, to a *coup d'état* inspired by the Jesuit General Lorenzo Ricci.[12] The one thing of which he did not accuse them, however, was inciting the Guaraní War: Campomanes agreed with the Society that the Treaty of Madrid that had occasioned it was deeply flawed, and not in Spain's interest, so instead he fell back on the widespread canard that the Jesuits had governed the Guaraní despotically and reduced them to the status of slaves.

It was not within the power of Campomanes himself to expel Jesuits from Spain; he had first to persuade the king. This did not prove difficult, despite a letter to Charles from the pro-Jesuit Pope Clement XIII: Charles told the French ambassador that the Society

---

[12] Colombo and Guasti, "The Expulsion and Suppression in Portugal and Spain," 129.

had fomented the Motín and conspired against him.[13] But it helped that Campomanes explained that, unlike the diocesan clergy, members of religious orders were not part of the divine dispensation but a human addition and therefore could fall under royal control.[14] A royal decree, dated February 27, 1767, but only put into action at dawn on April 3,[15] ordered the expulsion of members of the Society not just from Spain but from all the Spanish dominions, though it inevitably took time to reach all parts of the Spanish Empire.

How many Jesuits were affected is uncertain, though more than had been uprooted by the expulsion from Portugal and its dominions. In all, it seems that over five thousand Spanish priests and brothers, together with an indeterminate number from other European nations who were working in Spanish territory, had to be rounded up and shipped, not to Spain, but to the Papal States. These were already replete with something like a thousand Portuguese Jesuits, and Clement XIII refused to let more members of the Society enter the port of Civitavecchia, so they were taken instead to Corsica, which was then under the control of Genoa but shortly afterward became a dependency of France, which was unwilling to have them. Clement XIII relented somewhat, and the Spanish Jesuits finally entered the Papal States, though as time went on they spread across Italy.[16] The English Jesuit, and indefatigable letter writer, John Thorpe, who was resident in Rome, commented to a correspondent, "Rome was perhaps never so stocked with Jesuits as at present. There are near six hundred of them within the walls from almost every nation under the sun and, tho' persecuted almost all the world over, their pulpits, schools etc. are as much frequented and with as much credit as ever. The new guests from the Brasils and Islands give great edification in all places."[17]

---

[13] Van Kley, *Reform Catholicism*, 191.

[14] Ibid., 189.

[15] It was brought forward to overnight on March 31; Colombo and Guasti, "The Expulsion and Suppression in Portugal and Spain," 131.

[16] The change of heart, Colombo and Guasti suggest, came about when it became clear to the pope that the Spanish government was living up to its promise to pay pensions to the Jesuits (ibid., 135).

[17] Thomas M. McCoog, "Lost in the Title," in Burson and Wright, *The Jesuit Suppression*, 163.

Hostility to the Society in France because of their opposition to the "Gallican Liberties" and the tenets of Jansenism have already been recounted (see above, chapter 7 passim), but the chain of events that led up to suppression of the Society there began in 1755, at the beginning of the Seven Years' War. English privateers captured several French ships on their way from Martinique to Marseilles. The cargo of sugar and coffee on board these vessels had been intended to pay off the debts that had been incurred with a firm in Marseilles, Lioncy and Gouffre, by the Jesuit mission in Martinique, and as a consequence of the non-arrival of the cargo the Marseilles company went bankrupt. Whether the Jesuit procurator in Martinique, Father Antoine de Lavalette, who was very much of an entrepreneur, had exceeded the authority granted him by the Society was obviously not a matter of concern to the creditors, though equally obviously it very much concerned his confreres at home who forbade him to commit himself and the Society to any further borrowing.

Lavalette has, for the most part, been given an easy ride by historians of the Society. This, for instance, is the description of him by William Bangert: "An engaging, enterprising man with a flair for practical affairs. . . . Acting well within the limits on business by clerics set by canon law, he gained a fine reputation for commercial skill both at Martinique, at Marseilles, and other port towns in France."[18] The truth was much darker. It has already been mentioned that Jesuits owned slaves: in Brazil, as has been seen (above, p. 104), the missionary António Vieira even advocated the importation into the country of enslaved Africans so that his Amerindian converts would not themselves be subjugated by the European colonists. Slave ownership was widespread. It was common for slaves to be used on the Caribbean sugar plantations, such as the one run by Lavalette in Martinique that owned something in the region of two hundred enslaved men and women. The question remains, however: did the Jesuits treat their slaves better than did other plantation owners? The evidence gathered by Andrew Dial would suggest that on the whole

---

[18] Bangert, *A History of the Society of Jesus*, 373. He is not mentioned in the indexes of either Thomas Worcester's *Cambridge Encyclopedia of the Jesuits* or the recently published *La Compagnie de Jésus des Anciens Régimes au Monde Contemporain (XVIIIe–XXe Siècles)*, ed. Pierre Antoine Fabre and others (Rome: Institutum Historicum Societatis Iesu and L'École Française de Rome, 2021).

they were not much better, if at all, than their secular contemporaries despite frequent attempts by superiors in Rome to rein them in and despite expulsions from the Society for those found to have abused their slaves.[19] Lavalette, however, seems to have been particularly brutal: "Where other missionaries in the islands wrote of enslaved Africans as potential converts," Dial remarks, "who needed to be educated and Christianized, Lavalette wrote of them as investments."[20] The complexity and riskiness of Lavalette's financial dealings led eventually to unease in Rome and to the appointment of a visitor to report on his activities in Martinique. The visitor, Jean-François de la Marche, was a sixty-one-year-old priest from the Jesuit house in Nantes, the French city that was the center of the slave trade. His report to the Jesuit general, received just at the time when French members of the Society were on the verge of being expelled from the country, could not have come at a worse time. La Marche was shocked by what he had discovered. If the brutal treatment of slaves was commonplace, the killing of them was contrary to the local *Code Noire* that governed the relations between owners and their slaves, and la Marche could name four slaves who had been executed by Lavalette. The priest was indeed punished by his superiors, not, however, on account of his brutality, but for his financial dealings. He left the Society, though he did so not by expulsion but of his own volition. And there, as far as the Jesuits were concerned, the matter rested: General Lorenzo Ricci had other problems to face.[21]

Meanwhile one of the creditors of the bankrupt company, the widow Grou of Nantes, had obtained a court decision against the Jesuit procurator (finance officer) in France for the repayment of the money owed to her. But because of the vow of poverty, individual Jesuits, the procurator included, had no property of their own, and the cases effectively went against the whole Society: it was ordered to pay the company 1,552,276 in Marseilles livre. The provincial in Paris argued that each house of the Society was responsible for its own debts and refused to pay, but the matter had by now developed

---

[19] Andrew Dial, "Antoine LaValette, Slave Murderer," *Journal of Jesuit Studies* 8 (2021): 45.

[20] Ibid., 46–47.

[21] Dial's article, from which the above is taken, runs from p. 37 to p. 56 in the issue of *Journal of Jesuit Studies*, cited above.

a life of its own, the Jansenist party having sensed it had the Society on the run. As it was debated in the Parlement, it was argued that the Society had never been legal in France because it contravened the Gallican Articles and that it was also contrary to the French constitution because it was a despotism, all members having to swear obedience to the Jesuit general. And that meant that they owed obedience to someone who was outside France. On August 6, 1761, exactly a hundred years to the day after the death of Angelique Arnauld, the Society in France was forbidden to receive new members and was ordered to close all colleges. The French Jesuit provincial made concessions. That same month, August 1761, he rejected the common Jesuit theory, advanced by Bellarmine and others, that popes had indirect authority over the temporal power, also rejecting, as others had done before, that Jesuits were in favor of tyrannicide in certain circumstances. Two months later he agreed that the authority of the general did not extend to French laws, and he renounced all the privileges granted to the Society that had freed them from episcopal control. His final concession, in the following December, was to commit Jesuits in France to accepting the Gallican Articles.

Louis XV was sympathetic to the plight of the Jesuits, but at the time France was engaged in an expensive war, which meant he could not afford to alienate the Parlement. He tried to come to a compromise, proposing that the authority of the superior general be conferred on every provincial in France or, alternatively, that a vicar general be appointed in France to govern the Society. There were other significant changes suggested, but Lorenzo Ricci, the general in Rome, is said to have responded with a Latin tag, "Sint ut sunt, aut non sint": "Let them be as they are, or not at all."

On February 12, 1762, the Parlement, not of Paris but of Normandy, declared Jesuit vows to be invalid, and Jesuits living within its jurisdiction were to leave their houses. If they wished to continue as priests, they had to swear to uphold the Gallican Articles, which the provincial had already conceded. They were also to condemn teachings particularly distinctive of the Society.[22] Successive parlements

---

[22] It is questionable whether there were any such specifically Jesuit doctrines. In the midst of the disputes over Molina's teachings the general, Claudio Acquaviva, asked the advice of the theologian Alfonso Salmerón as to whether Jesuits should adhere to one particular interpretation of theology. Salmerón responded, "I believe

followed suit. In Versailles the king did nothing, Louis apparently resigned to the destruction of the Society in his dominions. That came in November 1764 when he ordered the dissolution of the Society in the whole of France, commenting, "I have no great affection for the Jesuits, but all the heretics have always hated them, which constitutes their glory."[23] The king was right to be concerned. As Dale Van Kley has written, "It is indeed difficult to avoid the conclusion that the Jesuits succumbed as the staunchest and perhaps last consistent defender of royal authority in France, and that monarchical government, at least as both Louis XV and his predecessors had understood it, was solemnly condemned with the Jesuit order in 1762."[24]

Jean Le Rond d'Alembert, who was, with Diderot, one of the editors of the *Encyclopedie* and indeed the person who composed its "Preliminary Discourse," in 1765 published *On the Destruction of the Jesuits in France.* He wrote that "these two accusations [made by Jansenists, that the Jesuit encouraged both despotism and regicide] might appear to be a little contradictory, but it was not a question of telling the exact truth; it was a question of saying as much evil as possible about the Jesuits."[25]

As d'Alembert's title indicates, the banning of the Society in France applied to all Jesuits, not just French ones. Among those affected by the 1764 decision were the English Jesuits who had run a successful college for the sons of recusant families in the city of St. Omer since the last years of the sixteenth century.[26] The college's procurator, aware of the possible closure of the school and the seizure of the property by the state, had already arranged for a new building in Bruges, which lay outside the jurisdiction of France in the Austrian Netherlands. "This extraordinary migration," wrote one of the priests

---

we should not draw up a list of propositions that we [his fellow Jesuits] may not defend. . . . But if a catalogue of this kind is actually composed, let it contain as few propositions as possible, lest the word go out that we wish to restrain the human mind within overtight limits and condemn by anticipation opinions and theses which the Church in no way has proscribed." Quoted by Bangert, *A History of the Society of Jesus*, 181.

[23] Van Kley, *The Jansenists and the Expulsion of the Jesuits from France*, 207.

[24] Ibid., 158.

[25] Van Kley, *Reform Catholicism*, 13; and also in *The Jansenists and the Expulsion of the Jesuits from France*, 161.

[26] The history of the college can be found in Chadwick, *St Omers to Stonyhurst*.

involved, "through such a length of way, was conducted with such caution and expedition, that nearly ninety students were brought safe to Bruges before the townsmen of St Omers knew that a single person had left the college."[27] The college was handed over to English diocesan clergy under the presidency of Alban Butler (1710–1773), a priest best known to Anglophone Catholics as the compiler of *The Lives of the Fathers, Martyrs and Other Principal Saints*, or, as it is more commonly known in its very many editions, *Butler's Lives of the Saints*.[28]

The closing of the school at St. Omer was, as it were, a byproduct of the hostility to the Society of Jesus expressed by members of the Parlement, particularly the Parlement of Paris, but also others. Before the general suppression in France in 1764, the Parlement had forbidden the Jesuits to receive novices, ordered them to close their colleges—colleges in towns where the Jesuit college was the only one were given a year's grace—and forced them to dissolve the congregations. The Marian congregations, sometimes called the Sodalities of Our Lady, rarely get noticed in general histories of the Society or feature in accounts of the suppression, but if Jansenists were largely responsible for the attack on the Society in France, they were opposed to much of the congregation's spirituality as it was fostered in the laypeople by members of the Society. They originated in the Roman College, founded by the Liège Jesuit Jean Leunis in 1563. Its members were to commit themselves to a weekly confession and a monthly, or more frequent, reception of the Eucharist. They were to consecrate themselves to the Virgin Mary, as Ignatius had done at Montserrat, and to say the rosary and other Marian prayers. Enhanced by papal bulls, they spread from Rome to anywhere that the Society was working: "Peter Canisius saw in the Marian congregations not only the instruments of Catholic reconquest, but also, and perhaps most of all, the means for a transformation of Christian society in its entirety."[29] Although they did not start out that way, by the end of the

[27] Quoted by Bernard Basset, *The English Jesuits* (London: Burns and Oates, 1967), 323.

[28] Not quite everyone abandoned the college. Two aged Jesuit priests, considered too old to travel, were left behind to be cared for by a Jesuit brother (ibid., 321).

[29] Louis Chatellier, *Europe of the Devout* (Cambridge: Cambridge University Press, 1989), 9. The original French edition, *L'Europe des Dévots*, was published in Paris, 1987.

seventeenth century the congregations were socially mixed and, as Louis Chatellier says, "a microcosm of the town,"[30] its members exercising considerable influence within the municipality:

> It was the mix of classes, already visible at the end of the seventeenth century, but which became systematic and willed, which gave the Jesuit associations of the eighteenth century their special character. Was it necessitated by fear of social unrest? Or was it rather the consequence to make men in the here and now reflect on their equality before God? . . . The disquiet displayed by certain adversaries of the Jesuits, who saw in their institutions destined for the laity potential instruments for the subversion of the social order, may well make better sense when looked at in this light.[31]

Chatellier does not spend much time on the Jansenists, though he comments on their attack on Jesuit moral theology, remarking that it would not have much importance in the world at large had it not been practiced by "hundreds of groups of active and respected men."[32] Nor does he dwell on the sharp divide in spirituality between, for example, the insistence in the sodalities of regular reception of the Eucharist and private devotions such as the rosary and the Jansenist practice of abstaining from both. Jansenists particularly detested devotion to the Sacred Heart, which Jesuits promoted from the late seventeenth century onward.

When he wrote the history of the Parlement of Paris Voltaire commented, "France was entirely Jansenist, except for the Jesuits and the bishops of the Roman party."[33] Hostility to the Society was not going to be placated merely by the expulsion of the Society from France: the aim was complete dissolution. In April 1764 the Duc de Choiseul, the French foreign minister in all but name,[34] wrote to the French minister at the Vatican, "If the Pope were prudent, enlightened and strong he would come to but one decision, to suppress the Society

---

[30] Ibid., 65.

[31] Ibid., 213.

[32] Ibid., 156.

[33] Quoted by Van Kley, *The Jansenists and the Expulsion of the Jesuits*, 28.

[34] Though he only held that title from December 1758 to October 1761 and again from April 1766 to December 1770, Choiseul was effectively in charge of France's foreign policy at least throughout the 1760s.

entirely,"[35] and at a meeting of the Council of State in May, he remarked, "What . . . would suit us best is if [His Majesty[36]], the King of Spain, the Empress Queen [of Austria] and the King of Portugal would unite in order to engage the Pope to dissolve the order of Jesuits completely."[37] In January 1769 France, Spain, and Naples presented Pope Clement XIII with a demand that the Society be disbanded: he rejected it.

There was no possibility of serious damage to the Jesuits while Clement XIII was pope: he had too many links to the Society. In the aftermath of the destruction of the Society in France he had published *Apostolicum pascendi* praising its achievements and reasserting his support, but his firm stance against the attempt of the duchy of Parma to limit the Church's rights in the duchy was the occasion for France to occupy the enclaves of Avignon and the Comtat Venaissin surrounding it that had been part of the Papal States since the end of the thirteenth century. The Bourbon Family Pact, signed in August 1761, committed its signatories to regard an attack on one of their number as an attack on all, and when Clement nullified Parma's decrees, they took this to be just such an assault by a pro-Jesuit pope. It was the final incitement the Bourbons needed to produce their demand for the suppression of the Society, to which Clement responded by calling a consistory, a gathering of cardinals, for February 3. The day before the cardinals were due to meet the pope had a stroke from which he never recovered. He died in the evening of February 2.

The chief obstacle to the Bourbons' plans now being out of the way, they had to ensure that Clement's successor was on their side. The conclave, which went on for three months, started on February 15, though it did not begin in earnest until after the arrival of the Spanish cardinals at the end of April. While it was indeed dominated by the fate of the Jesuits, the Catholic powers were not wholly in agreement as to the means of achieving the election of an anti-Jesuit cardinal. Spain, for example, wanted a prior agreement from any candidate that, once elected, he would abolish the Society, but the crown cardinals, those, that is, who had been appointed by the Catholic monarchs, warned, quite rightly, that this was verging on

[35] Bangert, *A History of the Society of Jesus*, 394.
[36] The king of France, who was present at the meeting.
[37] Quoted by Van Kley, *Reform Catholicism*, 197.

simony, and, in any case, such agreements, capitulations as they were called, were banned by Church law. Choiseul, on the other hand, was less concerned with the Jesuits than with maintaining French control of Avignon and its surrounding territory. And in an open flouting of the conclave's rule of secrecy, on March 15 Emperor Joseph arrived in Rome accompanied by his pro-Jansenist brother Leopold, duke of Tuscany, and both held long conversations with the electors. They assured the cardinals that they were in favor of suppression, adding that although their mother, Empress Maria Theresa, was close to the Society, she would not "move a finger"[38] to help it. Confirmation of this did not come until well after the conclave. For the Empress, her problem was marrying off her children into Europe's royal houses, so she could not afford to alienate them. She would not, therefore, oppose the suppression of the Society and told the Spanish King Charles III of her decision in April 1773.

In the usual meetings of cardinals before the conclave opened several candidates for the papacy were discussed, but the early front-runner was Lorenzo Antonio Ganganelli, a Conventual Franciscan who was renowned for twice refusing to be elected as head of his religious order. While this might have been taken as evidence of a proper humility, it was widely thought at the time that he had still higher ambitions for the office to which he was unanimously elected, except for his own vote, on May 19, taking the name Clement XIV. He had let it be known that he was not opposed to the suppression of the Society, and not only not opposed, but that he had the authority to do so: "It was a black day in the history of the Church," commented one historian.[39]

Members of the Society in Rome, however, remained hopeful—or at least, Fr. John Thorpe did so. He reported that the general had paid the customary visit to a newly elected pontiff and had been received kindly, and "the Jesuits continue to augment their hopes."[40] The recently ordained John Carroll was less sanguine. The future archbishop of Baltimore was shepherding the young Charles Philip Stourton, from 1781 the seventeenth Baron Stourton, on the grand tour. The

[38] Giancarlo Zizola, *Il Conclave, Storia e Segreti* (Rome: Newton Compton Editori, 1993), 143.

[39] Quoted by ibid., 144.

[40] McCoog, "Lost in the Title," 170f.

tour began in 1771 and lasted for almost two years, with the result that Carroll arrived in Rome shortly before the suppression of the Society. During his travels he wrote alarmed letters back to his community in Bruges, where he had been a schoolmaster, and to that in Liège, telling his confreres of the destruction of the Society that had already occurred and expressing anxiety for its future.

It was clear that Clement XIV was reluctant to dissolve the Society, but when Maria Theresa made it known she would not oppose such a measure, the Jesuits' last line of defense was broken. But just to make sure, the Spanish ambassador, José Moñino y Redondo, bribed the pope's two closest confidants, Innocenti Buontempi, like Clement, a Conventual Franciscan friar, and Cardinal Francisco de Zelada[41] to whom was entrusted the task of writing the required brief, known by its opening words *Dominus ac Redemptor*, "Lord and Saviour." It was signed by the pope on June 8, 1773, though it was not put into force until August 16 and communicated to the Jesuits in Rome two days later. In the brief the pope claims to be acting in order to bring peace to the Church, and though he praises the history of the Society, he also points to its failings and to what he regarded as its excessively privileged position within the Church. After what he claimed to have been mature deliberation, he said:

> We do, out of our certain knowledge, and the fullness of our Apostolic power, suppress and abolish the said company: we deprive it of all activity whatever, of its houses, schools, colleges, lands, and in short, every other place whatsoever, in whatever kingdom or province they may be situated; we abrogate and annul its statutes, rules, customs, decrees and constitutions, even though confirmed by oath and approved by the Holy See. . . . We declare all, and all kind of authority, the General, the Provincials, the Visitors and other superiors of the said Society to be for ever annulled and extinguished, of what nature soever the said authority may be, as well in things spiritual or temporal.

It could hardly sound more definitive, but that is misleading. There are many forms of documents emanating from the Holy See, of which papal bulls are the best known and most solemn, while papal briefs,

---

[41] Bangert, *A History of the Society of Jesus*, 398.

the format of *Dominus ac Redemptor*, are probably the least weighty.[42] This was no dogmatic definition. It could be reversed, and many of those rendered former Jesuits by the brief hoped—vainly, as it turned out—that it would be reversed by Clement XIV's successor, Pius VI. There was a second problem with this, as with all papal documents, that it was a maxim[43] that all such laws had to be promulgated in the territories that were affected by them, and there were two regions where the monarchs would not allow the brief to be published: Frederick the Great's Prussia and Catherine the Great's Russia. Both rulers had acquired territory with large Catholic populations and needed the Jesuits to continue to staff colleges to provide for their subjects' educational needs. In the case of Prussia, Frederick's support did not last long, only until 1780, when he seized all Jesuit property. In Russia, however, support from the monarch outlasted Catherine and continued until 1820, thus, as will be seen, providing an important bridge between the suppressed and the restored Society.

Elsewhere, however, Jesuits overnight became ex-Jesuits. Anyone who had not yet been ordained, novices, those in training, lay brothers, once more became laymen as states laid hands on the Society's property. If they were looking for cash, they were disappointed. Many of the houses that were seized had substantial debts, and Jesuits, because of their of vow of poverty, had for the most part lived frugally: there was little or no treasure to be found. Some former Jesuits were able to remain in the posts they had previously occupied. In China, for instance, those attached to the imperial court remained in place,[44] and, to take another example, in Canada, after a British administration had replaced that of France,

> The elderly Jesuits were permitted use of their chapel and residence in Quebec until the last of them died. . . . The priests were also permitted use of smaller properties at the Huron mission of Lorette and in Montreal. Additionally each man received a generous pension as a gift from the Canadian citizens to provide for their needs

---

[42] A papal bull takes its name from the seal attached to the document, *bulla* being the Latin word for a seal, while a papal "brief" comes from the Latin *brevia*, meaning "short."

[43] *Non obligat lex nisi promulgata.*

[44] Niccolò Guasti, "The Age of Suppression," in *The Oxford Handbook of the Jesuits,* ed. Ines G. Županov (Oxford: Oxford University Press, 2019), 930.

and a genteel life style in their last years. It was further agreed that the properties should be entrusted to the Canadian bishops of Quebec, so that they might be put to use again for their original purpose.[45]

There were a few other examples such as these of Jesuit missionaries being allowed to continue their endeavors, though most active in Portuguese or Spanish territory were deported back to their home countries.

One of the more remarkable survivals was that of the English Jesuits. Some were working on missions in Britain, and they were able to stay in post, but a relatively large number, some forty, were on the staff in one way or another of the Society's English seminary in Liège. At the suppression they were joined by the staff and some of the boys from the school at Bruges (see above, p. 219), and in Liège they maintained a community life according to the customs and traditions of the Society. Thanks largely to the support of the prince-bishop of Liège, the seminary and school were transformed into the "English Academy" with a (now former) Jesuit as its president. The sympathetic bishop advertised it across Europe and in 1778 obtained a papal brief transforming it into a pontifical seminary that could present candidates for ordination to the priesthood. It flourished for a couple of decades until, in 1794, the approach of French revolutionary forces made it wiser to return to the safety of Britain, where it reestablished itself both as a school and as a seminary at Stonyhurst, a house given them by a former student, in a remote part of Lancashire. Staff and students made their way there by various routes: the first of them to arrive at the academy's new home was Fr. Notley Young, from Maryland.[46]

Quite apart from hostility between Britain and France, the English ex-Jesuits had good reason to be afraid of the forces of the revolution. A good number of the French Jesuits were taken on by friendly bishops as parochial clergy. Others served as chaplains to convents or in other similar offices, but then, in 1791, they had to take an oath to the state if they were to continue as members of the "constitutional"

---

[45] Bronwen McShea, *Apostles of Empire* (Lincoln: University of Nebraska Press, 2019), 252.

[46] For the story of the "English Academy," see Walsh, *Heythrop College*, 43–54.

clergy; many refused to do so. In the September Massacres of 1792, 210 priests are known to have died in Paris, of whom twenty-six were former Jesuits; twelve more are known to have been executed in the French capital over the next two years. Many also died outside the capital, especially in Nantes and Rochefort, though the exact number is not known.[47]

For the most part, however, the lot of ex-Jesuits outside France was not quite so dire. Of those in the "East Habsburg Lands," Paul Shore writes, "The role of Hungarian ex-Jesuit bibliophiles and librarians looms unusually large in the nation's cultural history"[48] while those who had been unceremoniously dumped in the Papal States were freed by *Dominus ac Redemptor* to remain where Rome had placed them and to move to posts in whatever Italian city offered the more lucrative jobs.[49] Louis Caruana, SJ, writing on "The Legacies of Suppression," in particular its impact on Jesuit science, concludes that "many Jesuits became cultural outcasts, socially impoverished, and yet, precisely because of this, they became liberated from structures of approval and promotion. They gained more freedom to argue for the truth as they saw it, come what may."[50]

There was, however, no freedom for the general of the Society, Lorenzo Ricci (1703–1775), who had been elected in 1758. Along with his secretary and five assistants, he was arrested on August 17, 1773, and taken first to the English College, and then imprisoned in Castel Sant'Angelo along with his staff. The assistants were released one by one, but not Ricci, who died in prison. John Thorpe collected the general's Jesuit soutane and other bits and pieces and sent them off to his confreres in Liège for safekeeping; they in turn took them with them when they moved to Stonyhurst, and there they still remain.[51]

In the article cited above, Caruana writes of a Jesuit leaving the Roman College in tears, never to return. In the end, however, the col-

---

[47] D. G. Thompson, "French Jesuits 1756–1814," in Burson and Wright, *The Jesuit Suppression*, 196f.

[48] Paul Shore, "Ex-Jesuits in the East Habsburg Lands, Silesia and Poland," in ibid., 231.

[49] Niccolò Guasti, "The Exile of the Spanish Jesuits in Italy," in ibid., 251, though Guasti notes that they tended to cluster together and, as far as possible, keep in contact.

[50] Louis Caruana, "The Legacies of Suppression," in ibid., 276.

[51] McCoog, "Lost in the Title," 180.

lege (now the Gregorian University) fared reasonably well. The diocesan clergy were put in charge, overseen by a triumvirate of cardinals. Many of the diocesan priests who took over teaching at the college had been educated there, and the cardinals on the whole appointed suitable professors, including some ex-Jesuits. The cardinals made some improvements, including reestablishing chairs of liturgy and of Hebrew and erecting an astronomical observatory. "For some twenty years after the expulsion of the Jesuits the college continued to do well under the triumvirate of cardinals," one Jesuit historian has written.[52] It was closed only after, in 1798, forces of revolutionary France occupied Rome, and all clergy were required, as in France, to take an oath of loyalty to the new French constitution. To the distress of Pope Pius VI, with a single exception, the staff of the Roman College all did so.

The disappearance of the Society clearly left a gap that some tried to fill by establishing new religious institutes similar in character to that founded by St. Ignatius. The former Jesuit Pierre-Joseph de Clorivière (1735–1820)[53] started two new religious orders in France, one for women in 1790, the Daughters of the Sacred Heart, and one for men in 1791, the Institute of Priests of the Heart of Jesus. Three years later two former students of the Parisian seminary of Saint Sulpice created in the Netherlands the Society of the Sacred Heart of Jesus, while in Rome in 1797 the charismatic priest and eccentric visionary Niccolò Paccanari (1774–1811) founded the Society of the Faith of Jesus, more commonly known as Fathers of the Faith, which in 1799 incorporated the Institute of Priests of the Heart of Jesus, making it for a short time the most successful of Jesuit imitations.

It briefly flourished, gaining the support of Pius VI and then—also briefly—of Pius VII and embracing 130 members, attracting a number of former Jesuits. There were houses and schools in Germany, France, Holland, and England where, despite the anti-Catholic legislation not yet repealed, a school was opened in London, while a "Mother House" was opened in Rome in 1801. The Roman presence may have been a mistake. The same year that the house in Rome was opened,

[52] Caraman, *The University of the Nations*, 77.

[53] He was arrested and briefly imprisoned in 1804 on the charge of plotting against Napoleon. It was a case of mistaken identity: the true culprit in the Cadoudal Conspiracy was his nephew.

the lifestyle of Niccolò Paccanari attracted the attention of the Inquisition. In 1806 he was sentenced to prison for ten years for his pretence of holiness and sexual misconduct.[54]

The Paccanarists enjoyed for a time a reputation for leading missions and giving spiritual retreats,[55] rather as the Jesuits had done, but they melted away when the Society was restored in 1814. Though the Fathers of the Faith might be seen as a bridge between the old Society and that restored by Pius VII, it is questionable how similar they were to the Jesuits. Eva Fontana Castelli points to a number of significant differences between the two. Paccanari's institute laid far more emphasis on community life than did the Society: Jesuits were supposed to combine action and contemplation whereas the Paccanarists drew a distinction between the two, being more monastic in style, including separation from the world rather than being immersed in it, and laying greater stress on contemplation. Nonetheless, the Fathers of the Faith gave a home to some seeking a form of Jesuit spirituality, and they constituted a bridge between the pre-1773 and the post-1814 Society. Several members of the Fathers of the Faith came to play a significant role in the Society when Pius VII brought it back into being.

---

[54] The misconduct was, apparently, soliciting sexual favors in the confessional, which canon law treats as an especially heinous crime. See Eva Fontana Castelli, "Il Paccanarismo: una Compagnia di Gesù sotto altro nome?" in Fabre et al., *La Compagnie de Jésus*, 119.

[55] Cf. Jonathan Wright. s.v. "Paccanarists," in Worcester, *The Cambridge Encyclopedia of the Jesuits*, 577.

Chapter 9

Restored or Renewed?

There is a curious parallelism between the career of Jorge Bergoglio, Pope Francis, and that of the restored Society. Both began as sticklers for the Jesuit rule and, as will be seen, firmly pro-papal; then both had a conversion[1] experience and regained a measure of that inventive dynamism that had frequently brought the pre-suppression Society, despite its vows of obedience to the papacy in all that appertained to mission (see above, pp. 57–58), into sharp conflict with Rome. It is perhaps a little odd to suggest that Bergoglio as pope was in conflict with Rome, but there is no question that he has often been at odds with those, including cardinals and other senior churchmen, who were serving in Vatican offices.[2] Despite his obvious reforming zeal, Francis at first displayed a diplomatic caution. In the case of the restored Society, its caution was not exactly diplomatic, but, bruised by its suppression by one pope and grateful for its restoration by another, it became, as will be seen, throughout the nineteenth century and well into the twentieth extremely loyal to the Holy See and the person of the pope. This effectively put the Society into the distinctly theologically conservative camp, something that could hardly be said of the pre-suppression Jesuits.

The suppression had fallen upon the Society of Jesus in a brutal and sudden, if not entirely unexpected, fashion. The restoration, though formally announced by Pope Pius VII in 1814, shortly after

---

[1] Not all of the many biographers of Jorge Bergoglio would concede that in Còrdoba, during his "exile" from Buenos Aires, he underwent a "conversion," but this is the conclusion of one of the most successful biographies, *Pope Francis: Untying the Knots* by Paul Vallely (London: Bloomsbury, 2013; rev. and exp. ed., 2015).

[2] See, for example, Christopher Lamb, *The Outsider: Pope Francis and His Battle to Reform the Church* (Maryknoll, NY: Orbis Books, 2020).

his return to Rome from imprisonment by Napoleon, had been a rather longer, drawn-out affair, beginning in Russia. As has been seen in the previous chapter, partly because she was anxious to maintain the education system in that region of the Polish-Lithuanian Commonwealth that Russia had acquired in the partition of Poland in 1772[3] and partly to oppose the policy of the Bourbons and—especially—the Habsburgs, the Tzarina Catherine the Great had forbidden the promulgation of *Dominus ac Redemptor* in the territories under her control. The leadership of the more than two hundred Jesuits in White Russia fell to Stanisław Czerniewicz (1728–1785), who had recently been working in the Jesuit headquarters in Rome and had been named by Lorenzo Ricci as rector of the college at Polock. As a good Jesuit, Czerniewicz at first attempted to get Catherine's permission to suppress the Society, but that was denied. He was also reluctant to accept others into the surviving province, but pressure of work in the colleges forced him to admit Jesuits from other parts of the former Polish-Lithuanian Commonwealth while rejecting other requests from further afield. He then sought from the new pope permission to continue. He received an answer from Cardinal Giovanni Battista Rezzonico in his capacity of secretary of memorials that was ambiguous: it did not approve, but then neither did it condemn—popes are always reluctant to contradict their predecessors, especially their immediate predecessor. This tacit approval was enough for Czerniewicz to begin to reconstruct his province. There was a general congregation held in October 1782 at the Polock college where Czerniewicz was elected vicar general for life, "for life" implying he would be in office until a new superior general could be properly chosen.

While most attention has been paid to the role of Russia in the survival of the Society, and rightly so, it also survived—or, more correctly, was fairly promptly restored—in Parma. At the time of the suppression Duke Ferdinand was too young to resist the pressure from his Bourbon relatives and acceded to their demand for the abolition of the Society in his duchy. But then in 1794 the mainstay of the Bourbon alliance, the king of France, lost his head to the guillotine, having been stripped of his throne two years earlier. Ferdinand ap-

---

[3] White Russia, or Belarus.

pealed to both Catherine the Great and Gabriel Lenkiewicz, a Lithuanian who in 1785 had succeeded Czerniewicz as vicar general, for permission to restore the order in his territory. It was problematic. The Society was still under papal sanction, and Ferdinand felt he needed to get Pius VI's approval. This was granted, but only in a secretive fashion to avoid annoying the still hostile Spain, and when Ferdinand pressed further the pope told him that he might wish to restore the Society but could not do so while Spain remained opposed. Ferdinand wrote to the king of Spain, Charles IV, but to no avail. While it was clear that the pope was sympathetic, he was in no position to give his approval, and he died, a prisoner of the French, in August 1799.

Pius's successor, who also took the name Pius, was elected in Venice in May 1800 and was promptly approached in person by one of the Parma Jesuits. Pius VII told him that he was fully in agreement with Duke Ferdinand about the restoration of the Society and asked that his apostolic blessing be sent to the Russian Jesuits, now headed by Franciszek Kareu, together with the gift of a relic.[4] Kareu and his predecessors had enjoyed excellent relations with the Tzarina Catherine and her successor, the Tzar Paul I, and both, especially Tzar Paul, had encouraged their expansion. Paul had petitioned the pope to grant full recognition to the Society, and Pius undertook to do so, a promise fulfilled in defiance of Spanish pressure with the brief *Catholicae Fidei* of March 7, 1801, though the brief gave formal recognition only to those in Tzar Paul's dominions. The tzar was assassinated a couple of weeks later—he had alienated the aristocracy by his social reforms—and was succeeded by his son, Alexander I, who proved to be a great deal less friendly to the Society, banishing it from Russia in 1820.

Catholicae Fidei was something of a turning point. It was not a full restoration, or anything like it, but the Society once again had a corporate identity recognized by the Church. Almost the first to take advantage of this new status were the former Jesuits now in England with a school and a theology college at Stonyhurst. John Howard,

---

[4] Kareu was elected in February 1799 and died in 1802, after having appointed the Austrian Gabriel Gruber to assist him because of his failing health: Gruber succeeded him as vicar general. The name Kareu is an oddity. It is a Polish form of Carew, the name of a British family settled in Lithuania.

the head of the English Academy in Liège, had asked for affiliation with the Russian Jesuits when he had heard of their survival, but this had been rejected as being impermissible. Cardinal Consalvi, Pius VII's Anglophile secretary of state, had told Gabriel Gruber in July 1802 that the restriction on the Russian Jesuits accepting non-Russians had been lifted, and Gruber wrote to William Strickland, the effective head of the community, that those former members who wished to join the Russian province might do so. Strickland in turn wrote to former members of the English province inviting them to renew their vows. Although there were seventy-three surviving members of the province, only thirty-one took up the invitation. For some the hesitation was due to age; for others it was the lack of formal agreement by the papacy that the Society might be restored outside Russia.[5] The issue was pressing. The Jesuits had established a number of "missions"—effectively parishes—around the country; the income stream that funded them was under threat. Rome had ruled in 1786 that while the present incumbent of the missions was alive the income could continue to support them, but after their deaths it was to revert to the vicar apostolic of whichever district[6] to which the mission belonged. Strickland believed that most of the vicars apostolic would respect the Jesuit patrimony, but it would be much easier were the English province of the Society to be reconstituted. A novitiate was opened in a separate building on the Stonyhurst estate, and in 1803, on the recommendation of Strickland, Gruber appointed Marmaduke Stone as provincial. Gruber also requested that the newly constituted province take over the school the Paccanarists (see above, p. 227) had opened in London: Stone rejected the vicar general's appeal on the grounds that he did not want to encumber the province with their debts.

The English Jesuits presumed that the privilege they enjoyed at Liège of presenting candidates for ordination had been carried over to Stonyhurst, and eventually candidates were indeed presented, but

[5] On the reasons given for not renewing their vows, see Geoffrey Holt, "The English Province: The Ex-Jesuits and the Restoration," in *Promising Hope*, ed. Thomas McCoog (Rome: Institutum Historicum Societatis Iesu, 2003), 239–40.

[6] There were no dioceses in Britain, and therefore no diocesan bishops, until 1850, but instead there were "districts"—Northern, London etc.—with vicars apostolic who had the rank of bishop.

the issue remained as to whether they were being ordained as members of a religious order or as priests under obedience to the vicar apostolic. Most bishops took the latter view, fearing that the public restoration of the Jesuits as a religious order in England might hinder the restoration of civic rights to British Roman Catholics. The impasse remained until 1828 when, at the behest of an English Benedictine vicar apostolic who was visiting Rome, Leo XII effectively instructed that the Society be formally restored in Britain.[7] In the meantime, however, Stonyhurst had benefited from the considerable talents of Giovanni Antonio Grassi (1775–1849).[8] In 1782 the surviving (ex-) Jesuit priests in China, having heard of the reestablishment of the Society in Russia, appealed to Czerniewicz for new missionaries to be sent. At the time it was impossible, but in 1805 Gruber dispatched three: Norbert Korsack, a Polish priest; Johannes Stürmer; and a German lay brother. Grassi[9] would have seemed to the vicar general to be a particularly good choice as one of his specializations was astronomy, which had, of course, been one of the main factors attracting Chinese emperors to the Society. Grassi visited London in a vain attempt to find transport to China and also to purchase scientific instruments to take with him. When no ship would take him, in 1807 he was instructed make his way to Stonyhurst,[10] which was in dire need of learned men, and then in 1810 he was sent to the United States.

The restoration of the Society in the States was a somewhat low-key affair. At the suppression John Carroll (1735–1815) returned from Europe to Maryland where he was chosen by the other Maryland priests to be superior of what was, or rather had been, technically an English Jesuit mission with the vicar apostolic of the London district

---

[7] For a more detailed account of this complicated story, see Walsh, *Heythrop College*, 60–73.

[8] Grassi, rather oddly, given his importance in the history of Georgetown—it was he who negotiated the college's university status—does not have an entry in the *Cambridge Encyclopedia of the Jesuits*, not even in the index even though he is mentioned at least once. See instead Gilbert J. Garraghan, "John Anthony Grassi, S.J., 1775–1849," *The Catholic Historical Review* 23, no. 3 (October, 1937): 273–92.

[9] In 1806 four former Jesuits in China renewed their vows as members of the Society.

[10] Korsack also went to Stonyhurst and remained there, teaching theology in the seminary.

as its canonical superior. After the American Revolution this was no longer a feasible option, and indeed the vicar apostolic who in 1781 succeeded the great Bishop Richard Challoner as London's vicar apostolic refused to exercise any jurisdiction over the Maryland clergy. In place of the English vicar apostolic the clergy elected Carroll as the superior of the mission, a choice endorsed by Pope Pius VI in 1784. But this left them without a bishop. They approached Rome, which allowed them not only to choose the first cathedral city but also—and just for this one occasion—to name their favored candidate for the office of bishop. Carroll was nominated in April 1789, and in November of that year the pope again gave his approval. There being no other Catholic bishop in the States to perform the ceremony Carroll had to return to England, where in the chapel of the Welds of Lulworth Castle in Dorset he was consecrated bishop in August 1790.

In 1787 the Maryland clergy had decided on the establishment of a Catholic college, and in 1789 Carroll purchased the property in Georgetown on which it was to be built. He had wanted his old friend from England and most frequent correspondent, Charles Plowden, to come to the States to run the college, but Plowden, who was to become the novice master and eventually the provincial of the restored English province, decided against.[11] The first courses at what eventually became Georgetown University began in 1792, but its early years were fraught with difficulties. In 1803 Carroll and his assistant bishop, Leonard Neale, also a former Jesuit, wrote to Gruber that the priests in Maryland who had been members of the Society wished to re-join. Gruber replied a year later, and in 1805 five renewed their vows—though neither Bishop Carroll nor Bishop Neale did so.

---

[11] "How often have I said to myself; what a blessing to this country would my friend Plowden be! What reputation and solid advantage would accrue to the academy from such a Director! And what a lasting blessing would he procure to America by forming the whole plan of studies and system of discipline for that institution, where the minds of Catholic youth are to be formed, & the first foundations laid of raising a Catholic ministry equal to the exigencies of the Country! Could the zeal of a Xaverius wish a more promising field to exert his talents? But, my dear Sir, I am sensible, that I can indulge this happiness only in idea: Europe will hold you too fast to spare you to America." Letter dated January 22–February 28, 1787, in *The John Carroll Papers*, vol. 1, ed. Thomas O'Brien Hanley (Notre Dame, IN: University of Notre Dame Press, 1976), 242. See also Robert Emmett Curran, *The Bicentennial History of Georgetown University*, vol. 1 (Washington, DC: Georgetown University Press, 1993), 31.

The fortunes of the college did not greatly improve with the arrival of a few Jesuits, reaching its nadir in 1810 when only thirty-one students were enrolled. It was Grassi's arrival that same year, 1810, that made the difference. He increased the number of students by reducing the fees and increased the staff by recruiting more qualified Jesuits. He drew on his experience at Stonyhurst to improve the curriculum, in particular in the sciences, and he himself gave lectures on astronomy. The policy of "accommodation" that he might have been expected to develop in China, his original destination, he now transferred to the needs of the growing Catholic community in the United States.[12]

In 1817 Grassi reluctantly—he suffered badly from seasickness—returned to Rome on a mission for Bishop Neale, and, despite the fact that he had become an American citizen, he never again left Italy. He held a number of important posts, becoming rector of the College of Nobles in Turin, which became the premier Jesuit school, and attracted not just Italians but the sons of families he had known in England. He became provincial of the Turin province and reprised the traditional Jesuit role as confessor to princes, becoming the spiritual guide of the king and queen of Sardinia. Later he was appointed rector of the Pontifical Urban College in Rome, which trained priests for the foreign missions. His final post was as the general's assistant for Italy, in which office he died.

Italy as a unitary state did not, of course, exist. Grassi had been born at Bergamo, then part of the Venetian Republic, and had joined the Jesuits when he entered the noviceship at Colorno in the duchy of Parma. At Colorno his novice master had been José Pignatelli (1737–1811), who, despite his Italian-sounding surname, was Spanish by birth. He had been exempted from the 1767 decree expelling Jesuits from Spain because of his noble birth but instead preferred to go into exile with his confreres, first to Corsica and eventually to Parma, where in July 1797 he renewed his vows. In the meantime, however, he had solicited from Gruber some Russian-based Jesuits to create a new vice province with the authority to readmit to the Society any

---

[12] Or so argues Giovanni Pizzorusso in "The New World of the New Society of Jesus," in *La Compagnie de Jésus des Anciens Régimes au Monde Contemporain (XVIIIᵉ–XXᵉ Siècles)*, ed. Pierre Antoine Fabre (Rome: Institutum Historicum Societatis Iesu and L'École Française de Rome, 2021), 485–86.

who wished to join: Pignatelli had already gathered a number of former Jesuits, especially Spanish ones, to serve as teachers in the duchy's schools. The noviceship began toward the end of 1799, and by the end of 1802 there were some forty Jesuits in Parma. From Parma, under the continued leadership of Pignatelli, the revival had spread also to Naples, thanks in part to his aristocratic connections. The restoration of the Society in Naples was formally approved by the pope in a brief, *Per alias*, dated July 30, 1804, addressed to Gabriel Gruber. The king of Naples, Ferdinand IV (he was also Ferdinand III of the Kingdom of Sicily), was sympathetic despite being a Bourbon and attended the ceremonies to mark the Jesuits' return, but the Bourbon king of Spain was furious and suspended the pensions that had been paid to former Jesuits if they joined the Neapolitan province. With Napoleon's invasion of Italy, however, it was not long before members of the Society were again temporarily expelled from Naples and Sicily. This was a pattern that some provinces had to become accustomed to during the nineteenth and into the twentieth centuries.

In reviving the fortunes of the Society Pignatelli—who was canonized in 1954—played a central role, not just because he was in Italy but also because of his diplomatic skills even when Italy was invaded by Napoleon's armies. In order to pass on what he considered the true spirit of the pre-1773 Society he laid down three principles: the *Spiritual Exercises* of St. Ignatius were to be central together with the theology of Luis de Molina (for Molina, see above, p. 184); there was to be an active pastoral ministry in hospitals and prisons as well as teaching catechism and other works of charity; traditional Jesuit devotions were to be revived, such as that to the Sacred Heart, and the lay confraternities were to be reestablished.[13]

Pignatelli had been operating under the aegis of the vicar general—although Pope Pius VII allowed Gruber to be named as general—in

---

[13] Niccolò Guasti, "Il ristablimento della Compagnia di Gesù," in Fabre, *La Compagnie de Jesús*, 139. According to Guasti, it was the success of the educational work of the Parma Jesuits that played a part in persuading Pius VII to issue *Catholicae Fidei* (ibid., 140). In the same volume Emanuele Colombo's article, "Mission Is Possible: Italian Jesuits and Popular Missions between the Old and the New Society" (183–213), draws attention to Jesuit missionary activity in Italy and the plan devised by Luigi Mozzi de' Capitani (1746–1813) with the backing of Pignatelli, which also linked the pre-1773 Society with the apostolic activity after the limited restoration in Parma and Naples.

Russia. After the death of Gruber, Tadeusz Brzozowski (1749–1820), a priest of Polish parents but born in East Prussia, was elected general of the Society in a council held in Polock in 1805. On August 7, 1814, Pope Pius, fresh from Napoleonic captivity, issued *Sollicitudo Omnium Ecclesiarum*, a bull extending the privileges that had been granted to the Jesuits in Russia to all Jesuits around the world, thereby entirely reversing the brief issued in 1773 by Pope Clement XIV "of happy memory," as Pope Pius denominated his predecessor in the required traditional fashion. The bull was handed over in an elaborate ceremony at the Gesù. The pope first celebrated Mass in front of a gathering of cardinals and around one hundred old Jesuits, then handed over the document reestablishing the Society to Luigi Panizzoni (1729–1820), superior of the Italian Jesuits. Brzozowski was not present. He had been forbidden by Tzar Alexander I to travel to Rome, and the tzar also forbade the Jesuits to move their headquarters from St. Petersburg, though the following year they were banned from St. Petersburg and the headquarters was moved to Polock, which by this time had become a university. Brzozowski was never allowed to travel to Rome, and on January 25, 1820, he appointed as vicar general in his place, Mariano Petrucci, born in 1748 and at the time rector of the college in Genoa, a Jesuit from before the suppression.

It proved to be an unfortunate choice. Brzozowski died only a few days later, February 5, 1820, so there had to be called a general congregation to elect a successor.[14] It fell to Petrucci to organize it, but he was in no hurry to do so, perhaps fearing the problems that were likely to arise. For there were tensions, between those who had entered the Society before the suppression and those that had joined after, between those who had experienced Jesuit life in Russia and those who had been novices of Pignatelli, between those who had once been Paccanarists and the rest, and between those who had been diocesan clergy and had become accustomed to a more independent way of life than had hitherto been the practice of the Society and those who had not. There was, moreover, a group that threw doubt on the validity of vows taken by Jesuits before *Catholicae Fidei* or even, for some, before *Sollicitudo Omnium Ecclesiarum* and therefore on their right to vote in the election of a general.

[14] According to the entry for Brzozowski in the *Cambridge Encyclopedia*, at the time of his death there were 436 members of the Society and twenty houses.

Petrucci arrived in Rome at the end of April and set the date for the opening of the twentieth general congregation as September 14, 1820. By that date seventeen out of a possible electorate of twenty-one had gathered in Rome—some had been delayed by an apparent attempt by some in the pope's entourage, and perhaps by Pius VII himself, to postpone the opening of the congregation. Then, at the last minute, a letter arrived from Pope Pius to insist that before proceeding to the election, the assembled fathers should address the "irregularities" that had brought about the suppression.

Behind this last obstacle to the process of electing a new general was the figure of Luigi Maria Rezzi (born in Piacenza, 1785; died in Rome, 1857), who had entered the Society in 1803 and had taught literature—he later became a significant Italian literary figure—in Sicily. By the time of *Sollicitudo Omnium Ecclesiarum* he was in Rome, and a consultor to the Congregation of the Index, a post that enabled him to make influential friends among members of the papal curia, not least Cardinal Annibale della Genga, who, in 1823, was to succeed Pius VII to become Pope Leo XII. Pius VII after publishing *Sollicitudo* had been advised of the "irregularities" and had set up a secret commission to discuss them: Petrucci was aware of its existence, and Rezzi was the intermediary between the commission and Petrucci. It was only as the congregation was about to assemble that most members learned that the papal curia lacked confidence in the congregation and had ordered it—through della Genga—to be delayed, though in the meantime Petrucci was to enjoy the full authority of the general of the Society. The pope also instructed that assistants be appointed to represent the diverse parts of the order, and that they be given the same role as that which would normally, according to the Society's Constitution, be conceded by the general congregation.

The would-be electors were, not surprisingly, annoyed by the way their authority was being undermined and urged Petrucci to contact della Genga to protest. Ever dilatory, the vicar general failed to act, and the provincial for Italy, Giuseppe Sineo della Torre (1761–1842), who had come to the Jesuits by way of the Society of the Sacred Heart, threatened to resign. Petrucci would not accept his resignation—but he did so despite Petrucci's objections. In the meantime the French Jesuit Jean-Louis de Leissègues de Rozaven (1767–1851) had drawn up a memorandum for the pope pointing out that what the commission of cardinals had proposed was contrary to the Society's Constitution and therefore contrary to the will of St. Ignatius. Moreover, Rozaven remarked, the authority of a vicar general could only be provisional, and the longer the delay, the less confidence members would have in him.

It was a risky strategy, asking the pontiff to overrule a commission of cardinals. Rozaven took his memorandum to Cardinal Ercole Consalvi, Pius VII's very able secretary of state, and Consalvi sympathized with the Society's predicament. He had, it seems, little trouble in persuading Pius of the justice of Rozaven's arguments. On October 1, the pope wrote to Petrucci, saying that the congregation should start meeting without further delay, and, as all those attending had long ago arrived in Rome, it did so on October 9 and lasted until December 10. On October 18, at the second ballot, the assembled fathers elected Luigi Fortis (1748–1829) from Verona as the twentieth superior general. He immediately promoted a decree to reinstate all the decrees of previous congregations, all the rules and regulations that had governed the pre-suppression Society, of which he had been a member.

One of the congregation's decisions was to invite Rezzi and fellow conspirators to resign from the Society: when he refused to do so he was dismissed. Petrucci was also sanctioned. He was accused of being ambitious, which was somewhat unfair—when asked by Brzozowski to take on the role of vicar general, he had protested his incapacity— nonetheless he was deprived of any future role as a superior or of any "active or passive voice" in the governance of the Society and required to leave Rome.[15]

---

[15] This account closely follows Miguel Coll, "La primera Congregación de la Compañia de Jesús tras la restauración de 1814," in Fabre, *La Compagnie de Jésus*, 237–55. Fernanda Alfieri, "'Unearthing Chaos and Giving Shape to It': The Society of Jesus after Suppression; Hiatus and Continuity," in *The Historiography of Transition: Critical Phases in the Development of Modernity (1494–1973)*, ed. Paolo Pombeni (New York: Routledge, 2016), 110, rather suggests that the more official histories of the Society attribute the chaos that surrounded the twentieth general congregation to Petrucci's old age and debility rather than to intrigues and internal conflicts such as those described by Coll. The account of the congregation in William Bangert's *A History of the Society of Jesus*, while not dwelling on Petrucci's incompetence, passes swiftly over the machinations. The expression to deprive someone of "active or passive voice" is commonly used in the Society to indicate lack of authority to govern.

Despite all the problems on the sidelines, those electing the new general did so according to the Constitutions as laid down by Ignatius and clearly believed that the restored Society was a direct descendant of that suppressed in 1773. In doing so, they were entirely in keeping with the spirit of the age as exemplified by the Congress of Vienna that met to settle the affairs of Europe after the final defeat of Napoleon at Waterloo, a return to the *status quo ante,* across-the-board restoration of the *ancien regime.* But for the Society it was not quite so simple. The papal bull of 1814 had not restored to it all the privileges it has enjoyed before 1773. More significantly, *Sollicitudo Omnium Ecclesiarum,* while it laid great stress on the Jesuits' educational apostolate, made no mention of Jesuit missionary activity. And although there were some among the members who had been Jesuits before the suppression, they were inevitably elderly and not obviously mentors for the next generation of the Society. Luigi Fortis himself was over seventy years of age when elected and, having joined the Society when only fourteen years old, had only just over a decade of Jesuit life before the suppression. Despite this limited experience, he dedicated his period as general to trying to inculcate in new recruits—and there were many—what had been the main characteristics of Jesuit life and outlook as he understood them by writing letters to the novices and those in formation, as well as instructing that a new version of the *Ratio Studiorum* appropriate to the changing times should be prepared. It was completed in 1832, during the generalate of Fortis's successor, the Dutchman Jan Philip Roothaan (1785–1853).[16] Roothaan had been taught by an ex-Jesuit during the suppression and had joined the Society in Russia, serving there until the 1820 expulsion, after which he went first to Switzerland and then to Turin. In 1829 he was appointed provincial of Italy, a short-lived assignment as he was elected general in 1830.

In *Sollicitudo Omnium Ecclesiarum* Pope Pius VII had referred to "the urgent and pressing petitions coming to us day after day, by an almost unanimous consent of the Christian world, from our venerable brother archbishops and bishops and from the ranks of outstanding persons and associations on behalf of this same Society of Jesus." It is true that many, especially perhaps in France where some of the

---

[16] At the time of Roothaan's birth, Holland as a political entity did not yet exist. The term "Dutch" is used here simply for convenience.

Marian congregations had survived, still attracting high-ranking recruits to their style of Ignatian spirituality for laypeople, saw in the extirpation of the Jesuits a precursor of the Revolution and therefore were eager to see them restored—and not simply because of the Society's past contribution to education, although that was certainly also a factor.

Not everyone was applauding. John (João VI), prince regent of Portugal because of the incapacity of his mother at the time of the papal bull and, after his mother's death in 1816, monarch of the united kingdom of Portugal and Brazil,[17] wrote to Rome expressing his annoyance at the reemergence of the Jesuits and at not having been informed, let alone consulted, before *Sollicitudo Omnium Ecclesiarum*. He would not, he insisted, countenance any negotiations leading to the readmission of the Society to Portugal.[18] During this period the court was in Rio de Janeiro rather than Lisbon—João returned in 1821—and in its absence there were attempts to impose a more liberal constitution on the country. The liberal faction was even more hostile to the Society than the king, seeing it as a relic of the *ancien régime*, which the modernizers wished to overthrow.

This became the leitmotif of the opponents of the Society during the nineteenth century. Pope Pius VII had resurrected the order as one of the buttresses of the papacy, but the papacy was regarded by many as a major reactionary force in European society, and not unfairly so when one considers the pontificate of Gregory XVI from 1831 to 1846 or that of his successor Pius IX from 1846 to 1878, though Pius had begun his pontificate with a reputation for liberalism. "In this new century which seemed so promising," write José Eduardo Franco and Fernanda Santos, "the Jesuits showed themselves more than ever faithful to the papacy by way of compensating for the past disobedience of which they had been accused."[19] In the course of the nineteenth century Jesuits were to experience a bumpy ride, regularly a prey to political forces over which they had no control. This was particularly so in the countries that had led the way in demanding that Clement XIV suppress the Society.

[17] Brazil became independent in 1825.
[18] José Eduardo Franco and Fernanda Santos, "Echos politiques et idéologiques de la Restauration de la Compagnie de Jésus," in Fabre, *La Compagnie de Jésus*, 355–59.
[19] Ibid., 361.

This was clearly exemplified by the history of the restored order in Portugal. Jesuits were allowed back into the country in 1829, led by five Frenchmen, but then in 1834 the minister of justice, Joaquim António de Aguiar, "nationalized" all religious orders, not only the Jesuits, and seized their property, theoretically for the benefit of the poor but in practice largely for the benefit of the state's treasury. Jesuits were allowed back in 1858, and by 1880 there were 120 Portuguese members, enough to constitute a province.

The fate of the Society in Spain was even more turbulent. There was limited restoration in May 1815, when 112 priests and ten brothers returned, and full restoration a year later. It was not to be a peaceful return. Spain's economy was precarious and despite selling Florida to the United States for five million dollars, the government of King Ferdinand VII did not have enough money to pay his troops. In 1820 they rioted in Cadiz, and the rebel soldiers were joined by others from around the peninsula. The king was forced to accept the liberal Constitution of 1812, and the Jesuits were expelled, but not before twenty-five of their number had lost their lives. The liberal regime, detested by governments elsewhere in Europe, lasted only until 1823, and when a French army removed the liberals and restored Ferdinand, the Jesuits returned, growing in numbers to some 350 and establishing several colleges. Ferdinand died in 1833, having arranged that his daughter Isabella should succeed to the throne: as she was then only three years old she ruled with her mother as regent. Isabella's succession was, however, disputed by Ferdinand's brother Carlos, leading to the first Carlist war. The chaos of war was compounded by a deadly outbreak of cholera, for which the Jesuits were blamed. A mob stormed their college in Madrid and, after sending the pupils home, put to death fourteen Jesuits and over fifty members of other religious orders who were studying there. A year later the government of Queen Isabella once more sent the Jesuits into exile. When in 1851 Spain signed a concordat, or treaty, with the Holy See, one of the conditions was that some religious orders be allowed to return. A generous interpretation by the Spanish bishops of this clause in the concordat meant that the Society might reestablish itself in the peninsula. Though its beginnings were modest, numbers grew swiftly so that in 1862 the general decided to divide Spain into two provinces, but only five years later Isabella was sent into exile after a military coup, a republic was proclaimed, and a liberal government formed that again expelled the Society, the president of the Republic declaring, "Catholicism is dead in the conscience of humanity and in the conscience of the Spanish people."[20] In 1874 yet another military coup put Isabella's son Alonso XII on the throne, and he insisted that the 1851 concordat be respected, which meant that the Society could return yet again, in some ways more powerful than before because a new Constitution in 1876 effectively put education, and especially secondary education, in the hands of the Church.

Education also proved to be a major matter of contention in France, with its Jansenism, which still to some extent survived into the spirituality of the nineteenth century, and its Gallicanism. France had been the birthplace of the campaign for the suppression of the Society. After its restoration in 1814 Brzozowski named Pierre de la Clorivière (see above, p. 227) as provincial of France, and although eighty years old, he set about his new role with remarkable energy, taking charge of sixty novices, half of whom had already been ordained. Their arrival was welcomed by Catholics, still reeling from the impact of the Revolution, and requests to open schools poured in, far too many for the small province to handle. By 1826 they had taken on only eight,[21] the Society's policy being to keep a low profile, given its past travails. But then in 1828 Charles X was prevailed upon to ban from colleges anyone who did not belong to a body authorized to teach and, as the Jesuits had determined not to seek such a status, they were effectively removed from classrooms. Widespread hostility to the Society re-emerged after the July Revolution of 1830, with the result that most of its members fled France for safety in surrounding countries though they gradually returned, not to colleges but to parishes and the foreign missions. The anti-clericals in the government of Louis Philippe at one point threatened the Vatican that all religious orders would be banned unless the French Jesuits were dispersed. Gregory XVI conveyed this message to Roothaan, while assuring him of his support for the Society: Roothaan's response was to advise that the larger communities in France be reduced in size, something that, as he admitted, had won him no friends among the French Jesuits.[22] In

---

[20] Quoted in Bangert, *A History of the Society of Jesus*, 451.

[21] Ibid., 453.

[22] Robert G. North, *The General Who Rebuilt the Jesuits* (Milwaukee: Bruce Publishing Company, 1944), 239.

1850 the National Assembly passed the "Falloux Law" enabling religious institutes to open schools, and once again the Jesuits were inundated with requests, opening twelve new colleges before, in 1880, the Society was again banned and its French members had for the second time to flee the country, though once again they were allowed to drift back.

The hostility of the government is understandable. French Catholics were, for the most part, conservative monarchists, the Jesuits among them. In an effort to relieve the tension in 1890 Pope Leo XIII suggested to the archbishop of Algiers, Cardinal Charles Lavigerie, that he make some gesture of reconciliation toward the secularists. He gave a lunch in Algiers for the officers of the French Mediterranean squadron, had a band play the *Marseillaise*, and, most remarkably for a lifelong monarchist, toasted the Republic. This gesture, known as the *Ralliement*, did not have the desired effect, serving only to alienate many of the monarchists without winning over the secularists. Despite that, Lavigerie himself, because of his work in Africa, was a highly respected figure even in secular government circles, and as a consequence Algiers was exempt from the anticlerical legislation that had driven religious orders out of metropolitan France.

Jesuit historians tend to link Germany, Austria, and Switzerland together in their accounts of the society's revival, under the heading of "German-speaking lands"—though, of course, Switzerland is home to French and Italian as well as German. It was in the Republica Helvetica, set up under Napoleon, that the Society established itself, following the lead of the Paccanarists. From there Jesuits moved into what is now, but was not then, Germany. In both Switzerland and Germany there were disruptions. In Switzerland an indiscreet attempt by the Catholic cantons to have Jesuits take over the theological faculty of Lucerne, insisted on by Pope Gregory against the judgment of Roothaan, led to the Sonderbundskrieg, the short war between the Protestant cantons and the Catholic ones. In the war the Protestants were victorious, and when a new federal constitution was introduced in 1848 Jesuits were banned from the country. The ban was not removed until 1973, though by that time Jesuits had long been back at work in Switzerland.

Austria benefited from the expulsion of Jesuits from Russia and from the eagerness of Prince von Metternich to restore the *ancien regime*, of which the Society was to some extent a symbol. After he fell from power in 1848 Jesuits were briefly banned from the arch-duchy, returning in 1852. The exile from Germany lasted rather longer. They were casualties of Otto von Bismarck's campaign against the Church, the Kulturkampf, rather than against the Society in particular, but they had to go into exile nonetheless, largely to Holland and England. Bismarck lost his battle with the Church, but the anti-Jesuit legislation lay on the statute book until 1917, though German Jesuit numbers had grown in exile, and many had, despite the legislation, returned to their homeland.

Both England and the United States had benefited from the dispersal of German and other Jesuits, especially perhaps England, where the level of scholarship in its theology college, St. Beuno's in north Wales, notably improved. Neither country—nor Ireland, which was at the time governed from London, although there was a separate Jesuit province—suffered from political interference. The English province had more problems with the bishops (see above, pp. 232–33) than it did with politicians. If episcopal reluctance to embrace the revived Society was because they feared the presence of Jesuits might hinder the removal of anti-Catholic laws, they were possibly correct. When the Catholic Relief Act of 1829 was passed, all religious orders were banned from receiving novices or wearing religious habits in public,[23] although only Jesuits were mentioned by name. Schools and parishes were opened as numbers grew, but when the English provincial attempted to open a school in Manchester without the approval of the diocesan bishop, Herbert Vaughan, at the time bishop of Salford, later cardinal archbishop of Westminster,[24] he was forced to retreat, despite claiming the exemption of religious orders from the jurisdiction of bishops. The question of the relationship between religious orders and the bishops was taken up by the former (Anglican) archdeacon of Chichester, now archbishop of Westminster, Henry

---

[23] The London Eucharistic Congress of 1908 had been planned to end with a mile-long procession of the Sacrament, but because of complaints aired to the government, especially by the Protestant Alliance, that the procession contravened the terms of the act, it took place without the Host. "In obedience to the strict interpretation of the law, Religious wore ordinary clerical garb, although some carried their habits over their arms, 'by way of silent protest.'" Thomas Horwood, "Public Opinion and the 1908 Eucharistic Congress," *Recusant History* (now *British Catholic History*) 25, no. 1 (2000): 125.

[24] Vaughan had a brother who was a member of the English province.

Edward Manning,[25] who solicited from the pope a letter—technically an apostolic constitution—titled *Romanos Pontifices* in 1881, which basically sided with the bishops. The provisions of *Romanos Pontifices* were later applied to the United States and elsewhere, "mission" territories that operated under the aegis of the Propaganda Fidei.[26]

The "foreign" missions were slow to return to the role they had enjoyed pre-suppression. It was Roothaan's conversation with Pope Gregory XVI when he went to make the traditional visit for the head of a religious order to congratulate him on his election that brought them once more back into prominence. The pope expressed the hope that the Society would return to their former missions, and in 1833 the general wrote to the whole Society, reminding its members of past achievements and urging them to missionary activity. But it could never be quite the same. Some of the former mission territories in South America, for example, had become provinces in their own right even before the expulsion of Jesuits from Spanish and Portuguese possessions in the late eighteenth century. Like the provinces in Europe they gradually revived, but, again like European provinces, their fortunes depended on the whims of the government of the day. The Jesuits returned to Argentina, Pope Francis's own province, in 1836, were expelled only six years later, but were invited back in 1854. In China it was members of the French province who returned to the country in 1842, and in India British Jesuits arrived in Calcutta in 1834: Jesuit schools played an important role educating those who were to administer the British Empire. New mission stations were opened in Africa and even in South America, though in the years of competition among European nations for empire, such missions tended to be served by priests and brothers from the imperial power. That apart, in the nineteenth century the Society's global outreach matched, if it did not even exceed, the range of Jesuit missions of the heady pioneering days of the sixteenth and seventeenth centuries.

---

[25] Manning, in many ways a great archbishop, was no supporter of the Jesuits for complex reasons that had to do, in part, with their role in England during the years of persecution. There was no Jesuit school in London until after his death.

[26] The details of the conflict can be read in the introduction to *Bishop Herbert Vaughan and the Jesuits: Education and Authority*, ed. Martin John Broadley (Woodbridge: The Boydell Press for the Catholic Record Society, 2010), xxvi–xxxvii.

Together with missions, education had been one of the defining characteristics of the Society up to the suppression, but afterward these apostolates could no longer be quite so dominant. Many new religious orders had sprung up, some exclusively dedicated to teaching, others to missionary activity and often specializing in distinct parts of the world: Lavigerie, for example (mentioned above, p. 244), had founded the Société des Missionnaires d'Afrique, often known as the "White Fathers" from the color of their habit. Though the Society continued its traditional activities, new initiatives sprang up alongside them, one of which was the apostolate of the press, marked by the publication in April 1850 of the first issue of a new journal *La Civiltà Cattolica*, which was born out of the ideological conflicts that wracked Italy during the nineteenth century.

Inevitably, the Jesuits were caught up in the controversies of the day and were constantly being expelled from one part of the Italian peninsula or another, even from the Papal States, and in 1848 on the advice of Pius IX Roothaan fled Rome in disguise, remaining outside the city for two years. His successor, the Belgian Pieter Becks, left Rome for Florence in 1873, eventually settling with his curia in a monastery in Fiesole where they remained for more than two decades. In 1884 Becks gave almost all authority over to a vicar general with right of succession. The Swiss Jesuit Anton Anderledy governed the Society from Fiesole until his death. He was replaced in September 1892 by a Spaniard, Luis Martin, at a general congregation that was held in Loyola, Spain, rather than Rome, Rome still being considered to be unsafe for Jesuits. The general and his curia returned to Rome only in January 1895.

It was against this tumultuous background that *La Civiltà Cattolica* came into being, originally in Naples but shortly afterward transferred to Rome. It was edited by Carlo Curci (1826–1891) in an attempt to oppose "the ideology underlying 'the Revolution,' and asserting that Catholicism was the essential support for social and political order."[27] *Civiltà* remains in existence, the proofs of each issue still overseen by the Vatican, and Antonio Spadaro, SJ, the editor at the time of writing, is one of Pope Francis's closest collaborators. It is,

[27] Oliver Logan, "*La Civiltà Cattolica* from Pius IX to Pius XII," in *The Church and the Book*, ed. R. N. Swanson (Woodbridge: The Boydell Press for the Ecclesiastical History Society, 2004), 377.

however, a very different journal to the one founded by Curci. "In its ideological commitment up to 1958, a dominant role was played by polemic against secularist ideologies, notably liberalism, democratic radicalism, socialism and (in due course) 'bolshevism,' which were endlessly portrayed as forming a monstrous line of descent, stemming ultimately from the Reformation and the Enlightenment. There was polemic, too, against 'false brethren' such as 'liberal Catholics,' a contradiction in terms so our Jesuit journalists asserted."[28] This is too kind, failing to mention the journal's persistent anti-Semitism. As John Pollard has written, albeit about a later period, "*La Civiltà Cattolica* had been attacking the Jews in the most vituperative terms since its very inception,"[29] and that included regurgitating the hoary old myth of Jewish ritual slaughter, despite the canard having been comprehensively debunked by the English Jesuit historian Hubert Thurston (1856–1939).[30]

Its main purpose, however, was to promote the papacy. "During its first century *La Civiltà Cattolica* was strongly ultramontane and infallibilist. Furthermore, it constantly celebrated the historic role of the papacy and its contribution to 'civilization.' Along with other intransigentist journals it promoted 'devotion to the popes' and the personality cults attaching to individual popes."[31] This was likewise true of other Jesuit journals created in its image: *Études*, founded in France, as the name suggests, in 1856; *The Month*, begun in London in 1864 by the Catholic convert Frances Margaret Taylor[32] and taken over by the Jesuits a year later;[33] *Stimmen der Zeit*, the journal of the German Jesuits founded in 1865; *Razón y Fe* (Spain, 1901); *Brotèria*

---

[28] Ibid., 379.

[29] John Pollard, *The Papacy in the Age of Totalitarianism* (Oxford: Oxford University Press, 2014), 279.

[30] David G. Schultenover, *A View from Rome* (New York: Fordham University Press, 1993), 82.

[31] Logan, "*La Civiltà Cattolica*," 382.

[32] Frances Taylor was a quite remarkable woman. Her conversion in 1855 was inspired by John Henry Newman and his famous "Dream of Gerontius," which first appeared in *The Month* during her brief editorship—twenty years later the then-editor refused to publish "The Wreck of the Deutschland" by his fellow Jesuit, Gerard Manley Hopkins. Frances Taylor, who had nursed in the Crimea with Florence Nightingale, went on to found the Congregation of the Poor Servants of the Mother of God. She wrote over two dozen books, including novels and collections of short stories.

[33] Full disclosure: the present author was briefly *The Month*'s editor in the 1970s.

(Portugal, 1902); and the weekly *America Magazine* (United States, 1909). This commitment to periodical publication was not quite as much of a novelty as it is sometimes presented: the monthly *Journal de Trévoux* had been published in Trévoux, now a suburb of Lyon, and later in Paris, from January 1701 to December 1782, and it played a considerable role in combatting Jansenism. Nonetheless, Jesuit journalism has had a much more important role in the Society from the middle of the nineteenth century onward than in the earlier centuries.

Not every Jesuit was happy with the excessively pro-papal line taken by these periodicals in the nineteenth century. Carlo Curci himself, *Civiltà*'s founding editor, eventually rebelled, arguing after the fall of Rome that the pope ought to come to terms with the new situation in Italy and abandon its claims to temporal power. He left the Society, becoming increasingly attracted to socialism and increasingly opposed to what he termed "the royal Vatican." Some of his writings were condemned by the Inquisition, which did not greatly trouble him, and he was suspended from his priestly ministry, which did—not least because it cut off a source of income, though the unlikely figure of Henry Edward Manning, the very pro-papal archbishop of Westminster, offered to support him. At the end of his life, however, he submitted to the Holy See and was readmitted into the Jesuits.

Curci was one of the few who radically dissented, at least for a time, from the Society's pro-papal theology expressed in its publications. It had, of course, been a Jesuit—St. Robert Bellarmine—who was chiefly responsible for the much contested idea of the indirect temporal power of the papacy (see above, p. 166), but the political context had changed dramatically since the saint had engaged in controversy on the topic with King James I and VI in the early seventeenth century. Theology, the studying and teaching of which had always been a major part of the Society's mission, had to be rethought. In 1824 Pope Leo XII in his brief *Cum Multa in Urbe* returned the Roman College—after the suppression it had been staffed by diocesan clergy—to the Jesuits, and the teaching of both philosophy and theology, disciplines that were, and are, essential in the formation of the clergy, became increasingly dominant. The college's vicissitudes were not over. In 1870 the new Italian government confiscated the building in the Piazza del Collegio Romano, and it reopened in

1873 in the Palazzo Boromeo, at which point it was given the name of the Pontifical Gregorian University, the name change honoring Pope Gregory XIII (1572–1585), who had endowed it and provided it with its first purpose-built property.[34]

The first rector of the restored college was Luigi Taparelli d'Azeglio (1793–1862) who was, along with Curci, one of the founders of *La Civiltà Cattolica* and a particularly significant figure in the development of modern Catholicism, for not only did he help to revive Thomism as the predominant Catholic theology, but he also, with his Jesuit colleagues, emphasized the social dimension of the faith. He "contrasted the common human vocation to live by working with the terrible conditions inflicted on working people by liberal capitalist economic principles and practices."[35] Those familiar with Catholic social teaching will recognize in this a theme of Pope Leo XIII's 1891 encyclical *Rerum Novarum*, though that document, "On the condition of the working classes," was drafted by another of Taparelli's colleagues and cofounder of *Civiltà*, Matteo Liberatore (1810–1892), who was also a proponent of the thought—in Liberatore's case especially the philosophy—of Thomas Aquinas. A fourth member of this group was Giovanni Perrone (1794–1876), who wrote a book on the Immaculate Conception of Mary, which led to the proclamation of the dogma of the Immaculate Conception by Pope Pius IX in 1854. He was also influential in the preparatory studies for the dogma of papal infallibility, on which more below (p. 252).

John Henry Newman arrived in Rome shortly after the publication of his *Essay on the Development of Christian Doctrine* and was eager to discover what the professors at the Roman College thought of it. For the most part they were not enthusiastic, but when the future saint approached Perrone with a summary of his book's argument, the Jesuit was on the whole sympathetic. While Newman admired the

---

[34] The current building, at the foot of the Quirinal Hill, was opened in 1930. The Gregorian calendar was named after the same Gregory XIII, not after the university, though there was an additional connection because one of the professors at the Roman College, Christopher Clavius (see above, p. 152), was the chief "architect" of the reformed calendar.

[35] Paul Misner, *Social Catholicism in Europe* (London: Darton, Longman and Todd, 1991), 129. Luigi Taparelli is believed to have invented the term "social justice." It no doubt helped in the development of his thought that his brother Massimo, marquess of Azeglio, was a politician and for a time prime minister of Sardinia.

Jesuits he encountered for their austerity of life, he wasn't altogether sure of their teaching. He reported a conversation with one member of the Society, "asking whether the youths learned Aristotle. 'Oh no—he said—Aristotle is in no favour here—no, not in Rome—not St Thomas. I have read Aristotle and St Thos, and owe a great deal to them, but they are out of favour here and throughout Italy.'"[36] It is difficult to know what to make of this remark: the study of Aristotle and Aquinas were, of course, mandated by the *Ratio Studiorum*, though the latter was often interpreted through the writings of either Luis de Molina or Francisco Suarez, and certainly some Jesuit lecturers in philosophy continued to prefer the Suarezian version of Thomas to Thomas's own writings right down to the middle twentieth century.[37] Nonetheless, Newman's remarks are difficult to understand. Giuseppe Pecci (1807–1890), the elder brother of the future Pope Leo XIII and very much a scholar of St. Thomas, began teaching at the Gregorian in 1847 and became a major influence in the preparation of Pope Leo's 1879 encyclical *Aeterni Patris* promoting the study of Aquinas in the Church.[38]

The revival of the study of Thomas Aquinas in the nineteenth century was accompanied in the secular disciplines by a revival of scientific history. Newman was steeped in the history of the early Church, and the *Essay on the Development of Christian Doctrine* that had been so coolly received by most of Rome's Jesuits could be seen as one way of integrating history and theology. But history was not popular with those pressing, during the First Vatican Council, for the definition of papal infallibility.[39] Archbishop Manning, perhaps the

---

[36] Newman to John Dobrée Dalgairns, November 22, 1846, quoted in Juan R. Veléz, *Passion for Truth* (Charlotte, NC: Tan Books, 2012), 513. Despite this apparent disappointment at the level of theology in Rome, Newman described his time at the Collegium Urbanum, then run by the Jesuits, as "happy months." See Luca F. Tuninetti, "The 'Happy Months' of Newman at the College of Propaganda in Rome (1846–1847)," *The Newman Review* (August 2021), consulted online August 26, 2021.

[37] As the present writer can testify.

[38] Pope Leo appointed him a cardinal at his first consistory, alongside the Dominican scholar Tommaso Maria Zigliara, who also played a major role in the composition of *Aeterni Patris*. Dominicans would claim that there was no need for a Thomist revival, such as that briefly described here, as scholars such as Zigliara had been teaching him all the time.

[39] The council met from December 1869 to October 1870 when it had to be abruptly suspended: the French troops defending Rome against occupation by the army of King Victor Emmanuel II were withdrawn during the Franco-Prussian War.

leading proponent of the doctrine at the council, said that no one "who wishes to keep the name of Catholic may descend from the unshaken Rock of Truth, the Church's magisterium, into the swamp of human history when the truths of the faith are at stake,"[40] and Jesuits from the Roman College who were a significant presence during the gathering were of a like mind. The two members of the Society who had the most influence on the debates were the Austrian Johann Baptist Franzelin (1816–1886) and the German Josef Wilhelm Karl Kleutgen (1811–1883). It was Franzelin who was principally responsible for drafting the Dogmatic Constitution on the Catholic Faith, originally known as *Apostolici Muneris*, but after the revisions made because of comments by the bishops at the council it was renamed *Dei Filius*. The bishop in charge of the committee undertaking the revision, Konrad Martin of Paderborn, entrusted the redrafting not to Franzelin but to Kleutgen, an old friend, despite the fact that Franzelin was the better biblical scholar. The two, together with another Jesuit from the Gregorianum, Clemens Schrader (1820–1875), worked on the fourth chapter of *Pastor Aeternus*, the decree of Vatican I that included the definition of papal infallibility: "They stood clearly on the infallibilist side, strongly supported by Pope Pius IX. But Franzelin realized that the exercise of papal infallibility is a powerful instrument, which in some cases could lead to serious theological damage. He tried therefore to clearly define the conditions for infallible statements."[41]

---

[40] Quoted in August Bernard Hasler, *How the Pope Became Infallible: Pius IX and the Politics of Persuasion* (New York: Doubleday, 1981), 178. Hasler's book, with its introduction by the late Hans Küng, is undoubtedly a hostile account of the council, though that does not make it inaccurate. He points out that the leading Infallibilists had been taught by Jesuits (ibid., 178).

[41] Bernhardt Korn, "Johann Baptist Franzelin (1816–86): A Jesuit Cardinal Shaping the Official Teaching of the Church at the Time of the First Vatican Council," *Journal of Jesuit Studies* 7 (2020): 613. This article gives a fairly full account of Franzelin's life. For the life of the much more controversial Kleutgen, see Hubert Wolf, *The Nuns of Sant'Ambrogio* (New York: Alfred A. Knopf, 2015), *passim*. As the Jesuit historian John W. O'Malley puts it, "Kleutgen assumed an important role at the Council, even though a decade earlier he had been involved in a major scandal, the strange and erotic goings-on in the convent of Sant'Ambrogio in Rome, and fallen into disgrace. Somehow he had managed to survive and reestablish himself." See his *Vatican I: The Council and the Making of the Ultramontane Church* (Cambridge, MA: The Belknap Press of

In the end the decree on papal primacy and infallibility was approved by the council fathers on July 18, 1870, and became part of Catholic doctrine. But it has remained contentious. "The most basic problem with *Pastor Aeternus*," John O'Malley has written, "was its historical naïveté. It took the present situation as the norm for interpreting the past and projected present practice and understanding on to it. Since it ignored differentiation between present and past, it lacked a sense of development from past to present, even though Newman's *Essay on the Development of Christian Doctrine* was by then twenty-five years old."[42] In the end almost all bishops and theologians accepted the doctrine, and it crept into the textbooks, unfortunately usually in a maximalist interpretation. But the outcome was not what the Jesuits who had so readily collaborated in support of the primacy and infallibility of the papacy had perhaps expected. The chancellor of a recently united Germany, Otto von Bismarck, launched the Kulturkampf, alleging that the new decree turned bishops into mere functionaries of Rome. While the Kulturkampf was an attack on the German Catholic Church as a whole (a conflict in which Bismarck is generally judged to have come off worse), in the midst of the conflict there was a special "Jesuits Law" (Jesuitengesetz) in July 1872 that banned Jesuits and some other religious orders from German soil so that members of the Society had to take refuge in surrounding countries and in Britain where they established a new theologate at Ditton Hall near Widnes, not far from Liverpool, which had been a gift to the English province.[43] There was a similar reaction in France, originally more anticlerical than anti-Jesuit, perhaps, with the execution of the archbishop of Paris, but five Jesuits also lost their lives. In 1880 the Society was abolished in France, and its members, like the Germans, had to flee to other countries. In the end, however, the laws against the Jesuits were not strictly enforced, and the exiles gradually returned.

Harvard University Press, 2018), 167. It appears to have been Pius IX who summoned him back to Rome out of exile.

[42] O'Malley, *Vatican I*, 197.

[43] The German Jesuits engaged in pastoral work in the surrounding countryside and, as noted above, also taught in the English province's theologate. Cf. Walsh, *Heythrop College*, 89–90. One of those who did so, lecturing on canon law, was Franz Xavier Wernz (1842–1914), who was in 1906 elected superior general of the Society.

The response of politicians such as Bismarck was directed more against papal primacy than against the decree on infallibility. That was equally true of the reaction of the British prime minister at the time of the council, William Ewart Gladstone. His *The Vatican Decrees in Their Bearing on Civil Allegiance*, which appeared in 1874, argued that papal primacy made Catholics subjects of the papacy rather than, in the case of the United Kingdom, subjects of the crown. Newman, a long-time friend of Gladstone, refuted his arguments at length in *Letter to His Grace, the Duke of Norfolk*—the Duke of Norfolk being not only the leading Catholic but the senior nonroyal personage in the country. Newman's letter is the source for an often-quoted passage: "I add one remark. Certainly, if I am obliged to bring religion into after-dinner toasts, (which indeed does not seem quite the thing) I shall drink—to the Pope, if you please,—still, to Conscience first, and to the Pope afterwards."

Not all Jesuit provinces were impacted as a result of governmental hostility to the issues of papal primacy and infallibility: one recent history of Jesuits in the United States makes no mention at all of either Vatican I or even Pope Pius IX.[44] Though the experience may have been devastating for those affected by expulsions, some provinces benefited from them as learned members of the Society had to move elsewhere. That was certainly true for the English province's theologate at St. Beuno's College, picturesquely situated on a hillside in north Wales, with views much admired by the Jesuit poet Gerard Manley Hopkins.[45] But, as will be explained in the next chapter, what English Jesuits had somehow imbibed was definitely not to the taste either of Cardinal Vaughan, the archbishop of Westminster, or of the Spanish Jesuit Luis Martín García (1846–1906), elected superior general in 1892.

And "imbibed" is the word: one of Luis Martín's complaints was that the English Jesuits drank too much alcohol, a charge the provincial rebutted by sending to Rome the wine glasses that were used to

---

[44] Raymond A. Schroth, *The American Jesuits: A History* (New York: New York University Press, 2007).

[45] See Walsh, *Heythrop College*, 85, for arrivals to the theologate of foreign Jesuits professors. Hopkins was not, however, quite so enamored of the draughty, ill-heated building. For Hopkins at St. Beuno's, see Alfred Thomas, *Hopkins the Jesuit: The Years of Training* (Oxford: Oxford University Press, 1969).

indicate the amount of wine dispensed. A rather more serious issue was one already referred to (see above, p. 248), the accusation that Jews were responsible for ritual slaughter of Christian children. This canard was revived by the Dreyfus affair,[46] French members of the Society being firmly of the anti-Dreyfus party, which their English brethren found embarrassing. Complaints to the general about the French Jesuits, and also about the line taken by *Civiltà*, Martín did not exactly ignore, but he confessed to finding the evidence against ritual murder unconvincing.

An even greater problem posed by the English Jesuits, however, was that of "liberalism," the topic of Martín's first letter to the whole Society, which was titled "On some dangers of our times"—dangers that included, for example, reading newspapers, modern systems of education, and what he called "effeminate domestic training." Liberalism was exemplified in the articles by Jesuit writers appearing in *The Month* and in the Catholic weekly *The Tablet* that in his eyes were too sympathetic to Jews—see the Dreyfus affair—and Protestants. He was even moved, though not, of course, in the letter "On some dangers of our times," to complain that *The Month* had published an article on poetry by a woman when there were perfectly competent Jesuits to fill the pages. Martín's tirade against liberalism was well known to generations of Jesuits because it was mandated to be read to them, generally in the refectory, twice a year down to the 1960s, though how much of the letter they took in while they ate their lunch or supper one may seriously doubt.[47]

As examples of the detested liberalism, Martín found in John Gerard, a well-loved English provincial superior whom he dismissed from office after only one three-year term, the "tendency of the English to presuppose the innocence both of Dreyfus and of the Jews in general of the many charges brought against them." For Martín, "Protestantism was endemically pernicious, and the age called for duels, not dialogue. Those who had no stomach for the duels were

[46] Alfred Dreyfus, a French army captain of Jewish ancestry, was convicted in December 1894 of selling military secrets to the Germans. He was convicted on forged documents and the real (non-Jewish) culprit was exonerated. After serving five years in prison on Devil's Island, the sentence was quashed, and in 1906 the case against him was finally thrown out. He returned to the army and served throughout World War I.

[47] For an account of the letter, see Schultenover, *The View from Rome*, 68–74.

to be replaced by those who did, for indeed, toleration was but a platform of liberalism, which in turn was of a piece with English nationalism."[48]

Martín was not the only one to be alarmed at the growth of "liberalism" among the English; Cardinal Herbert Vaughan, the archbishop of Westminster, was similarly concerned, especially after a number of English Catholics, including Jesuits, had rallied in support of St. George Jackson Mivart, a distinguished zoologist who, at least in part, embraced the theory of evolution put forward by Charles Darwin. Some of his writings were put on the Index, and he was eventually excommunicated, though not, it should be said, over the question of evolution. Mivart had gathered a following, and Vaughan was at a loss about what to do. He consulted a quasi-Englishman in the Vatican bureaucracy, Bishop Rafael Merry del Val.[49] At Merry del Val's suggestion a pastoral letter was produced, condemning liberalism, with the assistance of two Jesuits appointed by Martín, one an Italian, the other an American with (distant) English connections. When it was in page proofs, Martín read it through and made a small number of corrections, which were accepted. Merry del Val then got the pastoral letter approved by Pope Leo XIII, so that when Vaughan presented it to his fellow bishops they could hardly refuse to add their signatures. But the question remained, when was it to be published, before or after Vaughan had made his ad limina visit to Rome? Merry del Val's answer was unequivocal: it should be published *before* the ad limina so that no one might think that this condemnation of liberalism had been influenced by anyone in Rome—where it had nonetheless been written. The deceit worked. The joint pastoral, joint because it was presented as the thinking of the entire English and Welsh hierarchy, was dated December 29, 1900, and it appeared, in two parts, in *The Tablet* for January 5 and 12, 1901.[50] It was a foretaste of the condemnation of Modernism that was to come.[51]

---

[48] Ibid., 77.

[49] He was born in London, his father being secretary to the Spanish embassy, and studied for the priesthood at Ushaw College in Co. Durham. He became a cardinal in 1903, after serving as secretary to the conclave that elected Pope Pius X.

[50] Cardinal Vaughan owned *The Tablet*.

[51] See also David G. Schultenover, *George Tyrrell: In Search of Catholicism* (Shepherdstown: The Patmos Press, 1981), 144–46.

Chapter 10

Thinking with the Church

Father Luis Martín, the twenty-fourth superior general of the Society, was, according to William Bangert, "a man of great energy and quick decisiveness";[1] in David Schultenover's view, however, the general's "memories of past and most painful days remained and cast a shadow of melancholy on his character."[2] The melancholy arose from the experiences, first, of the expulsion of the Jesuits from Spain in 1868 and then, shortly after they had been allowed back in Martín's homeland,[3] the destruction of the Society in France in 1880. In the midst of all this destruction he feared that Jesuit history might be lost. "The problem was that so much of the past was preserved only in [Jesuit] archives which at any moment could be destroyed or lost by confiscation, leaving the world without a reliable record of the Jesuit story—a record under constant threat of distortion from the liberal and revolutionary press."[4] He therefore encouraged the writing of provincial histories and, more important still, the collection, collation, and publication of documents relating to the Society's past in what has since become the massive *Monumenta Historica Societatis Iesu*, a series that began in Spain in 1894 and moved to Rome in 1930.

---

[1] Bangert, *A History of the Society of Jesus*, 439.

[2] Schultenover, *A View from Rome*, 192.

[3] He made little secret of his overriding patriotism (ibid., 199–203) and could hardly bear to be in the same room as American Jesuits after the defeat of Spain in its war with the United States. It did not help his views of the English that they were allies of the United States.

[4] David G. Schultenover, "Luis Martín García, the Jesuit General of the Modernist Crisis (1892–1906): On Historical Criticism," *The Catholic Historical Review* 89, no. 3 (July 2003): 435.

It was in Martín's generalate that the German historian and Thomist scholar Franz Ehrle (1845–1934) became pro-prefect then prefect of the Vatican Library, though he had been working in the Vatican Archives for some years before this appointment and was instrumental in making access to them easier for researchers, for, as he once remarked to a Protestant scholar working in the archives, "We are all servants of a single truth."[5]

In the latter years of the nineteenth and the early years of the twentieth centuries, however, such historical scholarship was dangerous, whether it was applied to the history of the Church itself or to the study of the Scriptures. In 1864 Pius IX had issued his "Syllabus of Errors," a list of eighty propositions that were to be condemned. It is anathema to suggest, read the final one, "that the Roman Pontiff can and ought to reconcile and adapt himself to progress, to liberalism and to modern civilisation":[6] the Church appeared to set its face firmly against the modern world, and that included critical history, the theory of which Ehrle explained to Luis Martín and to which the general was sympathetic. But the historical researches of a number of Jesuit scholars, including the Bollandists, who had been publishing critical editions of the lives of saints since the early seventeenth century, ran into trouble when they questioned the historicity of some devotions such as that to the "Holy House of Loreto" and the existence of some popular saints, such as Barbara, the patron of, among others, artillerymen and miners.[7]

Critical scholarship again came under attack when in 1907 there was published another "Syllabus of Errors" in the form of a decree of the Holy Office. *Lamentabili sane exitu* condemned a series of what the Church's doctrinal overseer considered to be deviations from the Catholic faith. *Lamentabili* covered a range of topics but concentrated

---

[5] Quoted by Owen Chadwick in his *Catholicism and History*, 139. This short book, containing Chadwick's Herbert Hensley Henson lectures delivered at Oxford in 1976, is a must-read for Catholic historians. Ehrle had studied at Ditton Hall (see above, p. 253), was ordained in Liverpool, and had ministered to the poor in Preston. He was created a cardinal in 1922.

[6] Romanus Pontifex potest ac debet cum progressu, cum liberalismo et cum recenti civilitate sese reconciliare et componere.

[7] Martín's problems with historians are discussed in the article by David Schultenover cited above in footnote 4. For the Bollandists, see David Knowles, *Great Historical Enterprises* (London: Thomas Nelson, 1963), 3–32.

especially on Scripture. Just two months later Pope Pius X followed the Holy Office's decree with an encyclical, *Pascendi dominici gregis*, which for the first time brought all these supposed errors under the umbrella title of Modernism.

Modernism is not a topic that is given much prominence in histories of the Society, possibly because only one Jesuit was deeply involved,[8] and he, though Dublin born, was a member of the English province and therefore perhaps doubly marginal. But George Tyrrell (1861–1909) was one of the major actors in a movement in the Catholic Church whose suppression cast a blight on Catholic scholarship, including Jesuit scholarship, for more than two decades.[9] Tyrrell joined the Society in 1880, a year after the publication of Leo XIII's encyclical *Aeterni Patris* commending the study of Thomas Aquinas, but when he started studying philosophy, after his two-year noviceship, he discovered that pure and unadulterated Thomism, which he espoused, was controversial, most Jesuits approaching St. Thomas by way of Suarez. A decade later, when Tyrrell found himself a teacher of philosophy, he wrote to Cardinal Camillo Mazzella, the man largely responsible for the encyclical and himself a Jesuit, to see if he would use his influence to have the English province replace Suarez with the text of Thomas. General Luis Martín learned of the letter and is reported as having said to Cardinal Herbert Vaughan that Tyrrell claimed to know more about St. Thomas than everyone else in the Society.[10]

Tyrrell had a wide circle of friends, especially among the liberal Catholics who had been criticized in the joint pastoral (see above, p. 256) and those who were undoubtedly the target of *Lamentabili* and *Pascendi*. He himself does not figure in either document, though he claimed that some of the condemned propositions were drawn

---

[8] The French literary scholar Henri Brémond, author, among many other works, of the eleven-volume *Histoire littéraire du sentiment religieux en France* and for a time editor of *Études*, had also been a Jesuit. He left the Society in 1904 though remaining a priest. He attended Tyrrell's funeral and gave a blessing.

[9] Maurice Bévenot, SJ (1897–1980), a world-renowned expert on the letters of St. Cyprian, once told the present author that he had originally wished to study Scripture, but because of the threat posed to scholarship by Modernism he chose instead to research the much less controversial fathers of the Church.

[10] Schultenover, *George Tyrrell*, 37.

from his writings by way of Italian authors.[11] Tyrrell had fallen foul of the Church authorities: it was the pope who eventually ordered the Jesuit general to dismiss him from the Society despite his being defended by his English Jesuit superiors and in particular by his friend Herbert Thurston,[12] something Luis Martín found especially irksome. The modernist crisis, at least in the active persecution of those labelled modernists, came to an end with the death of Pius X and the election of Benedict XV, but in the meantime, as has been suggested above, enormous damage had been done to Catholic, and Jesuit, scholarship. But if active persecution ended, the sense of living on a knife's edge continued because the Anti-Modernist Oath, required of all clergy, religious superiors, and professors in seminaries that Pius X imposed on the Church in 1910, remained in force until 1967.

The death of Pope Pius occurred in the same month, August, of the same year, 1914, as that of the Jesuit General Franz Xavier Wernz, who in 1906 had been elected to replace Martín. Delayed by the outbreak of World War I, the general congregation to choose a successor did not take place until the following February while the armies of the belligerents battled it out, the Catholic soldiers ministered to by British, Irish, French, Italian, German, Austrian, and eventually American Jesuit chaplains. For the twenty-sixth superior general of the Society the electors opted for the most obvious candidate: Włodzimir Ledóchowski (1866–1942) had been Wernz's assistant. Yet he was hardly a typical Jesuit. He was a count, a member of the Polish aristocracy, though Poland itself had ceased to exist in 1795, and Ledóchowski had for a time served as a page in the Habsburg court. He grew up in a deeply devout family of nine children, one of whom, Maria Teresa, has been beatified and another, Ursula, has been declared a saint. He had a brother who was a Polish general and an uncle, Mieczysław Halka-Ledóchowski, who was created a cardinal while languishing in a Prussian prison because of his opposition to the Kulturkampf.

---

[11] See the entry on Tyrrell by Patrick Maume in the *Irish Dictionary of Biography*, consulted online September 7, 2021, https://www.dib.ie. For a slightly more recent life of Tyrrell, see Nicholas Sagovsky, *'On God's Side'* (Oxford: Clarendon Press, 1990).

[12] See Robert Butterworth, *A Jesuit Friendship: Letters of George Tyrrell to Herbert Thurston* (London: Roehampton Institute, 1988).

Ledóchowski does not get good press. He was elected at the beginning of one world war and died soon after the start of another, his whole period in office beset with international politics, not least the culmination of the "Roman Question," the status of the Holy See in relation to the Kingdom of Italy. This was settled by the Lateran Accords of 1929, which set up the Vatican City as a sovereign state in its own right and, incidentally, returned property to the Society that had been sequestered after the fall of Rome in 1870, a result that enabled Ledóchowski to build the Jesuit headquarters on Borgo Santo Spirito, just around the corner from St. Peter's, and erect the rather grand-looking edifice that houses the Gregorian University.

Rather oddly, it was a Jesuit, Pietro Tacchi Venturi (1861–1956), who acted as the go-between for the Holy See in its negotiations with the Italian government—in other words, with Benito Mussolini. "The Jesuits, then," John Pollard has commented, "probably reached the peak of their influence in the Vatican in this period." Thanks to the opening of the Vatican Archives for the pontificate of Pius XI, Ledóchowski's "essentially behind-the-scenes, and sometimes malevolent, influence on many major decisions and papal public utterances can now be fully documented."[13] The "malevolence" lay in his unapologetic anti-Semitism, which was also reflected in the pages of *La Civiltà Cattolica*, which the Jesuit contributors to the fortnightly kept up even after the persecution of the Jews in Nazi Germany became known.[14] It is true that Tacchi Venturi was employed by the Vatican in an attempt to mitigate Mussolini's racial laws of 1938, but he was unsuccessful, and his influence over Il Duce, which had once been so helpful to the papacy, went into decline. It is also true that when Pius XI, almost at the end of his life, decided to produce an encyclical to defend Jews from persecution he asked an American Jesuit with a background in interracial relations in the United States to write it. John La Farge (1880–1963), later editor of *America* magazine, did so in an encyclical that would have been called *Humani*

---

[13] Pollard, *The Papacy in the Age of Totalitarianism*, 449.

[14] Bernauer, *Jesuit Kaddish*, 32. The author is himself a Jesuit and goes on to remark that Hannah Arendt "identified anti-Semitism as the special charism of the Society" (33). These paragraphs on Jesuit attitudes to Jews were being written just as the Jesuit pope visited Hungary and Slovakia, speaking out against anti-Semitism. Readers may recall that, when archbishop of Buenos Aires, he counted Rabbi Abraham Skorka among this friends and collaborators.

Generis Unitas ("The unity of humankind"), condemning the Nazi ideology though not, at least explicitly, Nazi racial theory, an omission Pollard attributes to the intervention of Włodzimir Ledóchowski.[15] The encyclical never appeared in print because, it seems very likely, the delaying tactics employed by Ledóchowski prevented the pope from approving the final version. The question remains, however, why Pius XI's successor, Pius XII, did not publish it—but that belongs to a different book.

Unhappily, these attitudes toward Jews were not confined to Germany or Italy. James Bernauer remarks that the US Jesuit magazine *America* passed in silence over the anti-Semitic diatribes of the radio priest (not a Jesuit) Charles Coughlin, and even the French paleontologist and quasi-mystical author Pierre Teilhard de Chardin (1881–1955) found something to praise in the rise of Naziism.[16] There were, however, Jesuit voices, including German Jesuit voices, raised against Naziism in general and its anti-Semitism in particular. While it survived (it was shut by the Gestapo in 1941), the Munich-based Jesuit journal *Stimmen der Zeit* was carefully critical of the Hitler regime. Others were not so careful, among them Rupert Mayer, who had won the Iron Cross as a chaplain to the German army in World War I—and lost a leg in a grenade attack—but was from the outset convinced that no Catholic could support Hitler and said so from the pulpit. Because he was so outspoken he was imprisoned by the Nazis, and, though he survived imprisonment, he died of a heart attack in May 1945 soon after his liberation. In 1987 he was declared a "Blessed."

For German Jesuits there was a hard choice between apparent patriotism and opposition to the program of the Hitler regime. This should not have been an issue in France, but, with the establishment of the traditionalist, anti-Semitic regime of Marshal Philippe Pétain at Vichy, it became one. In the confused situation of war-time Europe it was not possible to elect a successor to Włodzimir Ledóchowski. Conscious of his age, he had, in 1938, summoned a general congregation in order to appoint a vicar general: the choice was Maurice Schurmans. He had, however, left a letter to be opened on his death that named Alessio Ambrogio Magni (1872–1944), the assistant for

---

[15] Pollard, *The Papacy in the Age of Totalitarianism*, 268.
[16] Bernauer, *Jesuit Kaddish*, 49–50.

Italy, as vicar general instead of Schurmans. Magni, however, died after only sixteen months in office and was replaced by the assistant for France, Norbert de Boynes (1870–1954). It was an exceedingly curious choice. He had written on July 12, 1941, to all Jesuit communities in a militarily defeated France instructing them to obey the Vichy government. "We must first of all accept the established government," he wrote, "and obey it in all that is not contrary to the law of God, whatever our own political preferences. In no case may we oppose it, whether within our communities or outside. We must even use our influence . . . to guide souls toward the practice of that obedience which everyone, and above all Catholics, owe to the Head of State."[17] Given all the conflicts that the French Jesuits had been forced to endure from various arms of the French state, from the time of their arrival in Paris right down to the twentieth century, it was a curious letter to have been circulated. It was not well received, especially not at the Society's theologate in Lyon, Fourvière, where Pierre Chaillet (1900–1972) and Henri de Lubac (1896–1991)[18] were teaching. Chaillet was the main begetter of the clandestine publication *Les Cahiers du Témoignage Chrétienne*,[19] first produced in November 1941 in the form of an essay by Gaston Fessard (1897–1978) titled *France prends garde de perdre ton ame* ("France, beware lest you lose your soul") and continued to be circulated secretly until the liberation of France in 1944. *Témoignage Chrétienne* called on its readers to resist Naziism in the name of Christian values and argued, as Fessard did in this first contribution, that there was no obligation for Christians to obey the Vichy government. In writing this he was opposing not only de Boynes but the French bishops who did not, in the opinion of de Lubac in a note prepared for the philosopher Jacques Maritain when Maritain was named ambassador to the Holy See, properly understand Christian teaching. They were out of touch with the people, he argued, who mostly supported the French resistance while

---

[17] Quoted by Bernauer, *Jesuit Kaddish*, 80–81.

[18] De Lubac was created a cardinal in 1983—without, at his request, being ordained a bishop.

[19] The remarkable and courageous story of the *Témoignage Chrétienne* can be found in François Bédarida and Renée Bédarida, eds., *La Résistance Spirituelle 1941–1944* (Paris: Albin Michel, 2001).

the bishops appeared to back Pétain.[20] In all, some fifty Jesuits collaborated, one way or another, in the production and distribution of *Témoignage*. Distributing *Témoignage* was itself a crime, and one of those who had done so, Paul Petit, though he managed to avoid arrest when the Vichy police first came looking for him in January 1942, was eventually captured, deported to Germany, and executed.[21] One especially responsible for making it available in northern France was the remarkable Yves Moreau de Montcheuil (1900–1944), who in 1936 had become professor of philosophy at the Institut Catholique in Paris and who consistently spoke out against anti-Semitism. He served as a chaplain to the Young Christian Workers, and twice, in the summer of 1943 and at Easter 1944, he ministered to some resistance fighters in the mountains near Grenoble. When in 1944 they were attacked by German soldiers, the fighters fled with those lightly wounded, but the more seriously wounded were left behind, and Montcheuil remained with them. He was seized by the Germans, imprisoned in Grenoble, and there executed by firing squad.

The creation by French Jesuits of *Témoignage Chrétienne* marks a clear break with the policies pursued by Ledóchowski, and indeed with the attitudes adopted toward Jews by many French Jesuits during the Dreyfus affair. In their entry "Jews and Jesuits" in the *Cambridge Encyclopedia of the Jesuits*, Robert Maryks and James Bernauer recount the effort by predominantly Italian and Portuguese Jesuits to exclude *conversos*, or "new Christians," Jews who had converted to Christianity, from membership in the Society. As the authors point out, several prominent early members had been of Jewish ancestry, but the fourth superior general, Everard Mercurian (1514–1580), took steps to remove *conversos* from positions of authority within the Order, and in 1593 the fifth general congregation passed a decree denying admission to all those of Jewish—and of Moorish—ancestry. This ordinance was revoked only in 1946 because, Maryks and Bernauer comment, "Jesuits feared in the shadow of the Holocaust

---

[20] De Lubac's note is cited by Bernauer, *Jesuit Kaddish*, 20–21. In 1944 the newly appointed papal nuncio to Paris, Angelo Roncalli, the future Pope John XXIII, was faced with a desire by the French government to dismiss twenty-five French bishops for collaboration with the Vichy regime, including the cardinal archbishop of Lyon. Eventually Roncalli whittled the number down to seven. See Peter Hebblethwaite, *Pope John XXIII* (London: Geoffrey Chapman, 1984), 205–10.

[21] *Témoignage Chrétienne*, 162.

being accused of modern racism."[22] That may indeed be part of the explanation, but rigid, unimaginative, and anti-Semitic as Ledóchowski undoubtedly was, there had been during his generalate some far-reaching changes in Jesuit culture that made such anti-Semitic attitudes untenable.

At the same time that the Lyon Jesuits were producing *Témoignage Chrétienne* they were also engaged in another major enterprise: the publication, with notes, commentary, and a translation into French, of a thousand years of works by Christian theologians, philosophers, and historians in the *Sources Chrétiennes*, a series that, at the last count, runs to over six hundred volumes. The series was founded by Jean Daniélou (1905–1974), Henri de Lubac (1896–1991), and Claude Mondesért (d. 1990); Daniélou and de Lubac were both named cardinals. The first publication was a translation of a work by the fourth-century bishop Gregory of Nyssa, *Contemplation sur la Vie de Moïse*, which was a reminder to Catholics in the midst of the Nazi pogrom against the Jews that Christianity grew out of Judaism. That theme was echoed in a book published in Switzerland to avoid Nazi censorship, *Israël et la foi Chrétienne*. De Lubac wrote one of the four essays in the volume, and a second Lyon Jesuit, Joseph Bonsirven (1880–1958), contributed another. "Bonsirven argued that Christianity could understand itself only if studied in relationship to Judaism rather than to Greek philosophy."[23] This turn back by Jesuit scholars to the Christian thinkers of the first millennium overlapped with a renewal of the study of the Bible.

The Pontifical Biblical Institute (the Biblicum) was founded by Pius X in 1909 in the midst of the modernist controversy, which particularly threatened scriptural scholarship, and was shortly afterward handed over to the Society of Jesus. Its original purpose was to prepare candidates for the examination of the Biblical Commission, the Vatican entity that kept a wary eye on Catholic biblical research and was quick to condemn any opinion considered unorthodox, most of which views have since become commonplace teaching. Benedict XV unshackled it from the Biblical Commission and gave it degree-granting status of its own. Not only Jesuits passed through its doors,

---

[22] Worcester, ed., *The Cambridge Encyclopedia of the Jesuits*, 428; the article itself is on pp. 423–28.

[23] Bernauer, *Jesuit Kaddish*, 76.

but the Society remained in charge, down to the present day, and many of its members have studied there. Although it was not until September 1943 and the publication of Pius XII's encyclical *Divino Afflante Spiritu* that the historical-critical reading of the Bible was formally endorsed, it had by that time become widely used and gave a new impetus to Jesuit scholarship and a deeper appreciation of the Jewish context in which the canon of Scripture had evolved. Though the Biblicum was founded before Ledóchowski took charge, it was in his generalate that a house for its students was opened in Jerusalem, and it was during the same period that the Biblicum's original antimodernist stance was, for the most part, gradually abandoned.

It was also during his generalate that the Society was given charge of the Pontifical Oriental Institute—the Orientale—which was founded at the behest of Pope Benedict XV in 1917, at almost the same time as the Vatican's Congregation for the Eastern Churches with which it was closely allied. It was also closely linked to the Pontifical Russian College (the Russicum), which was set up in 1929 by Pope Pius XI and, like the Orientale, was entrusted to Jesuits. As has been seen (see above, p. 266) the Society had long been active in Russia, and, after a hiatus of almost a century (1820–1905), they returned largely to work with Polish Catholics. Their situation deteriorated after the 1917 Revolution, and particularly after the civil war that led to hardship, especially famine, for many. The Vatican attempted to help by setting up a mission overseen by an American Jesuit, Edmund Walsh. Walsh made a brief foray to Moscow, then returned to the States to raise money for the relief effort. His stay when he returned to Russia was short: "He upset the Soviet authorities with his 'Yankee manners,'" says Pollard who is apparently quoting Hansjakob Stehle, though the issue was more complex—steering a course between a suspicious Russian Orthodox Church and a potentially hostile Soviet government.[24]

One of the complications in the Vatican's attempts to establish relations with the Soviet Union was the role of another Jesuit, the French scholar of Russian philosophy, Michel d'Herbigny (1880–1957). In

---

[24] Pollard, *The Papacy in the Age of Totalitarianism*, 217, but see also the section on Soviet Russia, 216–20. Stehle's book is, in its English translation, *Eastern Politics of the Vatican, 1917–1979* (Athens: Ohio University Press, 1981). It has a good deal on Walsh's mission, but the present author could not find the direct quotation cited above.

1922 d'Herbigny was chosen to head the Orientale and then, in 1926, was sent on a clandestine mission to support Russian Catholics, for which purpose he was ordained a bishop behind closed doors by the papal nuncio in Germany, Eugenio Pacelli, the future Pius XII. While in Russia he secretly ordained a number of bishops who were swiftly rounded up by the Soviet government. He himself, however, returned safely to Rome and to his role as president of the Pontifical Oriental Institute and as president of the Pontifical Commission for Russia. But then in 1933 for reasons that have never been disclosed—ill health was alleged but that was obviously false—he was abruptly dismissed and sent back to the noviceship in Belgium, where he obediently stayed, still a bishop, for the rest of his life. Stehle argues that d'Herbigny had upset the hierarchy in Poland by his efforts to foster "a *russified* Catholicism on *Polish* territory,"[25] which might suggest that a staunchly nationalistic Ledóchowski had heard the bishops' pleas to rein him in: only the general would have dispatched him back to the noviceship. Not that, after the fall of d'Herbigny, the Society abandoned Russia. Pius XI appealed for missionaries to go there, and a number of Jesuits trained, and were ordained, as Russian Rite priests, largely serving the émigré community though some worked secretly, or so they hoped, within the Soviet Union itself.

Successive popes were asking the Society to undertake more and more "missions," including taking charge of Vatican Radio, inaugurated by Pius XI in 1931,[26] but with an ever more centralized and authoritarian Vatican, it became increasingly difficult to develop the imaginative initiatives that had been so much a part of the Jesuit presence in Japan, China, India, and elsewhere—though in China, after the overthrow of the emperor in the revolution of 1911 to 1912, the government itself declared that Confucian ceremonies were merely civic, thus opening the way for the Congregation for the Propagation of the Faith in 1939 to rescind the ban imposed in 1742 on the Jesuits' Chinese Rites. Foreign missions continued, though with the growing prominence of the Gregorian University, the Biblicum, and the Orientale, all under Jesuit direction, more and more

[25] Stehle, *Eastern Politics of the Vatican*, 156, but see also 157–67.

[26] On the Vatican Radio see Marilyn J. Matelski, *Vatican Radio: Propagation by the Airwaves* (Westport, CT: Praeger, 1995). The Society's relationship with the Holy See over its handling of the radio station was not always harmonious; see, for example, ibid, 40.

students from around the world came to Rome and put themselves at the feet of Jesuit professors so the Society's influence spread widely as a consequence.[27]

But to talk of "foreign missions" in a sense is something of an anachronism. Jesuits continued to leave the countries of their birth to work elsewhere, but many of these formerly mission territories had become provinces or vice provinces of their own with locally recruited members of the Society. In his apostolic letter of 1919, *Maximum Illud*, Pope Benedict XV urged missionaries to serve the interests of the people they lived among rather than the interests of the colonial powers and to form an indigenous clergy, a challenge—and to some religious orders it was a serious challenge—repeated by Pius XI in his 1926 encyclical, *Rerum Ecclesiae*.[28] To take one example, as has already been seen, the Chinese mission was restarted in 1842 with priests of the province of Paris, and over time other provinces sent more clergy, including from the province of California. Between 1899 and 1901, however, there was an uprising by Chinese militias (the Boxer Rebellion) against the Western powers and against the spread of Christianity. The rebellion was brutally put down by the Eight Nation Alliance of Austria-Hungary, France, Germany, Italy, Japan (the largest single military contingent), Russia, Britain, and the United States, but not before large numbers of Christians had been put to death, including at least thirty thousand Catholics and four Jesuit priests. After peace was restored the Society opened a university in Shanghai and established a large presence throughout the former empire, which was now a republic. At the time of the Communist takeover of the country there were more than nine hundred Jesuits in China; most of them, it is true, had come from abroad, but 250 of them were Chinese by birth. In 1949 the non-Chinese were expelled.

[27] For a history of the Gregorian, see Caraman, *The University of the Nations*.

[28] On the centenary of *Maximum Illud* Pope Francis wrote a letter to the prefect (head) of the Congregation for the Evangelization of Peoples—the Vatican department once called Propaganda—endorsing Benedict XV's text: "The Apostolic Letter *Maximum Illud* called for transcending national boundaries and bearing witness, with prophetic spirit and evangelical boldness, to God's saving will through the Church's universal mission. May the approaching centenary of that Letter serve as an incentive to combat the recurring temptation lurking beneath every form of ecclesial introversion, self-referential retreat into comfort zones, pastoral pessimism and sterile nostalgia for the past."

More than half of the Chinese Jesuits stayed behind, but many of them were imprisoned and some died behind bars; some Chinese Jesuits moved to Taiwan, not hitherto a mission of the Society, and the island nation—a status, of course, disputed by China—became part of the Chinese province with its headquarters in Macau.

The communist victory in China more or less coincided with the disappearance behind "the Iron Curtain" of large swathes of Central and Eastern Europe. For the most part Jesuits managed to keep working, often clandestinely, in the regions that had come under Communist governments, but in the persecution launched in the militantly atheistic Albania fifteen Jesuits died, along with sixty-five diocesan clergy and no fewer than thirty-three Franciscans.[29] Even outside the Soviet Union and its satellite territories, Communism gained ground in the 1950s and 1960s in the politics and trade unions of Western Europe. In Britain, in a rather odd approach to coping with the growing Communist influence, the confraternities, or Marian Congregations, were reorganized in the manner of Communist cells.[30] On a more practical note, however, and following the principle "know your enemy," Jesuits began to study, and to teach, Marxism and were active members of Marxist-Christian dialogue when that began in the 1960s.

But before members of the Society in Europe and the Americas were faced with this challenge of Marxism, they were confronted with a rather more traditional one, a major disagreement over theology—with the difference that this time Jesuits and Dominicans, for the most part, found themselves on the same side. The problem arose from a coming together of the historical-critical method of modern biblical scholarship—which Pius XII had encouraged in *Divino Afflante Spiritu* (see above, p. 266)—and the turn to the origins of Christian thought (hence the movement came to be known as *ressourcement*) exemplified by the publication of *Sources Chrétiennes*. Theologians, both Jesuit and Dominican, who pursued this path were reaching back behind the scholasticism that had dominated Catholic thought for almost a millennium. To many, however, this *nouvelle théologie* smacked of revived

---

[29] Jonathan Luxmore, *The Vatican and the Red Flag* (London: Geoffrey Chapman, 1999), 38.

[30] Since 1967 they have been known as Christian Life Communities.

Modernism. It was named *nouvelle théologie*[31] by the Dominican theologian Réginald Garrigou-Lagrange, one of its leading opponents, and although the term had been used before, the locus classicus is his article titled *La nouvelle théologie où va-t-elle?* ("The New Theology: Where Is It Going?"). It appeared in the February 1947 issue—though the issue is dated 1946—of the *Angelicum*, the journal of the Dominican college in Rome, also known as the Angelicum, though it is more formally the Pontifical University of St. Thomas, where he taught. In the first sentence of that contribution Garrigou-Lagrange criticizes the Fourvière theologian Henri Bouillard (1908–1981)[32] for suggesting that theological formulations might have to change: "In a recent book, *Conversion et grâce chez S. Thomas d'Aquin* [Conversion and grace in St. Thomas Aquinas], Father Henri Boulliard writes, 'Since spirit evolves, an unchanging truth can only maintain itself by virtue of a simultaneous and co-relative evolution of all ideas, each proportionate to the other. A theology which is not current will be a false theology.'"[33] The suggestion that Aquinas might need updating was not surprisingly anathema to the Dominican professor, but more problematic for the Fourvière theologians was the fact that it also proved to be anathema to Pius XII. Addressing a meeting of Jesuits in Rome in 1946 the pope declared, "A lot has been said not always with sufficient reflection, about 'a new theology' which, in a constantly developing world, would itself also be in constant development, always en route and never arriving anywhere. If such a view were thought legitimate, what would happen to immutable Catholic dogmas and to the unity and stability of the faith!"[34]

Four years later Pius XII's encyclical *Humani Generis* appeared. Even before that, however, the new general of the Society, elected in 1946, the Belgian Jean Baptiste Janssens (1889–1964), had thought it expedient to act. He had, perhaps, been warned of its content and

---

[31] See Gerard Loughlin, "*Nouvelle Théologie*: A Return to Modernism," in *Ressourcement: A Movement for Renewal in Twentieth-Century Catholic Theology*, ed. Gabriel Flynn and Paul D. Murray (Oxford: Oxford University Press, 2012), 36–50.

[32] On Bouillard, see James Hanvey, "Henri Bouillard: The Freedom of Faith," in Flynn and Murray, *Ressourcement*, 263–77.

[33] Réginald Garrigou-Lagrange, "La nouvelle théologie òu va-t-elle?," *Angelicum* 23 (1946): 126–45; the sentence quoted is the first line.

[34] Quoted by Joseph A. Komonchak, "*Humani Generis* and *Nouvelle Théologie*," in ibid., 145. Komonchak adds, "There is circumstantial evidence that Garrigou Lagrange was responsible for this passage."

imminent publication by a professor at the Gregorianum, the Dutchman Sebastian Tromp (1889–1975), who is known to have assisted
Pope Pius in the composition of several of his encyclicals, very possibly including, though it is not known for certain, *Humani Generis*.
Whatever the reason, Janssens ordered that de Lubac, Fessard, Bouillard, and others neither lecture nor publish and their books be removed from library shelves. Some Dominicans met a similar fate.
The encyclical, dated August 1950, did not mention any names, but
it was clearly an attack on some of the main tenets of the "new theology." Paragraphs 14 and 15 claim:

> In theology some want to reduce to a minimum the meaning of
> dogmas; and to free dogma itself from terminology long established
> in the Church and from philosophical concepts held by Catholic
> teachers, to bring about a return in the explanation of Catholic doc-
> trine to the way of speaking used in Holy Scripture and by the
> Fathers of the Church. . . . Moreover they assert that when Catholic
> doctrine has been reduced to this condition, a way will be found to
> satisfy modern needs, that will permit of dogma being expressed
> also by the concepts of modern philosophy, whether of imma-
> nentism or idealism or existentialism or any other system.

What perhaps was most troubling the pontiff became evident in
paragraph 18: "Unfortunately these advocates of novelty easily pass
from despising scholastic theology to the neglect of and even con-
tempt for the Teaching Authority of the Church itself, which gives
such authoritative approval to scholastic theology." And he added
(paragraph 19), "It is true that Popes generally leave theologians free
in those matters which are disputed in various ways by men of very
high authority in this field; but history teaches that many matters
that formerly were open to discussion, no longer now admit of discussion." As John O'Malley has commented, Pope Pius "challenged
the principle of *ressourcement* by affirming that the task of theology
was to discover how the present teachings of the Church's Magisterium are found in the past, which is precisely the opposite of what
ressourcement implied."[35] No theologian was mentioned, but one

---

[35] John W. O'Malley, *What Happened at Vatican II* (Cambridge, MA: The Belknap
Press of Harvard University Press, 2010), 41.

widely held opinion was declared unacceptable for Catholics: polygenism, that is to say, that there was no single ancestor to the human race, that *Homo sapiens*, or a variety thereof, had emerged in various places. This on the face of it contradicted the Bible and the story of Adam and Eve (shades of Galileo!), the historicity of which contemporary biblical scholarship had thrown into considerable doubt, but it was deemed by the pope to be essential for the transmission of the stain of original sin from humankind's first parents (paragraph 37). This defense of the Genesis story was aimed not so much at the Fourvière Jesuits or their Dominican counterparts but at Teilhard de Chardin who had been told in 1925 to confine himself to science and not to involve himself in theology. His best-selling *Phenomenon of Man*, completed in 1940, was not allowed by his religious superiors to be published during his lifetime, though it circulated in manuscript among his confrères. Even as late as 1962, more than half a dozen years after his death, the Holy Office issued a monitum (a warning) to rectors of seminaries ordering them to keep their students from the influence of Teilhard's writings. Seminary libraries were told not to stock them, and bookshops in Rome and Spain were instructed not to sell them despite the fact that his books were never put on the Index. Yet when the Jesuit journalist Pedro Miguel Lamet (b. 1941) visited Janssens's successor Pedro Arrupe (1907–1991) in July 1982, the general told him that the three Jesuit authors he read most often were Karl Rahner (1904–1984), Henri de Lubac, and Pierre Teilhard de Chardin.[36]

Humani Generis sent shockwaves through the Society—and, of course, not just the Society—with numerous professors being removed from their posts and more "reliable" ones brought in from elsewhere. It sent theologians such as Rahner loyally scrabbling to adapt their teaching to the papal instructions. The tension the encyclical produced lasted throughout the 1950s until the Second Vatican Council, where Sebastian Tromp, as secretary of the Preparatory Theological Commission and later secretary of the Doctrinal Commission, proved to be still a conservative force to be reckoned with. Before the council opened there was yet another shock. In February 1962 Pope John XXIII issued *Veterum Sapientia* ("The Wisdom of the

[36] Pedro Miguel Lamet, *Pedro Arrupe: Witness of the Twentieth Century, Prophet of the Twenty-First* (Boston: Institute of Jesuit Sources, Boston College, 2020), 431.

Ancients"), which reinstated Latin as the language of instruction in seminaries, it having largely fallen out of use except in institutions such as the Gregorianum with its multinational student body. The apostolic constitution sent Jesuit (and other) professors scurrying back to their lectures and hurriedly translating them into a language that few could understand and even fewer, except for the older generation of teachers, could speak.[37] As Peter Hebblethwaite puts it, "For the rest of that academic year—rarely longer—tongue-tied Anglo-Saxon professors exercised their rusty Latin on bewildered and sometimes uncomprehending students."[38]

The role played by Tromp did not bode well for the council Pope John had summoned to meet for the first time in October 1962 and that lasted to December 1965. He had his supporters among members of the Society who served on preparatory commissions or as *periti* (experts) or as advisers to individual bishops. They were heavily outnumbered, however, by Jesuits—there were fifty-eight of them as voting members—who were on the opposite side to Tromp in the ideological divide in the council chamber. If the Jesuit bishops present did not themselves make much of an impact, it was not necessarily for want of trying: the "maverick"—as he was often described because of his (then) unconventional views—English Jesuit Thomas d'Esterre Roberts (1893–1976), a former archbishop of Bombay (Mumbai), asked several times to address the council fathers but was not called.[39] Histories of the council detail the role played by members of the Society in the course of its proceedings, but some stand out. The theology of Karl Rahner underpinned many of the positions taken by the council fathers; Cardinal Augustin Bea (1881–1968), who had been rector of the Biblicum and from 1960 was the founding president of the Secretariat for Promoting Christian Unity, was instrumental in rejecting the document on revelation prepared by one

---

[37] For how one well-known English historian of philosophy coped with Latin, see Michael Walsh, "Frederick Copleston, S.J.," in *The Ministry of the Printed Word*, ed. John Broadley and Peter Phillips (Stratton-on-the-Fosse: Downside Abbey Press, 2018), 50.

[38] Hebblethwaite, *John XXIII*, 403. For the background to the document, see ibid., 403–5.

[39] Roberts had been a headmaster in Liverpool before he was unexpectedly called to serve as archbishop. He always believed that in selecting him there had been some bureaucratic mix-up in the Vatican.

of the preparatory commissions, while Karl Rahner was involved in producing the document that replaced it, *Dei Verbum*. A major talking point at the council was religious freedom. The theological commission working on the preparatory documents produced a draft, basically one that had been prepared by the Holy Office toward the end of Pius XII's pontificate, that demanded that civil authorities in majority Roman Catholic countries, while giving complete freedom to the Church, should inhibit non-Catholic teaching, whereas in religiously pluralistic countries Catholicism should not be subject to any restraint. Bea's secretariat objected strongly to this dichotomy. The man behind the alternative proposal, which eventually became *Dignitatis Humanae*, was the American Jesuit John Courtney Murray (1904–1967): he had originally been named as a council *peritus* but then was "disinvited," apparently on the instructions of the papal nuncio in Washington. The contentious issue of religious freedom was very important to American bishops, and Murray, who had written widely on the topic, was eventually "reinvited" as an adviser to the cardinal of New York.[40]

Janssens was the general of the Society for all but the final year of the council. Because of his failing health, however, in April 1960 he appointed a Canadian, John L. Swain (1908–1987), as his vicar general. Eighteen months or so later the Second Vatican Council began, which in its renewed vision of the Church's role in the world had many implications for all religious orders and not simply the Society of Jesus. After the death of Janssens, Swain consulted Pope Paul VI and decided that, although the council had not yet finished, the election of a new general took priority, so the thirty-first general congregation of the Society met at Easter 1965 and elected a Basque, Pedro Arrupe y Gondra (1907–1991), perhaps the most popular superior general the Jesuits have ever had since Ignatius and the only one since Francis Borja (or Borgia, 1510–1572), beatified in 1624 and canonized in 1670, to be a likely candidate for sainthood. After briefly studying medicine in Madrid, Arrupe had joined the Society in 1927, just four years before Jesuits were expelled from Spain under the Republic,[41] and

---

[40] For the story of Murray's role, see Michael J. Walsh, "Religious Freedom: The Limits of Progress," in *Unfinished Journey*, ed. Austen Ivereigh (London: Continuum, 2003), 134–48.

[41] Jesuits were expelled from Spain in January 1932, which explains why no Jesuits were killed during the civil war in that country.

then completed his studies in Holland, Belgium, and the United States before going to Japan in 1938. He began his pastoral work in Yamaguchi, where Francis Xavier had started out, but after Japan entered the World War he was briefly imprisoned as a spy. In 1942 he became the master of novices. The noviceship was in a suburb of Nagasaki, and after the atom bomb fell on the city in August 1945 Arrupe and the novices—Arrupe calling on his modest medical knowledge—entered the city and carried some of the wounded back to the novitiate, turning the chapel into an infirmary. When Japan became a province of the Society in 1958, Arrupe was appointed its first provincial superior, and it was in that capacity he attended the thirty-first general congregation, being elected general on the third ballot. There had been some speculation by commentators before the congregation began that Pope Paul might take the Society to task. Not only did this not happen but the pope greeted the delegates during the customary audience with warm words: it was on this occasion that he called on the Society to make a special point of combatting atheism. When he made his first intervention at the council, Arrupe made atheism one of his leading themes: his second intervention, suitably for someone who had spent so much time in Japan, was the Church's missionary activity, speaking of the need to accommodate Catholicism to the different cultures in which it found itself. He practiced what he preached. He had a room next to his office as a chapel furnished in Japanese style for his prayer and meditation.

Arrupe's responsibilities as general have been summarized by Pedro Lamet. The Society of Jesus was then by far the largest religious order in the Catholic Church, with over thirty-six thousand members.[42] "The Jesuits ran more than 4,600 colleges," reports Lamet, "618 parishes, sixty-four universities, thirty-eight seminaries and fifty-seven social centres. More than thirty members of the order were bishops or cardinals."[43] The large number of colleges occupied the work of roughly a third of all Jesuits, and it was inevitable that when Arrupe reconvened the thirty-first general congregation in 1966 to bring the Society into line with Vatican II the theme of education was to the forefront. What his approach was going to be he revealed in a

---

[42] It is now less than half that number, but almost all religious orders have lost members on a similar scale.

[43] Lamet, *Pedro Arrupe*, 235.

letter written in December 1966, ostensibly to the provincial of Mexico but with far wider significance. He called for the Society to be committed to social justice. He recognized that historically members had been particularly concerned with elites, but now the focus had to change, and that included colleges that "whether because of their exclusive clientele or their system of financing raise serious questions about their reason for existing, or their need for radical transformation."[44] Some colleges did indeed close, including an elite college in Mexico for the rich, which was then reopened for the poor, but the letter aroused considerable hostility among some members of the Society, especially in Spain, and among Jesuit alumni. Most of the other colleges and universities managed to survive, though with greater emphasis placed on inculcating the social teaching of the Church.

It was not easy for the Society to maintain its schools, particularly in Latin America. Where before the suppression it had funded them through its own haciendas, after the Jesuits' return they had perforce to turn to the wealthier classes to support their work in education. It had seemed to many, even before Arrupe's 1966 letter, that this was hardly ideal. In 1955 the Chilean-born José María Vélaz (1910–1985), working as spiritual director to students at the Catholic University in Caracas, Venezuela, created a school for poor children that was funded by his going from house to house seeking donations, aided by students from the university's Marian congregation. This was the first of many such institutions, usually in receipt of government funds but staffed by dedicated lay volunteers or members of religious orders, and under the general oversight of members of the Society in an organization called, since 1960, Fe y Alegría (Faith and Joy). The paradigm spread from Venezuela to Ecuador in 1964, to Panama the following year, and afterward to most countries of Central and South America:[45] it has since spread to some countries within Europe and more recently to Africa. It now educates well over nine hundred thousand students, two-thirds of them in formal education, the rest taught by radio and other means.

In Latin America the majority of Jesuits, if they were not Chilean, Venezuelan, and so on, were of Spanish origin and fitted into the

---

[44] Quoted in ibid., 272.
[45] Its headquarters are now in Bogota.

general culture of the region.[46] Not so in the United States, where Jesuit education was largely in the hands of priests from England, France, and Germany and was in the European style, still adhering to the *Ratio Studiorum*, and for the most part eschewing professional training. It was, in other words, out of step with what American parents wanted for their sons—for the education provided by the Society was certainly not coeducational. In 1899 the president of Harvard described Jesuit schooling in an article in *Atlantic Monthly* as "impossible and absurd."[47]

According to Gerald McKevitt, the motivation for Jesuits seeking university status for their colleges was the desire to keep their students within a Catholic environment,[48] but paradoxically, as a consequence, they became increasingly similar to secular institutions, seeking endowments not only from their alumni but also from the general public. Schools and colleges founded to educate the poor had become almost indistinguishable from their secular counterparts and therefore scarcely an obvious means for members of the Society to fulfill decree 4 of the thirty-second general congregation, which was held between December 1974 and March 1975. The decree was formally titled "Our Mission Today: The Service of the Faith and the Promotion of Justice." Though created much later than the Fe y Alegría group of institutions, the Cristo Rey schools in the United States perform a similar function of educating impoverished students. The organization began life in Chicago, the brainchild of John Foley (b. 1935), who had spent many years in Peru teaching poverty-stricken children. When he returned to his home province he found himself again working with poverty-stricken children, mainly Hispanic in origin, in Chicago. Their parents could not afford to pay for their education, and nor could the Church. Foley turned to a management consultant. The outcome of their collaboration was a system that allows the pupils of Cristo Rey schools to work in teams of five for five

[46] Guyana, as it is now known, was a British colony and was therefore served mainly by British (and later Indian) Jesuits—Indian, because of the large Indian community resident in the territory.

[47] Cited by Gerald McKevitt, "Jesuit Schools in the USA, 1814–c.1970," in *The Cambridge Companion to the Jesuits*, ed. Thomas Worcester (Cambridge: Cambridge University Press, 2008), 283.

[48] Ibid., 287.

days a month in an industry or a business, obviously at entry-level jobs, with their salaries being paid directly to the school. The unusual structure proved a great success. In an area where the drop-out rate from high school education had been 50 percent in the areas where these schools were established, it fell to 6 percent, and it enjoys a 90 percent college enrollment rate, far higher than other schools catering to the same type of student. At the last count, the group consisted of thirty-seven schools in twenty-four states, a growth that has been made possible not just from the collaboration of enterprises but also from donations from major foundations and, though in origin a Jesuit initiative, the support of many religious orders.

Both Fe y Alegría and the Cristo Rey initiatives demonstrate not only a new sense of purpose but also a regaining by the Society of imagination and enterprise and the ability for "accommodation" that had been evident in the history of its first two and a half centuries but that had been lacking in the restored Society. As the long-time editor, then director, of *Civiltà Cattolica*, Bartolomeo Sorge (1929–2020), put it in an interview published in 1989, "Until some forty years ago the way of life in our houses was ruled by 'customs,' timetables, bells. . . . But in fact the 'monastic' spirit which was common to all religious institutions could not easily be reconciled with the intuition of St Ignatius. . . . Jesuits aren't monks. . . . [W]e come together only to disperse, each with his own job to do."[49] Provincials in the United States seemed to share Sorge's view when, in 1966, they asserted, "Religious life as we have known it isn't suitable for the world of modern America. We seem to have stayed immobile in a period marked by change."[50] If change was on its way, Pedro Arrupe was the general to make it happen.

Change was indeed underway long before the thirty-second general congregation mentioned above. After a meeting of those engaged in the training of young Jesuits in September 1967 there was produced "an instruction on the spiritual formation of Ours" [i.e., Jesuits], which led to the move from rural locations into cities of houses of

---

[49] Quoted by Gianni La Bella, *Los Jesuitas: Del Vaticano II al papa Francisco* (Bilbao: Ediciones Mensajero, 2019), 49. This book is a Spanish translation—a fact the present writer did not realize until after purchasing it—of an Italian original, published by Guerini in Milan, also in 2019.

[50] Ibid., 50.

philosophy and theology: Woodstock in New York state to the city of New York, for example; Heythrop, located some twenty miles from Oxford, into London; Comillas on the north coast of Spain into Madrid. In 1968 Arrupe spent a month traversing Brazil, and after a meeting with Latin American provincials in a retreat house near Rio he produced what became known as the "Carta de Río," "the letter from Rio," which acknowledged the widespread injustice in Latin American society and called for a radical conversion in the Jesuits' apostolate in Latin America, making the "social problem an absolute priority in our apostolic activity." Such a stance, Arrupe claimed, marked a "clear break with some of the ways we have behaved in the past."[51]

That was perhaps something of an exaggeration. Janssens in 1949 had issued an instruction on the social apostolate, aimed particularly at Latin America, and had later urged each province to establish a Centro de Investigación y Acción Social, known by their initials as CIAS, and these had been endorsed by Arrupe. Nevertheless, there was a degree of unrest, mainly among Jesuits in Latin America and in Spain, at the direction the Society seemed to be moving under Arrupe's leadership. The older generation regarded the change of direction as an abandonment of the Society's mission, while younger members thought everything was moving too slowly. This was complicated in Spain by a residual loyalty of—mainly—older members to the aging Generalissimo Franco. After a conference on the *Spiritual Exercises* held at Loyola toward the end of August 1966 complaints were aired about the direction being taken by the Society, complaints that reached the Spanish bishops, who suggested a secessionist province, an idea backed by Jean Daniélou who even proposed separate houses for progressives and conservatives. In September 1971 the Spanish hierarchy gathered in what was called "The Asamblea Conjunta." It had before it the findings of a survey conducted by the Jesuit-run Instituto de Ciencías Sociológicas, which revealed that the faithful thought the bishops too complicit in the Franco regime and sought greater democracy in the Church. With some honorable exceptions, the bishops were indeed too close to the regime, many of them also being opposed to Vatican II, especially to the decree on religious

---

[51] For the Carta de Rio, see La Bella, *Los Jesuitas*, 100–102; the quotation is on 101.

freedom, and had allied themselves with the conservative faction in the Society in Spain, who called themselves "faithful Jesuits."[52]

The period from the mid-1960s to the mid-1970s, the period, in other words, leading up to the thirty-second general congregation, was a particularly problematic time for the Society, not least because of its rapid decline in numbers. To take one example, Pope Francis's own province of Argentina, where he was master of novices from 1971 to 1973 and then provincial until 1979, had recruited in 1961 twenty-five novices; in 1973 there were only two. The situation was made more difficult by the perceived identification of Jesuits with liberation theology. This was a mistake. The fundamental "primer" of liberation theology, *Teología de la liberación: Perspectivas*, published in Lima in 1971, was written by Gustavo Gutiérrez, a diocesan priest who later became a Dominican, though a Uruguayan Jesuit, Juan Luis Segundo, who had met Gutiérrez when both were students at the University of Louvain, was also one of the founders of the movement. Indeed, his book *Función de la Iglesia en la Realidad Rioplartense* ["The role of the Church in the context of the River Plate region"] appeared almost a decade before Gutiérrez's volume.

While it is true that a good many Jesuits were proponents of liberation theology,[53] there were also adversaries, including the Argentinian provincial Jorge Bergoglio[54] and especially the Belgian Jesuit, Roger Vekemans (1921–2007), who had been working in Chile but fled the country just before the election in November 1970 of Salvador Allende as the country's socialist president. He settled in Colombia, where he advised the archbishop, later cardinal, of Medellín, Alfonso Lopez Trujillo, a leading opponent among Latin American bishops of this new trend in theology. In Medellín Vekemans founded *Tierra Nueva*, which became a forum for attacks on liberation theology.

---

[52] Ibid., 109–23. The eventual outcome of the Asamblea was, however, progressive despite an attempt to challenge it, possibly because some of the more conservative elements boycotted the event. For a concerted effort to undermine it, see Michael Walsh, *The Secret World of Opus Dei* (London: Grafton Books, 1989), 136–40.

[53] There is a very helpful survey, highlighting differences as well as similarities among Jesuit theologians in Klaiber, *The Jesuits in Latin America*, 347–76. See also Mary Ann Hinsdale, "Jesuit Theological Discourse since Vatican II," in Worcester, *The Cambridge Companion to the Jesuits*, 301–5, where she also draws attention to liberation theology as developed by African Jesuits.

[54] Which is why many Jesuits, when his name was mentioned as a possible papabile in the conclave of 2005, expressed hostility to his election. (Personal knowledge.)

During Allende's brief period in office the Chilean Jesuit Gonzalo Arroyo (1925–2012) founded Christians for Socialism, which drew a great deal of popular support, but, because of its open backing for the left-wing regime, the hierarchy banned the clergy from being members. Though such open political commitment by Jesuits was not common, it certainly happened, most obviously perhaps in the case of the Vigo-born Fernando Hoyos (1943–1982), who had been the director of the CIAS in Guatemala. He chose to join the guerrillas opposing the particularly brutal regime, supported by the US government, of General Efraín Ríos Montt and was killed with weapons in his hands. Other Jesuits died: in Brazil defending indigenous peoples; in Zimbabwe; in Guyana where Bernard Darke, an English province Jesuit, was murdered while taking photographs of anti-government protestors. In El Salvador a right-wing militia assassinated Rutilio Grande (1927–1977) with an elderly man and a teenager who were with him. A dozen years later, in November 1989, regular Salvadoran soldiers assassinated six Jesuits at the country's branch of the Central American University, José Simeón Cañas, together with their cook and her daughter. After the murder of Rutilio Grande the "White Warrior Union" issued death threats against all Jesuits who did not leave El Salvador, while promising members of other religious orders they were quite safe, a promise the death squads did not keep as the murder of two Maryknoll sisters and an Ursuline in December 1980 bore witness.

Jesuits in this period were not always at odds with governments. Despite Peru having a military regime from 1968 to 1980, it was a reformist one and was supported by Jesuits. In Peru opposition to the Society came not from the military but from the Maoist "Shining Path" (Sendero Luminoso) guerrillas and from some prominent churchmen—and from Opus Dei. In Nicaragua members of the Society backed the uprising against the Somoza regime, which was overthrown by the Sandinistas in 1979. Fernando Cardenal (1934–2016), who had been the director of Fe y Alegría in Managua, became minister of education in 1984, and, under pressure from Pope John Paul II, Arrupe's successor as general, Peter Hans Kolvenbach, was obliged to dismiss him from the Society, but he continued to live in Jesuit houses, and he resumed his Jesuit life in full—though he was first obliged to endure a second noviceship—after he resigned his ministerial office. Few Jesuits played such a prominent part in their countries' political life,[55] though the Cambridge-educated economist and Gallego[56] Xabier Gorostiaga (1937–2003) had an important role in Nicaragua's Ministry of Planning and worked elsewhere in Latin America, including as adviser to the government of Panama in its negotiations with the United States over the takeover of responsibility for the Panama Canal.

This social activism owed something to liberation theology and, of course, to decree 4 of the thirty-second general congregation, though it had begun long before either. One issue of liberation theology was, however, a particular problem: its apparent dependency on Marxist analysis. Christians for Socialism in Chile or the Sandinista revolt in Nicaragua, both supported by members of the Society, were explicit in their embrace of Marxism, something that had given rise to considerable anxiety among Jesuit superiors in Latin America. Jeffrey Klaiber claims that "few Jesuits in Latin America actually embraced Marxism in all its totality. . . . A minority felt sympathy for leftist movements that broke with old-style Soviet Communism and espoused radical social change."[57] Latin American provincials had asked Arrupe for guidance, and this he provided in a letter to the whole Society in December 1980. Jesuits, he wrote, might make use of Marxist analysis provided they did not accept the atheistic dialectic materialism that went with it; much debate followed as to whether that was theoretically possible. But Arrupe also commented that Jesuits should come to understand what it was that made Marxism so appealing to people, the injustices from which they were suffering, and he went on to add that liberal capitalism had its own equally unacceptable ideology.[58]

Arrupe wrote this letter just two months after the cardinal archbishop of Krakow, Karol Wojtyła, had been elected, after the very short pontificate of John Paul I, to succeed Pope Paul VI. Pope Paul had always been sympathetic to, and admiring of, the Society, but in July 1973, in the lead up to the thirty-second general congregation

---

[55] The American Jesuit Robert Drinan (1920–2007) served for ten years as a Democrat in the House of Representative, but after pressure from the Vatican he did not stand in the 1980 election. The Code of Canon Law of 1983 forbids clergy from holding public office.

[56] That is, from Galicia, in northern Spain.

[57] Klaiber, *Jesuits in Latin America*, 272.

[58] Ibid.

the cardinal secretary of state, Jean-Marie Villot, wrote to Arrupe expressing concerns that Jesuits (1) had turned their houses into "bed-and-breakfast" accommodation, (2) had allowed laicised Jesuits to continue teaching, (3) had abandoned all Jesuit discipline, (4) had lost control of the editorial policy of their magazines, and (5) were all opposed to Pope Paul's 1968 encyclical on birth control, *Humanae Vitae*.[59]

It is certainly true that many Jesuits expressed opposition to *Humanae Vitae* and that some had abandoned their vocations as a consequence—as, indeed, did priests from other religious orders and from diocesan clergy. But the pope was disturbed by the attacks on him that arose not only because of his encyclical but also because of what seemed to many an overcautious approach to the implementation of Vatican II. This criticism had been expressed in Jesuit periodicals around the world, and as a result Arrupe called a meeting in Rome of Jesuit editors, ostensibly to discuss censorship. Apart from the general himself, it was presided over by Roberto Tucci (1921–2015), who was the director of Vatican Radio and had just ceased being editor of *La Civiltà Cattolica*. Under Tucci *Civiltà* had undergone a crisis, with many of its "college of writers" seeking to resign because of its more progressive, less apologetic theological slant: it had also become, in Gianni La Bella's words, more "Anglo-Saxon"; that is to say, the magazine began to distinguish news from comment![60] The discussion with the editors on censorship did not get very far after it became evident that rules drawn up for writers could not easily be applied to Jesuits who spoke on the radio or appeared on television.[61]

Arrupe complained that the Vatican was paying more attention to critics of the Society than to those in positions of authority; Villot responded with a thirteen-page list of criticisms that, as Lamet remarks, "could be summed up with the phrase 'Lack of responsible authority.'"[62] There were suggestions in the press that Arrupe, under such constant assault both from certain elements in the Vatican and from conservatives in the Society itself, was considering resigning his role as general. La Bella suggests that Villot was actively working

[59] La Bella, *Los Jesuitas*, 137.
[60] Ibid., 106. Tucci was created a cardinal in 2001.
[61] Personal knowledge.
[62] Lamet, *Pedro Arrupe*, 317.

to remove him from office, possibly by his resignation or by persuading Pope Paul to make him a cardinal, a status within the hierarchy incompatible with full membership of the Society. All this was going on in the run-up to the thirty-second general congregation, about which Arrupe kept Pope Paul fully informed. One of the items on Arrupe's agenda was to extend the fourth vow beyond those who hitherto had been solemnly professed. It will be recalled that there were—and still are, though with some modifications—several "ranks" in the Society: there are priests, brothers, and scholastics, i.e., those in training for the priesthood. All have taken the traditional three "simple" but permanent vows of poverty, chastity, and obedience. There are, however, two categories among the priests, determined by an examination *ad gradum*, "for status." When they come to take final vows, those who have succeeded in the examination are professed of the four vows; those who have not, the spiritual coadjutors, take three vows. The distinction matters, for there are certain offices, and voting rights, that are limited to the solemnly professed. This is what Ignatius laid down in the Constitutions, but in modern times such distinctions have had less and less significance. As the general congregation approached, Arrupe informed Pope Paul that he was going to propose that all members of the Society take the fourth vow of special obedience to the pope. Pope Paul did not forbid the discussion on the topic but indicated, through a letter written by Cardinal Villot, that if a change were to be made it would not have the necessary papal approval because it would mark a major departure from the founder's intentions. "The Society is governed by the general, not by cardinals," Arrupe told the assembled Jesuits,[63] and the debate went ahead, much to the annoyance of the pope, as Arrupe discovered when the two met. "When I left [the papal audience], I broke into tears," he later told Pedro Lamet:[64] the general congregation made no changes with regard to the fourth vow. There were to be more tears.

Pope Paul died August 6, 1978, and his successor, John Paul I, was elected twenty days later, only to die on September 28, 1978, thus precipitating yet another conclave: Karol Wojtyła became John Paul II on October 16. During this second gathering of cardinals a dossier

---

[63] Ibid., 332.
[64] Ibid., 335.

had been circulated to them that was highly critical of the Society: some of the complaints addressed to the new pontiff came from Jesuits themselves. Arrupe, who had by this time governed the Society for fifteen years, decided that he ought to resign in the face of all the criticism, but to do so he needed first to call another general congregation. Early in 1980 he began to make arrangements for the congregation, but when, as required, he informed John Paul II of his intentions, the pope wanted to know what his role might be in such a gathering and, when informed that constitutionally he did not have one, he banned the congregation from taking place.[65] Then, in the early hours of the morning of August 7, 1981, as he returned to Rome from a visit to Thailand, Arrupe suffered a cerebral thrombosis. He was to spend the next decade of his life, apart from the month in the Salvator Mundi hospital immediately after his collapse, being cared for in the infirmary of the Jesuit headquarters.

Arrupe had months earlier appointed the genial American Vincent O'Keefe (1917–2012) to be vicar general, and with the general incapacitated, in accordance with the Constitutions, it would fall to him to call a general congregation to elect a successor. It did not happen. On October 6 the papal secretary of state, Cardinal Agostino Casaroli, visited Arrupe and handed him a letter from the pope. Casaroli had asked O'Keefe to leave the room. When the cardinal departed O'Keefe returned to find Arrupe in tears. He read the pope's letter, to find that the pontiff had effectively sacked him from the office of vicar general and replaced him with his own nominees:

> After long reflection and prayer [the pope had written] I have decided to confide the task to a delegate of my own choosing, who will represent me more directly within the Society, will attend to the preparation of the general congregation, which should be called at an opportune moment, and will jointly, in my name, have supervision of the Society's governance until the election of a new superior general.[66]

This power grab by the Vatican, while not entirely unprecedented, was unexpected. Perhaps it should not have been. The Vatican, under the new Polish pope, was alarmed by who might be elected, were

[65] La Bella, *Los Jesuitas*, 196.
[66] Quoted in Lamet, *Pedro Arrupe*, 419.

the general congregation to go ahead under the supervision of O'Keefe as the Constitutions required. The pope, having lived so much of his life under a Communist regime, though an outspoken defender of human rights, was not sympathetic to some of the left-wing causes embraced by Jesuits, especially by those in Central and South America: liberation theology proved to be a particular papal bête noire.

The pope's actions sent shockwaves throughout the Society and, indeed, beyond. Even more astonishing was the person he chose as his "delegate." Paolo Dezza (1901–1999), originally of the Venetian province, had taught metaphysics at the Gregorian where, in 1941, he was the rector: Karol Wojtyła had been among his pupils even though not technically a student at the Greg. He had held many senior offices in the Society and had been confessor to both Paul VI and John Paul I. He was, however, eighty years of age and almost blind. John Paul II gave him an assistant, Giuseppe Pittau (1928–2014), a former provincial in Japan and rector of the Jesuit Sofia University in Tokyo, whom the pope had met during a visit to the Far East. The two moved cautiously to repair trust between the Society and the Vatican,[67] and, under pressure from his two "delegates," on December 8, 1982, John Paul II gave permission for a general congregation to elect a successor to Arrupe, to begin on September 1 the following year.

When the thirty-fourth general congregation opened, a very frail Arrupe—Don Pedro, as he was commonly known—made his way to the podium amid tumultuous applause and announced his resignation. On September 13, 1983, Peter Hans Kolvenbach (1928–2016), at the time the head of the Pontifical Oriental Institute, was elected on the first ballot. He was very different in character from his predecessor: a quiet-spoken man of few words—as La Bella put it, "able to speak several languages, but prefers silence"[68]—an academic specializing in linguistics, ordained not into the Roman Rite but as a priest of the Armenian Catholic Church in communion with Rome (hence the beard) but as committed as his predecessor to the Society's trajectory, something he made clear from the start of his generalate. Decree 4 of the thirty-fourth general congregation endorsed the de-

---

[67] So the sources all say, but little changed in the general trajectory of the Society during this period.

[68] La Bella, *Los Jesuitas*, 233.

cree on faith and justice passed by its predecessor-but-one in 1975. And he not only gave his backing to the Jesuit Refugee Service, which Arrupe had started in November 1980, but also told the Society that the Service was the responsibility of all Jesuits, not just those with special expertise.

Decree 5 committed the Society to interreligious dialogue, and there was perhaps no greater advocate for entering conversation with non-Christians than the Belgian Jesuit Jacques Dupuis (1923–2004). He had gone to India in 1948 and remained there until called to teach at the Gregorianum in 1984. When, in 1998, the Congregation for the Doctrine of the Faith (CDF), then presided over by Josef Ratzinger, the future Pope Benedict XVI, questioned aspects of Dupuis's most significant book, *Towards a Christian Theology of Religions*, Kolvenbach defended him vigorously, and no further action was taken. Dupuis, a retiring figure, was nonetheless deeply hurt. The same year the Indian spiritual writer Anthony de Mello (1931–1987) also came in for posthumous criticism by the CDF. The complaints continued. In 2004 Roger Haight (b. 1936) was banned from teaching at the Jesuit theologate in Cambridge, Massachusetts, because of his book *Jesus Symbol of God*, and he transferred to a non-Catholic seminary. In 2009 he was banned from teaching anywhere. In 2005 Thomas Reese (b. 1945) resigned from the editorship of *America* because of complaints by the CDF against articles he had published in his magazine, and in 2007 even the mild-mannered Jon Sobrino (b. 1938) was criticized by the CDF in what was clearly an attack on liberation theology as such. Sobrino protested, and no further action was taken either by the Vatican or by his Jesuit superiors. In Peru Jesuits were heavily involved—though it was not a Jesuit institution as such—with the Pontifical Catholic University located in Lima. Tarcisio Bertone, who became Benedict XVI's cardinal secretary of state in 2006, announced that it had been deprived of its titles of "pontifical" and "Catholic." Kolvenbach remained remarkably calm and successfully steered the Society through the many challenges of the last years of John Paul II's pontificate and the first ones of Benedict XVI, as well as, with the fall of the Berlin Wall, the reintegration of Jesuits still surviving in Eastern Europe. "Not even my parents knew I was a Jesuit," one Czechoslovak member of the Society commented.[69]

[69] Ibid., 323.

Kolvenbach's tenure of office had a lasting impact on the Society. He had a special interest in, and had written about, the *Spiritual Exercises*. They had always been central to the Society's mission, but under Kolvenbach they took on a new importance and a wider dissemination. And then there was discernment, a term that occurs often in Pope Francis's discourse. This too was something Kolvenbach had inherited from Arrupe, who had urged, without much notable success, community discernment on Jesuits. For Arrupe's successor, as he said in a letter of November 1986, it was "an indispensable instrument for the apostolate." Not all were convinced at the time, but "discernment" has since remained in frequent use in the Jesuit vocabulary.

In February 2006 the general, having received permission from Pope Benedict to resign his office, summoned the thirty-fifth general congregation to meet in January 2008 to elect his successor: by which time Kolvenbach, having served nearly a quarter of a century as superior general, would be in his eightieth year. As had become almost the norm in such gatherings during the pontificates of John Paul II and Benedict XVI, there was much politicking. Some cardinals, mainly from Latin America but including the Slovenian Franc Rode, the retired archbishop of Ljubljana who had spent his early years in Argentina to which his family had fled after World War II, saw this as an opportunity to bring the Society to heel. Bertone, the secretary of state, suggested that Cardinal Bergoglio be involved in the preparations for the meeting, but the archbishop of Buenos Aires refused. It would, he said, only add to the problems faced by the Society, not help to solve them.

When the congregation began, it did so with a homily from Cardinal Rode, now prefect of the Congregation for Institutes of Consecrated Life and Societies of Apostolic Life. He had first submitted his text to and received approval from Pope Benedict. His judgment on the Society was harsh. It had distanced itself from the hierarchy and no longer "thought with the Church": *sentire cum ecclesia*, as Ignatius instructed in the *Spiritual Exercises*. Before he offered his resignation, Kolvenbach read to the assembly a letter he had received from the pope, calling on members of the Society to recommit to a complete acceptance of Catholic teaching—liberation theology was mentioned, as was the relationship between Christianity and other religions. They then proceeded to an election. On January 19, 2008, on the second ballot, Adolfo Nicolás (1936–2020) was chosen as the thirtieth superior general: he had been a member of the commission set up to find Kolvenbach's successor.

Nicolás had a long and distinguished career as, for two decades, a lecturer in theology at Sofia University in Tokyo, followed by work in the Philippines, and then as provincial in Japan from 1993 to 1999. Kolvenbach had wanted him as rector of the Gregorianum, but the idea was vetoed by the Vatican.[70] In the discussions that followed, the congregation recommitted the Society to work for justice, but in the context of reconciliation of people with God, with each other, and with creation. And in an era when young Jesuits in particular were questioning the Society's involvement in education, the congregation reaffirmed the value of the intellectual apostolate in response to the very cordial, unexpectedly cordial, given Rode's homily, audience with Pope Benedict. But what Jesuits carried away in particular was decree 4, on religious obedience, famously one of the special traits of the Society. Obedience in the Society, the decree argued, was not simply to conform one's own will to the will of another but together to seek the will of God.

Then, on March 13, 2013, after the unexpected resignation of Pope Benedict, Cardinal Jorge Bergoglio was elected to the papacy, the first Jesuit in the Society's nearly five-hundred-year existence, to hold the highest office in the Church. The choice came as a surprise to many, despite the fact that Bergoglio had been among the papabile at the previous conclave. What was even more of a surprise—though, again, it should not have been, given the style of his tenure of the archbishopric of Buenos Aires—was the modest manner of life that he adopted as pontiff, a manner of life that immediately endeared him to many outside, as well as inside, the Catholic Church.

Shortly after the conclave Pope Francis rang Rome's Jesuit headquarters and asked if Nicolás could come to see him; they already knew one another slightly, having both attended the same meeting in Rome in 1987. On March 24 the general wrote to the Society about the encounter. He acknowledged that there had been tensions between Bergoglio and the Society; he had, for instance, been asked not to stay in Jesuit houses because so many Jesuits were opposed to the

[70] Ibid., 375.

line he had taken, as provincial in Argentina, on liberation theology. He was seen as a traditionalist and regarded as a source of division in the Society, as the attempt of some cardinals, reported above (p. 288), to recruit him as a conservative force. Nicolás did not gloss over the problems but insisted, as the pope himself did, that he considered himself a Jesuit. So much so, he told his first press briefing on July 28, 2013, as he flew back from Rio de Janeiro, "that in three days' time I will be joining them in celebrating the Feast of St Ignatius," as he did on July 31 in the Jesuit headquarters on Borgo Santo Spirito and has done ever since.

Pope Francis has perhaps shown himself as part of his order more than any previous religious has done in the past. When he travels he makes a point of meeting the local Jesuit community. The editor of *Civiltà Cattolica*, a journal that is enjoying a new lease on life freed from the constraints John Paul II imposed, has become a major conduit for Francis's thinking and a close confidant of the pope. Nicolás unexpectedly announced in May 2014 that he would resign as general for health reasons, and he summoned a general congregation to choose his successor to meet in Rome in October 2016. On October 14 the Venezuelan Arturo Marcelino Sosa Abascal (b. 1948) was chosen, a political theorist and unabashedly of the left. Instead of the delegates making their way to the Vatican for an audience with the pope, Francis went to them, gave an address, and answered questions. Two years later Sosa announced the Society's agenda for the coming decade: the *Spiritual Exercises* with an emphasis on discernment, accompanying the poor in their search for justice, accompanying the young, the care for creation. They were, said Pope Francis, very much the agenda that he himself had chosen for his pontificate.

Before Pope Francis there had never been a pope from Latin America; before Arturo Sosa there had never been a general of the Society from the New World. The fractious relationship between the papacy and the Society of Jesus, which had been a feature of Catholic history at least since the end of the Second World War, was over. At least for now.

Appendix
The Black Legend of the Society of Jesus

Jesuits have not always had good press. Even nowadays under the word "Jesuit" the *Shorter Oxford English Dictionary* says of the Society of Jesus that "its secret power and the casuistical principles maintained by many of its representatives, and generally ascribed to the body as a whole, have rendered its name odious not only in English, but in French and other languages and have given rise to sense 2." Sense 2, in the OED's definition, is "a dissembling person, a prevaricator." The examples given date, not surprisingly, from the seventeenth century in England, where Jesuits had long been the bogeymen for their loyalty to the papacy, especially after the attempt, known as the Gunpowder Plot, to blow up Parliament, a conspiracy in which Jesuits were implicated though they were in no way involved.

Such antipathy to the Society has not been limited to Protestant Britain. In 1816 the former American president John Adams wrote to Thomas Jefferson: "This Society has been a greater calamity to Mankind than the French Revolution or Napoleon's Despotism or Ideology. It has obstructed the Progress of Reformation and the improvement of the human mind in society much longer and more fatally."[1] It was a topic to which Adams returned more than once.

The Society encountered hostility from the outset, not least because of its name—it seemed to some an arrogant claim to be a "companion of Jesus"—but more significantly because it departed in many ways from the pattern of religious life as lived hitherto, by not having a specific habit, for instance, or having an obligation to sing the Divine Office in choir. It was known, moreover, that its founder Ignatius had

---

[1] Quoted McGreevy, John T., *American Jesuits and the World* (Princeton University Press, 2016), 1.

been investigated in Spain by the Inquisition, which was quite enough to set alarm bells ringing in some Catholic circles. Indeed, the earliest anti-Jesuit tract, dated 1564, comes from the pen of a bishop.[2]

To be more accurate, that was perhaps the earliest to attack the Society as a whole. In 1554 there was an anti-Jesuit work published that was aimed more specifically at the Jesuit attempt to establish themselves in France. Etienne Pasquier's *Plaidoyer de l'université de Paris encontre les Jésuites* presented the opening by the Society of the Collège de Clermont as an attempt to undermine the Gallican liberties of the French Church (for all this, see chapter 7, passim). The Society, for Pasquier, was a "monstrous" entity, a "hermaphrodite," neither secular nor religious.[3] In 1602 he returned to the attack again in *Le Catéchisme des Jésuites ou le Mystère d'iniquité*, presented as a conversation between two travelers, one of them a Jesuit. The Society marked a break with tradition, said Pasquier—by which he meant Gallicanism—and dominated the papacy. They met secretly and often in disguise, which in Elizabethan and Stuart England was certainly true, and Pasquier compared Ignatius himself to Machiavelli.[4]

Although Pasquier's *Catéchisme* proved popular—it was promptly translated into English and Dutch—it was far outshone by a pamphlet titled *Monita Privata Societatis Jesu* written by a Polish Jesuit who had been dismissed from the Society, though he was afterward readmitted, Hieronymus (Jerome) Zahorowski. First published in Krakow in 1614 and later renamed the *Monita Secreta*, it purported to be a version of the Jesuit Constitutions. It had enormous success despite, or perhaps because of, being condemned by the Holy Office in 1616. It too was promptly translated into various European languages and went into eighteen editions in the seventeenth century alone.[5]

> In effect, the pamphlet read as a set of behaviour protocols for the Jesuit. It had nothing to do with religion per se, but rather invited the members of the Society to extend their political and economic

---

[2] Pavone, Sabine, "The History of anti-Jesuitism" in Banchoff, Thomas and Casanova, José (eds.) *The Jesuits and Globalization* (Washington DC, Georgetown University Press, 2016), 112.

[3] Damour, Franck, *Le Pape Noire: Genèse d'un mythe* (Brussels, Editions Lessius, 2013), 14.

[4] Ibid., 34–36.

[5] Pavone, Sabine, "Between History and Myth" in O'Malley, John W. and others (eds.), *Jesuits II*, 52.

power by means of a slow but steady infiltration of society at all levels. This was to be effected through domination of the conscience, with the confessor serving in the role of principal protagonist. . . . At the same time, the *Monita* exhorted Jesuits to hide their real intentions whenever possible, by demonstrating humility before and submission to the reigning powers.[6]

Protestant Reformers regularly portrayed the pope as the Antichrist, and the Jesuits were his minions. The Society's success in effecting conversions could only be, some of its antagonists suggested, the work of Satan or of magic. Other of what might be regarded as Jesuit achievements, such as the reductions in Paraguay or their success in accommodating Catholic teaching to local cultures, were, as has been seen in the text of this book (see, for example, Voltaire's accusations, p. 210), used against them, especially in France. It was in France, for instance, that the first nineteenth-century publication of the *Monita* occurred.[7] Jesuits were suspected both of conspiring to bring about the French Revolution and of fostering the counter-revolution. Jesuits as conspirators was given renewed prominence with the reestablishment in 1814 by Pierre Ronsin (1771–1846) of the Marian Congregations, whose members were suspected of secretly seeking political power on the Society's behalf. Though they did not long survive, while they existed they were taken sufficiently seriously for the establishment, in Italy as well as in France, of organizations set up with the sole purpose of counteracting their influence.[8]

In 1843 two distinguished literary figures, both of them historians, both of them republicans, Jules Michelet and Edgar Quinet, combined to deliver a course of lectures on the Society at the Collège de France. "Study the writings of Jesuits," declared Michelet, "there you will find only one thing: the death of liberty."[9] Their lectures were followed avidly; the subsequent book, *Des Jesuites*, published the same year, a best-seller. They were contemporaneous with the serial publication, in a Parisian magazine, of the socialist Eugène Sue's reworking of the ancient legend of *The Wandering Jew*. The story, in Sue's telling, is less about the Jew condemned to walk the earth than about

---

[6] Ibid., 50–51.

[7] Cubitt, Geoffrey, *The Jesuit Myth* (Oxford, Clarendon Press, 1993), 58.

[8] Damour, *Le Pape Noire*, 62.

[9] Quoted ibid., 75.

the evil machinations of Jesuits, a secret society that is determined to lay hands on the inherited wealth of a family whose ancestors, as Huguenots, had once been persecuted by the Society. It is the role of the wandering Jew to protect this unsuspecting family from the wiles of the Jesuits. In a later novel Sue depicts Napoleon III as a secret Jesuit—an odd choice for a writer so hostile to the Society because Napoleon III was, at least until the defeat of the French in the Franco-Prussia war, a highly popular monarch. In Sue's account, however, the Jesuit general and Napoleon aim to dominate the world through the spread of capitalism.[10]

Wicked fictional Jesuits turn up in odd places. Dostoevsky presents his Grand Inquisitor in *The Brothers Karamazov* as a member of the Society, and Alexandre Dumas portrays the philandering musketeer Aramis not just as a Jesuit but, in the end, as the Jesuit superior general, the "Black Pope." Like so much of anti-Jesuit material, this title, which has now become commonly used without any particular pejorative sense attached, also first emerged in France in a hostile context. In 1865 there was published in Paris *Le Jésuite*, by l'Abbé ***. Hiding behind the asterisks was Jean Hyppolite Michon, who had indeed once been ordained a priest, though he had, in 1842, resigned from the ministry. He is remembered mainly as the founder of graphology, but he also wrote a number of books on the history of the Church. In *Le Jésuite* he has a crowd in Rome call out, "Long live the black pope." The name was not meant to be complimentary, but it was taken up by other writers and has survived, though not necessarily as a term of opprobrium, as originally intended.

Writing in a festschrift for the late John Bossy, once professor of history at the University of York, Peter Burke, emeritus professor of culture at Emmanuel College, Cambridge, recalls that terms derived from the word Jesuit "were often pejorative and tended to imply a lack of scruple, and especially hypocrisy."[11] But the hostility, he adds, has declined, at least for now:

If the Jesuit threat has been taken less seriously in the middle and late twentieth century, this is probably because the stereotype of the secret society was displaced on to the Communist Party, the CIA

---

[10] Ibid., 94.

[11] "The Black Legend of the Jesuits: An Essay in social Stereotypes" in *Christianity and Community in the West*, Simon Ditchield, ed. (Aldershot, Ashgate, 2000), 167.

and the Mafia, each of which has been lent certain characteristics earlier attributed to the Order. The resilience of stereotypes and the potential for their reactivation appears to be unending.[12]

Both Professors Burke and Bossy were alumni of the same Jesuit college in North London, so the Society must clearly still be getting some things right, despite its sometimes murky reputation.

[12] Ibid., 180.

Bibliography

Abbott, Walter, ed. *The Documents of Vatican II*. London: Geoffrey Chapman, 1967.

Alden, Dauril. *The Making of an Enterprise*. Stanford, CA: Stanford University Press, 1996.

Alencastro, Luiz Felipe de. "The African Slave Trade and the Construction of the Iberian Atlantic." In *The Global South Atlantic*, edited by Kenny Bystrom and Joseph Slaughter, 33–45. New York: Fordham University Press, 2018.

Alfieri, Fernanda. "'Unearthing Chaos and Giving Shape to It': The Society of Jesus after Suppression; Hiatus and Continuity." In *The Historiography of Transition: Critical Phases in the Development of Modernity (1494–1973)*, edited by Paolo Pombeni, 105–22. New York: Routledge, 2016.

Alvargonzález, David. "Relevance of the Metaphysical Discussion Concerning Divine Sciences in Molina's Concordia and Bañez's Apology." *International Journal of Philosophy and Theology* 3 no. 1 (June 2015): 89–95.

Amaladass, Anand, and Ines Županov, eds. *Intercultural Encounter and the Jesuit Mission in South Asia (16th–18th Centuries)*. Bangalore: ATC, 2014.

Aranda, Marcelo. "Deciphering the Ignatian Tree: The Catholic Horoscope of the Society of Jesus." In *Empires of Knowledge*, edited by Paula Findlen, 106–25. London: Routledge, 2018.

———. "The Jesuit Roots of Spanish Naval Education." *Journal of Jesuit Studies* 7 (2020): 185–203.

Aranha, Paolo. "Discrimination and Integration of the Dalits in Early Modern South Indian Missions." *The Journal of World Christianity* 6, no. 1 (2016): 168–204.

Araoz, Antonio. "On Father Nadal's Visitation." *Studies in the Spirituality of the Jesuits* 25, no. 4 (September 1993): 41–45.

Arzubialde, Santiago. "The Development of the Exercises." *The Way* 50, no. 4 (October 2011): 78–96.

Aston, Nigel, ed. *Religious Change in Europe, 1650–1914*. Oxford: Clarendon Press, 1997.

Bailey, Gauvin Alexander. "The Truth-Showing Mirror: Jesuit Catechism and the Arts in Mughal India." In *The Jesuits: Cultures, Sciences, and the Arts, 1540–1773*, edited by John W. O'Malley, Gauvin Alexander Bailey, Steven J. Harris, and T. Frank Kennedy, 380–401. Toronto: University of Toronto Press, 1999.

Bangert, William V. *A History of the Society of Jesus*. St. Louis: Institute of Jesuit Sources, 1986.

Barnes, Michael. "The First English Jesuit in India." *Thinking Faith*. October 29, 2019. www.thinkingfaith.org/articles/first-english-jesuit-india -remarkable-story-thomas-stephens-sj.

Basset, Bernard. *The English Jesuits*. London: Burns and Oates, 1967.

Beale, Derek. "Joseph II and the Monasteries of Austria and Hungary." In *Religious Change in Europe, 1650–1914*, edited by Nigel Aston, 161–84. Oxford: Clarendon Press, 1997.

Bédarida, François, and Renée Bédarida, eds. *La Résistance Spirituelle 1941– 1944*. Paris: Albin Michel, 2001.

Beltramini, Enrico. "Roman Catholic Government and Mission to Tibet: A Historical and Theological Study." *International Bulletin of Mission Research* (2020): 1–17.

Bernauer, James. *Jesuit Kaddish*. Notre Dame, IN: University of Notre Dame Press, 2019.

Bireley, Robert. *The Jesuits and the Thirty Years' War*. Cambridge: Cambridge University Press, 2003.

Blackwell, Richard. *Galileo, Bellarmine, and the Bible*. Notre Dame, IN: University of Notre Dame Press, 1991.

Bossy, John. "The Heart of Robert Persons." In *The Reckoned Expense: Edmund Campion and the Early English Jesuits*, edited by Thomas M. McCoog, 141–58. Woodbridge: The Boydell Press, 1996.

Bouchoff, Thomas, and José Casanovas, eds. *The Jesuits and Globalization*. Washington, DC: Georgetown University Press, 2016.

Broadley, John, and Peter Phillips, eds. *The Ministry of the Printed Word*. Stratton-on-the-Fosse: Downside Abbey Press, 2018.

Broadley, Martin John, ed. *Bishop Herbert Vaughan and the Jesuits: Education and Authority*. Woodbridge: The Boydell Press for the Catholic Record Society, 2010.

Brodrick, James. *Robert Bellarmine*. London: Longmans, 1950.

———. *Saint Ignatius Loyola: The Pilgrim Years*. London: Burns and Oates, 1956.

Buckley, Michael J. "Freedom, Election and Self-Transcendence." In *Ignatian Spirituality in a Secular Age*, edited by George P. Schner, 65–90. Waterloo, Ontario: Wilfrid Laurier University Press, 1984.

———. "Seventeenth-Century French Spirituality." In *Christian Spirituality Post-Reformation and Modern*, edited by Louis Dupré and Don E. Saliers, 28–68. London: SCM Press, 1989.

Burke, Peter. "The Black Legend of the Jesuits: An Essay in Social Stereotypes." In *Christianity and Community in the West*, edited by Simon Ditchfield, 165–82. Aldershot: Ashgate, 2000.

Burns, Jimmy. *Francis, Pope of Good Promise*. London: Constable, 2015.

Burson, Jeffrey D., and Jonathan Wright, eds. *The Jesuit Suppression in Global Context*. Cambridge: Cambridge University Press, 2015.

Butterworth, Robert. *A Jesuit Friendship: Letters of George Tyrrell to Herbert Thurston*. London: Roehampton Institute, 1988.

Bystrom, Kerry, and Joseph R. Slaughter, eds. *The Global South Atlantic*. New York: Fordham University Press, 2018.

Campion, Edmund. *Ten Reasons*. London: Manresa Press, 1914.

Caraman, Philip. *The Lost Empire*. London: Sidgwick and Jackson, 1985.

———. *Tibet: The Jesuit Century*. Tiverton: Halsgrove, 1997.

———. *The University of the Nations*. New York: Paulist Press, 1981.

Caruana, Louis. "The Jesuits and the Quiet Side of the Scientific Revolution." In *The Cambridge Companion to the Jesuits*, edited by Thomas Worcester, 243–60. Cambridge: Cambridge University Press, 2008.

———. "The Legacies of Suppression " In *The Jesuit Suppression in Global Context*, edited by Jeffrey D. Burson and Jonathan Wright, 262–76. Cambridge: Cambridge University Press, 2015.

Casalini, Cristiano, and Claude Pavur, eds. *Jesuit Pedagogy, 1540–1616: A Reader*. Boston: Boston College, Institute of Jesuit Sources, 2016.

Cervantes, F., and A. Redden, eds. *Angels, Demons and the New World*. Cambridge: Cambridge University Press, 2013.

Chadwick, Hubert. *St Omers to Stonyhurst*. London: Burns and Oates, 1962.

Chadwick, Owen. *Catholicism and History: The Opening of the Vatican Archives*. Cambridge: Cambridge University Press, 1978.

Chatellier, Louis. *Europe of the Devout*. Cambridge: Cambridge University Press, 1989.

Clooney, Francis X. "De Nobili's *Dialogue* and Religion in South India." In *The Jesuits: Cultures, Sciences, and the Arts, 1540–1773*, edited by John W.

O'Malley, Gauvin Alexander Bailey, Steven J. Harris, and T. Frank Kennedy, 402–17. Toronto: University of Toronto Press, 1999.

Clossey, Luke. *Salvation and Globalization in the Early Jesuit Missions.* Cambridge: Cambridge University Press, 2008.

Cognet, Louis. "Ecclesiastical Life in France." In *The Church in the Age of Absolutism and Enlightenment,* edited by Hubert Jedin and John Dolan, 24–56. London: Burns and Oats, 1981.

Cohen, Leonardo, and Andreu Martínez d'Alòs-Moner. "The Jesuit Mission in Ethiopia: An Analytical Bibliography." *Aethiopica* 9 (2006): 190–212.

Coll, Miguel. "La primera Congregación de la Compañia de Jesús tras la restauración de 1814." In *La Compagnie de Jésus des Anciens Régimes au Monde Contemporain (XVIIIᵉ–XXᵉ Siècles),* edited by Pierre-Antoine Fabre, et al., 237–55. Rome: Institutum Historicum Societatis Iesu and L'École Française de Rome, 2021.

Colombo, Emanuele, and Niccolò Guasti. "The Expulsion and Suppression in Portugal and Spain: An Overview." In *The Jesuit Suppression in Global Context,* edited by Jeffrey D. Burson and Jonathan Wright, 117–38. Cambridge: Cambridge University Press, 2015.

Colombo, Emanuele. "Conversioni Religiose in Calderón de la Barca: El Gran Príncipe de Fez (1669)." *Drammaturgia* 16 (2019): 49–79.

———. "Jesuits and Islam in Early Modern Europe." In *The Oxford Handbook of the Jesuits,* edited by Ines G. Županov, 349–78. Oxford: Oxford University Press, 2019.

———. "A Muslim Turned Jesuit: Baldassarre Loyola Mandes (1631–1667)." *The Journal of Early Modern History* 17 (2013): 479–504.

Conlan, Thomas D. "The Failed Attempt to Move the Emperor to Yamaguchi and the Fall of the Ouchi." *Japanese Studies* (September 2015): 185–203.

The Constitutions of the Society of Jesus and Their Complementary Norms. St. Louis: The Institute of Jesuit Sources, 1996.

Copleston, Frederick. *History of Philosophy.* Vol. 3. London: Burns and Oates, 1953.

Córdoba Salmerón, Miguel. "A Failed Politician, a Disputed Jesuit: Cardinal Johann Eberhard Nithard." *Journal of Jesuit Studies* 7 (2020): 545–69.

Cubitt, Geoffrey. *The Jesuit Myth.* Oxford: Clarendon Press, 1993.

Cunningham Graham, R. B. *A Vanished Arcadia.* London: Heineman, 1901.

Curran, Robert Emmett. *The Bicentennial History of Georgetown University.* Vol. 1. Washington, DC: Georgetown University Press, 1993.

Cushner, Nicholas R. *Why Have You Come Here?* New York: Oxford University Press, 2006.

Damour, Franck. *Le Pape Noire: Genèse d'un Mythe*. Brussels: Editions Lessius, 2013.

de Asúa, Miguel. *Science in the Vanished Arcadia*. Leiden: Brill, 2014.

de Castelnau-Estoile, Charlotte. "Jesuit Anthropology." In *The Oxford Handbook of the Jesuits*, edited by Ines G. Županov, 811–30. Oxford: Oxford University Press, 2019.

Deslandres, Dominique. "New France." In *A Companion to Early Modern Catholic Global Missions*, edited by Ronnie Po-Chia Hsia, 124–47. Leiden: Brill, 2018.

de Waal, Edmund. *The White Road*. London: Chatto and Windus, 2015.

Dial, Andrew. "Antoine LaValette, Slave Murderer." *Journal of Jesuit Studies* 8 (2021): 37–56.

Dinis, Alfredo. "Giovanni Battista Riccioli and the Science of His Time." In *Jesuit Science and the Republic of Letters*, edited by Mordechai Feingold, 195–234. Cambridge, MA: MIT Press, 2003.

Ditchfield, Simon, ed. *Christianity and Community in the West: Essays for John Bossy*. Aldershot: Ashgate, 2000.

Donattini, Massimo, Giuseppe Marcocci, and Stefania Pastore, eds. *L'Europa divisae i nuovi mondi*. Vol. 2. Pisa: Edizioni Normale, 2011.

Donnelly, John Patrick. "Antonio Possevino's Plan for World Evangelization." *The Catholic Historical Review* 74 (August 1988): 179–98.

Donohue, John. "Middle East." In *The Cambridge Encyclopedia of the Jesuits*, edited by Thomas Worcester, 520–21. Cambridge: Cambridge University Press, 2017.

Dupré, Louis, and Don E. Saliers, eds. *Christian Spirituality: Post-Reformation and Modern*. London: SCM Press, 1989.

Fabre, Pierre Antoine, et al., eds. *La Compagnie de Jésus des Anciens Régimes au Monde Contemporain (XVIIIᵉ–XXᵉ Siècles)*. Rome: Institutum Historicum Societatis Iesu and L'École Française de Rome, 2021.

Feingold, Mordechai, ed. *Jesuit Science and the Republic of Letters*. Cambridge, MA: MIT Press, 2003.

Flynn, Gabriel, and Paul D. Murray, eds. *Ressourcement: A Movement for Renewal in Twentieth-Century Catholic Theology*. Oxford: Oxford University Press, 2012.

Fontana Castelli, Eva. "Il Paccanarismo: una Compagnia di Gesù sotto altro nome?" In *La Compagnie de Jésus des Anciens Régimes au Monde*

Contemporain (XVIIIe–XXe Siècles), edited by Pierre Antoine Fabre, et al., 119–32. Rome: Institutum Historicum Societatis Iesu and L'École Française de Rome, 2021.

Franco, José Eduardo, and Fernanda Santos. "Echos politiques et idéologiques de la Restauration de la Compagnie de Jésus." In *La Compagnie de Jésus des Anciens Régimes au Monde Contemporain (XVIIIe–XXe Siècles)*, edited by Pierre Antoine Fabre, et al., 351–72. Rome: Institutum Historicum Societatis Iesu and L'École Française de Rome, 2021.

Franco, Juan Hernández, and Pablo Ortega-del-Cerro. "A Jesuit Utopian Project on Behalf of the Conversos: Fernando de Valdés and the Statutes of Purity of Blood (1632)." *Journal of Jesuit Studies* 8, no. 2 (2021): 214–32.

Friedrich, Markus. "Jesuit Organization and Legislation." In *The Oxford Handbook of the Jesuits*, edited by Ines G. Županov, 23–43. Oxford: Oxford University Press, 2019.

Ganson, Barbara. *The Guaraní under Spanish Rule*. Stanford, CA: Stanford University Press, 2003.

Ganss, George E. *The Constitutions of the Society of Jesus*. St. Louis: Institute of Jesuit Sources, 1970.

Garraghan, Gilbert J. "John Anthony Grassi, SJ, 1775–1849." *The Catholic Historical Review* 23, no. 3 (October 1937): 273–92.

Garrigou-Lagrange, Réginald. "La nouvelle théologie òu va-t-elle?" *Angelicum* 23 (1946): 126–45.

Gay, Jean-Pascal. *Jesuit Civil Wars: Theology, Politics and Government under Tirso González*. London: Routledge, 2012.

Gernet, Jacques. *China and the Christian Impact*. Cambridge: Cambridge University Press, 1985.

Grendler, Paul. "The Culture of the Jesuit Teacher, 1548–1773." *Journal of Jesuit Studies* 3 (2016): 17–41.

Guasti, Niccolò. "The Age of Suppression." In *Oxford Handbook of the Jesuits*, edited by Ines G. Županov, 930. Oxford: Oxford University Press, 2019.

———. "The Exile of the Spanish Jesuits in Italy." In *The Jesuit Suppression in Global Context*, edited by Jeffrey D. Burson and Jonathan Wright, 248–61. Cambridge: Cambridge University Press, 2015.

———. "Il Ristablimento della Compagnia di Gesù." In *La Compagnie de Jésus des Anciens Régimes au Monde Contemporain (XVIIIe–XXe Siècles)*, edited by Pierre Antoine Fabre, et al., 133–81. Rome: Institutum Historicum Societatis Iesu and L'École Française de Rome, 2021.

Guerrero Mosquera, Andrea. "Los jesuitas en Cartagena de Indias y la evangelización de africanos. Una aproximación." *Montalbán: Revista de Humanidades y Educación*, no. 52 (2018): 1–27.

Hamilton, Alastair. *The Copts and the West*. Oxford: Oxford University Press, 2006.

Hamilton, Bernice. *Political Thought in Sixteenth-Century Spain*. Oxford: Clarendon Press, 1963.

Handy, Robert. *A History of the Church in the United States and Canada*. Oxford: Clarendon Press, 1976.

Hanley, Thomas O'Brien, ed. *The John Carroll Papers*. Vol. 1. Notre Dame, IN: University of Notre Dame Press, 1976.

Hanvey, James. "Henri Bouillard: The Freedom of Faith." In *Ressourcement: A Movement for Renewal in Twentieth-Century Catholic Theology*, edited by Gabriel Flynn and Paul D. Murray, 263–77. Oxford: Oxford University Press, 2012.

Hasler, August Bernhard. *How the Pope Became Infallible: Pius IX and the Politics of Persuasion*. New York: Doubleday, 1981.

Hebblethwaite, Peter. *Pope John XXIII*. London: Geoffrey Chapman, 1984.

Hill, Elizabeth. "Roger Boscovich: A Biographical Essay." In *Roger Joseph Boscovich*, edited by Lancelot Law Whyte, 17–111. London: George Allen and Unwin, 1961.

Hinsdale, Mary Ann. "Jesuit Theological Discourse since Vatican II." In *The Cambridge Companion to the Jesuits*, edited by Thomas Worcester, 298–318. Cambridge: Cambridge University Press, 2008.

Holt, Geoffrey. "The English Province: The Ex-Jesuits and the Restoration." In *Promising Hope*, edited by Thomas McCoog, 219–58. Rome: Institutum Historicum Societatis Iesu, 2003.

Höpfl, Harro. *Jesuit Political Thought: The Society of Jesus and the State, c. 1540–1630*. Cambridge: Cambridge University Press, 2004.

Horwood, Thomas. "Public Opinion and the 1908 Eucharistic Congress." *Recusant History* (now *British Catholic History*) 25, no. 1 (2000): 120–32.

Hosne, Ana Carolina. "The 'Art of Memory' in the Jesuit Missions in China and Peru in the Late Sixteenth Century." *Material Culture Review* 76 (Fall 2013): 30–40.

———. "*Dios, Dio, Viracocha, Tianzhu*: 'Finding' and 'Translating' the Christian God in the Overseas Jesuit Missions (16th–18th Centuries)." In *The Rites Controversies in the Early Modern World*, edited by Ines G. Županov and Pierre Antoine Fabre, 322–44. Leiden: Brill, 2018.

———. *The Jesuit Missions to China and Peru*. London: Routledge, 2013.

Hyland, Sabine. *The Jesuit and the Incas*. Ann Arbor: University of Michigan Press, 2003.

Imbruglia, Girolamo. "The Jesuit 'Made in China': A Meeting of Empires–Spain, China, and the Society of Jesus, 1586–1588." Accessed online at https://www.academia.edu/19703108. March 23, 2020.

Innes, M. J. "Robert Persons, Popular Sovereignty, and the Late Elizabethan Succession Debate." *The Historical Journal* 62, no. 1 (2010): 57–76.

Ivereigh, Austen, ed. *Unfinished Journey*. London: Continuum, 2003.

Jedin, Hubert, and John Dolan, eds. *The Church in the Age of Absolutism and Enlightenment*. London: Burns and Oates, 1981.

Jedin, Hubert, ed. *History of the Church*. Vol. 5. London: Burns and Oates, 1980.

Kainulainen, Jaska. "Virtue and Civic Values in Early Modern Jesuit Education." *Journal of Jesuit Studies* 5 (2018): 530–48.

Klaiber, Jeffrey L. *The Jesuits in Latin America, 1549–2000*. St. Louis: Institute of Jesuit Sources, 2009.

Knowles, David. *Great Historical Enterprises*. London: Thomas Nelson, 1963.

Komonchak, Joseph A. "*Humani Generis* and *Nouvelle Théologie*." In *Ressourcement: A Movement for Renewal in Twentieth-Century Catholic Theology*, edited by Gabriel Flynn and Paul D. Murray, 138–56. Oxford: Oxford University Press, 2012.

Korn, Bernhardt. "Johann Baptist Franzelin (1816–86): A Jesuit Cardinal Shaping the Official Teaching of the Church at the Time of the First Vatican Council." *Journal of Jesuit Studies* 7 (2020): 592–615.

La Bella, Gianni. *Los Jesuitas: Del Vaticano II al papa Francisco*. Bilbao: Ediciones Mensajero, 2019.

Lacouture, Jean. *Jesuits: A Multibiography*. London: The Harvill Press, 1995.

Lamb, Christopher. *The Outsider: Pope Francis and His Battle to Reform the Church*. Maryknoll, NY: Orbis Books, 2020.

Lamet, Pedro Miguel. *Pedro Arrupe: Witness of the Twentieth Century, Prophet of the Twenty-First*. Boston: Institute of Jesuit Sources, Boston College, 2020.

Lavenia, V., and S. Pavone, eds. *Missioni, Saperi e Adattamento tra Europa e Imperi non Cristiani*. Macerata: EUM, 2015.

Law Whyte, Lancelot, ed. *Roger Joseph Boscovich*. London: George Allen and Unwin, 1961.

Lee, M. Kittiya. "Cannibal Theologies in Colonial Portuguese America (1549–1759): Translating the Christian Eucharist as the Tupinambá Pledge of Vengeance." *The Journal of Early Modern History* 21 (2017): 64–90.

Letso, Douglas, and Michael Higgins. *The Jesuit Mystique*. London: Fount, 1996.

Logan, Oliver. "*La Civiltà Cattolica* from Pius IX to Pius XII." In *The Church and the Book*, edited by R. N. Swanson, 375–85. Woodbridge: The Boydell Press for the Ecclesiastical History Society, 2004.

Lopez, Donald S., and Thupten Jinpa. *Dispelling the Darkness: A Jesuit's Quest for the Soul of Tibet*. Cambridge, MA: Harvard University Press, 2017.

Loughlin, Gerard. "*Nouvelle Théologie*: A Return to Modernism." In *Ressourcement: A Movement for Renewal in Twentieth-Century Catholic Theology*, edited by Gabriel Flynn and Paul D. Murray, 36–50. Oxford: Oxford University Press, 2012.

Lucas, Thomas M. *Landmarking: City, Church and Jesuit Urban Strategy*. Chicago: Loyola Press, 1997.

Luxmore, Jonathan. *The Vatican and the Red Flag*. London: Geoffrey Chapman, 1999.

Maclagan, Edward. *The Jesuits and the Great Mogul*. London: Burns, Oates & Washbourne, 1932.

Madigan, Daniel. "Global Visions in Contestation." In *The Jesuits and Globalization*, edited by Thomas Bouchoff and José Casanovas, 69–91. Washington, DC: Georgetown University Press, 2016.

Mahoney, John. *The Making of Moral Theology: A Study of the Roman Catholic Tradition*. Oxford: Clarendon Press, 1987.

Martin, A. Lynn. *The Jesuit Mind: The Mentality of an Elite in Early Modern France*. Ithaca, NY: Cornell University Press, 1988.

Maryks, R. A. *Saint Cicero and the Jesuits*. Farnham: Ashgate, 2008.

Matelski, Marilyn J. *Vatican Radio: Propagation by the Airwaves*. Westport, CT: Praeger, 1995.

Matignon, Ambroise. "Les Doctrines de la Compagnie de Jésus sur la Liberté." *Etudes* (July 1867): 1–24.

McCoog, Thomas M. "Converting a King: The Jesuit William Crichton and King James VI and I." *Journal of Jesuit Studies* 7, no. 1 (2020): 11–33.

———. "'Lost in the Title': John Thorpe's Eyewitness Account of the Suppression." In *The Jesuit Suppression in Global Context*, edited by Jeffrey D. Burson and Jonathan Wright, 161–80. Cambridge: Cambridge University Press, 2015.

————, ed. *Promising Hope*. Rome: Institutum Historicum Societatis Iesu, 2003.

————, ed. *The Reckoned Expense: Edmund Campion and the Early English Jesuits*. Woodbridge: The Boydell Press, 1996.

McGinness, Anne B. "Between Subjection and Accommodation: The Development of José de Anchieta's Missionary Project in Colonial Brazil." *Journal of Jesuit Studies* 1 (2014): 227–44.

McGreevy, John T. *American Jesuits and the World*. Princeton, NJ: Princeton University Press, 2016.

McKevitt, Gerald. "Jesuit Schools in the USA, 1814–c.1970." In *The Cambridge Companion to the Jesuits*, edited by Thomas Worcester, 278–97. Cambridge: Cambridge University Press, 2008.

McShea, Bronwen. *Apostles of Empire*. Lincoln: University of Nebraska Press, 2019.

Meissner, W. W. *Ignatius of Loyola: The Psychology of a Saint*. New Haven, CT: Yale University Press, 1992.

Méndez Alonzo, Manuel. "El derecho a la vida y la salvación en los subyugados." *Bulletin de la Sociètè d'Étude de la Philosophie Médiévale* (2020): 1–11.

Milward, Peter. *Religious Controversies of the Elizabethan Age*. London: Scolar Press, 1977.

————. *Religious Controversies of the Jacobean Age*. London: Scolar Press, 1978.

Minamiki, George. *The Chinese Rites Controversy from Its Beginnings to Modern Times*. Chicago: Loyola University Press, 1985.

Misner, Paul. *Social Catholicism in Europe*. London: Darton, Longman and Todd, 1991.

Moran, J. F. *The Japanese and the Jesuits*. London: Routledge, 1993.

Morello, Gustavo. *The Catholic Church and Argentina's Dirty War*. Oxford: Oxford University Press, 2015.

Mujica Pinilla, Ramón. "Angels and Demons in the Conquest of Peru." In *Angels, Demons and the New World*, edited by F. Cervantes and A. Redden, 171–210. Cambridge: Cambridge University Press, 2013.

North, Robert G. *The General Who Rebuilt the Jesuits*. Milwaukee: Bruce Publishing Company, 1944.

Obirek, Stanisław. "Jesuits in Poland and Eastern Europe." In *The Cambridge Companion to the Jesuits*, edited by Thomas Worcester, 136–50. Cambridge: Cambridge University Press, 2008.

O'Malley, John W., Gauvin Alexander Bailey, Steven J. Harris, T. Frank Kennedy, eds. *The Jesuits: Cultures, Sciences and the Arts, 1540–1773*. Toronto: University of Toronto Press, 1999.

———. *The Jesuits II: Cultures, Sciences and the Arts, 1540–1773*. Toronto: University of Toronto Press, 2006.

O'Malley, John W. *The First Jesuits*. Cambridge, MA: Harvard University Press, 1993.

———. *The Jesuits and the Popes*. Philadelphia: St. Joseph's University Press, 2016.

———. *Vatican I: The Council and the Making of the Ultramontane Church*. Cambridge, MA: The Belknap Press of Harvard University Press, 2018.

_____. *What Happened at Vatican II*. Cambridge, MA: The Belknap Press of Harvard University Press, 2010.

Palazzo, Carmen Lícia. "Jesuits: Favored Agents of Image Transfer from China to Europe, 16th to 18th Centuries." This is an English translation, accessed online March 28, 2020, of an article in Portuguese that appeared in *Tuiutí: Ciência e Cultura* 48 (Curitiba, 2014): 13–31.

Pasquale, Sofia. "Iglesia Católica en America Latina: La Teología de Liberación." *Cuestiones Políticas* 37, no. 65 (2020): 48–65.

Pavia, José Pedro. "The Impact of Luther and the Reformation in the Portuguese Seaborne Empire." *Journal of Ecclesiastical History* 70, no. 2 (2019): 287–91.

Pavone, Sabine. "Between History and Myth." In *The Jesuits II: Cultures, Sciences, and the Arts, 1540–1773*, edited by John W. O'Malley, Gauvin Alexander Bailey, Steven J. Harris, T. Frank Kennedy, 50–65. Toronto: University of Toronto Press, 2006.

———. "The History of Anti-Jesuitism." In *The Jesuits and Globalization*, edited by Thomas Bouchoff and José Casanovas, 110–30. Washington, DC: Georgetown University Press, 2016.

Pavur, Claude, trans. *The Ratio Studiorum*. St. Louis: The Institute of Jesuit Sources, 2005.

Pizzorusso, Giovanni. "The New World of the New Society of Jesus." In *La Compagnie de Jésus des Anciens Régimes au Monde Contemporain (XVIIIᵉ–XXᵉ Siècles)*, edited by Pierre Antoine Fabre, et al., 483–99. Rome: Institutum Historicum Societatis Iesu and L'École Française de Rome, 2021.

Po-Chia Hsia, Ronnie, ed. *A Companion to Early Modern Catholic Global Missions*. Leiden: Brill, 2018.

Pollard, John. *The Papacy in the Age of Totalitarianism*. Oxford: Oxford University Press, 2014.

Pombeni, Paolo. *The Historiography of Transition: Critical Phases in the Development of Modernity (1494–1973)*. New York: Routledge, 2016.

Rafferty, Oliver. "Gunpowder Plot." In *The Cambridge Encyclopedia of the Jesuits*, edited by Thomas Worcester, 354. Cambridge: Cambridge University Press, 2017.

Rahner, Hugo. *Ignatius the Theologian*. London: Geoffrey Chapman, 1968.

Rockett, June. *A Gentle Jesuit*. Leominster: Gracewing, 2004.

Ronan, Charles E., and Bonnie B. C. Oh, eds. *East Meets West: The Jesuits in China, 1582–1773*. Chicago: Loyola University Press, 1988.

Roufe, Gai. "The Reasons for Murder." *Cahiers d'Études Africaines* 55, no. 3 (2015): 467–87.

Rubiés, Joan-Pau. "The Concept of Cultural Dialogue and the Jesuit Method of Accommodation: Between Idolatry and Civilization." *Archivum Historicum Societatis Iesu* (2005): 237–80.

———. "Ethnography and Cultural Translation in the Early Modern Missions." *Studies in Church History* 53 (2017): 272–310.

———. "Real and Imaginary Dialogues in the Jesuit Mission of Sixteenth-Century Japan." *Journal of the Economic and Social History of the Orient* 55 (2012): 447–94.

———. "Reassessing 'the Discovery of Hinduism': Jesuit Discourse on Gentile Idolatry and the European Republic of Letters." In *Intercultural Encounter and the Jesuit Mission in South Asia (16th–18th Centuries)*, edited by Anand Amaldass and Ines Županov, 113–55. Bangalore: ATC, 2014.

Russell, Camilla. "Imagining the 'Indies': Italian Jesuit Petitions for the Overseas Missions at the Turn of the Seventeenth Century." In *L'Europa divisae i nuovi mondi*, edited by Massimo Donattini, Giuseppe Marcocci, and Stefania Pastore, 179–90. Vol. 2. Pisa: Edizioni Normale, 2011.

Russell, John L. "Catholic Astronomers and the Copernican System after the Condemnation of Galileo." *Annales of Science* 46 (1989): 365–86.

Sagovsky, Nicholas. *'On God's Side'*. Oxford: Clarendon Press, 1990.

Saint Ignatius of Loyola: Personal Writings. Translated with introduction and notes by Joseph A. Munitiz and Philip Endean. London: Penguin Books, 2004.

Sarreal, Julia J. S. *The Guaraní and Their Missions: A Socioeconomic History*. Stanford, CA: University of Stanford Press, 2014.

Schner, George P., ed. *Ignatian Spirituality in a Secular Age*. Waterloo, Ontario: Wilfrid Laurier University Press, 1984.

Schroth, Raymond A. *The American Jesuits: A History*. New York: New York University Press, 2007.

Schultenover, David G. *George Tyrrell: In Search of Catholicism*. Shepherdstown: The Patmos Press, 1981.

———. "Luis Martín García, the Jesuit General of the Modernist Crisis (1892–1906): On Historical Criticism." *The Catholic Historical Review* 89, no. 3 (July 2003): 434–63.

———. *A View from Rome*. New York: Fordham University Press, 1993.

Schwartz, Stuart B., ed. *Early Brazil: A Documentary Collection to 1700*. Cambridge: Cambridge University Press, 2010.

Shea, William R., and Mariano Artigas. *Galileo in Rome*. Oxford: Oxford University Press, 2003.

Shell, Alison. "Campion's Dramas." In *The Reckoned Expense: Edmund Campion and the Early English Jesuits*, edited by Thomas M. McCoog, 103–18. Woodbridge: The Boydell Press, 1996.

Shore, Paul. "Ex-Jesuits in the East Habsburg Lands, Silesia and Poland." In *The Jesuit Suppression in Global Context*, edited by Jeffrey D. Burson and Jonathan Wright, 229–47. Cambridge: Cambridge University Press, 2015.

———. "Jesuits in the Orthodox World." In *The Oxford Handbook of the Jesuits*, edited by Ines G. Županov, 318–48. Oxford: Oxford University Press, 2019.

Spence, Jonathan D. *The Memory Palace of Matteo Ricci*. London: Faber and Faber, 1985.

Stehle, Hansjakob. *Eastern Politics of the Vatican, 1917–1979*. Athens: Ohio University Press, 1981.

Steinkerchner, Scott. "Introduction: Dominicans and Jesuits through the Centuries." *Journal of Jesuit Studies* 7 (2020): 357–76.

Strathern, Alan. "Catholic Missions and Local Rulers in Sub-Saharan Africa." In *A Companion to Early Modern Catholic Global Missions*, edited by Ronnie Po-Chia Hsia, 151–78. Leiden: Brill, 2018.

Stucco, Guido. *When Great Theologians Feuded: Thomas Lemos and Leonardus Lessius on Grace and Predestination*. Privately printed, 2017.

Swanson, R. N., ed. *The Church and the Book*. Woodbridge: The Boydell Press for the Ecclesiastical History Society, 2004.

Thomas, Alfred. *Hopkins the Jesuit: The Years of Training*. Oxford: Oxford University Press, 1969.

Thompson, D. Gillian. "French Jesuits 1756–1814." In *The Jesuit Suppression in Global Context*, edited by Jeffrey D. Burson and Jonathan Wright, 181–98. Cambridge: Cambridge University Press, 2015.

Tuninetti, Luca F. "The 'Happy Months' of Newman at the College of Propaganda in Rome (1846–1847)." *The Newman Review* (August 2021).

Vallely, Paul. *Pope Francis: Untying the Knots*. London: Bloomsbury, 2013; rev. and exp. ed., 2015.

Vanderstappen, Harrie. "Chinese Art and the Jesuits in Peking." In *East Meets West: The Jesuits in China, 1582–1773*, edited by Charles E. Ronan and Bonnie B. C. Oh, 103–26. Chicago: Loyola University Press, 1988.

Van Kley, Dale. *The Jansenists and the Expulsion of the Jesuits from France*. New Haven, CT: Yale University Press, 1975.

———. *Reform Catholicism and the International Suppression of the Jesuits*. New Haven, CT: Yale University Press, 2018.

Veléz, Juan R. *Passion for Truth*. Charlotte, NC: Tan Books, 2012.

Walsh, Michael. "Frederick Copleston, S.J." In *The Ministry of the Printed Word*, edited by John Broadley and Peter Phillips, 335–67. Stratton-on-the-Fosse: Downside Abbey Press, 2018.

———. *Heythrop College, 1614–2014: A Commemorative History*. Heythrop College, University of London, 2014.

———. "The Publishing Policy of the English College Press at St Omer, 1608–1759." *Studies in Church History* 17 (1981): 239–50.

———. "Religious Freedom: The Limits of Progress." In *Unfinished Journey*, edited by Austen Ivereigh, 134–48. London: Continuum, 2003.

———. *The Secret World of Opus Dei*. London: Grafton Books, 1989.

Whitehead, Maurice. *English Jesuit Education: Expulsion, Suppression, Survival and Restoration, 1762–1803*. Farnham: Ashgate, 2013.

———. "On the Road to Suppression: The Jesuits and Their Expulsion from the Reductions of Paraguay." In *The Jesuit Suppression in Global Context*, edited by Jeffrey D. Burson and Jonathan Wright, 83–99. Cambridge: Cambridge University Press, 2015.

Witek, John W. "Understanding the Chinese: A Comparison of Matteo Ricci and the French Jesuit Mathematicians Sent by Louis XIV." In *East Meets West: The Jesuits in China, 1582–1773*, edited by Charles E. Ronan and Bonnie B. C. Oh, 62–102. Chicago: Loyola University Press, 1988.

Wolf, Hubert. *The Nuns of Sant'Ambrogio*. New York: Alfred A. Knopf, 2015.

Worcester, Thomas, ed. *The Cambridge Companion to the Jesuits*. Cambridge: Cambridge University Press, 2008.

————. *The Cambridge Encyclopedia of the Jesuits*. Cambridge: Cambridge University Press, 2017.

Wright, Jonathan. *The Jesuits: Missions, Myths and Histories*. London: Harper-Collins, 2004.

————. "Paccanarists." In *The Cambridge Encyclopedia of the Jesuits*, edited by Thomas Worcester, 577. Cambridge: Cambridge University Press, 2017.

————. "The Suppression and Restoration." In *The Cambridge Companion to the Jesuits*, edited by Thomas Worcester, 263–77. Cambridge: Cambridge University Press, 2008.

Zeron, Carlos. "Political Theories and Jesuit Politics." In *The Oxford Handbook of the Jesuits*, edited by Ines G. Županov, 193–215. Oxford: Oxford University Press, 2019.

Zizola, Giancarlo. *Il Conclave, Storia e Segreti*. Rome: Newton Compton Editori, 1993.

Županov, Ines G., and Pierre Antoine Fabre, eds. *The Rites Controversies in the Early Modern World*. Leiden: Brill, 2018.

Županov, Ines G., ed. *The Oxford Handbook of the Jesuits*. Oxford: Oxford University Press, 2019.

Index